M'aii Trouble

Book Two
in The War
This Side of
Heaven series

by

Sharon

Evans

To Aunt Ruth
Thank you for all the love & encouragement,
Much love,
Sharon
11-6-2015

Copyright © 2015 by Sharon Evans

All rights reserved. No part of this book, including cover art/interior design, may be reproduced in any form, stored in a retrieval system, transmitted by any means, used or reproduced by any means including electronic or mechanical means, without written permission from the author, except by a reviewer when quoting brief passages in a review. For information, contact Sharon Evans by email at **thewarthissideofheaven@gmail.com.**

Published 2015 by Sharon Evans

First Edition

ISBN-13: 978-1517256500
ISBN-10: 151725650X

* * * * *

DISCLAIMER:
This book is a work of fiction.
The characters and the incidents detailed in
Man Trouble and all the volumes and/or related works of
The War This Side of Heaven are fictitious,
and any resemblance to actual persons living
or dead is purely coincidental.

* * * * *

Cover art and design by Sharon Evans
Interior design by Sharon Evans

"In all thy ways acknowledge him,
and he shall direct thy paths." Proverbs 3:6

ACKNOWLEDGMENTS
Special thanks to God for my cousins Luster and Olivinia Jackson of Chicago, IL, and to Father Kenneth Brin and other priests for their help in researching Teddy. Thanks also to a certain Mr Archer for his help with Johnny Angrahm.

This volume of the series is dedicated to
my sister, the late Wanda Coleman,
for all her love, support and inspiration
down through the years.

Table of Contents

1. Temptation Calls
2. The Trouble With Helen
3. Christmas Jeer
4. Teddy Molloy
5. The Brush Off
6. Hearts and Flowers
7. Intimacies
8. Torn Between
9. The Passion Ploy
10. My Hand in Marriage
11. Nedra Bates

Albuquerque, New Mexico

★ 1968 - 1969 ★

Chapter One
Temptation Calls

WEDNESDAY, OCTOBER 9:

My boogie woogie dancing days were over–for the time being. In a way I was glad, since it made life slightly less complicated. But my partner, Alan Haskell, was crestfallen when I gave him the news. Old Jacob Noonan's boots had done me in to the point that I couldn't handle that kind of jumping around in time for the talent show. So Alan would have to go it alone.

Even though the Noonan incident was still big news, my world was getting back to normal. With a week's time having passed since the ordeal of my kidnaping and the apprehension of this nasty killer, not as many people asked questions and life began to go on as usual.

Well, there was one change.

"Bon jour, Mademoiselle."

"Ah, Monsieur Conrad–bon jour."

I was in my usual spot over in the lunch pavilion, juggling *Rashi's Commentary* with the book of Genesis and about to make some notes when, for the third consecutive day that week, my handsome, blue-eyed and heroic teacher, David Conrad, interrupted my morning studies to invite me to breakfast in the teachers' cafeteria. It became apparent that what had only happened a couple of times was to become a daily routine. This time of morning was set aside for Torah study, but this guy seemed to think I should feed my face instead of my spirit at that time of day, and in his company. His reason seemed to be a preoccupation with my talent as a songwriter, for the topic of conversation was always Music Theory. No polite hints had discouraged him and my present look of displeasure was totally ignored. So I gathered my things and followed along with a feeling of losing my touch when dealing with faculty members.

Most girls would have been thrilled to ecstasy and trotted happily alongside this tall, beautiful dark blond specimen of manhood; but me–I wanted to be careful. I had to be. Even with the surety of the close friendship that was developing between me and this exclusive and rather mysterious man, I was no fool. Though I certainly appreciated his kindness and gallantry in my rescue from Jake the Snake, by this time, with studies to focus on again and a bit of catching up to do, my head was back on a bit more securely, and the last thing I wanted was to make an idiot out of myself by falling into the quicksand of infatuation. But just as important was not giving Conrad–or anyone else–even the slightest impression that I was sweet on him. That would mean trouble no matter how you sliced it. So the adoring gazes, smiles and whatnot that he had received from me in gratitude the week before were history. In their place was the prior cool, calm and collected demeanor becoming of a mature and discriminating woman whose head was not turned simply because someone in an expensive suit and tie was being nice to her. But on the up side was the knowledge that his attentions to me were a sure-fire sign that when enough time had passed, the man himself would reveal to me the secrets he now guarded so carefully.

We settled into a remote corner of the cafeteria. I expected the usual once over lightly visual admiration after I removed my little beige jacket to reveal a marvelous white and navy blue silk number with a square neckline, but he kept his eyes where a teacher ought to, something very important in the presence of other faculty. Then, while I sipped hot tea and picked at a biscuit and fruit, Mr C talked about my last assignment in Music Theory.

"Here, I'll show you what I mean," he said, reaching for his briefcase. My paper just happened to be on top. He took it and showed it to me. "It's much better than the last one. You're doing fine with the figured bass."

"That's good to know. It does make more sense now."

"What we're working on now is too elementary for you to do much with this, but your melody here is very nice. Does it have words?"

"No, not yet."

"Then see what you can come up with. What I'd like is to spend time with you on an arrangement. Would you mind?"

"Of course not. What I do mind is–"

"Good. Maybe we can start this afternoon. Just be sure to let your parents know that you'll be late coming home. I don't want them to worry. And that reminds me. We ought to do that little recording session we talked about and soon. I'll give your parents a call so we can set something up."

I had tried to tell him that while I appreciated his help with Theory, I also loved and needed the time I spent studying Torah. While we chatted, I also spoke with HaShem (God) and expressed my anxiety over this new development which, if it continued, meant flat out refusing him or finding a new time and place for my personal studies.

Okay, God, what's going on here? Opportunity's knocking and he's dressed to kill. Is this your setup? I sure hope so, 'cause this is just too, too hard to resist. Finally I gave my mind a rest and left the problem alone. Since there was nothing I could tactfully do at the time, I relaxed, enjoyed my teacher's company and allowed myself a few minutes to delight in the way my oddball existence was finally beginning to pay off.

That afternoon marked my fourth encounter of the day with David Conrad–nicknamed "The Fox" by the female student body. The way he'd latched onto me reminded me of what I'd heard about being responsible for the life of the person you save, which made me wonder about this man even more. In other words, something just didn't jive. At his penthouse apartment that afternoon, it didn't feel quite the same as I began my lessons, and yet all appeared as usual. After I paid a proper amount of attention to Pirate, the old cat curled up on the love seat and began to purr while I went through my assigned pieces at the black grand piano. It would take a few days for me to realize just what had changed.

"Janette, you did very well," said Mr C when I finished the last piece.

"You may become a decent pianist yet, if you keep up the hard work and stop playing favorites. It's obvious which composers you like best."

"I can't help it. Some of this music is just too boring."

"Boring or too hard?"

"Both. Too hard because it is boring. Oh, some of it's nice, but it just seems I've heard it all before. A lot of it, anyway."

"But if it's pretty enough, you can learn to play anything. Is that it?"

"Just about."

"That's something you need to overcome . . . and so that you will–" He reached over my shoulder and turned a few pages past what I'd just played. "Yes, this is it. Have this one ready for me in two weeks."

Withholding comment, I watched in dismay as he scribbled the date at the top of the page. It was the very same piece I'd murdered at my first lesson. I had heard of haunting melodies, but this was too much.

"Now, I know you can do it," he went on. "I don't expect it to be perfect, but you should be able to play it adequately in two weeks."

I wanted to say how overburdened I already was, and how I needed all the motivation I could get to keep up the pace. But his point seemed valid, so I said nothing; only all the joy and anticipation I'd felt moments before was suddenly gone. Mechanically I arose from the bench and let him take my place. Then I stood alongside the piano for my voice lesson.

"Janette, is it really that bad?" He was surprised at my dour expression.

I almost responded with, "No, I'm a big girl. I'll survive." But suddenly I remembered the harpsichord and how I still had yet to play it. I glanced over at the lovely instrument and despaired of ever touching its keys. Then with my eyes on the rug, all I wanted was to go home.

Following my gaze, he quietly said, "I did promise you that, didn't I?"

"Yes, you did. I was supposed to play it on the day I was kidnaped. Remember?"

"I do now. All right, Janette, move to the harpsichord."

At last!

There was a twinkle in his blue-gray eyes as he spoke, and then a smile arose on his face when he saw how excited and happy I had suddenly become. And I was also nervous. As I took my place at the instrument, he set my book of Bach inventions before me and I began to play my assigned piece. I stumbled at first, but only for a second. The unique sound threatened to distract me so that I worked much harder in order to play. And I did it.

"Well, Janette, are you happy now?"

"Yes, I am."

"Then this'll knock you for a loop. Close your eyes." I did as I was told and waited. While my eyes were closed I heard movement and then the rustling of paper. "You can look, now," he said.

"What?" After opening my eyes, it took a second for it to register. The title of the handwritten music he'd set before me was his arrangement of a harpsichord tune that had hit the charts the year before and was still popular: "Love is Blue" by Paul Mauriat. I had fallen madly in love with this song and now he was giving it to me to play on his harpsichord. When the realization hit, all I could say was, "Oh! Oh! Oh!"

First he began to chuckle, then he threw back his head and laughed long and hard. "I knew it! I knew it! Oh, I've gotcha now." He slapped his knee. "Yeah, you just pretend to be hard boiled. Ha! You're a romantic!"

Gaping in astonishment, I turned to look up at him. When he caught my expression, he laughed even harder.

"I'm sorry, Janette," he finally said. "It's just that I was so terrified of you in the beginning."

Angry and embarrassed, I shot him a deadly look. "Well, don't take me for granted now. The school year isn't over yet. As a matter of fact, we're just getting started."

"Uh, uh. You don't scare me, so stop trying. Now, turn and look at the music." Sobering up, he leaned over, and reaching around me, played a few measures. "It's a duet, see?"

"Oh . . . yes, I see." Now only chagrined, I swallowed my pride and shifted my focus to the music.

"I'll play the other part on–no, wait a minute. I bought a little synthesizer for this." Against the wall was a keyboard beneath a vinyl cover. Mr C brought it close, uncovered it, turned it on and began pressing buttons. "It may not sound like much, but I thought it'd be fun to try. Are you game?"

"Of course I am. You big stinker–I ought to punch your lights out." One look at the happy grin on that handsome kisser and I immediately forgave him. "I guess you do have my number, don't you?"

He winked. "Ain'tcha glad?"

Now it was my turn to laugh. I couldn't believe what I was seeing. What a disarming contrast to the personality he'd shown thus far.

When we finally quieted down, Mr Conrad helped me through the entire song. My vocal lesson was pushed aside to make room for it. We were both pleased with the way I executed the piece for the first time, and then he joined me in playing the last few measures at the synthesizer. By the time we were done I was very happy and satisfied.

"I tell you what," Rising from the keyboard he took my other book from the piano, leafed through it and said, "You know, we have the rest of the school year to work on music. I suspect you've got a pretty heavy work load with all of your extracurricular activities. Am I right?"

"Yes. It'll be a bit better once the talent show is over, but being so busy does overwhelm me at times."

"I thought so. Well, I don't want you to burn out. Here. Learn this Ravel number. I think you'll like it. And work on the Mauriat piece. Forget the other piece–for now."

"Will it come back to haunt me next semester?"

"Probably." I laughed. "There! That's a better outlook. You know, maybe we'll forget that piece altogether. I'll feel much safer around you if you're happy and smiling. Plus I think I know of a better way to improve your playing." He winked and smiled again. "Now, do you feel up to working on your song, or would you rather do it some other time?"

"No, I want to stay."

"Good."

After getting cookies and coffee from the kitchen, he returned and we went to work on my composition. I sat in an armless padded chair pulled close to the bench so I could watch what he was doing as he wrote. At first we did work together as he asked what I heard and felt regarding the music; it began as a personal lesson in Theory. But as he expressed his thoughts on what it should do, it wasn't long before he began to lose me. Still I could hear what he was doing and that helped me understand his explanations. Other times he ignored me while working out parts, writing furiously and then playing it for me. I liked what I heard very much.

Had it not been for the ring of the telephone, we might have been at it well into the evening. By the time I left, it was nearly six o'clock.

As I hurried home, it was hard to stop laughing. Scenes from the afternoon and the music that went with it played in my head, and the remembrance of my teacher's jocularity still amazed me. I couldn't recall ever having this much fun while learning. It was something I would long remember and hoped to have more of.

Up the front steps and then to my room, I softly sang the words that were beginning to come that fit the tune and new arrangement we had worked on. Once inside the door to my little sanctuary, I dropped my books in a convenient spot, went to wash my hands and then rushed back down to join the family. Even though Mommy had waited past the usual time, dinner was already in progress and almost over by the time I sat down at the table.

"My goodness," said Mommy as I filled my plate. "I didn't expect you'd be this late. How did it go?"

"Wonderful. We aren't done yet, but the song is taking shape just fine."

"You were at Mr Conrad's all this time?" asked Charlotte. "Man! What were you guys doing, singing?"

"No, we were counting his money," I replied jokingly, which made her smile. "We were working on a piece I wrote for Music Theory. He's helping me to arrange it."

"Yeah? Do you think the choir might sing it?"

"I don't know. I hadn't thought about that, but I guess it's possible. Once I put words to it, that is."

Everyone broke forth with comments over this possibility, especially Mommy and Daddy. I could almost see the buttons popping off their chests as they declared how proud they were that Mr Conrad was showing such an interest in me. When someone used the word prodigy, it raised my eyebrows. *No, protégée is more like it,* I thought. *Or just teacher's pet.*

THURSDAY, OCTOBER 10:

All the fuss my teacher was making about my musical abilities at last silenced any opposition my parents had to my choice of a career in music. The following evening they got his phone call about the recording session, just as I was heading out the door to rehearsal for the talent show. That news on top of what they had heard the night before seemed to have a sobering effect on them, and it changed the way they looked at me from then on out.

SATURDAY, OCTOBER 12:
The talent show at Paseo Verde High was a big deal in the neighborhood and always well attended. Every year the event was heavily advertised. An admission price of $1.75 was charged for adults and $1.25 for students, so the show had to be good, and it always was. Singers, dancers, actors with short skits, magicians and all kinds of performers were included in a show that ran for at least two hours, not including intermission.

No back number dresses this time. Black leather pants with silver studs and ruffles with lace from the pale pink blouse under a leather vest was my outfit for this gig. For my set I had ten pieces backing me, which included brass, strings and rhythm section: all members of Rock of the Witness, the Jesus People group I had fallen in with. Aside from my vocals there was prominent jazz musician David Richardson, plus three others on backup. Janette West and the Rockin' Witness Band were scheduled to play just before intermission. As the time for our spot approached, we got into position and waited for the introduction.

The house was filled to capacity with a lively audience. The atmosphere was electric and the crowd had been warmed up very well by the preceding acts. We caught the energy and began playing as the curtain rose.

Our opening number was genuine rock and roll with a hard driving beat designed to pull people up out of their seats to move and groove. They jumped out into the aisles to dance as we played, and before I knew it, my feet were moving, too.

After the opening number I introduced the band members. Richardson's name caused a small murmur as well as applause from those who recognized him. While the attention was on him, he told the audience that I had written the song we'd just done and all the music in our set. Then we went on with the next tune. The tempo was moderate and the song had the flavor of blues.

That night I did things I still don't remember. I was so high from God's presence that I just zoned out. The joy intensified when, slowing the tempo way down, we started up the last number. As his spirit moved over and around me, I played with a joy and confidence I had never known.

With our last song already being sung at services, members of the congregation joined in, causing it to build and then go on for several repeated choruses as it developed with added harmonies and counterpoint on and off stage. When it finally ended, there was a brief silence followed by an outbreak of thunderous applause and shouting.

Mr Johnson, our emcee, brought us back for one more song at the end of the show and then it was over. As we packed up, we talked of concerts in the park and other possibilities for our music. It was then that I knew what I wanted most to do with my talent. Nothing beat the joy I found in HaShem's presence.

SUNDAY, OCTOBER 13:
The next morning brought a big and very welcome surprise. At breakfast, my parents announced that the whole family would go to services with me that day.

"I want to hear more of that delightful music," said Mommy, all excited.

"Yeah," said Daniel. "Your group was really good last night. I wish our church had a band like that."

"You're not the only one," said Daddy.

And so they came along for more of the Rockin' Witness Band and got slightly more than they had bargained for. It seemed as if the sermon was tailored just for them (Daddy, especially), and they were slightly over dressed for our casual hippie crowd. Still they enjoyed it and said that they would like to come back, only the service was much too long to attend every Sunday. Then they got to meet the pastors and chat with them; they even met David Richardson, which was the highlight for my parents. They were thrilled when we went out with the Richardsons afterward and found out that David still had some old albums that Daddy had never bought: more music for his huge record collection.

That evening Margo Townsend phoned to complement my performance and just to chat. That's when I updated her on Mr C and the upcoming recording session.

"Wow, kiddo," she said. "You and The Fox have really connected. Almost makes me wish music was my major."

"It's too late, Muggsy," I replied dramatically. "Stay where you are. He's mine now and no one else can have him."

"Oh, is that so?"

"Actually, it's more like I'm the one being owned. He seems obsessed with my music. I don't think I could shake him if I wanted to."

"Maybe it's not just your music he digs."

"Yes, but to what degree–and in what fashion? He hasn't come on to me, and to be honest, I feel pretty safe."

"That's good–depending on how you look at it. You said you couldn't shake him if you wanted to. Do you?"

I was silent for a second or two until laughter erupted from my throat.

"Yeah, I figured as much." Margo laughed with me. "Don't pull any of Georgia's stunts and end up in trouble."

"Funny, but I think about that cousin of mine a lot when I'm sitting there with him and my hair is done up nice and I'm wearing something that's really cute. It's awful tempting but–"

"Can't handle it, huh?"

"It's no way to solve a mystery, Muggs, at least not in my book. But seriously, I do like him a lot. I'm starting to see some of that personality you told me about and it's like being with a Jekyll and Hyde. Most of the time he's all business and then this really fun guy pops up."

"Yeah, he's loads of laughs when he wants to be. Say, why not let me come along to your recording session?"

"Sure, you can come. Think it's news worthy?"

"Yes, I do. But it's also something else."

"Oh? What's that?"

"A chance to get more photos of Conrad's digs. Didn't you say that he'd added a lot since I took the pictures you saw?"

"Yes. Still everything seems void of any real clues, unless I just don't know enough to understand what I'm looking at. If I were an art expert, I'm sure I could dig up something of interest, but I'm not. What I'd be interested in are the photos he's got on his wall. There are a few in the hallway where the bathroom is that look like family photos; though they're nice, I don't think they're what we want. He's got more around the corner, but I've never had the chance to venture there for more than a second."

"Well, maybe I can. If we work it right, I'll get pictures of whatever is there, including the stuff by the bathroom."

"Great. Just keep in mind that my folks will be there."

"That won't be a problem. I'll use that new spy camera I got when we shopped for the Noonan case. I'm surprised you haven't used yours."

"He keeps me pretty busy, Muggs. Also, since I don't have a decoy to distract him, I'd be taking a big chance of getting caught. That would ruin things big time."

"You're right. Not worth the risk. Anyway, let me know the date and time, and make sure he knows I'm coming to cover it as a news item."

In another moment our conversation ended, and as I hung up the phone with my thoughts running backward over our discussion, it dawned on me what had changed at my private lessons. Mr C had stopped wearing his horn-rimmed glasses.

MONDAY, OCTOBER 14:

Returning to school on Monday naturally brought more reactions to the talent show. It started first thing when, once again, Mr Conrad interrupted my reading. Just as I got started, along came his footsteps. Reluctantly I gathered my books and walked beside him. (Please keep in mind that we don't always speak English. I simply write it that way to make it readable.)

"Mademoiselle West," he said "You are full of surprises."

"I don't mean to be," I replied innocently. "I assume you are referring to the talent show?"

"You bet I am. Your performance was fantastic! And how on earth did you meet up with David Richardson?"

"He goes to my congregation. He's the Minister of Music."

"Honestly? That old hep cat–a minister? The last time I saw him was at some club in Hollywood. He was so bombed he almost fell off the stage, but he could still play. Of course, that was almost fifteen years ago; then he just faded from the scene. I always wondered what happened to him."

"Would you like to meet him? I know he'd be glad to tell you about it."

"Sure, that would be great. How should we arrange it?"

"Just come to a service and I'll introduce you afterward."

"Oh. . . . Uh, Janette, I don't think I could–handle one of your services. Maybe I could come once it's over."

"The only thing about that is they never let out at any particular time."

"They don't?"

"No. When God is done, that's when it's over."

"I see. Well, I could just–"

"Oh! I know what. The congregation is having a picnic–next weekend, I think. Yes, next weekend. That'd be perfect. We're going up to Fourth of July Canyon to see the trees."

"I've never been there, but I've heard it's absolutely gorgeous in autumn."

"It is."

"Then count me in. I don't believe I have anything else planned for that day, but if I do I'll cancel it."

"Great. You'll have a good time, I promise you."

"Thank you. And now, Miss West, about those songs of yours. You really wrote all that you sang the other night?"

"Yes."

"What about the one at the end of the show?"

"Yes, that one, too. We planned an encore, just in case."

"I had no idea you were so prolific. And what about the arrangements? Was any of that you or did Richardson do everything?"

"It was a group effort, but he did most of it; all except for the third song. I wanted it to sound a certain way, so they followed my lead pretty much."

"I see. He hasn't been helping you with theory, has he?"

"No." *But that's not a bad idea.* "Why do you ask?"

"Because I want to know just what you're capable of doing on your own. There were things I heard the other night that were distinctly Richardson, while other parts weren't at all typical. The way you're coming along so fast in Theory–well, I thought I should ask."

"Like maybe he was helping me a little too much?"

"No, it just confirms that you've chosen the right major. You know, your stage presence was wonderful. When an artist is that in love with what they're doing, it's truly a pleasure to watch. You'd really make a marvelous entertainer."

"Oh, I suppose, but I don't know how much heart I could muster up for it. Making entertainment a career somehow doesn't have the same appeal that it once did. Ideally, sacred music would be more my bag, but only if

I were a bonafide Christian could I find an avenue for that."

"There are countless people that perform in churches who aren't Christians, so don't worry about that. But it doesn't have to be one or the other; you could do both."

"I never thought of that. Maybe I could."

"Of course you could."

"You know, it's funny, but Cowboy and his folks thought I'd make a good country singer."

"You're kidding. I never dreamed you would like country music."

"I don't particularly. But good music is good music even if it has a twang, so there are some songs or artists that I do enjoy. For the most part, though, it all sounds the same after a while."

"You're right. But my girlfriend won't listen to anything else. Sometimes it drives me nutty."

"That's how it was with me and Cowboy. But since I couldn't get away from it, I decided to make fun of it. I'd sing along with the music and put on a real strong country twang. You may not believe this, but they didn't realize that I was joking and thought I sounded pretty good." Mr Conrad laughed heartily at the imagery. I let him calm down a little before I went on. "As a matter of fact, Cowboy suggested I could make a living off of doing that when I got to Canada. But I just couldn't see myself singing in honky-tonks."

"For honkies?"

"That's an interesting point. But there is a black man that does that kind of music, and he's real popular, too. I could do some of his songs and have myself billed as Charlotte Proud."

He chuckled again and I added to his enjoyment by quietly singing one of Papa Halstead's favorites that called for yodeling. It kept our conversation on a humorous note until the first bell rang.

Getting settled into class took our thoughts away from the jokes, but much later in the hour, when they seemed forgotten, Mr Conrad's truck drivin' girlfriend showed up at the door.

"Excuse me," said Miss Marshall in a low voice. "Mr Conrad, may I see you for a moment?"

Laughter escaped from my lips as soon as I set eyes on her, and so it did with Mr C. Immediately I turned my head in hope that she wouldn't think it was directed at her. Conrad did the same, but he had to look at her sooner or later. The rest of the class just sat there amazed, wondering if we'd lost our minds. When we couldn't stop the chuckles and Mr Conrad refused to acknowledge her, Miss Marshall finally walked away in a huff.

My teacher waxed sober when he realized that the woman was now extremely ticked off. He thought for a second and then arose from his chair. "Everyone read silently till I come back," he said and went down the hall.

"What was that all about?" asked Helen B. with a dubious look.

"Well, the joke is about country music," I explained. "Miss Marshall's a big fan of it and Mr Conrad said that he really doesn't care for it. We laughed about it earlier and I guess we still think it's kind of funny."

Helen grinned and said, "She sure won't think it's funny. I wonder what he's going to tell her?"

"It won't be the truth, that's for sure," said another girl.

"We've got eleven more minutes of class," said one of the boys. "I'll bet he won't make it back before the bell rings."

He didn't. But he was there for my other classes and not looking any the worse for wear. Then when he looked at me, the laughter was gone from his eyes.

"I see you're still alive," I remarked to him on my way out to lunch.

"Yes, no thanks to you."

"What? I'm no more to blame than you. You'd have laughed anyway."

"No, I don't think so. . . . No, you're right, I would have."

"So what did you tell her?"

"I told her the truth."

"You did?"

"Well, not the whole truth. I didn't want her upset with you, so I took all the blame. Besides, what else could I come up with? After all, you and I were the only ones laughing."

"What did she say?"

"I don't think you want to hear it, but we did come to an understanding and she's forgiven me."

"Good. How much is it going to cost you?"

"What? How did you–"

"How'd I call it right? I've known her a lot longer than you have."

"Well, it's none of your business how much. Now, she's still a little uptight or else I'd ask you to lunch. But right now you're kind of dangerous to be around, young lady, so why don't you, uh, make yourself scarce?"

"All right, I will. And maybe you'd better have breakfast with her tomorrow. That way she'll be happy and I can get some studying done."

As I hurried on to lunch, a little dark cloud cast a shadow over my happiness. In spite of my casual reply, the thought that he just might start keeping his distance, even for a little while, bothered me quite a bit. I was growing accustomed to his attentions and at that moment discovered just how much I did enjoy them. With it being too late to recant, I asked God to keep him from taking my words too seriously.

TUESDAY, OCTOBER 15:

In vain I tried to accept the possible consequences of my hasty words, believing that my teacher would take me seriously and leave me alone the next morning to read. But to my relief, there he was again on Tuesday, as regular as the sunrise. This time I happily closed my books and trotted blissfully alongside him, vowing never again to suggest anything like I'd done the day before.

As we sat down in what was becoming our usual spot, I found myself trembling and a bit self conscious. Since the previous afternoon, a feeling arose in me that I had offended him and had to win him back. That morning I had made myself especially pretty and hoped he would be pleased.

"You said yesterday that I was keeping you from your studies," Mr Conrad remarked as he doctored his coffee. He was his usual stoic self, as he always seemed to be in public, appearing to ignore my new hairstyle and pale pink flowered dress. "Is that for your bat mitzvah?"

"No, I do that at home. Morning study is mainly personal. It starts the day out right."

As he looked at my Bible and the other books I carried–a Hebrew dictionary, a small concordance and a translation of *Rashi's Commentary on Genesis*–fear of losing the morning breakfast routine rose up again.

"So you honestly enjoy all this?"

"Yes."

"No wonder you always look like a walking library. Well, I am sorry, Janette. I just assumed I was rescuing you from something unpleasant. I know it would be for me; now I feel like a heel. Well, if you'd rather be left alone in the morning, that's fine, but I'll be very lonesome and awfully bored without you."

At that my heart sank, but I said nothing. I really didn't want to give up my studies, nor did I want to give up him.

"Look," he said. "It's my guess that you need help with your bat mitzvah. Am I right?"

"You sure are."

"Then let's work a compromise. Bring a small portion of it each day and we'll work on it. Or if you prefer, you can read me some of whatever Torah portion you're studying and show me what you find so exciting. Then if there's time left, we'll deal with music. Will that work?"

"Yes, to perfection. Thank you."

"It is I who should thank you. A man could die of boredom in this place. But now I'm curious to see what you find so enthralling in all that; and a little religion never hurt anybody . . . I suppose. Now, you are still coming tonight, aren't you?"

That evening I was skipping band rehearsal and going to celebrate Simchat Torah at Mr Conrad's synagogue.

"Oh, yes. I'll be there, and my parents are coming, too."

"Good. I've been wanting to talk to them."

"Oh?" I said with suspicion in my voice. "What about?"

"Oh, about you. . . ."

About us.

". . . And about us."

I saw the twinkle in his eyes and laughed out loud. "You're nuts!" I said in English. Heads turned.

"Nuts about your music. That's what I want your parents to know. You have a lot of potential; I saw that when you turned in your first theory assignment. I'm planning some changes in my schedule pretty soon and then I'll be able to spend more time with you on it. If I come to your house, we can work as long as we want."

"Mr Conrad, one thing I'd really like to work on is where I'll be going to college. I know that UCLA and USC have very fine music departments and I plan to apply."

"Wherever you go, you ought to get a scholarship. Now, don't worry. We'll get to that soon enough."

I sure hope so.

At last it was clear what was going on: I provided an entertaining distraction for him, which included developing my talents, all of which was in line with his teaching M.O. That was safe enough—for him and for me. In turn, he provided some things that were important to me. But the topper was that Mr C's Hebraic heritage made him one of the few people in the daily grind that I could truly relax and be myself with, making our friendship like a green oasis; a treasure that was certainly worth keeping.

Since it was Tuesday, that meant Madrigals at noon. After Choir, with the group gathered around the big grand piano, Alan Haskell and I looked over some new music together while it was still being passed around. Having perfect pitch and being an excellent sight reader, he had picked out his part right away and was learning it already. I read along with him until Mr Conrad got things started.

Alan and I seemed to be getting used to each other. Always together in Music Theory, Choir and then at Madrigals, we were blending into a comfortable relationship. At least that's how it felt to me. We weren't yet going steady in an official sense, but it seemed a matter of course as things continued; especially since Alan had finally accepted the way I felt about petting and was behaving himself. This was good. This was safe. This was what I wanted. No worry about getting too deeply involved with this cute, coffee colored underclassman; just nice, non-threatening companionship.

That day when Alan walked me to class after Madrigals, he took my hand. We talked a little bit about the talent show and then he sprang a new idea on me.

"You know, the talent show was fun," he said. "But it just wasn't enough–especially since you weren't able to dance with me. Wouldn't it be a trip to do a big show with the choir, or even just the madrigal group and the stage band? We could do swing music. I'm not the only one that knows how to tap and Lindy, so we could put in some real together dance numbers. We could have costumes and everything. What do you think?"

"I get visions of Mickey Rooney and Judy Garland," I replied casually while remembering how Alan had mentioned something like this before. "But yeah, it'd be fun. We'd just have to get Mr Conrad to go for it."

Alan's smile faded suddenly. "Yeah, that's the thing. I mentioned it to him last year and he didn't go for it at all. He didn't seem to think anybody else would, either. But you're getting real buddy-buddy with him, so maybe you can help me sell the idea."

"Well, I'll do my best, but I can't make any promises. Let me think it over and I'll see what I can do."

"Great! I'm sure if anybody can persuade him, you can. I wouldn't be surprised if you could even get him to dance. I imagine he's pretty good."

"Oh, really?" I couldn't recall anything in Mr C's file about dancing, but then remembered what he'd said about being in vaudeville. "That's right. He danced when he was a child."

"Only as a child? I'd say he'd been dancing longer than that, but that's my opinion."

"How'd you find that out? Did he tell you?"

"No, he didn't have to tell me. Next time you see him, dig the way he walks. People who dance–who really dance–have a different way of walking. You'll see what I mean."

A show with dancing and singing? The more I thought about it the more it appealed to me. Suddenly my head filled with images and speculation so much that I hardly noticed the kiss on the cheek Alan gave me when we said goodbye at the door to the gym. By the time I made it home from school I knew what I wanted to do with this idea. But I put those thoughts aside shortly after because of the evening ahead at Temple Ner Tamid.

"Do I have to wear one of those little hats?" asked Daddy as he drove us to the synagogue.

"I think you ought to, Rich," Mommy answered before I could. "Besides, it's only for one night."

"I'll help you with it, Daddy," I said, although I'd never put a *kippah* on a nappy black head before. Fortunately he kept his hair short.

"What kind of hats?" asked Daniel.

"Little round hats," I told him. "The men wear them and so do the boys."

The youngest, Gregory, Amelia and Daniel, also came. That made me a little nervous because they often got fidgety and bored in church. Hopefully they would find this new and exciting enough to hold their interest.

We were a bit early, but still Mr C was there to greet us as soon as we arrived. He started us out with a brief tour of the synagogue after we took to covering Daddy's head. Mommy and I both wore hats, and the young ones wouldn't hear of it.

The building was nice, but nothing fancy: a simple red brick exterior with lots of wood paneling on the inside. The beauty was mainly in the artwork that lined the walls and other items encased in glass in the vestibule. There were paintings, a few photographs and a couple of works of bronze done in relief; but most outstanding were the framed works of Hebrew calligraphy. They were so beautiful and detailed that it was difficult to tear ourselves away. Then there was the lovely Judaica for sale in the window of the sisterhood shop that I longed to browse over. But window shopping would have to wait. It was time for the evening service.

Simchat Torah means, "Rejoicing in the Torah," and so the holiday is meant to be very joyful. The highlight is when the Torah scrolls are taken out and paraded around the sanctuary. People touch them, kiss them and dance with them. But this was mostly an older congregation, so I didn't expect much in the way of celebration. Still, the hour and a half that the service lasted was an absolute blast. I became so absorbed in the celebration that I forgot my family and joined right in as if I were still at kibbutz Aleph Tav. I took my turn with the scrolls and was even blessed to be called up to receive an *aliyah* (a chance to go up and recite a traditional blessing).

For me the service was over too soon. But afterward the joy continued with *oneg, i.e.,* refreshments. Conversation was lively as we lined up at the table and then balanced cups and plates in an effort to consume our selections. Mr Conrad was doing his best to have the talk he'd wanted with my parents concerning my music, but was constantly interrupted. Then someone pushed through the crowd and approached us. It was the rabbi.

"David," said the gray haired man, a twinkle in his warm, dark brown eyes. "This must be the young lady you were telling me so much about."

At those words a chill went through me. What had he been told? What had everyone in this place heard about me? Whatever it was wouldn't have been bad, and yet this man still might see me as a Christian and not accept me as Mr Conrad had. He seemed nice enough, but I knew from experience that they could get pretty nasty if they even suspected you were a Christian trying to convert someone. I didn't want to get politely raked over the coals and put in my place.

Mr Conrad introduced us all to the rabbi and then, just as I feared, the man wanted to talk to me. Just me.

I followed Rabbi Birnbaum back to the sanctuary where we sat down. He asked about Alef Tav and how it was started, as well as the life there and the direction of study. Being just a bit careful, I told him what I knew about its beginnings and purpose and then about my experiences there.

As I spoke, he listened intently, interrupting with only an occasional question. To my relief I saw no signs of anger or displeasure of any kind, only a keen interest and curiosity. When I had told all that I believed he would care to know, he smiled and thanked me for indulging his request.

"Janette?" My father approached us from the rear of the sanctuary. "We're ready to go."

"So soon?" said the rabbi. "Is the food gone already?"

"Oh, no, there's still plenty. We just need to get these kids home to bed or we would stay longer."

"Where's Mr Conrad?" I asked. "I want to say goodbye."

Daddy laughed. "A couple of ladies have him over in a corner talking him to death. You may not be able to get a word in, but you can try."

Boldly, but with tact, I rescued my teacher from the two women. Being free, he was then able to walk us out to the car where we said our goodbyes.

The drive home was full of talk. As I listened to and occasionally joined in with the chatter, all sorts of thoughts danced in my head. There were the new things I had learned that night that I didn't want to let slip. Uppermost, however, was the joy in knowing that after this night, my parents would be more accepting of my love for Judaism, even though Daddy declared that such a service still wouldn't be worth fifty dollars even with twice the food. Having had them experience just this one holiday was certain to make life easier in that regard. This was an answer to prayer, which is what David Conrad seemed to be–one big, beautiful hunk of answered prayer.

WEDNESDAY, OCTOBER 15:

But as warm feelings prompted doubts and questions to rise up again the next day at breakfast with Conrad, I looked squarely at this amazing gift horse and wanted to see every last one of his teeth. It was only natural to suspect that something was amiss with this too-good-to-be-true setup, and though I wanted to guard my heart, I didn't want to spoil a situation that might be innocent. So I imagined myself as a moth happily about to be toasted, the thought of which suppress any fanciful romantic notions.

While eating, we naturally discussed the previous evening and my music as well. Then as he had asked, I brought out my Hebrew studies. Having his assistance was such a joy and relief that by the time the first bell rang, those doubts about spending my mornings with him seemed foolish.

A discussion over the text nearly made us late to first period, and a certain party sure took notice of us coming up together. Helen Bombardner said nothing and I pretended not to notice her reaction. So what if she had it bad for The Fox? I wasn't about to live my life to please her. So the thing that happened right after class caught me completely off guard.

As I stepped out the door, Helen slipped her arm through mine and clung to me as we walked down the hall.

"Janette, please don't be upset with me," she said. "But I need your help again. Look, I know you don't really need me for French anymore, but I don't have anyone else to turn to. Please say you'll help me? Please?"

"Well, what is it that you need, Helen?"

Leaning close, she whispered, "Can you teach me how to dance?"

"Dance? I don't know. I honestly don't know any of the latest dances. You really should ask someone else."

"But I don't know anybody else. Not that I can trust. And not that can really dance. Oh, please?"

How do you know I can really dance?

Helen continued to plead desperately and look forlorn, while telling me of the dance she'd been invited to by a "super cute guy," so I took pity.

"All right," I said, beginning to feel relieved that it was something so trivial. "But you'll have to come to my house. When is your date?"

"Next week. Uh—Wednesday night at the Elk's Lodge."

"That's not a lot of time, but we'll give it a shot."

"Oh, merci, Janette! Merci, merci beaucoup!" Helen gave my arm a grateful squeeze and ran off to class while I thanked God she was excited about someone other than The Fox. Maybe she'd lose the crush all together.

That day at lunch I went to see Mr Johnson. He took me out for a burger and we talked and laughed like old times. He was naturally very pleased when I told him how Mr Conrad had asked me to read to him from the Scriptures and offered me help with bat mitzvah studies. Then I mentioned Alan's idea for a big band show, and he also thought it would be fun to do.

As we talked it over, Bob Johnson smiled soberly and nodded to himself. He didn't say why, but he wasn't surprised that Mr C didn't want to do it, and agreed that getting his friend's approval might take some effort. "But I think we can convince him," he said, while thinking things that I wished he would share. "At least I hope we can, because he needs this. If we can't, we'll do it without him. You and Alan come see me on Friday like you said you would and we'll talk about it."

"That's odd," I said casually. "Why Mr Conrad would need this show?"

Mr J thought for a second, then shook his head. "We won't go into that. Let's just do this and see what happens."

Later that afternoon, as promised, Mr Conrad began taking me in a different direction with my lessons. When I arrived, a large piece of old sheet music was sitting on the piano. Titled "Bethena" by Scott Joplin, it had the picture of a lovely Negro woman on the cover wearing a long string of pearls. There were other sheets as well that would eventually replace most of the standard classical pieces that I'd been learning.

"Are you familiar with this composer?" He opened the cover of the music before taking his place in the overstuffed chair. When I said that I wasn't, he took a few minutes to tell me of this once popular American composer.

"Let's trade places and I'll play it for you," he said.

As I listened to this lovely waltz a whole new world seemed to open up for me. There was an enchantment in this old time music that carried me back to my visits with grandfather in Chicago and the silent movies he loved to watch at an old theater. Other thoughts filled my head along with the music as it changed and then returned to its original theme. I couldn't wait to learn it.

"What do you think?" Mr Conrad turned to me with a slight smile and a definite twinkle in his eye.

"Oh, I love it. Can I try?"

He had me join him on the bench and there he guided me slowly through the first section. This kind of instruction was something he'd only done once before and the piece didn't seem difficult enough to warrant it. Were I not so excited about the music, it would have been a big distraction to be so close to him. As it was, the music helped me to steel myself against falling into the pit of desire and becoming a silly, starry-eyed fool.

"You should do very well with that piece," he said. "I have photocopies of this and the others for you to take home. I'll keep the originals."

"Okay."

"Would you like to hear the rest of these?"

"Sure. But let me get out of your way."

Immediately I returned to the chair and happily listened as Mr Conrad played "Magnetic Rag" and "Solace", both of which were Joplin compositions. He also helped me get started on these, even though they would not become my assignments until later. Working on the new music took up most of the lesson time, except for one enchanting new vocal piece from the same era, "Bohemia Rag".

My mind was in a happy whirling haze all the way home, as I anticipated learning the new music and as the memory of the afternoon occupied my thoughts. I would have completely forgotten Helen's request for a dance lesson had my thoughts not jumped onto a track that eventually led in that direction. So as soon as I got in, I took care of the details, enlisting my sister Olivia to help out.

THURSDAY, OCT. 16:

With great relief, Helen's dance lesson was successful and soon out of the way, thanks to a lot of persistence on everyone's part. The gratefulness Helen expressed afterward increased my hope that the attentions she now received from classmates would leave me to enjoy my favored status with The Fox with no reprisals. So I relaxed and set myself to enjoy the daily routine once again. I'd grown used to it; comfortable now with the pleasant privileges and all the piquant variations. Seeing Mr C in the morning, the afternoon, the occasional evening had come to feel quite normal. Even his good looks and other charms appeared to be less of a jolt to my hormonal system. And with Torah study and Hebrew lessons thrown in, it bordered on the heavenly, this being asked to provide an entertaining distraction for this man. But while he and I were getting comfy-cozy, somebody else was severely out of sorts.

FRIDAY, OCTOBER 17:

"Oh! Well, look who's here," said a familiar feminine voice. Vicky Marshall had come into the cafeteria right behind Mr Conrad and I. Smiling sweetly, she chirped, "How are you this morning?"

In red, three inch spiked heels and bouffant blond hair, she stood almost as tall as Mr Conrad. Instead of the provocative necklines and tight sweaters she wore in the days preceding the regime of our principal, Constance MacGregor, she was into frilly, yet conservative attire for the sake of her job; and the buttons on her ruffled red Victorian blouse did their best against the forty plus inches of her bust, while her average hips posed no problem for the simple gray A-line skirt she had on. Outwardly she was perky and sweet, her long thick hair bouncing on her shoulders as she bobbed happily along. But the lack of a smile in her big green eyes betrayed the real mission she had of discovering just what went on with her boyfriend and me.

"Hello, Vicky," said Mr C, who seemed to feel the same displeasure at her presence. "How come you're up so early?"

"Oh, nothing special. I seldom have a real breakfast and it's just not a good meal to skip. Mind if I join you?"

Inwardly I grimaced. *Yes, I mind. But you're not asking me. Why don't you just shove off, lady?*

"Well, I don't mind if Janette doesn't mind," said Mr C.

A polite smile and a nod was all I gave her. I said nothing until we were seated, nor did I broadcast my feelings. The Fox and I sat across from each other while Miss Marshall sat next to him as I often did.

"I brought the kibbutz pictures this morning," I said.

"You found them?" My teacher's eyes lit up and he smiled slightly. "Great! Let me see."

"Say *ha motzi* first."

Together we sang the Hebrew prayer to bless HaShem for his provision of bread and then translated for the sake of Miss Marshall. Then I dug out the envelope of photos from my book bag and placed it in his hands.

As Mr C went through each of the snapshots, I explained them. Miss Marshall looked on and feigned interest. However, both were impressed with the photos taken of me in action with our small heard of cattle, roping and riding, *etc*. The best were saved for last. Those were the posed for pictures of us in our fancy new cowboy getups with some of the men wearing the knotted fringes called *tzitzit*. Doffed hats in one scene revealed *kippot* (yarmulkes) on their heads. There was even a couple of me with a fake mustache and *payess*.

"If I hadn't seen it with my own eyes," laughed Conrad. "I never would have believed it. These are wonderful! If only you'd had a movie camera. I'd like to see this in action."

"What are they wearing this other stuff for?" asked Miss Marshall. "I don't get it."

"They're orthodox Jews," explained Mr Conrad. "Those fringes they have on are worn all the time."

"Do they sleep in it?"

"I don't think so. Janette, may I borrow these for a few days? There are some people I'd love to show theses to."

"Like Rabbi Birnbaum? Sure."

"And I promise to take good care of them. Now, since Miss Marshall is here, why don't you select something to read?"

"Well, let's see. How about Proverbs? Chapter 31 looks very interesting."

Not catching my humorous inference to the "virtuous woman," he went on to say, "Wait a minute. You know, you haven't read anything to me from the New Testament. Let's hear something from that for a change. I've never really read it before and I'm kind of curious."

"You are? Okay." Turning pages to no place in particular, I found one of my favorite chapters. "Ah! Here we go. John's Gospel, chapter three."

As I read the entire chapter in my usual expressive manner, I realized that certain passages were likely to make my listeners uncomfortable or even upset. But I read on anyway and let the chips fall wherever.

"My!" Miss Marshall remarked haughtily. "I don't remember any of that being in the Bible. Is that a regular Bible or some kind of Jewish thing?"

"It's the authorized King James version," I replied.

"Well, I guess we can't believe everything that's in the Bible anyway."

"Why not?"

"Well, it's outdated and it's full of contradictions."

"It only seems that way if you haven't unlocked the means of interpretation. Miss Marshall, the Bible is a spiritual book. To understand it fully, a person has to be spiritually equipped. It takes sincere prayer and intense study, not to mention faith, especially if the reader is to make sense out of all of those strange visions and prophesies. So don't knock it until you've made that kind of effort yourself. Have you?"

"Well no, I can't honestly say that I have."

"But, Janette," said Mr Conrad. "Didn't you tell me that there were also some serious problems in the translation?"

"Oh, yeah, the *goyisms*."

"The what?" Miss Marshall wrinkled her nose.

"Oh, I made that up. That's what I call the gentile twists on certain things that turn up in English translations, mainly in the New Testament. You see, over the centuries, many pagan traditions were introduced into the faith and labeled as true worship. Even though the New Testament is a Jewish book, it's been translated for us by people that didn't want to be Jewish and didn't want Jesus to be either, so they altered the meaning of a few things."

"Well, I sure as he-heck have never heard that before."

"You're not alone by any means."

"So what are some of these whatever you call them?"

"The biggest example I can think of is this whole business called church, especially when church refers to people and not just a building. Now, in the Greek New Testament, the Greek word that church comes from doesn't appear anywhere in the manuscripts. So with the people in the Bible, the church as a group of people or even as a building didn't exist at all."

"So you're saying that those people who wrote the Bible didn't know anything about church, right?"

"Correct."

"Then where did people go on Sundays?"

My eyes widened and for a second my mouth hung open in amazement as I held back the laughter. Then I reminded myself that I hadn't heard any of this before studying at kibbutz Alef Tav, and then her question didn't seem so silly.

"Because they were Jews, they had no Sunday worship. They gathered in the temple or the synagogue, and they also met in homes; their day of weekly worship was on the seventh day. I believe Sunday worship was something brought in by Constantine."

"This makes a lot of sense," said Mr C. "You know, if the New Testament is a Jewish book, then there needs to be a Jewish version."

"That's right. They're working on that up at Alef Tav."

"That's all well and good, Janette," said Miss Marshall. "But then how could regular people understand it? If its made to read Jewish, then how will Christians know what it says? There ought to be another way to fix it."

"They'll just have to convert," said Mr Conrad in a serious tone that almost made me lose my composure again.

"Are you serious?" Miss Marshall was incredulous.

"It would certainly make a difference in how they see things," I said, avoiding the temptation to make fun. "If the traditions of the Bible ceased to be foreign, then it would be much easier to understand and more enjoyable to read. That's how I see it."

"Now, why don't you read a little something from the Psalms," said Mr C. "Then we'll go up to the room."

By the time we got upstairs, any need to laugh vanished. I even felt a bit sorry for the ignorant Miss Marshall and regretted the levity. Even though her reason for joining us had been phony, some of her questions had seemed in earnest. I could only hope that her curiosity was satisfied enough for her to leave me and Mr Conrad alone.

While this was happening, Alan and I were having a brown bag lunch with Mr Johnson in the band room and talking over ideas for a program of swing music and dance. First Alan shared his basic idea, then we were told what could be expected. By the time lunch was over, we had a sketch of a program down on paper. With that done, it was entirely in Mr Johnson's hands and all we could do was pray that Mr Conrad would go for it.

SATURDAY, OCTOBER 19:
Saturday morning I sprang out of bed and sang my way through the early morning hours, happily anticipating the church picnic. I knew it was going to be a perfect day.

Aside from my teacher, I'd also invited my family. But too much was going on that morning for us to all ride together. Daddy usually had to work anyway, so he was coming later, and Mommy would also arrive just a little late with the rest of the brood, except for Charlotte who had plans with some of her school chums. That meant that at least for a little while, I would have The Fox all to myself.

The day was gorgeous, with a slight chill in the air, very little wind and big fluffy clouds decorating a sky of electric blue. Most everyone from The Rock had met earlier at the church to share the ride and caravan, which is what I had originally wanted to do. Mr Conrad, however, preferred to take his time and drive his own car; so I showed up at his apartment at ten. We went on up by ourselves, listening to the radio and enjoying the scenery.

At this time of year, Fourth of July Canyon in the Manzano Mountains was at its best. Brilliant, fiery maple trees filled the canyon floor with bright fall colors that were as lively as a fireworks display. Enthralled by the sight, Mr Conrad drove slowly to the end of the picnic area and a little beyond, enjoying the drive a bit longer before turning back to park.

We arrived along with many of the others. The big, long psychedelic bus with the destination sign that read "Heaven" marked the spot where our people were gathering to set up camp. We joined the happy hippy crowd and I introduced my teacher around, almost losing him right away to David Richardson. But I was being torn in another direction anyway. As soon as the children from my Sunday school class set eyes on me, they swarmed around with hugs and kisses, wanting to know if we were going to dance. I said yes, then sent them off to find a good level spot for our feet, while Mr Conrad and I set up camp. Then he sat down with David Richardson and we parted company for a bit.

The kids found a nice spot of ground and we cleared it of sticks and leaves. Since no one else was there who could play the songs for us, the only accompaniment would be our voices. Joining hands, we made a circle and started with "Hiné Ma Tov".

Soon I lost track of time. Our happy voices and clapping hands drew others, both children and adults. Some joined our circle while others were content to watch. I became so wrapped up in dancing that I forgot about Mr Conrad until he suddenly showed up and joined our circle.

We had already been dancing for a while, getting hot and sweaty on the more vigorous songs; wanting to stay on the fresh side, I was almost ready to quit when Mr C stepped in. The idea of dancing with him kept me going.

Not all the dances were traditional, so I called out some of the steps for him as we went along. He followed with ease and moved with a grace and lightness of foot that told me Alan Haskell knew what he was talking about. A short time after that, my mother showed up with my brothers and sisters. They were pleasantly surprised at what they saw and I could hear some of their comments as I whirled around. If only they could have come a little sooner and seen more. The adults were beginning to drop out and take some of the children with them.

"Okay," I said as we ended a song. "Enough dancing."
"What?" Mr Conrad was disappointed. "Can't we do one more?"
"Huh? One more?" I looked at him like he was crazy.
"Just one more. Please?"
"Well, all right. If it's a slow one."

"Do you know 'Ma Na Vu'?"

"Sure."

We'd already done it once, but the dance was a favorite; so those who remained joined in to do it again.

That was beautiful," Mommy said as we came over to greet her. "What kind of dancing is that?"

"It's Jewish folk dancing," I told her. "I learned it on the kibbutz."

"Can I learn to do that?" asked Amelia.

"Sure. If you come to our Sunday school, you can dance with the kids."

"Mommy, why don't we start going to Janette's church?" asked Daniel. "They do fun stuff."

"We do fun stuff at our church," she replied.

"No, we don't," said Adrian. "They hardly have anything fun to do. And they sure don't have anything like this."

"Well, ask your father about it when he gets here, and if he says we can go to Janette's church then we will."

Just then was the call to come and get it. There was the usual picnic food of hamburgers, hot dogs and chicken; then there were big roasted ears of corn, plus giant pots of the most wonderful green chili stew and freshly baked, hot buttered tortillas, as well as sopapillas. It would take a lot of willpower not to over do it with that kind of food, and I was starved from the workout I'd just had.

As we sat down to eat and relax, I let my mother and Mr Conrad do most of the talking. When my father arrived, the conversation got even more interesting. They discussed the song writing and recording sessions Mr C had in mind in pursuit of a scholarship for me; but once the excitement from this was overcome, they waxed casual and my parents made attempts at getting better acquainted with my mystery man. That's when my ears really perked up in hopes of collecting more data. But David Conrad was expert at dodging questions about himself that even looked like they might probe too deeply, conveniently finding rabbit trails to run along. Nothing came forth in their discourse that I didn't already know in some shape, form or fashion, but I paid special attention just in case; no clue was too small or unimportant.

While the adults chatted, I took out the tablet I always kept with me and sketched, occasionally making notes in code of anything I thought I might forget. But then I got tired of sitting, and the conversation waxed boring as my teacher asked Daddy about business. It looked like time to go for a walk, so I arose, stretched and headed off into the maple trees.

As I wandered the trails that led in through the wooded area, I gathered a child or two, or three. After a while, we started a game of tag and went running and laughing. This only lasted a short time, though, because all I really wanted to do was enjoy the beauty and quiet of the canyon.

A large fallen tree provided a good spot to rest, so I sat down there with a tiny toddler on my knee. Cradling her in my arms, I sang quietly and looked up at the trees. Moments later she fell asleep and then someone else came along the trail. It was Mr Conrad. Lowering his 5' 11" frame to sit beside me, he said nothing and neither did I, until some of the children came running up and changed the mood a bit.

"They certainly do like you," Mr Conrad observed. "They follow you like the Pied Piper."

"I know," I said happily. "I wouldn't have it any other way. They're so sweet and so much fun. If it weren't for them, I wouldn't have anyone to dance with. I also get to fill their little heads with some of the other stuff I picked up in Colorado, so that I don't forget it all."

Sarah, the little girl in my arms, suddenly awoke and began to squirm. When I tried to pass her to her older brother, Zach, she reached insistently for Mr Conrad. He took her, and she promptly grabbed for his glasses.

"No, sweetheart," he said, carefully pulling the gold wire spectacles from her grasp. He folded them and put them in his shirt pocket. For her next move she put her hands on his head and began praying in tongues. "Is she doing what I think she's doing?" Mr C lowered his voice for this question.

"She's praying for you," said Zach.

"That's what I thought. That's a pretty good imitation."

"It's not an imitation, mister," said Zach. "She's for real."

"Oh! Hurts!" Sarah exclaimed, patting Mr Conrad just below the left shoulder blade. "Bad lady hurt you. In Jesus' name be all better. All better."

Mr Conrad's countenance suddenly changed to wide-eyed amazement before he blanched and broke into a serious sweat. Slowly he pulled Sarah away from him and placed her in the arms of her brother; then with an expression of disbelief, he rubbed the spot on his shoulder the child had touched. It then occurred to me that Sarah had prayed over the exact same spot that I had when teaching him to shoot.

What happened to this man? A bullet? Stabbing? It's a wound of some kind. If only I could get a look at that shoulder . . . that is, if it's not too late. With Sarah's prayers, whatever was there is likely gone by now.

"Are you okay?" I asked him.

"I, uh, I don't know." Shaking his head to clear it, Mr C tried to get hold of himself, and not very successfully. "I–I don't really know."

I sent a boy off to get him a cold drink while I stayed close. When he returned with a cup of punch, I sent all of the children away.

"Thank you," said Mr Conrad, after a few sips. "I guess I feel a little better now. That was rather–intense."

"What happened?"

"Well–first it was like a jolt of electricity went through my shoulder, and then for a split second all the lights went out. It was as if the universe–blinked."

"Wow! So what is it that happened to your shoulder?"

He shook his head. "No, Janette. This is one thing I cannot talk about, not with you or with anyone else. It just–doesn't help. Talking only brings it all back and that's the last thing I need."

"Well, whatever it is, I can tell you this: HaShem knows every detail, and he wants to take care of it. That's why he had both Sarah and I pray over that same shoulder."

Again he shook his head, then rubbed his eyes. Reaching for his glasses, he put them on and said, "Maybe God can heal my body, Janette, but he can't change the past. If you see him do any miracles like that then be sure to let me know and I'll be the first in line." Drinking the last of the punch, he crushed the paper cup in his hands and got to his feet. "I think I'll go."

"Go where and do what?" I stood up and stayed close to him. "Sit around and mope? Uh, uh."

"Janette–"

I had made a quick move. "My, my! Look what I have!"

"That's my wallet. Hey! How did you–" He reached out to grab the billfold but I kept it just out of reach.

"Can't drive without a license." Smiling impishly, I danced a few paces away, dangling the wallet in front of me. "Come and get it."

First he sighed and looked exasperated, then shook his head and smiled. Finally there appeared a gleam in his eye and the smile twisted into a mischievous grin. "You'd better be fast, young lady," he said just before he lunged at me. "Real fast."

I took off running, afraid the man I had just robbed might take out his frustrations on me with a spanking. Then it occurred to me that he just might not, and that being caught wasn't such a bad idea after all.

Chapter Two
The Trouble With Helen

SUNDAY, OCTOBER 20 - MONDAY, OCTOBER 21:
Bad lady . . . bad lady. . . . What kind of a bad lady caused David Conrad to sustain a wound to his shoulder?
Knowing how attractive he was to women, it wouldn't be at all far fetched to assume that the perpetrator was a jealous girlfriend. His apparent propensity for choosing unsavory or low brow female companions (as evidenced by his ties with Vicky Marshall), made it even more likely that the incident was connected with his love life. And was it a bullet wound? And if it was, had it been intentional? If this was the incident that ended his career in show business, it was certainly no accident.

Mrs MacGregor always checked for criminal activity in the background of any teacher she hired, so David Conrad had no jail time or convictions, but then neither had serial killer Jacob Noonan. Still, Conrad was not the criminal type. Then, type aside, anyone pushed to the limits can commit a crime or become involved in one. He might have been duped, or more than likely he'd been a victim, as in blackmail. *Was he a victim still–that he had to leave Los Angeles to come here?* Off and on throughout the weekend I worked and reworked all that I knew about my precious teacher, but again had to shelve my cogitation for more immediate things.

On the Monday following the picnic, Mike O'Connell had decided to join Mr Conrad and I for breakfast. For some reason or other, Mr C was rather quiet, and my senses told me there was turmoil going on far beneath his calm exterior. Mr O'Connell sensed it as well, but when this somber mood was alluded to, Conrad denied there being any problem. Rather than make an issue of it, we went on and read from the Scriptures and had our discussion. Eventually he perked up.

Again Mr C and I were almost late to French class and again Helen B. took notice. As I took my seat, she leaned over and whispered in my ear. "My, but aren't we getting cozy with teacher," she said.

My only response was to look bored and shrug before opening my text book to the day's lesson. But I knew she would take up the subject at length once class was over, so I had to be ready for her.

"So what gives?" asked Helen, running to catch me as I hurried out to second period. "Are you and Monsieur Conrad getting into extracurricular activities?"

"Not the kind you're suggesting, Helen. We've been having Bible study in the mornings. Today Mr O'Connell joined us, so the discussion ran long and made us late. Miss Marshall was there last week, and I wouldn't be surprised if a few other teachers decide to show up."

"Are you serious? That tramp came to your Bible study?"

"Oh, she was just being nosey. Fat chance she'd be interested in anything the Bible has to say."

"So do you do this every day?"

"Pretty much, but I don't know how long it'll last. Most people can't take too much Bible if they're not seriously interested in God. Look, I have to go to my locker before class and I don't want to be late. I'll see you in Choir."

I hurried off before she could say anything else, and as I went, prayed about the jealousy dear Helen was obviously feeling. That kind of irritation I did not need.

TUESDAY, OCTOBER 22 - WEDNESDAY, OCTOBER 23:
Tuesday morning was reminiscent of Alef Tav, except that I got to be the rabbi. Mr O'Connell returned to join Mr C and I, plus three other faculty members, two of whom I'd never met formally. Again I read from the Scriptures, gave bits of commentary for the sake of clarity, and a discussion ensued. Some questions were rather pointed and tinged with anger from disappointment with religion, but the Spirit of God worked in a way that was positively dazzling from my end. He made things come out of my mouth that I'd never even heard before. Otherwise I never could have answered these people. Then on Wednesday there were even more wanting in on the study, but God told me that it wouldn't last and it didn't.

THURSDAY, OCTOBER 24:
Helen was quiet and sullen all that week. Even when I had asked about the dance, she only answered in one brief sentence that it had been nice. Knowing what was bothering her, I hoped that if I just ignored it, maybe it would go away. Fat chance, of course. Thursday after first period, she asked if I could come by after school to study and talk. Figuring I might as well get it over with, I agreed.

We didn't study much, although we started out going over the day's lesson. After a while Helen fell silent. Tears began to roll down her pale cheeks and her chin slowly dropped to her chest. Not quite what I was expecting.

Putting my books aside, I reached out a hand to offer a comforting touch. "What's wrong, Helen?"

"I'm sorry. I'd like to be strong like you are, Janette, but I don't know how. I just can't help the way I feel about him."

"Who?" As if I didn't know.

"Monsieur Conrad. I've loved him from the first day I saw him, but he's never really noticed me. At least not the way I want him to; and certainly not the way he notices you."

"But he notices you more than he used to. He thinks you're very pretty. I can tell."

"Well, that may be so, but it's not enough. You're the one he spends all the time with. You get private lessons and–and you get to have breakfast with him! And me–he hardly gives me the time of day. But you know what? He used to spend time with me in the mornings before you came along. Yes. I used to come in early and sometimes catch him when he'd first open up the room. Then we'd have conversations all in French. But this semester, it's only happened a couple of times, and I think it's all because of you."

It was on my tongue to say, "Well, have you considered that maybe Mr Conrad knows you have a crush on him, and that maybe he's trying to send you a message that he's not interested? And have you considered that maybe the reason he's with me so much is that I'm not after him, and therefore he feels safe and comfortable?" But feeling the words were too frank, what I said was, "Helen, I can't control what Mr Conrad does. Besides, haven't you noticed that my personality is different than yours? It's different from his, too, which is important. See, he tends to be quiet and withdrawn and so do you. That combination doesn't always work when it comes to getting a love interest going. Opposites do attract, which is probably why he's more interested in my company, because it's certainly all been his idea. Lessons, breakfast and anything else have all been initiated by Mr Conrad. I would never have dreamed of approaching him myself, and you know that."

"Well, what else can I do? I just don't know how to be outgoing like you. I don't have anything new and exciting to get his attention. How do I make him want to be with me?"

"Helen, I hate to say this, but maybe you shouldn't do anything. Maybe you should just forget about him and enjoy getting to know the cute guys that are noticing you. At least they are interested in having your company."

"But I'm not in love with them! I was hoping to tell Mr Conrad about my dates and all the attention from these boys, so he'd be jealous or more interested. You know. With other men–young men wanting to be with me, he might begin to think of me as nice to be with. But I don't know when or how to even tell him about those boys–or to tell him anything! I was thinking that maybe I could come with you to your morning Bible study. There's a Bible here somewhere and I could start reading it."

"That's not what a Bible study is for. Besides, I would still upstage you. Another thing is that it might not be correct to take the liberty of inviting you, since we meet in the teachers' cafeteria. The only reason I can go in is because Mr Conrad invited me. I'd have to ask him first."

"He'd probably say no."

"Look, Helen, if you're really in love with him then–"

"Then what? What should I do?"

Knowing her case was pretty hopeless, I figured it might be best to let her experience the easy let down from Mr Conrad himself. Margo had gone through the same thing with Mr Fletcher her freshman year, and his talk with her had set her straight. But in order for that to happen in this instance, there had to be some sort of confrontation. Although Mr C was probably aware of Helen's crush, he wasn't about to do a thing but sidestep her.

"Helen, I think that if you're in love with Mr Conrad and you believe you've really got something he should want, then you ought to be more up front about it. Otherwise you'll just go on the same way you are now."

"Yes, but how?"

Hmmm . . . now what would Georgia do? My saucy, high yellow cousin knew what to do to get a man's attention. Actually, with her beautiful face and figure, she didn't have to do anything. But if she wanted to flirt, she could come up with the darnedest ideas.

"I know," I said after a moment's cogitation. "Yeah! This ought to be a good way to get the point across. Helen, go to the market and buy a bunch of the biggest, sweetest apples you can find, and make sure they're red. Then every morning give teacher an apple."

"Okay. Is that all?"

"Not if you want to get really bold. If they have a stem, tie a nice ribbon on them. Or if you like, you can slip him a little note along with each one."

"Notes that say what? Like a poem maybe?"

"Well—maybe; if it's real short. I was thinking more about writing something like—like, 'I just wanted to sweeten your day.' Or you could say, 'This fell when someone shook my tree.' Get the picture?"

"Oh, yes, I see. It might even be corny, but it would get the point across."

"Exactly. But write your own material. You can skip the cute quips and just tell him you miss talking in the morning like you used to. Try saying it simple with, 'I miss the way we used to talk.' Just be sure to make your notes short and to the point, and don't get too sexy or he'll get the wrong idea–and you don't want that."

"No, I don't."

"Oh! Wait a minute. Here's one." *Thank you, Lord!* "Roses are red–"

"Roses?"

"Let me finish. Roses are red, a passionate hue—"

"And?"

"Red is this apple, from me to you."

"Not bad! And very appropriate. Where'd you get that?"

"It just came into my head."

"*Magnifique!* I'll use it. I may wait a while for that one, but I'll definitely use it."

"Fine. Then if Mr Conrad is interested in you and your fruit, he'll tell you. I'm sure that if you employ this apple a day gimmick, you'll be having a nice long talk with The Fox in no time. And it'll be just the two of you."

"Excellent. Thanks ever so much, Janette. You're a real friend. Now I feel better about the party I'm going to have. I naturally wanted to invite you, but I was upset because you've been taking Mr Conrad away from me. But since you're helping me get him back–well, I guess we can stay friends. Look, I'm having a pajama party on November 2nd with some of my new girl friends. I don't think I'm ready yet for a party with boys. Anyway, I'd like you to attend. Bring a friend with you, if you like. Can you come?"

"Sure. I don't see why not."

"Good! Now I've got to get ready for it. It's been years since I've had a party or even very many friends that I could invite."

"I'm glad things have changed for you, Helen."

"Look, Janette, could you do me one more favor?" She got up and went over to her bureau. "I need to get some practice in on something. I do it all the time for myself, but not for other people, so I'd like to try it on you." Helen resumed her seat on the bed and motioned me over. "Here. Sit facing me and get ready to cut the cards."

In her hands was a small, red velvet pouch from which she brought a deck of Tarot cards. I'd never seen any before, but I was pretty sure I knew what they were. While she shuffled the ornate deck, I began praying on how to handle this one.

"Helen, are you going to tell my fortune?"

"Yes. I'm really getting quite good at it. One of these days I want to read Mr Conrad's fortune. That should be fun. And they can tell the past, too. Wouldn't that be interesting to look into his past to see what he's hiding?"

Fortune telling, astrology and all other types of divination are strictly off limits for anyone keeping covenant with the God of Israel. The Bible makes it abundantly clear, so I was not about to touch anything dealing with the occult. The warning I had received was that to do so was very dangerous, opening up doors to the realm of hellish spirits. But how could I explain that to Helen?

"Here." She set the deck before me face down. "Cut the cards three times to the right."

"No, Helen. I can't let you tell my fortune."

"But why not?"

"Because–well, because it's witchcraft; it's divination, so for me it's strictly taboo. God doesn't like for his children to be involved with things from Satan's world. It just isn't healthy."

"Oh. Well, it is witchcraft; I know that, so I guess it would be against your religion. But I sure would like to read for you. You'd be surprised at what you can learn from them, and it sure couldn't hurt to do it just once."

"Helen, I don't intend to do it and find out. I know you mean well and I'm sure it must be exciting for you, but I'm going have to pass."

A knock came on the door. Mrs Brown opened it and poked her head in. "Helen, could you come here a minute?" she said. "I can't find where you put the new blender. It must be some place where I can't reach it."

Helen sighed and left to do her aunt's bidding. While she was out of the room, I looked around again at the myriad knickknacks I had gotten used to seeing and generally ignored. Some had given me the creeps at first, but I had never said anything. Now I understood better what was going on. Around the room were crystal balls in various sizes and enthroned on odd looking or grotesque little pieces of furniture; there were votive candles, figurines some of which I now recognized as gods and goddesses, and other objects that, to me, looked as if they could have been talismans. Obviously Helen was deeply fascinated by the occult, and if she kept going, she would no doubt get completely swallowed up in it.

This business was totally out of my league; just thinking about it gave me the willies. With no desire to sit one minute longer with all that weirdness, I got my things together and prepared to exit as soon as Helen came back.

Look under the bed.

The thought came into my mind so loud and clear that I couldn't ignore it as just being me. Afraid of what I might find, I got up anyway and lifted the bed spread to see what was hidden there. Stacked neatly underneath were about eight or ten books on various occult topics and two Ouija boards in boxes. One box was very old and falling apart while the other was fairly new. After a quick peek at this, I dropped the edge of the bed spread and returned to the chair. Seconds later, Helen was back and it was time for me to get out of there.

"Okay," said Helen. "So I won't tell your fortune, but you are coming to my party and I can look forward to that. We'll have lots of fun, I promise."

FRIDAY, OCTOBER 25:

By Friday the morning devotional crowd was dwindling. Most who had come out of curiosity were satisfied, and I was almost glad to have them gone. I needed to speak privately with Mr Conrad and didn't know when either of us could find the time. He had to know about Helen.

"You weren't quite yourself this morning," said Mr Conrad as we walked to first period. "You seemed a little distracted when you started out. Is something wrong?"

"Yes, it is, and I need to talk to you about it."

"During lunch period?"

"After school would be better, if you're not too busy."

"I've got one student at three thirty for half an hour. Why not drop by my place a little after four?"

"All right, after four is fine. Thank you."

The entire business with Helen had me bothered, but I wouldn't tell it all to Mr Conrad, only the part that concerned him. The rest I would share with someone else.

Mavis "Peaches" Washington, the girl who sat next to me in choir, was brought up old style Pentecostal, much like Mr Johnson. Tall, with a deep ebony complexion, and a little on the heavy side, she looked slightly older than her years. The shock of gray hair which decorated her left temple was said to be a birthmark. With long skirts, hair always plainly styled and no cosmetics on her face, her appearance reflected that brand of holiness found amongst certain Christians. Naturally there were some beliefs we didn't agree on, but she had far more experience than I did in spiritual matters, and her love for God was an inspiration. Certain that her knowledge of some subjects was greater than mine, I asked her to have lunch with me. While we lunched, I told her about Helen's involvement in the occult.

"Prayer and fasting," she responded, patting the worn black leather cover of her old King James Bible. "That's how you deal with that witchcraft business. And don't be afraid of it, either. That doesn't mean there's no power in it. There is. But Jesus has far more power than Satan ever dreamed of, and he lives in you, so don't be afraid."

"Okay. But what about this party she's invited me to? Should I go? I mean, I just know she's going to break out the Tarot cards or the Ouija board as part of the entertainment."

"So what? Don't be so uptight over this, Janette. You're talking about paper and wood, not a coven of witches. The main thing is being prepared spiritually. It also helps to have others covering the situation in prayer. If she does drag out the hocus pocus, then you deal with it. If not, then you just relax and have a nice time."

"But I know so little about this kind of thing."

"Then it's time you learned."

"But–well, I can't do it alone that's for sure. It wouldn't be wise. Helen said I could bring a friend to the party. Would you like to come?"

"I can't think of anything I'd like better."

The way she smiled when she spoke assured me there was nothing to worry about. Now having Peaches to stand with me in this strange and awkward situation, I could even look forward to Helen's little shindig.

That afternoon I waited till someone with music books left Mr C's place before ringing his bell. When he answered the door, there he was again doing his Clark Kent routine, wearing those ugly horn rimmed glasses. It affirmed that he intentionally stopped wearing them for my benefit.

After fixing me an ice tea, we sat down together. He took the love seat while I sat on the couch.

"Now, what's wrong, Janette? I haven't upset you, have I?"

"No, that's not it at all. This is about Helen Bombardner. Mr Conrad, you've got to do something. Did you know that she's in love with you?"

"Oh, I've known for some time that Helen has a crush on me. What's the problem? Is she jealous of you?"

"I'll say she is. Helen has always been somewhat aware of the attention you pay me, but now it's worse since she's seen us coming to class together the past few days. She's been making remarks and asking questions. Now, I think I've convinced her she has nothing to be concerned about; but even though Helen knows we couldn't possibly be carrying on, the fact remains that I'm spending time with you and she's not. Therefore she's been upset with me. But that's not all. It's unfortunate, but this isn't something that will go away simply by ignoring it. She's so obsessed with you that nothing I say can convince her how pointless it is to go on like that. I mean, she's got a good looking guy from the football team asking her out and still she's only thinking of how she can use him to make you notice her more."

"That's too bad. She should be thrilled to have that kind of attention."

"Of course. But Helen doesn't live in the real world. She has plans to come after you very soon and that's mainly what I wanted to tell you. I think you ought to be forewarned, and I also think you should consider having a chat with her. Maybe if you talked with her openly like another teacher did with a friend of mine, she might come to her senses and forget about you. After all, she won't graduate for another year, and if you don't handle this now, she'll just grow worse and worse."

"She's going to come after me? How?"

"Oh, it's real cute. You'll see, probably on Monday. Don't worry about her causing a scene or anything. Still, if you don't do something, it could escalate. If I were you, I'd do something before it gets out of hand."

"If what you're saying is true, then I guess I'll have to. At any rate I'll give it some serious thought."

"Good. It may or may not work, but at least it's worth a try. Thank you."

"Thank you, for bringing this to my attention. I'll do what I can."

SATURDAY, OCTOBER 26:

It was the weekend to set our clocks back, and soon it would get dark early. This was a prelude to the season which began with my least favorite holiday, Halloween. All week Charlotte had been trying to get out of taking the little ones out for trick-or-treat because she had a party to go to that night. Thank God the band was putting on a concert that evening, which required my presence, or I'd have been in a very awkward position. The job usually fell to the oldest, and that was me, since Aaron was away at school. So my sister resented my not taking the kids out, just as she resented almost everything about me. (In this instance her complaint was that I was in church all the time.) But the perpetual animosity was her problem, and I could no longer let it be mine as well.

But this weekend had lots of things going on. After dinner on Saturday evening, Mommy and Daddy drove me over to Mr Conrad's for my very first recording session. I could tell that they were both excited, even though they said very little. I would later learn that Mr Conrad had told them to downplay the event so that they wouldn't add to my anxiety.

We arrived promptly at 7:30 and Mr. C ushered us in seconds later. To my surprise, Margo had arrived ahead of us and rose to greet us in the living room when we walked in. Her professional flash camera was on the coffee table ready for work. She greeted us happily and explained her presence to my parents who thought it was great to have the event captured on film.

"Now, before we begin," said Mr C. "Would anyone like a beverage?"

"I'd like a little brandy," my father said.

"And you, Mrs West?"

"I'll have the same," said Mother.

"And how about you ladies?"

Margo and I looked at each other, wishing we could join the adults in their choice. Thinking better of it I said, "I'll have some hot tea. Earl Grey, if you have it."

"I'll have the same," said Margo.

"Two Earl Grey teas coming right up," he said and stepped behind the wet bar. "After I serve the brandy."

The first twenty minutes or so were taken up with a discussion about the possibilities for my recording while we sipped our refreshment. Mr Conrad again explained that the recording would be part of a package to send with applications for scholarships. Margo made notes and took a picture or two. Then it was down the hall to the room that was Mr Conrad's studio.

The penthouse apartment held three bedrooms, two full baths and one half bath. One of those bedrooms was the recording studio. It seemed a simple set up, with sound proof walls, a large reel to reel tape recorder, mixing board and several microphones. There was also a piano and a glass booth. The arrangement was, as he had said, adequate for small projects. So we set about to first record our arrangement of Edward Purcell's "Passing By." If time allowed, we would add another song which would be the flip side of a small 33 1/3 disc. As we were all getting settled into our places, Margo excused herself to go powder her nose, taking only her purse with her. Knowing her true errand, I smiled from excitement of a different kind.

The big camera that Margo had brought with her wasn't necessary for the pictures she would take of what now hung in the back hallway. Thanks to the benevolence of Mr Conrad in financing our efforts to solve the Noonan Case, Margo had a top of the line espionage style camera that was slender and fit into pocket or purse. It took great pictures in any kind of light.

The distraction of the secret photo shoot helped my nerves a bit, but still I started to feel on edge. Before I knew it, I was trembling all over and my throat was tightening up as we tested the recording levels. Since Mr Conrad noticed most everything about me, he picked up on this, too.

"Just relax, Janette. Take a few deep breaths and you'll be all right."

"Mr Conrad,"

"Yes?"

I want brandy! "Oh, never mind. I'll be okay."

"Just remember, Janette, this is not Capital Records. It's only a spare bedroom filled with gadgets. I have some water here for you if you need it, or you can have more tea."

Closing my eyes for a few moments I searched inward for peace. Then when I looked up, my eyes met with Mr Conrad's.

"Ready now?" he asked.

"I'm ready."

My teacher looked around the room to make sure everyone was in place. It was then that Margo quietly slipped through the door to again take her seat. Looking at me she raised her eyebrows slightly to say that her mission was successful. Then she lifted the big camera and took my picture.

To our amazement, we did the song without numerous takes. I sang the melody first, then over dubbed the harmony. Mr Conrad added his voice as well, a special treat for all of us. We did it again before doing the next song.

It wasn't a long evening. We finished in less than three hours. After we'd gathered up our jackets, my mother went and studied the painting that hung over the fireplace: the beautiful Monet. The subject was that of a woman and a toddler in a field of flowers and tall grass with a beautiful sky above, filled with fleecy clouds.

"Mr Conrad, I just love that painting," she said. "How on earth did you come by an original like that?"

He didn't answer right away. Margo and I froze, our eyes on him as we all waited.

"It was a gift," he finally said. "From a very dear friend."

Margo and I exchanged glances, then made a date to talk the following afternoon by phone. Then we all said our goodbyes and headed home.

SUNDAY, OCTOBER 27:
I slipped out of church just before the sermon to get home before the family got back. I grabbed the phone and called Margo as planned.

"I couldn't wait," she said, excited. "I've been up all night developing film. Can you come over?"

"Be there in ten minutes or less."

Back down the stairs and out the door, I soon arrived at the Townsend residence and let myself in.

"In here," she called from the diningroom.

Margo had laid out most of the photos she'd taken on the diningroom table. All were enlarged to 8x10 for the sake of viewing fine detail.

"Now, these over here look like family photos," she said, pointing to the ones on the right. They were all on the same wall. "But they're older than the ones next to the bathroom. Now these–"

"Wow! That's Buster Keaton."

"Autographed and personalized. All of them are."

"Good grief! Charles Laughton, Jimmy Stewart, Bette Davis, Loretta Young."

"Who's this George Chandler?"

"That old guy on *Lassie* that played Uncle Peachtree or something."

"How about this guy, uh, J. C. Flippen?"

"Character actor. He was in *Oklahoma*."

"Man! I really need to start reading the credits more. Good stuff, huh?"

"It's fantastic! But we need to take a closer look to see if there's anything really important here."

"That's what this is all about."

"Let's look at the women first."

"My thoughts exactly. I'm sure I've already figured out which one gave him the painting."

I selected the face of a lovely brunette with pink cheeks and an upswept hairdo. "Hmmm . . . I've never heard of this one. She doesn't even look familiar."

"How about her?"

"Nope. . . . Say! Look at this one."

"Ah! Do you know her?"

"Not sure. My grandfather used to take me and Aaron to watch silent movies. If she's an actress, maybe I saw one of her films."

"Well, check what she wrote."

"'To my dearest David, with love and affection, Nedra.'"

"Yes, but Nedra who?"

Except for Grandpa West, the most knowledgeable person I knew on the subject of silent screen stars was Helen. "Look, I'll ask around or I'll check the public library."

Margo wagged her head suggestively. "She's not bad to look at, her picture is in the nicest frame and it's the biggest of all of these. If she's an actress, that says that he was much more than a fan. She's the one, alright."

"I'm sure you're right about that."

For almost an hour we studied the photos, looking for clues. But in the back of my mind was something I finally had to express because it wouldn't let me alone. "Maybe I'm wrong but I really don't see Conrad as the criminal type. If there's anything dark and dirty in his past, I'd peg him as the victim."

"Well, Jan, I'm inclined to agree, but–"

"So what are we being so nosey for? Do you think maybe he needs a good rescue?"

"It's possible. But we can't know that until we discover what the problems are and he's not telling."

"I don't know, Muggs. . . ." For the first time it dawned on me that I wanted to protect him. And I wanted to protect him because I loved him. David Conrad was very good to me. I didn't want anybody or anything to hurt him–including me and Margo. Only if we could help him would it be worth digging for dirt. "Maybe we're just wasting our time."

"Or maybe you're just going soft over this guy. Yeah. I think you're falling for him and you don't want our Mister Nice-Nice to get hurt. I ought to slap you back into your right mind. Look, Jan, I like him, too, but we don't know what may have happened a few years back that the police didn't nab him on. People do feel remorse and change their ways. But on the other hand, if the man does need our help, we can't do anything if our heads aren't on straight, so wake up! Lady J, you're the best friend I've got, so listen to me when I tell you to get a hold of yourself. Conrad's no choirboy, and his chances of joining your hallelujah crowd are slim to none. He may be extra-specially dreamy, but he's a poor choice for somebody like you unless you can turn him around."

"Oh, I know that. But thanks, anyway. A girl needs a good reminder."

"Glad to be of service. Now, we both figured that whatever the problem is, it's got to be wrapped around a dame. Well, maybe he hasn't committed a crime, but you can bet a cool million that he didn't end up in trouble by being virtuous. I'd lay you ten to one that where he went, he went willingly. It just turned out to be more than he bargained for."

"I think you're right. But whatever happened, I'm pretty sure there's a crime connected to it."

"How so?"

"Little things. That night when you guys got me away from Noonan, I was with him all the time after that. One thing I noticed was how uptight he got whenever the cops showed up. Then there was his reaction when I first put a gun in his hand. He was so terrified, I though he'd blow a gasket. I know that's not enough, but I think there's more; it's just a lot of little stuff that when you get enough of it together, it suggests–"

"Murder?"

"Perhaps. He's got a wound on his shoulder that could be from a gun."

"How'd you find that out?"

"Prayer has its advantages."

"Uh–you prayed and so he took off his shirt? Hey, that's not bad!"

"No, Muggs, he didn't. The knowledge came through revelation and Mr Conrad confirmed that I was right."

"Well, that's no fun. Aw, anyway, I figured his problem was blackmail. He is a man with a lot of money."

"I thought of that, too, but let's table this for now. I've got a date."

"Oh? Who with?"

"Alan Haskell."

Alan had called that Saturday afternoon to ask me out on Sunday. He wanted to take me to a movie. He'd have asked me sooner but had just gotten access to an automobile.

"Okay. Come by tomorrow after school. I'll have some more done by then anyway."

Back home again, I pushed aside sober thoughts on David Conrad in anticipation of the evening ahead. My date was to go see a musical. It promised to be was a very good one, so ignoring the check in my spirit, I'd said yes. It was so long since I'd had a real date that it made me feel like an honest to goodness normal teenager. You know, just like you see on TV. Cowboy and I had gone to a drive-in once in the old pickup truck and saw a shoot 'em up, but his youngest brother had hidden in the bed under a blanket and come along for the ride. Not only that, we'd gone to the drive in theater only because Cowboy thought that going to a walk-in might cause problems with folks that didn't care for mixed couples. With

Alan, though, it would be a regular date, and I was sure looking forward to that.

It was a real pleasure having a beau again. Alan had borrowed a car so he could take me in style. He didn't even suggest a drive-in, saying that films were better seen up close in a dark theater. He came by at four fifteen driving a red '67 Chevy Impala–and did he look sharp! My heart rate increased at the sight of him in his tailored gray flannel Nehru suit, navy blue turtleneck sweater and silver medallion. He'd had a haircut and his short Afro sported a nice sheen. Mommy and Daddy were also favorably impressed. But it surprised the heck out of Charlotte that I would be dating him at all, since he was barely sixteen.

"What it is, baby," said Alan as he escorted me to the car. "Can you dig the wheels?"

"Yes, indeed."

"I knew you would. My cousin Frank's been laid up sick, so I knew he wouldn't need the car. If I'd known it sooner, we could have gone out last night or even Friday night."

"I go to services on Friday night, but Saturday nights are usually open."

"That's nice to know." He started the car and pulled out into the street. Then a couple of blocks away from the house, he turned to me and said, "Say, what are you doing way over there? Get over here next to me."

I slid across the divided bench seat and sat next to Alan leaving two or three inches between us.

"That's more like it." Alan slipped his arm around my shoulder, stole a kiss at the boulevard stop and drove on.

Our evening began with Chinese food at a nice little restaurant near the theater. After a pleasant meal, we went on to the show.

Earlier that year, Warner Brothers-Seven Arts had released a film version of the 1947 Broadway musical *Finian's Rainbow*. Fortunately the Kimo theater was running it again, because both Alan and I had missed its first showing. Starring Fred Astaire, it was rumored to be the last movie Mr Astaire would dance in. Many wonderful actors were featured in this film, a guarantee for the viewer's enjoyment; we were delighted for the chance to see it on the big screen.

Since Alan and I were both so interested in seeing the show, he didn't try any necking. For the most part, my date kept his arm around me and kept his eyes glued to the screen. Only when we occasionally turned to each other with a laugh or comment over something of particular amusement did he plant a kiss on my cheek. But after the show was over.

. . .

"It sure is a lovely evening out." Alan looked up at the clear night sky and sighed. "I hate to go home so early. Why don't we go for a little drive and look at the constellations?"

Constellations? Is he into astronomy or is this just a line? I figured it was probably both, but wasn't sure what I wanted to do about it. "I don't know, Alan. It really isn't that early, and we do have school tomorrow."

"Your curfew is ten thirty, right?" He paused to look at his wrist watch. "That gives us almost an hour and fifteen minutes. Why not use it?"

I'd forgotten about that curfew. Usually I didn't have one, so it had bothered me a bit when my parents mentioned it; then I realized the difference was that this wasn't church but a first date, and that smoothed my ruffled feathers. With just over an hour to kill, I figured this wouldn't be such a bad way to spend it; I was in the mood for a touch of romance anyway, especially after the romantic theme of the movie. Tommy Steele had made an adorable leprechaun and Don Francks was a real turn on, not unlike David Conrad. Since Alan knew where I stood as far as limits on necking and petting, I saw no reason not to go look at the stars.

In those days, the distance was fairly short to the outskirts of town from downtown, especially when driving as fast as Alan. Just a few minutes heading west on Central took you past Tingley Beach and the last of the cheap motels for motorists who travel Route 66. Then you were out in the desert where it's really dark, and only the occasional howl of a coyote breaks the silence. It's a different place at night with a strangeness and mystery so unlike the daylight hours. Stars can be seen quite clearly there.

Songs and scenes from the musical still danced in my head as we sped along the highway, putting me more in the mood for singing than anything else. The night was indeed lovely, and the stars plentiful. I watched the darkened landscape go by and relaxed.

With so little time, Alan didn't waste it. He chose a spot on the side of the road less than five miles from town. As soon as he turned off the motor, he put both arms around me and gave me a nice tender squeeze. "Mmmm, you smell so good." Alan started with a soft kiss on my temple.

"We are going to look at the stars, aren't we, Alan?" I said and slipped away from him.

"Oh, sure, sure. But can't I just hold you for a little while before I have to take you home?"

"Well—I guess so."

For maybe ten or fifteen minutes, Alan and I looked at the shooting stars and tried to pick out constellations; but being so close and warm with each other, hormones got the upper hand.

Alan started up again with kisses on my cheek. Then as I turned my face to his he placed his mouth on mine. But this was different than before. His kisses weren't usually very soulful, so this one took me completely by surprise. Alan liked kisses of the French variety, which happened to be my favorite as well. But now he was turning up the heat and it had my thought processes going a little foggy.

It was quite chilly outside in the desert night air, but not inside that car. Kiss after long kiss, the windows began to steam up just like my head. Something told me it was time to end the evening before it got any hotter.

"Alan, we'd better go," I wanted to say, once I could come up for air, but then I was distracted by a breeze down my back. I tried to ignore it until I felt his hands touch my skin where he shouldn't have been able to.

Immediately the fog lifted.

My outfit was a straight skirt that fastened in the back and a simple sweater that buttoned down the back as well. Alan, deft as a pickpocket, had undone them both.

"Stop it!!" I shouted and yanked myself away. "Stop it right now, Alan, and take me home!"

Instead of doing as I asked, he reached for me again with a seductive touch, stroking my skin and pulling me closer. "Look, just relax," he said softly. "We won't do anything bad. We'll just cuddle close for a minute, that's all."

What a touch! This guy knew his stuff, and had I been a weaker person, it would have posed a real problem. But I stood firm and kept up my efforts to elude his grasp. "Alan, I mean it. Stop it and take me home!"

Still he would not comply and continued his attempts to make love, pulling me close again as he said, "Don't worry, baby. I'll be good. I promise, I'll be real good."

But that didn't work. Squirming until my hands were in front of me, I pushed against his arms with all my might. And still he wouldn't give up. Once free from his embrace I didn't expect him to keep going, but he grabbed me again to hold me tenderly, keeping me from putting my clothes back together and causing them to be even looser.

That was the last straw. This time I got away and jumped back to the far side of the seat. When he came after me again with more love and kisses, I made sure it was the last time.

Alan drove us home slowly with one hand on the steering wheel while the other nursed a bloody nose and a swollen eye; his lip was also cut. I thought of offering to drive once I saw the awful damage my little fists had done, but believed the lesson might be better learned without trying to make things easier. So I sat next to the door and fumed all the way home, just as angry at myself as I was with Alan. The Lord had already warned me about keeping such company with him, and I had already learned what kind of boy he was from my own experience. How stupid can a girl get? Even though I'd made it clear that I didn't go in for petting, I should have known better. Of course I had been sure I could handle something like that, and I had after a fashion; but still it would have been better not to have fooled around with it in the first place. The dirty feeling it gave me was awful. It was stupid to have put myself in that position.

But even while I sat there kicking myself, every now and then I would look over at Alan holding his swollen eye and trying to drive. What a beauty! That must have made him see a few constellations. I couldn't help but smile, and finally laughed out loud with no thought for his feelings.

Well, I'd learned my lesson. That evening before crawling into bed, I had a long talk with God. Not only did I repent for my disobedience, I also laid on him all the things that bothered me about my always being so different from most kids and the absence of a love life. In a firm but loving manner, he set me straight so that I was able to feel better about myself and have more patience when it came to boyfriends.

MONDAY, OCTOBER 28:
   Monday morning it was back down to me and Mr Conrad for study. We didn't chat much as we were both anticipating what Helen might do later on.
   This time we were not late for class, although we did show up together. Helen arrived shortly afterward and gave Mr C one of the biggest red delicious apples I had ever seen. It was all bright and shiny and the stem was decked with a white ribbon. Then they chatted *en Français* for a few minutes before class started.
   "Oh, Janette! Did you see?" Helen squealed as we walked down the hall after class. "He liked it! He said it was a sweet thing to do. He even smiled!"
   "See? What'd I tell you?"
   "I had a hard time finding apples that size but at least I know where to get them now. The ones without stems Aunt Jessica can put into pies. I can't wait until tomorrow! That apple's going to have a note along with it."
   Before she could get away, I remembered what I needed to ask her. "Say, Helen, wait a minute. Have you heard of an actress named Nedra something or other? She did silent films."
   "Nedra? The name is familiar, but I don't know her work. I'm only into certain ones, especially if they worked with Rudolph Valentino."
   So much for that.
   The day flew quickly by and soon I was sitting at Margo's dining room table going over photos. They were all done, now, and she had separated them into groups: family, girl friends, famous stars, and miscellaneous. We sat mostly silent as we examined them with magnifiers.
   "There are four photos of Nedra," said Margo. "She's got to be our girl."
   "But our 'girl' is probably twenty years older than him. Just look at her in that color shot. She's still a knockout, but she's no ingenue. And with so many photos, she can't be all that bad."
   "We just need more information. There may have been a scandal. God knows Hollywood has always been full of them"
   "I talked to Helen today, but she couldn't tell me a thing. Guess I have to call Chicago." I dug into my purse and handed her a ten dollar bill. "Here's some dough. Make me some copies. If this isn't enough, I'll get more. I'm getting little bits of inspiration from these that just might lead somewhere."
   "You got it."
   Bad lady hurt you, I thought later on as I sat in my room remembering the pictures. If the lady was that evil, her picture wasn't anywhere on that wall. But it was just possible that those that were there could lead to the right question or comment that would get this man to open up.

TUESDAY, OCTOBER 29:
"So, what's Helen going to do today?" asked Mr C, smiling slightly as he closed the music theory book and slipped it into his briefcase. This morning had been mostly school work.

"What? Oh. She'll probably just give you another apple."

"Was this apple business her idea or was it, uh, somebody else's?"

His question provoked a guilty smile that was impossible to restrain. Still I replied, "You ask a lot of questions, mister."

"It's one way to get answers. Personally, I think that if Helen had thought of it on her own that she'd have done it a long time ago. And the way she's been getting help from you–well, I think you're the madness behind her method."

"You're entitled to believe anything you want. I already feel like a turncoat and you want me to tell all of Helen's secrets? Uh, uh. You'll just have to go on wondering."

The first bell rang. I got to my feet but Mr Conrad remained seated. That meant he would stop off somewhere before class and I would go up alone.

"Okay," he said. "Have it your way. Say, how about helping me chose some more Christmas music this afternoon?"

"Sure. Glad to."

"Good. Do you like what I've picked so far?"

"Yes! Especially the Bach and that Fauré number."

"I thought you would. Look, I've got a half hour lesson at 3:30, but after that I'm going over to Fielding's Music. You know the place, don't you?"

"Of course I do."

"Then meet me there around 4:20."

"I'll be there." *With bells on!*

Alan had not shown up for school on Monday. But with it being Tuesday, he had to come because that week's madrigal rehearsal was very important; we had another performance coming up soon. He showed up wearing dark glasses and doing his best to keep a low profile. His story to explain the his injuries was that he tripped over some furniture in the dark.

I casually kept my distance from Alan as we went over the music. In spite of efforts not to draw attention to the rift between us, it was still noticed by others. Eyes looked questioningly at us both, but no one said a word, and neither Alan nor I volunteered any information.

But after rehearsal he still walked me to class so we could talk about Sunday evening's little episode.

"Look, Janette," said Alan. "I'm sorry about the other night, but I thought sure we were on the same wave length."

"How could you have possibly thought that?"

"Well, because some girls like to play hard to get. Look, let's try it again and I promise you I'll behave, all right?"

"No. It is over. I am not going out with you anymore."

"It's over? But it can't be. Please? We just got started. You mean I can't kiss you anymore?"

"Above all, please don't kiss me anymore."

"But–but what about the show? We're partners. Please at least say you'll still be my partner, okay?"

I wasn't too sure about that. What if he got grabby at a rehearsal just like before? *Lord?*

"Please! Janette, that show means more to me than anything. Don't cop out on me. Please!"

I listened in my spirit to hear what HaShem was saying and responded accordingly, keeping my voice low but angry.

"Alan, I'll be more than happy to be your friend and work with you on the show whenever I have the time, but only so long as you understand that I don't want you ever–EVER–to get kissy-touchy-feely with me again. And I mean that. Do you understand me?"

"Okay, fine. Fine. If that's the way you want it, that's the way it'll be. But I sure do like the way you kiss; and you have to be the softest thing I've ever held in my arms. Janette, you like so many of the same things I do that most other Colored girls around here aren't even interested in. Couldn't you give me one more chance?"

He moved closer and reached out to touch me. I stepped back and pushed his hand aside.

"No, Alan, I mean it! Get it straight right now. I say what I mean and I mean what I say, and I'm telling you it's over. From now on we're going to be nothing more than friends, or you can kiss your show goodbye."

With that I went into the gym and shut the door behind me.

Glad to have that over, I pushed the whole business out of my thoughts and turned to more pleasant things, such as my date with The Fox that afternoon. As the day came to its close, I couldn't hold back the excitement.

Before it burned to the ground in 1971, Fielding's was Albuquerque's oldest and largest music store. Situated a few blocks east of our drug store, Little Pueblo, it was one of my favorite places to browse and dream. Especially happy to have this excuse to go there, I headed over as soon as I could get home and change clothes. Then until Mr Conrad showed up, I spent my time in that giant warehouse of instruments and sheet music playing the guitars that were on display.

"Stop that racket."

"What?" I hadn't heard Mr C's approach, so he startled me. "Say! You've got a lot of nerve," I said with a sneer.

"So when are you going to give me a concert?" He smiled as he spoke; something he was doing more of lately.

"Mr Conrad, there are many worthwhile things I'd like to do, but there's a problem. A certain teacher I know gives too much homework. I should be home doing it now."

"What do you mean, 'too much homework'? Do you get homework in Choir? Now, if that were a regular class–"

"Oh, yeah? You seem to forget that we have to memorize the music. That's homework. Look, just admit it. Nobody gives homework like you do. Nobody."

"Seriously? Is it really that bad?"

"Without a doubt. Especially in French."

"Oh. I didn't realize I was being such an ogre. All right, I'll see what I can do to cut back."

"You will? Oh! Thank you so much!"

"Come on. Let's go look at that music."

Holiday music had a section all its own. The recently published works were what he was interested in. Most everything else he'd already heard. After making several selections, we sat down at one of the little spinets that the store provided and sampled the music.

"That's awful!" Mr Conrad tossed aside a very modern piece after playing a few bars of dissonant and angry chords. "I can't believe some of the trash being published these days."

"Try this one." I handed him one with text that I especially liked. He played through the first few measures and it also sounded modern, but with warm, rich chords and harmonies.

"This one's a keeper. Pick another."

It started out being fun, but then to my horror and agony, I felt myself falling, and falling deeply, for David Conrad. So far I'd managed to keep such feelings in check. As long as I saw him chiefly as a mystery to be solved, it was okay. But with so little to go on and the two of us being together constantly, I realized that even the pursuit of clues was leading me down a path to becoming that starry-eyed fool. Sure, we were growing more familiar, just as I'd hoped, but it was the perfect breeding ground for both love and infatuation, turning my objective mind set for deductive reasoning into mush under the constant attention from, and contact with my quarry.

The obvious cure would be to cut the amount of time spent together, but after looking at all the angles, I saw that this entanglement which was our friendship was too far advanced. To withdraw would make people talk–and they wouldn't say anything nice. But one thing that I could do was make sure our mornings were even more centered on Torah than music. That should be like a cold shower to those fanciful feelings.

A strong diversion was also needed. What it would be, I didn't know, but I had to find one. After all, there seemed to be no reason, other than amusement, that I needed to delve into whatever dark issues lay in Conrad's past. He wasn't looking to be rescued, and since he was a decent, kind and caring man with no rap sheet, there seemed no real need. So I decided then and there that it was best to close my casebook on David Conrad until such time as it proved necessary to open it again.

With that decision made, it was as if a door had actually closed. Passions and desires suddenly seemed easier to manage . . . for about ten minutes. With such close contact, holding on to a sane and sober state of mind was next to impossible. As I sat next to my Mr Wonderful, nonchalantly going over music, I had to withdraw in order to fight the battle. Naturally I prayed through all this, but God was moving like a needle stuck on a turntable. So summoning my ability to reason, I looked again at the consequences of entertaining infatuation.

Every day I saw them: the Helen Bombardners, the dreamy-eyed desperate ones that he casually ignored. There was a good chance that if he saw me looking that way for too long, he would get bored and I would join their ranks as a has-been. That I could not afford. But there was something else even more frightening, and that was being seduced and thrown away. That look of love could be seen as a come-on, an opportunity to indulge his attraction to me. I couldn't afford that, either.

I had read more than once that infatuation, mistaken by many for love, was nothing more than a combination of hormonal urges and flight of fancy, and that those who were foolish enough to let it rule their hearts were likely to pay dearly for it. From all the broken-heartedness I had seen others go through and endured myself, I was certain those writers had been correct and so refused to let myself fall victim to the euphoria. That I loved David Conrad was true. But this thing called being in love was something I had yet to experience in a genuine sense, and I was more than willing to wait for a more profitable opportunity.

In about an hour–a painfully long hour–we had managed to wade through quite a bit of music. I was about ready to run out of the store, but kept my cool, or so I thought. Mr Conrad seemed to notice everything about me, so naturally he saw that I wasn't quite as chipper as when we started.

"What's the matter?" he asked. "Tired?"

"I suppose so."

"You're not getting bored, are you?"

"No, not in the least."

"Good. I'd say we're about done anyway. Except that I just remembered something. We haven't picked out anything for Hanukkah. Since we're probably the only Jews in that place, do you think we can get away with adding it to the program?"

"It's possible." I smiled at Mr Conrad's idea and he responded with a charming grin. That was a little too much. Before he could see me lose my composure, I got up and walked quickly back to the holiday section and began looking for Hanukkah music. Mr Conrad caught up to me and stood very close, looking over my shoulder. So close was he that I could feel the heat of his body as if we were touching. "You know what I really like," I said, unable to concentrate on the titles. "Uh–Handel's J–Judas Maccabaeus. Most people have–never heard it, but they know his music."

"That's a good suggestion. All right, the madrigal group can handle that very well."

"Are you making a pun?"

"What? What'd I say?"

"Never mind."

"Oh! Handel and handle. That's pretty good but it wasn't intentional."

"I'll bet you pun in your sleep."

It wasn't long before we decided on two choral works for Hanukkah and then we were done. Then I had to get home for dinner.

While Mr Conrad wrote out a check for the music, I casually looked around at the hanging instruments, all the while aching to leave. Then we finally walked out to the parking lot together, and still he wasn't ready to let me go.

"Now that we've got the music picked out," he said. "You can help me put the program together. Are you game?"

"Uh, well. . . ."

"I'll buy you dinner."

"Mr Conrad, the way to a man's heart is through his stomach; not so with teenaged girls."

"I can't buy you diamonds, Janette."

"Oh? What's stopping you? You can afford it."

He wasn't expecting that response and the look of surprise on his face sure tickled my funny bone. Yes, and thank God! Laughter was just the antidote. So I let go and chuckled away my anxiety and the flood of infatuation with it.

"Young lady, if you don't stop that–. All right, keep it up, then. You'll see just how much homework I can dish out."

That provoked more laughter; soon I felt close to normal.

"Okay, I'll help you," I said. "But you'd better make it worth my while."

"I'll see what I can do."

A smile returned to his face and this time the charm did not overwhelm me. I hopped on my Indian Scout, and as I rode by him, tried to knock the music out of his hand.

That had been such a close call that it made me seek advice and support. That evening I went early to rehearsal and talked about it to Holly Ann Richardson, David's wife. Being an older, experienced and very godly woman, she could be trusted for what I needed. But because of time and interruptions, I was only able to give an abbreviated version of my story. She listened carefully, a grave expression on her sweet, sun tanned face as I told her of all the attention given me by Mr Conrad. She stopped me only to ask if he had a wife or girlfriend, then I revealed what I knew of his love life. Seeing her grim reaction, I wasn't too sure I wanted to hear her response.

"Janette, you've done really well so far," she said, twisting the ends of her long brown hair. "I don't know many grown women, let alone young ones, who can control themselves the way you have. Now, I can see that God put you close to this man in the beginning, but I think the way you keep getting closer and closer isn't what God has in mind, even though you can reach him with the Gospel. If you keep on going in that direction, you'll not only be out of God's will, you could also be in some serious trouble. Now, it may not be easy to pull out of this situation, but it has to be done, okay? You need to do things like go back to reading your Bible alone instead of having breakfast with him. In the meantime, make sure that you take care of yourself physically so that you can stay in control of your emotions. Get plenty of rest; eat right and all that kind of thing so you'll stay sharp. Maybe he means well and everything is just the way you say, but you shouldn't take the chance that it'll stay that way, especially since you're starting to feel differently about him. Okay?"

"Okay," I replied, but for some reason didn't feel that it was okay. Still, what she said seemed to be correct and wise, so I went along. Feeling right about it could come later.

The doorbell rang just then and David came out to answer it. People were starting to arrive for rehearsal so we couldn't continue much longer.

Holly got to her feet. "Let's go in the other room. I want to pray for you. You can't possibly do what you need to do on your own strength."

We went into her sewing room and closed the door. I sat in a chair while she stood in front of me, laid hands on my head and began praying in tongues. Closing my eyes, I lifted my hands in worship to the Lord as she spoke aloud over me in a prayer language that sounded similar to Navajo. Then when God's anointing came strong upon us, I felt Holly's hands suddenly lift and heard a thud on the floor.

I opened my eyes and was amazed to see the woman laid out on the carpet in front of me, eyes closed, arms outstretched and hands poised in an expression of praise to God. Whatever the Holy Spirit was doing, I didn't want to interrupt, but having heard how hard she'd hit the floor, I was a little bit concerned. I made myself wait until her eyelids fluttered open and then asked, "Are you okay?"

"Sure, I'm okay," she said with a smile.

I offered her a hand and she got up laughing.

"It didn't hurt?"

"No, not a bit." Holly pulled up a chair next to me and sat quiet for a bit, grinning and laughing occasionally as she shook her head and thought. "This is hard to believe," she said, and laughter bubbled out after the words. She paused again and opened her mouth to speak, but more laughter bubbled out. Then she sighed and I could see her trying to control it. "Jesus," she said and giggled once more before saying, "I'm going to have to eat my words, Janette. Your Mr Conrad is okay, so don't stay away from him like I told you to. You're right where God wants you to be. That doesn't mean you should throw caution to the wind, of course; after all, he is a man and he's not a Christian that you can pray with over things. But just keep doing as God shows you. When the Lord took me down in the Spirit just now, he told me that this is not an ordinary circumstance, but something that he has arranged for a purpose. Yes, God does want you to minister salvation to this man, but there's a whole lot more to this than you think. The only thing is that I can't tell you about it."

"Why not?"

"Because–" She laughed again. "Because some of it I just don't know how. Things in the spirit don't always translate well into English. Then again, some of what I could tell you I don't feel God wants me to. But don't worry about it. The Lord said for you not to be afraid of anything that's happening now or that will happen. He's going to strengthen you to be able to deal with it, so don't back off from your relationship with this Mr Conrad. God also said that he'll reward you greatly for your faithfulness, and that's the part that really blows my mind. Oooo! Glory!"

Holly laughed freely for a while and then let go a shout of, "Hallelujah!" The joy was almost starting to get on me, but not being able to see as she did, I could only smile in awe while wondering what could possibly happen in the future.

"Now, listen, Janette," she said in a serious tone. "Because this part is very important. No matter what happens or how things appear, you must keep trusting God and make sure that you're listening to *his* voice and not just figuring things out on your own. Remember that. Do NOT lean on your own understanding. Even though what you want to do may seem like the most logical thing, make sure that you're being led by the Holy Spirit. God has placed you with this Mr Conrad for reasons that can't be put into words. And rest assured that I will keep you in prayer, because you are going to need it. There are more trials for you and him down the road."

"That sounds like fun. As if we haven't been through enough already."

"Oh, don't worry. You'll see. God hasn't allowed anything to happen that there wasn't a good reason for. The same goes for whatever happens down the road. You may not be able to see it now, but you will when you look back on it."

What on earth God had cooked up, I could not begin to fathom, and wouldn't even try to figure it out. I only purposed in my heart to wait and listen to his voice the best I knew how. Whatever he was going to do, I did not want to mess it up.

WEDNESDAY, OCTOBER 30:

After the morning Torah portion, Mr Conrad and I worked on the Christmas program. Why he even wanted my opinion was beyond me. Certainly he was capable of doing it by his self, but remembering how he said I provided amusement and good company, I made no protest.

We tossed around ideas until time for class and decided to talk more about it after my lesson that afternoon. It was then that he would reward me for all of my assistance.

Once lessons were out of the way, it didn't take long for us to figure out a plan. When we were done, Mr Conrad sent me over to the harpsichord. Just inside the open lid was a rectangular box of black velvet.

"Are you serious?" I asked, shocked at finding what was obviously a jewelry case.

"Maybe. Open it and find out."

Rhinestones. A lovely and delicate necklace with earrings to match. The shimmering stones were caressed by dainty gold electroplated leaves.

"Mr Conrad–I was only joking when I–"

"I know that. But would you rather have had a book or a–a fancy pen?"

"Well . . . I don't–"

"That's what I figured. So if it's what you really want, Janette, it's what you should have."

"I–I suppose so. The set is very beautiful. Thank you."

"I'm glad you're pleased. Just let everyone else think you bought it for yourself, okay? Otherwise. . . ."

"My lips are sealed. You know that."

"Thank you."

Any guilt I had over accepting these lovely trinkets became almost nonexistent with his words–and his look. Then with the thought that the diamonds weren't real and there were no strings attached, it disappeared all together. There was no doubt that this was all just for kicks, and because it was, I wanted to throw my arms around his neck and kiss him for making life so much fun lately.

"And now, Miss West, before you start asking for fur coats, I'd better throw you out."

"Oh, but–"

"Out!"

Laughing happily, I quickly stashed the jewelry case in my purse, grabbed my books and left.

At home in my room I took out the velvet box and looked at my beautiful and obviously expensive costume jewelry. There would be no immediate need for any kind of story about where I'd gotten the pieces because no one else would see them. Except for the occasional stage band concerts, I had no place to wear such things. The set was much too nice for school and certainly too dressy for the hippie setting of The Rock. Unless I went to the prom or some other dressy affair, the set would be nothing more than a keepsake.

Burying Mr Conrad's gift in a drawer where it was likely to be forgotten, I then put on a record album and did my best to concentrate on homework. But thoughts and questions arose and whirled around in my head unprovoked, as if someone demanded I reopen his casebook. Helen had described him as tragic, and I was beginning to get a strong sense of this tragedy from the things I'd seen and because he clung so to me. Attention in the name of academic advancement of a student was one thing, but to risk his teaching career and reputation by giving me a gift as he had just done–that was something else. But what could I do if he wouldn't confide in me?

Unable to study and with no further clues to help me work this thing through, I pushed my books aside, brought the phone into my room and called Grandpa West.

THURSDAY, OCTOBER 31:
Since every silver lining must have it's dark cloud, so my red letter day of Wednesday was made imperfect by a phone call from Helen who just had to tell me of all her hopes, fears and anxieties over The Fox. She even had the gall to suggest that I voluntarily step aside and not spend so much time with him. It was starting to get on my nerves, so at breakfast on Thursday I mentioned to Mr C what I was going through.

"So are you happy now?" I said to end my tale. "Are you satisfied that you're causing me all these problems? Do you have any idea what it's like being teacher's pet? Do you? This is all your fault. God knows I didn't ask for this."

"If I want guilt, Janette, I'll call my mother," he said. "Or better yet, I can call Vicky and save on the long distance."

"You know I'm only teasing, don't you?"

"Of course I do. You haven't been at it long enough to make it work even if you meant it. Sorry, but I think you have to be born Jewish to really do the guilt right."

"Anyway, you've still got to fix this for me with Helen, so please don't forget."

"I'm almost as anxious as you are. Today's apple number four. Look, I'll do my best, but I just don't know what to say. I really don't. I've never had to do this before."

"You haven't? That's amazing."

"Well, just think about it. If I had to talk to every girl that got a crush—"

"You'd be an extremely busy man. I see your point. Well, talk to Bill Fletcher. He could give you some pointers."

"I take it he was in a similar situation?"

"Yes. It worked out fine for him and for the young lady."

Mr Conrad sighed and shook his head. "I like Helen and I don't want to hurt her feelings, but there doesn't seem to be a way around it. And I suppose I ought to do it now and get it over with."

"Well—no. I hate to say this, but maybe you should wait till next week. She's having a party this weekend and that would put her on a bummer. It's her first party in ages and I wouldn't want it to be spoiled for her."

"Okay. That way I'd have more time to think of what to say and how."

"Would you like to know what I told her? It was a strong enough argument to make her talk about something else besides you, so maybe if she heard the same thing coming from you it would hit home."

"Sure. What did you tell her?"

I repeated the important parts of my conversation with Helen at the drug store on the day of her make over the month before. He listened casually at first but sat up straighter in his chair and fidgeted slightly as I recounted the logical reasons I'd given her for not letting myself fall prey to infatuation in such a hopeless case. It puzzled me as I saw amazement, dismay and incredulity in his facial expressions and body language. By the time I finished I was shocked to also see exasperation and a touch of anger. What on earth had I said that was wrong?

"Janette–" Mr C bit his lower lip and seemed to think better of what he started out to say.

"What's the matter? What did I say that bothers you?"

"It's nothing. Never mind."

"No, it's not 'nothing.' I can see you're upset. Tell me."

He sighed and thought for a long moment. As he did, I felt the anger subside. "Well, you've given me some ideas, but Janette, there are times that you are so–so doggone logical that you remind me of that pointed-eared Vulcan on Star Trek. It just seems so unnatural for a young woman–like when you compared marriage to walking the last mile."

His reference to Spock wasn't meant as a complement and I knew it, but still I couldn't help but be pleased. When I smiled slightly in response, he just shook his head again.

"And another thing," he said half smiling. "You sure know how to bruise a man's ego. Young lady, I have a reputation to uphold. Don't you ever tell people you're not the least bit interested in me. They'll think I've lost my touch."

Now he was joking, but at the same time I felt he wasn't. Did he want me to be interested in him? Was he that vain? Possibly. There were occasions that I had suspected he was flirting with me but thought he was just having a bit of egotistical fun and simply dismissed it. If that was where his head was at, his ego needed some bruising, and not just a little; so I said, "And they'd probably be right."

If I'd only had a camera to capture his dumbfounded expression as he gaped at me. He sat that way for almost half a minute before he said, "Why you little–so help me, I'll–"

"You and what army?"

At last a smile spread across his features and he told me, "Just you wait."

"Now, Mr Conrad, don't forget that I also have a reputation to uphold. I don't get crushes on teachers, I eat them for breakfast. Instead I get a teacher who feeds me breakfast. What am I going to do with you? Go get your apple."

"I guess I should. It's about that time."

"What do they taste like?"

"They're really very good. Find out where she gets them, will you?"

Later, at lunch, I was able to tell Margo the latest. We sat back in the morgue and spoke in low tones.

"Nedra Bates? She was some stuff, huh?"

"Oh, yeah. That's what Grandpa said. But aside from the films she made, all he could tell me about her personal life was that she'd married her director when she was young and then that she died about ten years ago."

"It does give us a time line, though. And with a full name, now we know where to start digging."

"Well, sort of. We need resources. In the meantime, I've got to figure out how to use what we do know to get something out of Mr Conrad."

SATURDAY, NOVEMBER 2:

Thursday evening at sundown I had begun a fast in preparation for Helen's party, which didn't end until Saturday afternoon when Peaches and I finished with prayer at her house. Then I came home from there, had a bite to eat, grabbed a nap, and got myself ready for the pajama party.

Arrival time was eight o'clock. Several girls were already there when I walked up at a quarter past. Helen seemed to have made a fair number of new friends since becoming a beauty. With them bringing others to her party, she had a crowd of sixteen girls. Then with the great spread Aunt Jessica had laid out, she was bound to get rave reviews and broaden her social circle even more.

We did have a great time. Helen knew some delightful party games. The one she started with, called "Newspaper," had us howling with laughter while we learned each others names so that we'd never forget them. Those first few hours were loaded with fun for all of us, but as the witching hour approached, things took a turn toward the dark side. Just as I figured, Helen eventually brought out the hocus pocus.

"And now it is time," our little hostess said with an air of mystery and melodrama. "Madam Helena knows all, and you will have the opportunity to know your future!"

A murmur arose from the group at her announcement. One of the girls dimmed the lights while she left the room. Then in a moment or two Helen was back. There were bangles on her forehead, a long red scarf covered her head and shoulders, and she carried her Tarot cards and Ouija board.

All watched as Helen ceremoniously arranged her apparatus on the coffee table, then lit candles and incense. She then sat cross-legged on the floor, closed her eyes and mumbled inaudible words. Halloween wasn't over yet.

"Now, who shall be first?" she asked looking around at the group. Three or four raised their hands. Gesturing with an open hand toward a chubby little redhead, she said, "Linda, you may come forward."

Helen gave a choice between using the Ouija or the Tarot cards and explained the pros and cons of each. The session began with her using the Tarot with each one who came to sit at the coffee table, but she was having trouble interpreting the way the cards fell in relation to each other and her readings weren't very clear. So after a few frustrating sessions she put them away and brought out the Ouija board.

"This Ouija has been in my family for two generations," Helen announced, even though this modern version had not been around that long and she'd bought it at a second hand store. "It has proven to be very accurate. Who will be next?"

There came another volunteer and sat down at the coffee table. Placing their fingers lightly on the planchet, they asked a question of the board, but the triangular piece that would move their hands along and spell out the answers wouldn't budge. They tried a different question, and when it finally did move, it only wandered aimlessly and then went over the edge. Helen became upset.

"I don't understand this," she complained, shaking her head and looking perplexed. "It never acted this way before."

"I'll bet I can make it work," said Peaches to my complete surprise. Not waiting for an invitation, she got up and went to the table and stood next to our hostess.

"Do you know what's wrong with it?" asked Helen.

"Sure I do. Move back a little, okay?"

Peaches did not sit down or even touch the board. Instead she looked down and spoke to it.

"Ouija board, in the name of Jesus I command you to tell me your name."

Everyone sat stock still while, without the touch of anyone's fingers, the planchet slowly began to move. Back and forth it went over the letters of the alphabet until it spelled out a foreign sounding name.

"Are there other demon spirits with you?" Peaches asked.

Again the planchet moved. The answer was yes.

"See, Helen, this board and your Tarot cards are influenced by demonic power; especially this thing. The reason why they haven't worked tonight is that Janette and I have been praying so that those evil spirits won't speak."

"I don't believe you," she said. "It doesn't have demons."

"But the board just told you what it was."

"I don't like this," said a girl named Frieda. "I don't want to be calling on evil spirits or–or demons."

"I thought it was just a game," said one named Mona. "You know, like that Eight Ball game."

"It's not just a game," said Peaches. "This stuff can be for real and it's nothing to be played with. You need to get rid of this Ouija thing."

"No! Leave it alone!" Helen shouted with rage. Getting to her feet, she looked at Peaches and then squarely at me. "How dare you! How dare you interfere with my party! First you throw yourself between me and Mr Conrad, and now you come in here with this person and your–your Jesus stuff, and try to make me look like a fool in front of my friends. Well, I've had just about enough of you, Janette West."

Raising her hands with occult significance, Helen began to speak something undecipherable under her breath and made a slow but deliberate step in my direction. It was then that I sensed a change in the room's atmosphere, and as it grew heavy with oppression, I was distracted from prayer and began to puzzle over what she was doing. I could hear little noises, like the ones I sometimes heard when sitting in her room. Before I knew it, I felt myself becoming paralyzed by fear and the dark and heavy oppression that was filling the room was pressing down upon me.

At five foot eleven and over two hundred pounds, dear Peaches could have relied on her physical presence to stop Helen. Instead she simply stepped between me and her with hands raised in praise to God. She then turned and directed her right hand toward the girl's head. Without being touched, Helen stopped, and with a look of wonder on her face, went backward onto the couch and didn't say another word.

Turning to me, my friend said, "Come on, Janette."

Now the oppression was broken. Relieved, I went back to praying in the Spirit and joined Peaches on the other side of the coffee table. That's when the Ouija board began to have conniptions. First the planchet moved from side to side and then the board began to vibrate. At that a couple of girls screamed in terror, which brought Mrs Brown running into the room. Peaches and I determined to ignore it all. We spoke in the name of Jesus and commanded the sprits in the board not to speak and to leave the house. Then everyone else went into hysterics as the board danced wildly. It then sailed across the room where it slammed against the wall and shattered into a hundred pieces, sending several knickknacks and a photo to the floor. Then as the group made efforts to collect their wits, the front door flew open, there was a great flurry of wind and then stillness.

It was a minute or so before anyone moved. Peaches and I naturally were the first to do anything. The girls clung to each other and some were whimpering, but my first thoughts were for the elderly Mrs Brown. The poor woman had gone so white that I feared she might faint, so I grabbed a chair and put it under her, while Peaches got her a glass of water. We prayed as it was administered lest something worse than fainting happen. Then I felt my second errand of mercy should be to Helen.

As soon as Mrs Brown's state of being improved, I went to sit with Helen. Understanding how she was horribly upset and embarrassed at the turn of events, I offered her my hand in comfort and friendship.

"Get away from me!" She yelled and quickly turned to bury her face in a pillow where she poured out her tears.

"Are the spirits gone now?" asked Mona.

"Yes, they're gone," said Peaches.

"But could they come back?" asked Frieda.

"Sure. Maybe not tonight; but if this house isn't spiritually cleaned and sanctified, then there's nothing to stop them."

"I'm not spending the night in this house," said Frieda. The others agreed.

"And I won't have that evil junk in my house anymore!" screamed Aunt Jessica, still shaken up by the whole business. "I never wanted it here in the first place, and every bit of it is going in the trash tonight!"

Phone calls were made until everyone had a ride home except for Peaches and I. Mrs Brown begged us to stay and help get rid of all of Helen's occult paraphernalia and we agreed. As we sat waiting for parents to come, Peaches took the opportunity to share in greater detail the power of God's goodness over evil. Then came a time of prayer for which all expressed their gratitude. All but Helen, of course.

When the last of the girls had gone, it was time to clean house. However, I felt it necessary to talk with Helen to make sure she understood just what had happened, so that she would willingly give up her things. Peaches agreed.

By this time, most of the fight had gone out of our little fortune teller. With her occult toys and their power shown up for what they were in front of her friends and her guardian, there was nothing else she could do but give it all up.

I sat down again with Helen and offered her my hand.

"You are not my friend," she said. "Don't try to act like it."

"But I am your friend," I said, taking her slender digits and rubbing them gently. "That's why I'm sitting here instead of trashing your room right now. You may not have a choice in losing your stuff, but your feelings about it are still important."

"Huh?"

"Look, remember what I said when you wanted to tell my fortune?"

"Sure, I do."

"I couldn't let you do it because it was witchcraft, right?"

"Yes."

"And witchcraft is evil, isn't it."

"Well–maybe it is–evil."

"Maybe?"

"It's confusing. Sure there's lots of evil a person could do with spells and curses, but–well, what's wrong with just trying to know the future? If something helps you, how is it evil?"

"Helen," Peaches interjected. "Evil only pretends to be your friend in order to gain control of you. Evil only wants to use you under the guise of giving you something. I don't know how far you've gone into the occult, but what were you looking to get out of it?"

"I don't know. It was fun, something mysterious and fascinating."

"What about power? That's generally what interests people the most when they get into witchcraft."

"Okay," Helen conceded. "Power to know the future."

"And the past," I said. "You told me that your cards could tell about past events. You wanted to use them to look into the past of someone you like. With things like that, you'd like to gain power to not only know the future, but to change it. You'd like to gain power over that person."

"Well–yeah, sure."

"How would you feel if someone was trying to manipulate you and control your life for their own selfish gain?"

"I never thought about that. But it's not like I'm trying to hurt anybody with this."

"If someone made you mad enough, you would," countered Peaches. "Look what you wanted to do to Janette."

"I never thought about that, either," said Helen. "Yes, you're right. I almost wanted to kill her."

"Helen, what happened to your Ouija tonight?" I asked.

"It committed suicide. You and Mavis made it freak out."

"That's because it couldn't handle the power of God. If the Ouija had been from the same power source as ours, there wouldn't have been a conflict. Those spirits you were looking to for help turned tail and ran. Do you understand why?"

"Because–they were afraid! They were afraid!"

At last she was getting the idea. We sat sipping cider, letting her mull it all over quietly until she finally said, "I've been in church all my life and never knew there was any real power in Jesus. I've found power in the Tarot, the Ouija, and a few other things, but this is the first time I've ever seen anything supernatural connected with Jesus. Is there more?"

It was a long evening, but the ending was a happy one. Helen willingly gave up divination and opened her heart for something more satisfying. Down came every last idol, including the ones from the silver screen.

SUNDAY, NOVEMBER 3:

On Sunday morning Peaches went home, but I stayed behind and went with Helen and Mrs Brown to their church, remaining at their residence until late afternoon. Then on Monday morning, Mr Conrad's ego received another bruise when the last idol in Helen's life fell. One final apple and a letter to go with it told him of the change that had taken place in her heart toward him and life in general, because of her newfound peace and joy.

Chapter Three
Christmas Jeer

MONDAY, NOVEMBER 4:

Mr Conrad was almost scowling as he watched Alan and I go through our dance routine at lunch time.

Don't look at him! Concentrate, stupid, or you'll blow it. Just dance!

Chiding myself, I determined to focus on Alan whose smile was practically a grimace from the strain on his nerves over this audition. The boogie woogie music seemed to go on forever and both of us were sweating more than usual as we threw ourselves and each other around.

At last the needle reached the center of the 78 rpm record, and Alan and I sighed aloud in unison, our bodies weary from the exertion and the tension.

"Not bad," remarked Mr Conrad. "But that's just you two. What about the other kids? How many of them are into this? It isn't exactly the latest craze, you know."

That was much the same argument he had given before when Alan had approached him with a similar idea.

"Listen, man," Mr Johnson told his old friend. "There are plenty of kids that would jump at the chance to do something like this, and a few of them have studied dance just like Alan has. Besides, David, they put up with the rest of the stuff we throw at them, so why shouldn't they go for this?"

"Well, maybe they would, but that's not the only thing to consider. A show like this means costumes, sets and countless rehearsals, which amounts to a great deal of time, money and sweat. And what about the choreography? Alan, you dance very well, but are you good enough to choreograph this show and then rehearse all of the other dancers?"

"Uh–I never thought of that," replied Alan, beginning to look hopeless. "B-but–"

"Do you expect me to do it or should we dig up Busby Berkeley?"

Again Mr J came to the rescue, saying, "Look, I've already talked to Mike O'Connell about this. The drama department can do the sets, the lights and handle the props and costumes. I'll help rehearse both the choir and the band. That way you'll have the time to work with the dancers."

"Bob, I haven't done this kind of work in years. I can't–" My expression caught Mr Conrad's eye as he spoke. I must have looked terribly disappointed because suddenly all of the fight went out of him. "You'll, uh, rehearse the choir, too?"

"Yes, I'll take care of any extra rehearsals for the choir so that you can work with the dancers."

"Well . . . all right then. I'll give it a chance. Let's you and me talk over the details before we tell Mrs MacGregor. If she goes for it and our budget can handle it, then we'll do it next spring."

"We can also sell tickets," I added.

Alan was stunned for a moment and then literally jumped for joy as he realized that the show was going to happen. "Oh! Thank you, Mr Conrad," he said. "Thank you all! You have no idea what this means to me. Thank you, thank you, thank you!"

Alan was so ecstatic that he kept dancing and singing all the way to walk me to gym class. It made it seem worth all the trouble just to see how happy he was.

TUESDAY, NOVEMBER 5:

Tuesday was different. I didn't see Mr Conrad until French because he had taken the morning to vote and therefore didn't get in as early as usual. But Tuesday was special, too. That day the Paseo Verde Highschool choir and madrigal group had a show off campus.

By the start of third period, the choir room was a lively sea of black and pink as we socialized and rehearsed. The boys in the choir wore simple black suits and neck ties with white shirts, while the girls wore pale pink dresses in the popular empire style. But for the madrigal group, the boys wore tuxes and the girls wore empire dresses that were a darker, dusty rose pink complemented by black velvet sashes. Many stood and talked about everyday things or the election (Humphrey and Muskey vs. Nixon and Agnew) and their parent's politics, while the risers were being loaded on the bus. Others primped and fussed over their appearance or rehearsed their parts and tried to deal with being nervous, especially soloists like me.

We were booked to perform at an elementary school in the northeast heights. Because it was Election Day and because of the up coming season of Thanksgiving, our program was one of patriotic songs and religious Americana, including a Negro spiritual. It was the choir's second concert outside of school, and for me–for all of us–it was exciting. Of course, any legitimate excuse to get out of school like this was fun.

Helen, Peaches, and I had gathered together with four other believers in the choir for a time of worship with our favorite sacred songs from the program, which helped me to take the focus from myself and calm my nerves. By the time we filed out of the classroom and got on the bus, the shakes were almost gone.

"Save your voices," shouted Mr Conrad before taking his seat up front. "You're singing and talking way too much. Keep it to a minimum so you'll still have something to sing with and so you won't drive me crazy. Now!"

The whole group fell suddenly quiet and the only sound was that of the bus' engine. After a word to the driver, Mr C took his seat and the bus pulled away from the curb.

"You know what?" Peaches leaned forward and whispered low after a few minutes passed. "We should start a prayer meeting or Bible study here at school."

"Good idea," said Helen. "We can do it during lunch."

While I remarked that I was often obligated at lunch period, I turned to look at Mr Conrad to see if our talking had caught his attention. His head still faced forward, and so I was about to speak when suddenly he turned around and looked in my direction. He made a beckoning motion, but when I made a move to get up, he shook his head.

"No," he said. "Helen. I want Helen."

She was sitting next to me by the window and holding on to my arm. We looked at each other for a second and then I moved aside to let her pass.

Due to the concert, there hadn't been time for me to talk to Mr C alone since he had received the last apple, so I didn't know what he could possibly be saying to Helen. Whatever he said it was brief. About a minute or so later, she was back.

"Well?" I asked her.

"I'll tell you later," was all she said.

It wasn't long at all before we reached our destination. The head of the music department was our hostess and the first clue to prove my theory that Mr Conrad did not limit his self to the likes of that cheap, green-eyed walking bust line with hair teased as high as a ten gallon hat. This woman was a lovely brunette with no wedding ring and a certain look in her big dark eyes for our teacher. A look that was more knowing than wishful. More than a couple of times she slipped into calling him by his first name. I knew, of course, that there could always be other explanations for the familiarity, but somehow I didn't think I was off track in my first assumption. Besides, it was just what my heart needed to help keep those romantic feelings in check.

Our concert was performed before the entire school. Though we were the main attraction, ours was not the only part. There were a couple of short speeches and a great amount of flag waving, complete with color guard, marching boy scouts and ROTC. It seemed a statement against the strong anti-American spirit so prevalent during these times.

After the show I mingled with the rest of the choir as we prepared to go back to our school. It was then that Helen took me aside and revealed what Mr C had said to her on the bus.

"He said he was very happy to know that I had decided to be sensible," she whispered, a note of satisfaction in her voice. "Monsieur said he was proud of me and wanted me to know that such a mark of maturity is what becoming a woman is all about. Then he told me to keep using my head so that someday I can marry a man worthy of my talents and beauty."

"Did he say it just like that?"

"No, not exactly, but still it's what he said. And he's right. I can see now that he feels pretty safe around you whereas he didn't around me; and you really do have much more in common with him than I do. Oh, well. That's the way it goes. But I'm glad to give him up since it really was so hopeless. I've got a lot more to choose from now, anyway, and the choices are pretty good ones."

"They sure are."

"Thanks, Janette." Helen squeezed my arm and kissed my cheek. "God sent an angel when he sent me you."

Well, praise God! One more problem is out of the way. Is there anything else that can happen? I couldn't think of a thing to dread. At day's end I breathed a great sigh of relief and prayed that HaShem would allow me a few weeks of trouble-free living until Christmas vacation.

Since it was Tuesday, it was rehearsal night for The Rock's worship band. As much as I enjoyed our sessions, this time I was a bit sorry to be going out. The sound of partying and the smell of hot buttered popcorn followed me out the door as I left, and those just arriving greeted me as I rode down the driveway on my Indian. Watching the election returns was something we usually did with family and friends, but I knew which was more important and more edifying to my soul. However, had I stayed home I would have seen a very special, local news report that came on the tube.

I have purposely omitted the gory details of the aftermath of my kidnaping because I don't care for such things. They are oppressive to the soul, mine in particular. There were, as you know, other victims that never lived to tell their stories, and the details are ghoulish. Unwilling to take the rap alone, Jacob Noonan confessed in a strange, roundabout way, and not only to his own crimes; he blew the whistle on his buddy Farquart and the other teacher that we had suspected. Of course, with all the photographs and video that he'd taken of the various girls, as he would have done with me, there was no way he could deny his evil crimes. The police found several volumes of photos and their negatives, in Noonan's home after finding more recent photos at the apartment. A large stash of drugs was also found. Then there were the bodies, nine of them so far with more to come. It was enough to make you vomit.

That night, however, the news was not concerning the victims, but Noonan himself. It seems he had hung himself in his cell. How he ever got hold of anything to do it with was a mystery, and there was commentary on the possibility of rope burns on his wrists. But it was never looked into very deeply, and soon any suspicions of foul play would be dropped.

It was the strangest feeling to come home and get the news. My parents told me as soon as I returned from rehearsal. Then thoughts about it colored my dreams that night. Having gotten to where I could pray earnestly for my former tormentor's salvation, it was odd to have him suddenly gone. Yet all in all, my soul was at peace concerning it.

WEDNESDAY, NOVEMBER 6:
At breakfast the next day, little was said about Noonan's alleged suicide, but it was the first topic for discussion with the Guild at lunch.

"Well, at least we know that he can't come back to haunt us," said Katie McMichaels as she peeled the wax paper from a sandwich.

"You're right on about that," said Emily Fisk. "And he can't get out of jail to hurt anybody else."

"That may be true," said Mr Fletcher. "But the sad part is that Noonan won't be around to testify against his cohorts. Now it'll take longer to nail them, even with the information he gave the police."

"Yeah, that is too bad," said Tommy McMichaels. He reached for a deck of cards and began to shuffle. "It even makes me wonder just who had Jake the Snake knocked off and why. But that's not our case to solve. Let our illustrious police department or the FBI take care of that. Who wants in?"

"You can deal me a hand," I said.

"No, don't play, Janette," said Estrelita Salazar and drew me aside. "I want to ask you something."

"Never mind, Tommy," I told him. "Maybe the next hand."

"Janette," said Estrelita with a look of concern. "Is it true that you don't celebrate Christmas at all?"

What on earth?

This was not my favorite topic for conversation. I'd already learned from experience with family and from the stories of friends, that most people were highly prejudiced when it came to the holidays of Christmas and Easter. It made no difference what the truth was, they would hold to their keeping till doomsday. With Estrelita being a Guild member, I had felt there might be some chance she would have the smarts to at least accept my viewpoint, whether she agreed with it or not; so this was a disappointment. In my response, however, I tried not to let my feelings show.

"Why do you ask?" I replied. "Are you planning to buy me a present?"

"Well, no. I hadn't thought of that."

"Then why discuss it? You heard what I said before about the half truths and fairy tales. No, Star Baby, I have no personal celebration of Christmas. It's not in the Bible. Of course, it's almost impossible to keep from taking some part in it when you're involved in things like Choir, and that's what I limit myself to. Now, is there a point in all this?"

"Some kids from my biology class were talking about it. You probably don't know them, but one girl said she heard it from your sister."

Charlotte strikes again. "Oh. Well, so what? Is it supposed to be some kind of big deal? What's your point?"

"Sure, I know what you said, but I talked to my pastor about it and he says things differently. He said you need to be careful with that Jewish stuff because it'll get you on a good works trip and trying to keep the law."

She was referring to trying to work one's way to heaven as a do-gooder and/or provide one's own salvation through strict adherence to Jewish law instead of finding salvation through God himself.

"The man doesn't know what he's talking about, Estrelita."

"Then why can't you celebrate the birth of Jesus? There's nothing wrong with it. Since you're a real Christian now, it should have even more meaning. It sure has for me. Then there's the fact that so many people get saved that time of year because it's a good time to preach the Gospel. How can you be against that?"

God! A real Christian? Wasn't she paying attention?

Whatever I was–whatever I'd become up at Alef Tav–it wasn't "a real Christian." Christianity didn't embrace Judaism and its traditions as having any spiritual value, which is why it was absent from their teachings and their worship. I only went to church because it was the best thing available at the moment. But if I told her plainly that I wasn't a Christian, it would really get her panties in a ruffle.

"Estrelita, Christmas does have more meaning to me, but it's not the same meaning most people give it. Look, it's not a situation where I can't celebrate it, as if I'd lose my salvation or something. It's something that I just don't choose to do. I don't need it and God doesn't require it. You can do what you like; I won't condemn you, but I don't need any kind of half-baked, hypocritical garbage like Christmas that's based on pagan customs, and where blasphemers can join right in and make believe they're worshiping God. I've simply found something I like better. And frankly, I'm glad to be free of all the hassles of shopping for obligatory presents, and all the other hoopla. As long as I can remember, it's been a royal pain and a perpetual disappointment, and it feels real good to let go all of that."

"Garbage?! It's about the birth of Jesus, not Santa Claus or the shopping and presents. Being a Christian, you should know that and it should mean something good to you."

There she goes again. I'm gonna– "But it's not about the birth of Jesus. I'm surprised at you, Star Baby. You know as well as I do that Jesus wasn't born on December 25th and that the Christmas customs are all pagan."

"They are?" piped up Billy Osborne. "I didn't know that."

"Neither did I," said Emily.

The card game suddenly halted and all heads turned in my direction.

"Janette is right on," said Margo with a happy grin. "The Christmas season was originally dedicated to the birth of the Unconquered S-u-n (not S-o-n) and a few other things that are totally unrelated to Jesus. It was actually banned in this country until the early 1800's. I've been telling Fletcher about this for ages, but he won't believe me. I sure am glad to finally hear somebody else say it."

"All right then, girls," said Mr Fletcher. "If what you're saying is factual, then when exactly was Jesus born?"

"If I tell you, then can I just play cards?"

"I'd like to hear this answer myself," said Margo. "Go ahead, Jan."

"Okay. I can't give you an exact date because the changes in the calendars over the centuries make that impossible. But I do know that he was born at the Feast of Tabernacles. The Bible, history and Jewish tradition all point to that. It can be calculated in relation to the birth of John the Baptist and the schedule of his father's service in the temple, not to mention the messianic prophesies. Now can we just play cards?"

I was never dealt a hand, nor was the game in progress ever finished.

From there the discussion went into the story behind December 25th being chosen to mark Christ's birth, and for once Margo and I were in agreement on religion. She knew as much on the subject as I did, and through what she said, I discovered her other reasons for not embracing Christianity. With so many of its traditions being phony and contrived, she had come to doubt that any of it was valid outside of the general philosophy.

To my relief, the others received what we had to say, except for Estrelita who insisted on telling us what her pastor had told her. She even wanted me to meet with the guy so I could hear for myself and be convinced.

"You know," said Margo derisively. "You talk about that pastor of yours like he wrote the Bible himself. But it seems pretty obvious that he doesn't know beans about this. Either that or he's on the make. If I were you, Estrelita, I'd find another church."

"And find yourself a brain while you're at it," said Billy. "You need to learn how to think for yourself, kid."

"Yeah," said Tony Gutierrez. "I don't know why you're on Janette's case about this anyway. Leave her alone."

She did, but I knew that she was only keeping quiet in the face of opposition. Then the bell rang and ended it for good. But this had not been the first time the subject of my religious beliefs had been brought up to me in the past few days, so it was beginning to concern me. And it was more than the questions. I was beginning to see that the little whispers and odd looks in my direction were not just my imagination.

Twice that afternoon fellow believers stopped me to express concern that I wasn't a true follower of Messiah as they had first thought. Talking to one girl made me late for U.S. Government because the conversation had been such a difficult one. What she had heard from others had made her believe I was a counterfeit and it had really upset her. That naturally made me upset as well, so after coming home from music lessons, I went looking for Charlotte so we could have a nice little chat about what she was telling her friends. I found her on the back porch taking laundry out of the dryer.

"I heard you've been talking about me," I said before she knew I was there. She gasped and whirled around. Then when her fear faded, guilt took its place for a split second before she put up the usual careless facade.

"Yeah? So what?" Charlotte casually folded the skirt that was in her hands and reached for more clothes.

"So what are you doing, telling people I'm a heretic or something?"

"All I've done is tell a couple of my friends that I have this weird sister who thinks she's Jewish and thinks she's too good to celebrate holidays with her family. That's all. Now, if they decide that they want to tell other people about it, there's nothing I can do. That is not my fault."

"Your attitude is your fault, Charlotte. When are you ever going to get that big, ugly chip off your shoulder and stop feeling sorry for yourself?

You're nothing more than a great big cry baby. It's always, 'Janette did this,' and 'Janette won't do that.' Charlotte, it's time to grow up!"

"What's going on out here?" Mommy suddenly appeared from inside the house and stood glaring at us from the other side of the screen door.

"Nothin'," said Charlotte.

Not sure it was worth the risk of what this might turn into, I kept my mouth shut.

"Well, it had better be 'nothin'.' I am so sick and tired of you two always picking at each other. Janette, you get in here and set this table. Charlotte, you hurry up and finish that laundry."

I went and set the table as my mother had asked, all the while steeped in anger and frustration. *Too good to celebrate holidays with my family–as if she cared. When did she ever get me anything decent for Christmas? Not since she was old enough to do the buying for herself did she ever get me one single thing I didn't end up giving or throwing away.*

For years I had tried to reach my sister and get her to understand that I was not the source of her problems, and that she needed to get over the things teachers and others had done to make her feel inferior. When I discovered I couldn't beat it into her, I sincerely tried to love her, to teach her to like herself, and gain more confidence. Eventually she did improve, so some of it must have hit home. Not only did her grades come up to a B average, she got involved in extracurricular activities and brought home an award or two. But still she was bound and determined to keep me as a scapegoat for all her pain, and to hurt me any way she could. Even many of her achievements were acquired with an attitude of trying to out do me. Also, it bugged me that her ire was only directed at me, even though Aaron was the real genius. Miles ahead of us all, he had started college at age fifteen with a full scholarship. All of us kids had had to follow in his wake, and for me it wasn't easy at times. Charlotte had to be the slow one, the late bloomer. But that wasn't my fault, and I was sick of taking the blame.

Years ago Charlotte and I used to sit next to each other at the dinner table. Because of our constant bickering, we now sat at opposite ends. But with all the anger flowing between us that evening, we might as well have sat in each other's lap. Everyone could feel the tension, and our angry expressions made it obvious just who was upset.

"All right," Daddy said, throwing his napkin down on the table. "What is it now? Charlotte, are you picking on your sister again?"

"Why is it always my fault," Charlotte complained.

"Because it usually is. Janette, tell me what happened."

"Well," I began, searching for a place to start. "She's got people at school thinking that I belong to some kind of cult or something. I don't know everything that she's saying, but I do know for a fact that she's made a great big deal out of my not celebrating Christmas, and she doesn't have to tell anybody about that. The people I go to church with don't even know. So now I can hardly get to class on time because kids are looking at me weird and asking all kinds of questions."

"You're sure it's all because of what Charlotte said?"

"Positive. The teachers know about my beliefs, but as long as Queen Constance has been principal, teachers almost never swap gossip with students. They don't dare. Besides, Estrelita told me that friends in her biology class were talking about this from what they had heard from Charlotte. And it's only been the past week or so since she was mad at me for Halloween that there's been this problem."

"Charlotte, what do you have to say for yourself?"

My sister hemmed and hawed and looked sullen while trying to come up with a plausible defense. She knew that they knew that I was not in the habit of lying and could always prove very well the things that I told them.

"Don't we have enough problems in this house without you causing more?!" Daddy bellowed. He was quite an imposing figure anytime, but especially when livid as he was then. It seemed he grew another foot as his chest heaved with anger and the veins bulged in his neck. His thick black eyebrows met in the middle, and as he spoke he slammed his fist down more than once, shaking the entire table and spilling water all over. "Here you are half grown and still acting like a damned baby! Well, this shit's gone on long enough. We're going to put a stop to this right now!!!"

Mommy was rather upset, too, but she was also a little afraid for Charlotte as Daddy got up from the table, grabbed her by the arm and literally dragged her away. She followed quickly while the rest of us stayed right where we were, not saying a word or cracking a smile lest we get some of it, too.

The screaming, crying and pleading didn't last long. The general consensus of those of us remaining at the table was that Charlotte had gotten a spanking with Daddy's belt which was the ultimate punishment for all us kids. Then would follow the lecture. In this case she would get one from Daddy and one from Mommy as well. But as much as I wanted to listen in, this was one instance when I didn't dare.

As we cleared away the dinner dishes, the others talked in low voices, giggling and making funny comments about Charlotte's situation. Even though I couldn't help but smile at some of the things they said, I found no joy in what my sister was going through. It didn't matter that she'd brought it all on herself and that little else would make her toe the line. It bothered me not knowing if her heart would ever change toward me. Daddy was right. It had gone on long enough.

It so happened that the events of that afternoon were a turning point for Charlotte, and her attitude toward me showed a marked improvement from then on. But even so, it did nothing to stop what she had already started. The situation at school got even worse. Because I had so unabashedly declared my faith to the whole school, many had put me on a spiritual pedestal of sorts. Since the talent show, a great many believers had remarked to me in passing how my boldness and love for God had inspired them. So as they discovered through the grapevine that I had what seemed to them peculiar and rather unorthodox beliefs, it not only made them ask questions, it lessened me in their esteem.

THURSDAY, NOV. 7 – MONDAY, NOV. 11:
Being different has its advantages, and it seemed I'd finally reached a place where I could relax and enjoy some pretty good perks. But now, as the week ended and the next one began, the disadvantages once more had me wishing I could blend in better, as I was more and more accosted in hallways and in the courtyards by other students demanding to know just what I did believe. "Are you a Jehovah's Witness?" and "Was that kibbutz place you went to some sort of a cult?" were some of their queries. I couldn't just say it was none of their business, so to let them know that I believed the same basic things they did concerning Jesus and the Gospel, I would recite a reworked version of the old Apostle's Creed, eliminating the words "holy catholic church," replacing them with, "the body of Christ" which, to Christians in general, is a more accurate and contemporary expression. Most were satisfied with that while a few still wanted to argue. They were usually the ones who felt I was condemning them for the way they believed simply because I didn't worship as they did.

TUESDAY, NOVEMBER 12:
It was on Tuesday, just after a rough day of very difficult conversations that a curious and rather frightening incident happened as I left the campus to head for home. Trying to quiet my mind and focus on the evening ahead, I almost didn't notice the big green and white Oldsmobile parked across the street. There were two men in the front seat and one in the back. Something told me that it didn't belong there. Its engine started as soon as I walked out of the gate and immediately my spirit began to pray.

The routine was so old it had whiskers. The idea was to follow me, and probably at gunpoint, force me into the car. If they played it right and nobody saw the gun, it would just seem that I was getting in uncoerced. I walked across the street as usual, pretending not to notice the Olds as it slowly followed a few feet behind. Their reason for wanting me was not important at the moment. That they posed a threat was.

In the old days of childhood fantasy of being a detective, I'd have had a pair of phony glasses with rearview mirrors so that I could see anyone following me. Having discarded the ugly horned rims as silly, I suddenly wished I had them. But I couldn't let the thought linger and distract me. Continuing with nonchalance, I palmed my two-shot derringer and prayed for good aim, something not as easy with a small caliber gun. Then, as I heard the car slowly approaching, I turned, took a short second to aim and fired at the front left tire. Hitting the mark, the car rolled a little more and then stopped to avoid damage to the rim. The looks on the men's faces were priceless, but I didn't dare take time to enjoy them.

Walking quickly backward, I turned and looked as closely as I could at my pursuers and then memorized the license number before turning to run a block or so toward home. Not being followed any further, I slowed my pace and made it to my doorstep without further incident.

As soon as I was through the door, I hurried up the stairs and called "Charlie," our ADG connection with the DMV and asked him to run a make on the Oldsmobile. Then I collapsed on my bed until I could relax and find some comfort in prayer. Then I called Margo and related the incident to her and everything else that was going on. Whether or not it was connected to the current controversy over my faith couldn't be determined, but it looked as if Billy would be walking me home from school again.

WEDNESDAY, NOVEMBER 13:
Then, as if life wasn't interesting enough, it waxed more colorful on Wednesday, the 13th.

"Janette," called a feminine voice. I turned and saw Vicky Marshall out in the hallway, hands on hips and staring at me with an expression strongly suggestive of being put out. The smile on her lips was strained, her head was tilted, and the daggers coming from her big green eyes were almost visible. Her voice was pleasant, however as she said, "Janette, could you come here a minute, please? I'd like to talk to you."

Oh, God! Now what is it? I could have ignored her, but decided to get whatever it was out of the way. I followed along to her classroom and she closed the door behind us.

"Janette, have you been telling Mr Conrad that he ought not to go out with me?"

"What? No, of course not."

"Are you sure of that?"

"Yes, I'm sure. We never talk about that sort of thing."

"Well, I'm sorry but I don't believe it. And I'm telling you right now that I don't appreciate the way you've interfered in my relationship with him. You come along and then he starts asking me questions about God and what I think about faith and religion; now he's called things off with us for no good reason. The only thing he had to say was that what we were doing wasn't right, and that he just didn't think we should see each other anymore. Now, why else would he say something like that if you hadn't influenced him?"

Am I hearing things? He said that? That's tough to believe. For a moment I was too stunned to answer. When I did find my voice I asked, "Are you sure that's what he said?"

"I most certainly am. I made him repeat it. Then I asked him several times if I had done anything wrong and he said that I hadn't."

"What else did he say?"

"He said that if God was real then he needed him on his side and didn't want to offend him. Now, naturally I asked him if there was somebody else he was interested in, but all he said was that it wouldn't make any difference one way or the other because it was over with us."

"Well, I'll be! I had no idea. Honestly, Miss Marshall, Mr Conrad rarely mentions you or any of his other girlfriends."

"Other girlfriends?"

"Oh, I just figured he had others. I don't know for sure. Anyway, I never told him he shouldn't see you anymore or even suggested it. Now, if you'll please excuse me, I'd better get to class."

"Not just yet." She blocked the door until she could finish saying her piece. "Now, since you were the one that messed things up, I want you to have a little talk with Mr Conrad and fix it. Do you understand me?"

Lady, what side of stupid did you get up on this morning? Do you know who you're talking to? A smile spread across my face and I nearly laughed out loud. "And if I don't fix it?"

"Then maybe people might find it interesting to know that you're trying to take my place with Mr Conrad, because I'm beginning to think you are; turning his head with your fancy clothes and that religious talk. Maybe the other woman he's got is you."

Now I did laugh openly. "Oh, man! You can't be serious!" It felt like old times, having a teacher call me on the carpet. My anger didn't rise up like it used to, though. Actually it was rather amusing, and would have even been flattering had the place she held with Mr Conrad not been such a low one. Finally, since this whole business was making me late to class, I began to get annoyed and decided to bring this conversation to a close. "Miss Marshall, do you have any idea why you still have a job at this school? Maybe you think it's because you've changed the way you dress and stopped all those little games you used to play with the boys, but that's not the reason. The reason is that certain friends of mine weren't willing to give you up as a hobby, so they withheld evidence against you. Well, Miss Vicky, I have some of that evidence, and there are others who have collected even more since then. Now, if at any time you feel you would like everybody else to have it, too, then you just try and make good on your threat. Now, please step aside so I can go to class."

Miss Marshall turned pale and swallowed hard. Then without another word, she moved aside and let me pass.

I wasn't sure I would mention the incident to Mr C because it would likely upset him far more than it did me. Still, I was dying to know what was going on with him. Was that his real and only reason for dumping her, because it "wasn't right"? I'd often thought he'd tire of her eventually and find another main squeeze, but this looked like something else. Well, whatever his reason, this news was a bright spot in an otherwise dismal season. But then I hadn't made it to my next class yet.

Even though the halls weren't very crowded, there were still quite a few students bustling about. As I headed down the stairs to my locker, I distinctly heard the words "dirty Jew." Assuming they meant me, I wasn't interested in having a confrontation and didn't so much as turn a hair in the general direction. Then since my involvement with Judaism was relatively new, the remark didn't cut as deep as was intended. Still it was unsettling.

Coming out of English class, uneasiness about the awful words returned. Someone was after me. At lunch time I would mention it to Margo and Mr Fletcher to see what they thought should be done about this trouble my sister had started.

Suddenly a hand pressed on the middle of my back and shoved hard. A passer by in my path helped to soften the fall, but still I ended up on a dirty floor with people stepping over and around me. One kind young man offered me a hand up, but in the meantime some of my books, including my Bible, were kicked out of reach as people walked carelessly by.

I made myself recover quickly. Ignoring jarred bones and bruised dignity, I got to my feet and thanked the young man who assisted me in rising and in retrieving my books. Then after a trip to the restroom to fix myself up a bit, I simply ran on to class. But a few minutes into Music Theory (I was late, by the way), my stiff upper lip began to tremble. I could only control it intermittently for about five seconds at a time. Then to my dismay, my whole body began to shake.

I knew what it was like to be called ugly names, to be hit and spat upon for preaching a Jewish Gospel. When sharing Y'shua out on the streets with my friends from Alef Tav, it had been very scary at times. But afterward we'd all go home and be safe, since on the kibbutz people left us alone. This, however, was different. Now there was no secluded country home to retreat to and my persecutors weren't complete strangers. They at least knew me if I didn't know them. What if it got out of control? How could the ADG or anybody else protect me against a mob if one got started?

Tears and mascara rolled silently down and moistened the pages of my text book. Lost in anxiety and fear, there was no such thing for me as Music Theory until I heard Mr Conrad softly speak my name.

"What's the matter?" he asked, standing close and bending down to look at me. I only looked at him for about a second and worked hard on trying to gain composure. "Would you like to go to the nurse?"

I shook my head and this time looked him in the eye long enough for him to see the fear before I looked down again. Still I said nothing.

He thought for a second or two and then dug keys out of his pocket. "Here. Go across the hall to the auditorium and sit there. We can talk about it after class, okay?"

Silently I took the keys, gathered my things and left.

It was very dark and cold inside the auditorium. I entered reluctantly, not really wanting to be alone. Going to see Margo or Mr Fletcher seemed like a much better idea so I could tell them how I was being persecuted. But I did have to get myself together first, and here there was no one to hear me cry. I turned on some lights, dropped my things in one of the wooden seats and let myself go.

After crying and praying for what seemed a long time, I didn't feel much better; just worn to the point that I couldn't do it anymore. Anger and fear still had their grip on me, and now I trembled from cold as well as emotion. The remedy I sought was to think of other things.

There were many warm and happy memories for me in that place. Getting to my feet, I went to the foot of the stage, trying to remember the first program I'd ever been in. *A play, I think. No, my first time had to have been the talent show, and the second time was with the choir. But there was a one act play the fall of my first year and I was the only freshman in it. What was the name of it?*

"Janette?"

I hadn't heard the door open behind me. In walked Mr Conrad. He came and joined me by the stage.

"So how is teacher's pet doing now?" he asked with a smile. That made me smile, too.

"I don't know. Better, I guess."

"What happened today?"

"Where do I start? You know, I'm beginning to wonder if I'm going to make it through this semester alive."

"I think you will."

"Oh, yeah? Well, guess what Charlotte's been up to."

I gave him a very succinct rundown of what I'd been going through, including the part about the guys in the car. His brow knitted with concern and his complexion paled as he listened.

Just as I finished, the bell rang, which meant that Mr Conrad had let class out early on my account. As the shrilling tone sounded, he reached for me and held me tightly in his arms for a moment that was brief and yet long enough for me to draw strength and comfort from his touch. As he released me he sighed heavily, and shook his head.

"Janette, this is too much. You shouldn't have this kind of a problem, especially if it's not necessary. Do you have to be a Jew? You have enough to deal with in life just with being a Negro. Why take on something else that will only make life more difficult? Maybe you should just give it up."

"It's a little too late for that."

"It's not too late. Baby, this is just highschool. What about when you go to college? What about the rest of your life? You keep this up and you will have the rest of your life to deal with it. Are you sure that this is what you want to do? Are you sure that you really want to be a Jew? Janette, you don't need to be Jewish to believe in Y'shua."

Just then the door opened and in walked Mr Johnson.

"Somebody said you two were in here," he said. "What's the matter?" He walked up and touched my tear stained face and then slipped an arm around my shoulder.

"Janette's had some trouble with people who don't like her religion."

"You know, I heard something about that the other day. Somebody was asking me what I thought about Janette being Jewish. I told them I didn't see anything wrong with it and that God didn't either."

As Mr Johnson held me, the tears returned and I began to sob. "Here," he said. "Let me pray for you right quick." He took his arm from around me and placed me directly in front of him. Then he motioned to Mr Conrad. "Say, Dave, get behind her in case she falls."

"What?"

"Just stand a few inches behind her."

Without really understanding what he was being asked to do, Mr C came and stood behind me. Mr Johnson held his hands just above my head and began to pray in tongues. Almost immediately the Holy Spirit began to pour over me in powerful waves, addressing the issues of my pain, fear and anxiety. Within seconds my whole being relaxed and I found myself falling backward into my teacher's arms. Still Mr Johnson prayed, but he was winding down and spoke mostly in English.

I became so lost in the sweet presence of God that I didn't hear the second bell when it sounded. But Mr Conrad couldn't hold onto me forever. To my dismay, he soon set me upright again, bringing me back to the earthly realm.

"You want to go on to class, Dave?" Mr Johnson asked.

"Uh–are you finished now?"

"Almost."

"No, I'll stay till you're done."

"Okay, but stay there behind her. Now, Janette," Mr Johnson looked me right in the eye. "You have a very high calling of God on your life. It may be a lot different from what most people are called to, but don't you let anybody–not anybody–cause you to doubt for a minute that you are in the will of God. He's allowing you to go through all these trials because he is going to grow you up fast and purge you of a lot of things as you go through all this fire. He's preparing you for what you will endure in the days ahead, and what you're going to endure the rest of your life. Now, I'll tell you more later, but there are two verses the Lord gave me for you. One is, 'Think it not strange concerning the fiery trial which is to try you; but rejoice, inasmuch as ye are partakers of Christ's sufferings. . . .' The other is, 'Trust in the Lord with all thine heart, and lean not unto thine own understanding.'"

As he spoke the last few words, Mr J slowly raised a hand and lightly touched a finger to my forehead. At that the power of God hit me again, sending me back onto Mr Conrad. This time, however, I didn't go out and brought my own self upright again.

"You feel better now?"

"Yes. I feel fine. I'm not so overwhelmed. Thank you, Jesus! And thank you, Mr Johnson." I reached up and pulled his head down to hug his neck and kiss his cheek.

"Now, say thank you to Mr Conrad," he said, turning me in his direction.

Getting just a little red, Mr C lowered his head to my level. I hugged his neck to show my appreciation, leaving two faint lip prints on his cheek.

"I'd better get to class," Mr Conrad said when I'd let go.

"Not like that, you don't," said Mr Johnson, grinning as he reached for his handkerchief. "Wipe the lipstick off first."

"Oh, yeah.... Janette, now that you're feeling better, why don't you go fix yourself up and then come to class?"

"I will." Quickly and happily, I grabbed my things and ran down the hall.

At lunch I updated Margo, Fletcher and the gang on the details of this ugly persecution. Estrelita looked uneasy but said nothing; Billy was especially angry and feeling frustrated since he couldn't do much more than escort me home. They'd already had their ears to the ground so that they would pick up anything that might ID the jerks trying to hurt me, but coming up with a real plan of action didn't seem possible until someone could check in with Charlie and get the info on the green Oldsmobile. Billy promised to take care of that before school was out.

That day, my private lesson hour was especially welcome. Having the music to concentrate on and being with Mr. C kept me at peace. At the end, as I prepared to leave, my teacher asked me to sit down because he wanted to talk to me. He sent me into the living room and poured me a glass of ice tea. Then we sat on the couch.

"First of all, I have something to give you," he said.

There on the coffee table was a medium sized cardboard box. He reached into it and then handed me a small 33 1/3 rpm record in a plain white sleeve. The label read, "*Passing By* Janette West, soprano, David Conrad, baritone." I was also listed as vocal arranger and Mr C as pianist.

"Oh! My goodness!" I almost shouted, and found myself bouncing up and down on the cushions. "I almost forgot. Oh, Mr. Conrad, thank you!"

"I had quite a few pressed. I thought you might like to do more than just send them off to universities, so take the whole box. Maybe some of your family might like a copy."

"Yes, I'm sure they would. Oh.... Talk about perfect timing. I really needed this."

"Yes, I know."

I was able to enjoy looking at it for a second more and then it was taken from my hands and returned to the box. He had something else to say.

"Janette–I've been thinking about what you told me a while back about hoping for a life of adventure rather than–well, settling down and getting married. In light of what's going on now and what happened to you with Jacob Noonan, don't you think you've had enough adventure? I'd say you've had enough to last a life time."

"I know what you're saying, and I guess I've seen plenty of trouble this semester–"

"And it's not over yet."

"Mr Conrad–when I say adventure, it's not synonymous with trouble or intrigue. What I want is to travel and see other places and do things I can't do here in New Mexico. I want to go sailing on the Atlantic Ocean or the Pacific, both of which I've never seen. I want to see Europe and New York City and lots of other places. I know you've traveled a lot. That's what I'd like to do before I settle down."

"Well, there's nothing wrong with that, but the way trouble seems to follow you–I guess I'm just a little concerned."

"I see what you mean. But from what I can tell, it's all been connected with school. I think once I graduate, I'll be okay."

"I certainly hope so. This business has me very worried, Janette. There's a good possibility that you could get badly hurt over this."

"But I can't run and hide. Look, don't worry. I'll be fine."

"You know, I never thought I'd say anything like this, but I'm glad you carry a gun. I had it rough when I was young. My family started out in a neighborhood where there weren't many Jews, so I had it pretty bad for a couple of years. I don't know all the things that my parents or even my sister went through, but I don't think it was nearly as bad for any of them as it was for me. I had my glasses smashed so many times that I lost count. Then for a while there were two big Catholic boys that would call me names and rough me up once a week whether I needed it or not, and always on a Friday. Because of things like that, Dad finally decided we should move into a neighborhood where there were more Jews. But the saddest thing is when it's a part of your own family, like with my Dad's people. That can be a never ending battle."

"I believe it."

"Now, there's something else for you to consider. Are you going to marry a Christian or a Jew?"

"A Jew who believes in Y'shua, I guess, not that there are very many."

"Would you ever consider a Jew who doesn't believe in Y'shua?"

"No, not really. The next best thing would be a Christian who would willing embrace Jewish tradition. I wouldn't dream of marrying an unbeliever. I'd be an old maid first."

"I figured as much. But you might change your mind down the road."

"That would take a miracle. So, what about your family? How did that work out?"

"Even though my father converted to Judaism, his people were Lutheran. Every time we went back to Iowa for holidays or whatever, I had my nasty little cousins to deal with. Some of the adults weren't much better; they were just more subtle and devious. The things my poor mother and sister went through! Fortunately my baby brother wasn't even born for most of that time, so he missed out. Of course, my dad didn't exactly have a great time either, because we weren't happy, and because he could never completely relax. There was no way he'd tell them he'd converted because they wouldn't understand, so Dad pretended he was still Lutheran. On the first trip out he wanted us to fake it, but it would never have worked and my mother told him so. Well, every visit was a disaster, but he gave it the old college try about four times and then, thank God, he gave it up. Then any trips he made back to Iowa were without us."

"Did it ever change? Do you ever see those people?"

"No. Sometimes my grandparents would come to California to see us, and it was nice. They'd bring gifts and try to get along; but then my father died and that ended their visits. Oh, there were letters and a phone call once in a while, but only from my grandparents and never anybody else. So when they died, that was it all together. But I'm not sorry, believe me."

"Can't say I blame you."

"You know, I've been wondering. How do you handle being Jewish with people at church? And how do they feel about all this that's going on?"

"They don't know. All they know is that I used to be involved with a ministry that reached out to Jewish people. It's not the whole story, but it's enough to explain the things I do, like the folk dancing, Yiddish and Hebrew. As far as I'm concerned, that's plenty. If they don't ask me, I don't say much; then when I do, I'm careful about how I say it. See, they assume that since I'm with them that we're not any different in our beliefs. Since they stick so closely to the Scriptures in most of their worship, there actually isn't much difference with the truly important things. That's fine with me. I really can't ask for better where church is concerned, and I want to keep it just the way it is. So for the first time since I've been at The Rock, I haven't taken a major problem to them for prayer because it just might open up a can of worms. I don't want to be the one to tell them the truth about things like Christmas, and I don't think it's what God wants. Since I'm no big named preacher or theologian, they wouldn't listen to me, no matter how much proof I had. So if God wants them to know the truth about that stuff, I'd much rather he use somebody else."

"Sounds like a smart way to play it."

"Right now it's the only way."

Mr Conrad fell silent but didn't dismiss me. There was more he wanted to say, and I could sense it. But what it was, I couldn't begin to fathom. As I waited patiently for him to speak, I felt the rise of my feelings for him that corresponded to his feelings for me, which were apparent but unconfessed. Not once had he ever said that he loved me, but his continued care and attention declared his affection and friendship plainly. I could only imagine that he wanted to verbalize what he felt, but his position as my teacher naturally made it awkward and therefore difficult.

"Janette–" Looking up at me, he sighed, seeming unsure.

Yes?

"I–I just dread the thought of anything happening to you." He paused again and said, "You're very–precious to me. I know you have no idea what it means for me to–well, I can't really explain now, but the time we spend together, especially on music, does a lot for me. I wish–" He looked at me as if to add more, until at last he said, "I'm sorry, Janette, I won't keep you any longer. Just be very careful going home."

After that, how could I be careful of anything–especially my heart? It seemed he had finally said it–that he loved me. Not that he was in love with me, but that he cared as deeply for me as I did for him. As I left the apartment I held onto his words and the way he had looked as he said them, and then had to stop dead in my tracks to compose myself. As I went down the hall to the stairs and down to the parking lot, that and all else faded to the background until my focus was completely on my surroundings for the sake of my own survival. I would have to wait for a more convenient time to further enjoy the tenderness expressed by my teacher.

THURSDAY, NOVEMBER 14:
Though I longed to continue replaying the sweet episode on Wednesday afternoon, staying sharply tuned in on the present was all important, if I was to protect myself from danger. Getting enamored by the pleasures of being teacher's pet had clouded my head before with the Noonan case and I had paid the price for it. It would be foolish to let it happen again, especially with an enemy I didn't know. And that fact was confirmed in a very big way the following morning.

It could be seen from down at the far end of the hall. When I first noticed the black mark, I found it interesting that it was so near my locker. I didn't need to change books yet, but I went down anyway to take a look. The closer I got, a feeling of dread made me certain that the thing was on my locker. Yet when I saw it up close, I found it hard to believe.

A full minute must have passed while I stared at the crudely painted swastika on my locker door. The shiny black paint had splattered and dripped, and it looked to have been done in a hurry. Feeling unruffled, I opened the narrow metal door to see if any had dripped inside. Only an insignificant amount had gotten through, damaging nothing. So I shut it up and started to go on to senior English when I felt a check in my spirit.

Show it to Mr Fletcher.
That was a good idea, but it could wait until after class.
No. Do it now.
Fletcher's door was just down at the other end of the hall, so it didn't take but a moment to get him there.

"I don't believe this!" Bill stared in amazement at the ancient symbol done in reverse and followed the strokes of paint with his fingers. "My God! This had better be a joke."

That's when the seriousness sank in, although I was still unafraid.
"When did this happen?" asked Bill.
"It's completely dry so it was probably done yesterday after school. I didn't see it until a few minutes ago."
"Mrs MacGregor needs to see this."
Mr Conrad needs to see it, too.
Okay. Thank you, Lord.
"Do you want her to see it now, Bill, or wait till later?"
"This looks pretty serious, Janette. Go back to my room and wait there

while I go get her."

"No, I'll meet you there. I need to run upstairs for a minute and then I'll be right back."

Wearing high heels and a straight skirt, I couldn't take more than one step at a time, but I made my steps quick all the way to the third floor to Mr Conrad's, hoping he would still be there. It was the first opportunity for me to see what he did after my French class, and I found him correcting papers.

"Didn't I just get rid of you?" he said as I stuck my head inside the door.

"Have you got a minute? I need to show you something."

"All right, come in."

"No. I need you to come with me. It's downstairs."

Mr Conrad got up but came no further than the door. "Just what is it you want me to see?"

"Someone painted a swastika on my locker."

Without another word, he locked up his room and followed me down.

Soon we all had seen the Nazi trademark and before long, Mr Conrad, Bill Fletcher and I were seated with Old Mac in her office. The full story was laid out and all plans for the hour were put on hold while we tried to figure out what to do.

"I must be frank with you all," said Mrs MacGregor from behind her desk. "And confess that I simply don't know how to handle this. It's so upsetting that it's difficult to think. I've never faced anything quite like this before, at least not since I became an administrator. Any suggestions you have will be greatly appreciated."

We sat in silence, all of us overwhelmed by the task. Finally Mr Fletcher spoke up with the first suggestion.

"A good article or editorial in the school paper might help defuse the situation. We could put out a special edition."

"Perhaps. What do you say to that, Mr Conrad?"

"It's a fine idea, if handled properly, and I'm sure Mr Fletcher is quite capable. But another thing that would help is to give the kids something more exciting to think about. At the moment I don't have any specific ideas, but if we can come up with something that will distract the majority of the student body–preferably in a positive way–then perhaps we can get their minds off of this all together."

"And now, Janette, since you're the one who's the center of this ugly business, what do you have to say?"

"I like both ideas and I think that both are necessary. As for a diversion, a big dance party is always something that will get the kids excited. Maybe if we add to that some door prizes or a raffle, we can get a sizeable turnout. As for the article, that's going to be more delicate to handle. I suggest some serious prayer go ahead of that."

"I agree," said Mr Fletcher.

"So do I," said Mrs MacGregor. "What I will do is call an emergency faculty meeting and do what I can to get teachers to assist in seeing that this does not escalate. God help any of them that are adding fuel to the fire."

Everyone made this project a priority. Bill and I alerted everyone in the ADG, and then that evening he and I worked on his editorial by phone. Fletcher couldn't take sides to prove whose viewpoint on religion was correct, but somehow had to encourage people who saw themselves as Christians to behave in a manner that better reflected a life devoted to God. Mr Conrad volunteered to provide the prizes for the dance, so that was his job, which he took care of at home that evening.

FRIDAY, NOVEMBER 15:
The next morning, something felt odd but I couldn't put my finger on it. I kept my hand within easy reach of my derringer in its new carrying place all the way to school and took special care to check my surroundings before settling down to wait for Mr Conrad. Then, as usual, I began to read a bit of Torah before he came to escort me into the teacher's cafeteria.

Keeping a heightened awareness of my surroundings, I was soon unable to focus on my reading, the reason being that fifteen minutes had passed and Mr Conrad had not yet come. It was his habit to tell me in advance of any changes in his schedule that effected me, so this was upsetting. Maybe he wasn't feeling well and was staying home today. But that explanation didn't satisfy the growing uneasiness in the pit of my stomach.

Beginning to feel desperate, I began to think of other things that might delay him. Car problems? The silver Jag was always kept in tiptop condition, but flat tires happen to everybody. A car accident, maybe? *God! What is it? Where is he?* Finally I got up and went to the faculty parking lot to look for his car, which wasn't there. Last of all, I went to the library to spend the rest of my time before class in thought and prayer.

The first twenty minutes of French class was spent standing outside the classroom door waiting for Mr C. He never showed and the teacher from across the hall helped us to get inside.

It was tempting to forget the trouble that dogged my steps and think only of my teacher's absence. While in the classroom going over lessons, it was easy to put it aside because I was safe there and knew that I would be in any classroom. But as I left French for second period, I forced my thoughts to return to my own dilemma. Then the whole inconvenience of the business got me to thinking about the outcome of the remedy that was in the works. Rather than being sharp, my thoughts returned to Mr C and the way he was always there to help, except that now he might be in need of help. That's where my head was when my enemies decided to show themselves.

She couldn't wake him. It was as if he were in a coma. Lovely darkhaired Lisa Overton cradled the head of her estranged lover in her arms and cried in desperation. Even though she was still somewhat angry, she hadn't planned to hurt him. She had only wanted to talk things over in the hope that he would be willing to change his plans and let her back into his world. But at the sight of the .38 caliber pistol pointed at his heart, his eyes had grown wide and rolled back in his head as he fainted dead away.

All this had happened late last night. It hadn't been easy to get David Conrad to come over, but he was a good man at heart and finally gave in to her pleading. Then this had to happen. If only he'd been willing to reason. But no. He wasn't interested in hearing about being together on a more permanent basis. He didn't want to look at the pictures that showed how happy they'd been together. Instead he'd interrupted her so he could explain their breakup much the same way as he had before with that business about God. The heavy threats she had saved for last, the final tool of reasoning being the gun. With that he would have to listen and really think things through. Only he couldn't listen to her now.

The night's rest didn't refresh and awaken him as she had hoped. She'd tried talking to him, pinching him, and gently slapping his face. Were it not for the fact that his heart was still beating, she would have thought he was dead. A time or two she was sure he had moved. Mostly he lay still, and now she was afraid that his health, if not his very life, was in jeopardy. Finally she picked up the phone and was ready to call for an ambulance when suddenly David moved. His eyes remained closed while his body twitched. He mumbled incoherently. In the hope that he would soon return to consciousness, she put down the receiver and gently stroked his hair.

Laughter accompanied by quietly spoken remarks of "Jew" and "nigger" followed me closely down the stairway as I made my way to Senior English. A very strong sense of their malevolence urged me to pick up my pace and zigzag through the crowd wherever I could. Anticipating the possibility of being pushed again, I did not want to fall down the stairs. But even wearing more practical, low healed shoes, I couldn't ditch them. The two boys stayed close behind me and a feeling in my gut said I didn't dare let them catch up.

I had just made it down to the first floor but was still several feet from the classroom door when a foot almost tripped me up. They were right behind me, and I could hear their laughter. If I could only make it into Mrs Tharp's room, I would be safe; but that didn't seem likely because of the hand that grabbed my arm.

Fingers pressed firmly and painfully into my flesh, then were suddenly gone, snatched away. To make sure the hand didn't return I made a mad dash for the open door of the nearest classroom, but stopped just a few feet inside the threshold when I heard the sound of scuffling behind me.

At first glance, students were getting out of the way, giving me a very brief look at the scene of three boys that were fighting. Seconds later a crowd formed around them that completely blocked my view. It must have been a dandy display, the way it excited the onlookers. Even above their noise, the angry yells and painful grunts of the fighters reached my ears along with the sound of hard-hitting fists. But thinking it unwise and impractical to explore the scene of the altercation, I stayed put while the teacher whose class I'd entered pushed past me to go and break things up.

When the crowd parted and began to disperse, there was Billy Osborn standing over the groaning body of one of my tormentors, a tall, muscular, blond boy with freckles. He held the other boy, a dark haired, overweight kid, with one arm twisted behind his back. They were two of the three occupants in the car that had followed me. Billy's wiry appearance and easy going demeanor were deceptions he counted on for surprise at such times. Strength, agility, a bit of boxing, and the martial arts made it easy for him to take care of jerks like these two boys who were much bigger.

The teacher, whose name was Mr Proctor, demanded that Billy loose the one boy's arm while he stooped to help the other to his feet. Ignoring the request, Billy looked over at me, tossed his flaxen hair back and grinned.

"What happened," asked Fletcher, who came running from down the hall.

"These boys were bothering Janette," said Billy and finally released his prisoner. "I got hold t' them 'fore they could get hold t' her."

Mr Proctor looked up as he struggled along with the fallen boy to get him up. "Help me with this boy, Fletcher. We need to get him to the nurse."

"Aw, he'll be all right," said Billy. "T'ain't nothin' broke."

The boys did get to see the nurse, but only after a visit to Mrs Mac's office. Our "Queen Constance of the Moors" made them stand the whole time they were being interrogated. It was almost worth it just to see them tremble and cower in her presence. As she walked the room with her father's gnarled walking stick in hand, Mrs MacGregor was not only able to make them confess to painting the swastika, but to apologize and beg for mercy so as not to be expelled. Still she made no promises. She would talk first to their parents and see just what kind of people they were to bring up such ignorant hoodlums. In the meantime they were suspended from school.

"Janette," Mrs Mac turned to me once the boys were escorted out. "Would you happen to know what's become of Mr Conrad?"

"No," I replied, the uneasiness returning. "I was going to ask you the same question."

"He hasn't called in and no one is able to reach him at home. I'm very concerned."

"So am I. Do you want me to try and find him?"

She paused. "I don't want to take you out of class . . . and yet–wait here."

She went quickly over to the Boy's Vice Principal's office where Billy had gone along with Fletcher to take the two boys. She returned shortly with both Billy and Fletcher.

"I know virtually nothing of Mr Conrad's personal life," she said to us all. "But I do know that it is not like him to simply not show up without first calling the office. Also, it is common knowledge that he is a Jew, and it could be that the problem which has accosted Janette has reached him as well. I've sent for Mr Johnson in the hope that he might shed some light on what's happened to him and where he might be."

"I think we should call in the police on this," said Bill. "Sure, we can look for him, but this is a big town and we'll need all the help we can get."

"I say we start with his apartment and the surrounding area, then work out from there," said Billy.

"That's what I was thinking," I said. "We can call in here to report our findings."

It was then that Mr Johnson appeared at the door, a look of deep concern on his face while clutching the note that Mrs Mac had sent him.

"Mr Johnson, please come in and close the door behind you," said Mrs Mac. "I'm going to call the police and then we can talk about how to find Mr Conrad."

While waiting for the officers to arrive, Mr J did his best to overcome his anxiousness and tell us what we wanted to know so that finding Mr Conrad would be easier. Making notes, we then set about to take action. Billy, Fletcher and Mrs MacGregor pulled the rest of the ADG out of class while Mr Johnson and I took off to start the search.

There were no signs of Mr C at home. As we were getting back in the car, I suggested we make the rounds of some of the restaurants or night spots that he was known to patronize, but even as I spoke, I knew it wasn't the answer. Finally I gave way to what kept running through my head, and that was my recent encounter with Vicky Marshall.

"Mr Johnson, what about some of Mr Conrad's girlfriends. Do you know any of them or who they are?"

He looked at me like I was crazy, then laughed. "You may have the right idea, Janette, but who knows how many he might have and what their names are. I can only think of two in this town that I've ever met, and that includes Vicky Marshall."

"Well?"

He took a moment to try and recall the other lady's name, saying, "Lisa ... Overstreet? No. Over-something. I've seen her a couple of times, and we went to some sort of shindig together a little more than a month ago."

"Let's find a phonebook and we'll see if any of the names ring a bell."

At a nearby market we found a phone booth and Mr J looked through the listings. There weren't many that matched, so it didn't take him long to discover that she wasn't listed.

"Overton is the name," he said. "But there's no Lisa."

We then went restaurant hopping, taking into consideration that, had he indeed had dinner out, only someone working the evening shift would have seen him; so it was simply a search for his car. Then, after about an hour, we called in and were relieved to hear that the police were on the job and would also be on the lookout for Mr C. We were instructed to return to school, but neither of us wanted to go.

"I guess we'd better get back," said Mr J. "I know Connie doesn't want to call us in, but the cops are on this now."

"Mr Johnson, can't you remember anything else about that Lisa what's-her-name?"

"I've been trying. I remember she said that she'd just moved into a brand new complex that had fireplaces and beautiful views of the city lights. . . . My wife talked to her much more than I did. Let me give Letty a call."

He put another dime in the slot and called home. He didn't upset his wife with the problem, but simply asked about the woman. In just a couple of minutes he was reaching into his pocket for pen and paper so he could write down the address and phone number. Once he got the information, he told her what had happened and asked her to pray.

"Let's go," he said as he hung up the phone.

It only took about ten minutes to find the address–and David Conrad's car. We were both feeling anxious as we rode the elevator up and finally knocked on Lisa Overton's door.

"Who is it?" She opened the door as much as the attached chain allowed.

"Bob Johnson. Remember me?"

"Uh . . . oh, yes! Please come in. Maybe you can help." She unlatched the chain and let him in. I followed right behind and she looked at me with curiosity. "Oh, is this your daughter?"

"Uh, no, this is Janette, a friend from school." Mr J went straight to the couch where Mr Conrad lay, fully clothed, a light blanket over him and a pillow under his head. The coffee table had been moved aside and an ottoman was there where Lisa had been sitting next to him. "We didn't know what happened to David since he didn't call in sick. I thought he might be over here."

"What's the matter with him?" I asked.

"I don't know. He passed out and I haven't been able to wake him up."

"Did you call a doctor?" asked Mr Johnson.

"No. For a while he seemed like he would snap out of it. He moves around sometimes–as if he's trying to wake up."

"Does he say anything?"

"He just mumbles."

"I'm going to call for an ambulance. He needs medical attention."

Mr Johnson looked worried and shook his head as he stood by the phone and dialed the operator. But I was boiling with rage at the foolishness of this woman who had neglected to see that my Mr Conrad got whatever help he needed. Instinctively I went to the couch and knelt by his head, felt his body temperature and then his pulse, praying quietly as I touched him. His breathing came evenly, and his temperature and heart rate seemed regular.

"Your name is Janette?" Miss Overton stood looking down at me from behind the couch.

"Yes," I answered quietly.

"Janette West?"

Uh, oh.

"You are Janette West, aren't you?"

"Yes, I am."

"Oh, so you're the one. And here I thought you were just a kid. Well, you don't fool me. Take your hands off of him and get out of here–right now!"

Somehow I knew this was coming, or something like it. After all, Vicky Marshall had given me the clue. Feeling the need to release my anger, I got to my feet, looked her straight in the eye and said, "Make me."

The voluptuous Lisa O, with her long, thick black hair and large cobalt blue eyes was about seven inches taller than me and outweighed me by about forty pounds. I faced her as she came around the short end of the couch in a fury, then quickly dodged her as she swung hard with her right. When the momentum carried her past me, I sent my right into her midsection and then came down hard on her back with my left. As she went down, I grabbed her wrist, held it to the middle of her back and sat on her.

"What did you do to him?" I demanded.

"I didn't do anything. Get off me, you–ow!" I repeated my question and twisted harder. She only protested louder and then began to cry, "I'm sorry! I'm sorry! I didn't want to hurt him. I swear it!

Suddenly Mr Conrad sat bolt upright, eyes wide open, and began to scream. Bob Johnson dropped the phone, went to put his arms around him and called his name. Still he screamed and screamed, looking at something that only he could see.

Shocked and surprised, it took a moment, but forgetting Lisa, I jumped up and sat instead on the ottoman, reaching for Mr Conrad's hands that desperately clutched the blanket. Immediately both Mr Johnson and I began to pray aloud in the Spirit. A few long seconds later, the screaming stopped. Now he only stared at the unseen, while his shoulders drooped and tears flowed down his cheeks. He wept bitterly.

Mr Johnson's tone bordered on desperation and it was almost catching, but I knew that I didn't need to go in that direction. Instead I lay my right hand on my teacher's forehead and began singing in tongues. It was then that God instructed me to sing the song I'd written that he and I had worked into a choral arrangement. As the song came forth, my Mr Conrad grew calm and the stream of tears lessened and finally ceased. Last of all, he closed his eyes and lay down once more with his head on the pillow. Seconds later a loud knock came on the door. The paramedics had arrived.

While Bob Johnson talked to the men who gave aid to Mr Conrad, I listened intently to what he told them and heard him say that this had happened before but not in a very long time. But when asked what it was that could trigger such an episode of hysteria, he wouldn't reveal what that trauma was.

I paced, thinking only of what could possibly cause so much mental anguish. *Is this a part of his deep, dark secret? If so, it's no wonder he won't talk about it.* My pacing took me toward the little dining area where some things were laid out on the table: photos and a scrap book, the subject being Lisa O. and David Conrad vacationing in some exotic, faraway place. They looked happy, her especially. But as I reached for one of the 8"x10" photos, I happened to see a revolver.

"Mr Johnson." I spoke calmly and quietly.

"What is it?"

I motioned him over and I pointed at the gun; while he looked at it and the contents of the scrap book, I stepped over to the phone and called Mrs Mac to tell her that we'd found Mr Conrad. In regard to his condition, I thought it best to protect him and told her that he'd fallen very ill while at a friend's house and was finally getting the proper care.

Subdued and feeling deeply ashamed, Lisa Overton had come to her senses and sat passively by while the man she loved and had lost was being tended to and then loaded onto a stretcher. It was as they were lifting him off the couch that his eyes fluttered open and he called my name.

"Wait!" I told the men and rushed over to stand where Mr Conrad could see me. "Here I am."

"You *are* here!" With a wild light in his eyes, he reached for me and I gave him my hand. "I thought I heard you singing."

"Are you okay? How do you feel?"

"I don't know. All right, I guess. A little tired. And I could sure use something to eat."

"Can we put him down, please? I think he's all right now."

"I think so, too," said a happy and greatly relieved Mr Johnson. "I'll call Letty and tell her we're coming for lunch."

Later, a few miles away at the Johnson's residence, Mr Conrad was able to freshen up and shave, while I helped Mrs J prepare a big lunch. Once we were all together around the table, it was time to catch up on events.

"Janette, I'm glad that you were there today," said Mr C. "But at the same time–well, it's rather embarrassing."

"So what happened?"

"I'd already broken up with Lisa and explained to her my reasons why, but she called last night crying and saying she needed to talk it over with me. I felt sorry for her and went to her place, hoping that if I made it a little more plain that she'd have a better time of it. Well, it didn't work, and when I tried to make my exit, she–well, she pulled a gun on me. That's the last thing I remember. How'd you know where to find me?"

"You have Vicky Marshall to thank for that."

"What?!" they chorused.

"Well, just the other day she collared me after class, told me that you'd dumped her so that you could please God instead. She demanded that I send you back to her."

"Oh, really? What did you tell her?"

"I laughed in her face and told her to watch her P's and Q's or she'd be looking for a new job. She knew that I meant business, so I don't expect she'll bother me anymore. Anyway, when you turned up missing, Old Mac thought the same people were after you that were after me. But that chat with Vicky kept playing in my head, so I figured God was giving me a clue. I asked Mr Johnson what he knew about your girlfriends and he told me about Lisa Overton."

"David, I'm amazed that you let that Lisa girl go," said Letty. "She was so sweet and intelligent. I thought sure she'd be able to straighten you out."

"Straighten *him* out?" said Mr J. "They don't make women like that."

"Oh, yes they do," Mr Conrad said quickly. "You've got one right here. She's my angel." He put down his fork, turned to me and gave my hand a little squeeze. "Janette, I am so sorry to have made you a target. I didn't realize it would cause you any kind of trouble at all. I don't even remember mentioning your name."

"You didn't have to with Vicky, but Lisa somehow knew who I was."

"Oh, no!"

"Oh, yes. She told me to get out and attacked me when I refused. But she didn't hurt me and I don't think I hurt her too badly. So now that those two dames are out of the way, are there any more I should know about?"

"No. No, I'm sure I haven't mentioned you to anyone else. Janette, please, please forgive me. I truly am sorry."

"I'll forgive you on one condition."

"What's that?"

"I don't know. I'll think of something."

"A new car," said Letty as she set out a light dessert. "After what you've been through–make him buy you a convertible!"

"Now, that's an idea," I said. "Besides, all of these crazy jealous women want me out of the way and I'm not even in the running. I ought to have some compensation."

"I agree," said Bob, laughing. "Get her a car, Dave, or whatever else she wants."

Mr C smiled slightly and said, "I'd do it, too, if it wouldn't cause even more trouble. But I'll come up with something."

"Mr Conrad, I don't want anything," I said, remembering his gift of jewelry. "I was only joking and you know it."

In reply he smiled crookedly and winked at me. That was reward enough.

We never went back to school. Less than an hour after our leisurely lunch, Mr Johnson took me home and the peace that was in the house felt strange after all the excitement of the day. It was not yet three o'clock and feeling the need to talk rather than study, I jumped into a pair of jeans and rode over to Margo's for a much needed drink and to tell her the latest.

SATURDAY, NOV. 16 - MONDAY, NOV. 18:
It wasn't long before the controversy surrounding my faith ceased to be an issue. That weekend the staff of the Warrior Gazette and the ADG worked long and hard to put together our special edition and get it delivered, slaving away down at the school, setting type and running the ancient presses. The front page story, written by Margo, reported the circumstances surrounding the two suspended boys and was accompanied by a large photo of the swastika. Then in an editorial along the same lines as Bill's, she portrayed the situation from the standpoint of an unbeliever. For filler, incidentals about sports and other campus activities were added. But this edition also carried teasers strategically placed throughout that announced the big Winter Wonderland Dance coming in December.

First thing Monday morning, the paper was being read in every classroom at Paseo Verde. Teachers and students alike devoured the news. Margo's article seemed to have just as much, if not more impact than Fletcher's editorial in settling the religion issue. Both, however, caused certain overzealous Christians to hang their heads in shame at their crass behavior, while others made believe that nothing had ever happened. And as predicted, all the kids chattered with excitement about the dance and which prize they wanted most. But before the day was over I received several apologies. The most important one came from Estrelita.

Chapter Four
Teddy Molloy

FRIDAY, NOVEMBER 29:

"No, let me show you," said Mr Conrad and joined me on the piano bench. He played the cadence correctly. "Now, you try it."

"Down here?" I had moved over to make room for him and was now way down at the bass clef. Played in that range, it would sound like mud.

"No," he said. "Use the next octave up."

Reluctantly I moved as close to him as I could comfortably get and reached for the keys. As I touched the ivory, his arm went around behind me, allowing more room for me to play. As best as I possibly could, I executed the measures the way my teacher had shown.

"Was that right?" I asked.

"Close enough."

Mr Conrad didn't get up from the piano bench. Instead the arm he'd slipped behind me embraced me and brought me even closer. As I looked at him in astonishment, his face turned to mine and there on temple and cheek he planted soft kisses until he reached my mouth. Unsure of his motives, I squirmed to try and make a getaway, but his other arm quickly imprisoned me and brought me back. Again his lips found mine with even more passion. With no hope of escape I simply gave up, gave in and let him have his way.

"Well, if you're done with the test, Janette, bring your paper up."

Mrs Tharp's gravelly alto voice shattered my daydream and rudely snapped me back to reality. On one hand I was pretty peeved, but on the other hand I was grateful. With the absence of any major problems to occupy my mind, I was becoming more and more prone to such sappy imaginings about my handsome teacher–and it wasn't healthy.

I took my test up to Mrs Tharp and resumed my seat. Ten minutes were left in the class period, so I put them to good use.

On a blank sheet of paper I began listing all the things I wanted in a husband. It's not as if I didn't know, especially since thoughts of matrimony had been popping up in my brain for the past month or so. To keep myself on level ground, I had then made myself think it over in great detail. The point of this present exercise was simply further discipline for those unruly emotions and hormones. I kept it up throughout the day.

I ended up going over the same old business about how David Conrad, though oh-so-dreamy, just didn't stack up since he couldn't fulfill my deepest spiritual needs as a marriage partner, nor was he likely to remain faithful (all of which was moot, since he wasn't likely to ever pop the question). However, this argument had lost much of its strength since the incident with Lisa Overton. It was clear that the man was doing his best to turn over a new leaf by dumping his old flames, plus he was including God in the equation, which suggested I might move to the top in the romantic ranks, were he so inclined. Apparently our discussions and study had had an effect on him, and I couldn't help but be pleased–and tempted.

But I didn't dare yield to it. It was a hope that was foolish to entertain. Just because he wanted to get closer to God, it wasn't tantamount to a marriage proposal. I had no idea what kind of demons had been driving this man, and though he seemed headed in the right direction, he had yet to arrive. So loving him was one thing; getting involved was another. If he wanted me for more than a plaything, he was smart enough to know how to win me. And he hadn't come that far yet.

And there was something new to add. I'd always known my mystery man was a playboy, but seeing the sad results of his escapades up close was something else. Lisa O wasn't a tramp like Vicky Marshall, so it was easier to feel empathy. I was sorry for that poor woman who had foolishly cheapened herself with him while expecting a lasting relationship. And look what she got. Would I fare any better?

There was so much to think of in regard to this man. I still shuddered at the memory of his screams, and then the crying. What was that about? He had no military background, so it wasn't war related. And he had changed since that incident, becoming more like when we'd first met, only somber, at times even sad or depressed. Even so, he still called me pet names, as he'd started doing about a month or so before *(ma petite fleur, ma petite amie, ma petite rose,* and even sweetheart*)*, but the jokes, puns and teasing had all but ceased. At times I wanted to comfort him but had no idea how to go about it. Whatever had happened to my Mr Conrad, I wasn't about to broach the subject after seeing him flip out. At least not until some time had passed and he was out of the gloom.

That night I took my troubles to bed. Tears streamed down my face as I lay against my pillows, and in desperation I began to sob while trying to get a grip. I had that "follow him anywhere"syndrome, making me envy the ones who had known his kiss. What made the battle even more difficult was the fact that David Conrad had never hidden his attraction to me. Though he didn't ogle suggestively or put the make on me, our friendship was just a step below open flirtation and romance. All I had to do was let him know when I was ready. If only someone could help me. I again considered a question that had come to mind some time ago as to why Mrs Mac hadn't broken up our morning encounters. It would have been a mercy if she had, but then I was certain that I knew the reason she left us alone. Like Bob Johnson, there was no doubt that she was praying that my influence would help to change Mr Conrad into a believer. So there was no hope of rescue coming from that quarter. I was trapped indeed. Then with these thoughts I began to see the whole supernatural setup in finer detail. It was God's doing, obviously in answer to all those prayers for this man. He chose me for the job, sending me to Alef Tav for prep. And thus I had the reason why God was remiss in extricating me from this predicament. But this part didn't bother me. I just didn't see why it seemed necessary for me to be so in love with the man. Who's prayer was that?

Torment and frustration brought more tears and now my chest heaved with violent sobbing, but I had to keep the noise down. The last thing I needed was a family intrusion into my private anguish. By this time I was through with praying for a release from these deep feelings for my Mister Wonderful. An exercise in will power seemed the only salvation, so I reached for something else and recounted my warning from Mrs MacGregor when she had told me not long ago of her marriage to a man with no genuine faith in God. Hell on earth she had called it. She hadn't given any details, but I could still imagine: a divided household and lifestyle, enduring profanity, blasphemy and maybe even pornography in the home, married to someone who had nothing but disdain for what I loved and held sacred. No. Old Mac's marriage had cost her a great deal and for a good number of years and that was not going to happen to me. So I worked through this scenario for a good while to embed the consequences of such a relationship in my mind. It did the trick and the flow of tears subsided. The pain of unfulfilled longing lost much of its intensity. But taking no chances, I went for reinforcement. Getting up, I went to the window seat and found my worn out copy of *Jane Eyre*. Turning to the place where Jane makes a decision to leave Edward Rochester, I began to read where, in spite of his deep love and desperation to have her in a phony marriage, she leaves and faces destitution, rather than live a life of sin and deception while enjoying his embrace. Now that was a strong woman. So what if she was fictional? Jane's thoughts and actions were in the heart of the woman who created her.

Now my head was reasonably clear and my heart was, for the moment, in submission to good old common sense and logic. How long it would last, I wasn't ready to make book on. If I could just stay halfway sober until Christmas vacation, those weeks of being apart from my Mr Conrad might be just the ticket to getting over him once and for all.

SATURDAY, DECEMBER 7:

As winter approached and the days passed into the year's final month, I managed to keep my head fairly level, slipping only occasionally. In light of my deplorable condition, when Alan Haskell asked me to the Winter Wonderland Dance the week before, I did not refuse. The sight of my knuckles in front his nose when I greeted him at the door on Saturday was sufficient to remind him that things had not changed. Alan got the message and we had a fine time. He even won a door prize, which was a fifty dollar savings bond. But all the time I was there, it was an effort to concentrate on the evening in spite of the fun. Some of the faculty attended as chaperons, so I found myself looking for my man. With the dance being partly his idea and with the prizes being his donations, it only seemed natural that he would attend. But he never came.

SUNDAY, DECEMBER 8:

I did, however, see him on Sunday morning. The Paseo Verde Madrigals had been booked to perform at the big, new United Methodist church in the northeast heights. Naturally our program was one of sacred music, most of which had a message of Advent. But one of the pieces in our repertoire was a composition of mine which Mr Conrad had arranged.

To my dismay, he was his old stoic self, just as he'd been so often lately, even at my lessons. It gave me the feeling that he was shutting me out. Still I approached him.

"So where were you last night?" I asked as our group gathered before the service. "Why weren't you at the dance?"

"You were there? You didn't go alone, did you?"

"Alan took me. But what about you? You should've been there. Why didn't you come?"

"I didn't want to stand around and watch others dance."

"But you could have brought a date. Other teachers did."

"Yes, but I'm not seeing anyone right now."

"Oh, that's right."

"So, how was it? Did you have a good time?"

"Yes, it was very nice. For the first time in my life I had lots of boys asking me to dance. I didn't need Alan after all."

"Did you win a prize?"

"No, but Alan did. He got one of the savings bonds."

"Good. That's nice to know."

Someone else needed him, so I took a seat and waited for us to do warm-ups. This wasn't the time and place, anyway, to ask what bothered him.

After the performance and the reception that followed, I went home and slipped into jeans. Sitting out front by the stone lions, Marvin and George, I pondered the age old question: What do you get the man who has everything? After all, it wasn't just Christmas time; Hanukkah was only days away. Though technically it wasn't a gift giving time for Jews, with the tradition having been added to compete with Advent, it was still a good excuse to show love and appreciation for my teacher; it might even put a smile on his face. That was if I could just decide what to get him. It was one of the things I hated about gift giving, especially on the allowance I got; and in this case, after having forfeited my Christmas money.

Lord, what should I do?

Ask your father. He'll make good suggestions and he'll even pay for it. Hotcha!

So, inside I went to the family room where Daddy was watching TV, and told him how I was at a loss to buy Mr C something nice for Hanukkah. "I don't want to get him the usual stuff, like a tie or a book," I explained. "Can you give me some ideas?"

"Well, let's see. . . ." Daddy squeezed the remote to turn down the television and then poured a beer before answering. "Now, there's always a gift certificate from a nice store, but that's kind of a last resort gift. Or–he likes baseball, doesn't he? Yes, I believe he's a big Dodger fan. He might like football, too. A souvenir of his favorite team would work."

"Okay. Can you think of anything else?"
"Well, he doesn't smoke, but he does drink, doesn't he?"
"Yes."
"Right, I remember. Well, get him a nice big bottle of his favorite gin or whiskey. And if you want, add some nice glasses for him and his girlfriend. I'm sure he'd like that."
"I'm a minor, Daddy."
"That never stopped you before. But all right. If that's what you think he'd like, I'll get it for you. Just find out what brand he likes best and let me know. But whatever you decide to get him, Janette, it's always best to buy it specially packaged, like in a nice decanter or fancy carrying case; also, you can have it monogrammed, if it's appropriate, okay? And don't worry about the cost; I'll be more than happy to pay for it."
"Oh, thank you, Daddy!" I gave him a big hug and kiss. "You've really been a great help."

As my father spoke, the Lord told me which idea would work best, so I took a magnified look at the photos from Mr C's file that showed the bar in his livingroom in order to make my selection. Then later on that week, Daddy and I went shopping together. We called around first because the brandy I spotted on his bar was not a common one. But there was one place in town that had it. Then we bought a lovely decanter, beautiful crystal glasses and a silver tray to set them on. All were arranged together, boxed and wrapped for me to give him at my last music lesson before the holidays.

MONDAY, DEC. 16- THURSDAY, DEC. 17:

As I faced the final week of school before Christmas, I felt old, tired and anxious. There were a few activities to look forward to, but not enough to fill up my days and keep my thoughts from where they had no business. Already some of the plans I'd made for my vacation had been dashed.

I had expected to spend most of my time with my cousin Georgia, the best friend I had in the whole wide world; she'd become a believer not long after I had, making us closer still. But she wasn't coming because the Holisters would not spend the season in Albuquerque as usual. I couldn't even remember when they had missed a party. Even when Uncle Calvin had passed on of a heart attack in `64, they still came that year. This time they would be in England, of all places. Aunt Laura had met a man there while on summer vacation with friends, and from what Georgia said in a letter, it was serious. My heart ached, as I desperately needed my cousin, especially in light of what I was going through. It had been two years since I'd seen her last, and now it would be even longer. It didn't seem fair.

So I would just have to get by on the diversions that remained. My oldest brother Aaron would be home soon and that would be nice. We got along pretty well and I did miss him at times. Maybe we could have some fun together. If the weather was good, he could help me paint Marvin and

George. Also, Mr Conrad had announced a caroling party to his private voice students and the Madrigals. Because the choir was so large, only the madrigal group and the choir's very best were invited. I accepted the invitation with pleasure, remembering what I'd heard about last year's party. The date was Saturday evening, the 21st, the first day of vacation.

Then the street witnessing teams at church had plans to go caroling on Christmas Eve. There had already been one meeting and another was planned a few days before the event, to take care of the final details. The intent was to reach out to the lonely and share the good news of the Messiah. Food and blankets would be given to the needy.

Still, in spite of weariness and disappointment, it seemed a burden was lifting as the days dwindled down to the last week of school. Relieved that so much trauma was now behind me, I was able to pull my chin completely off the ground and allow myself to get excited over the immediate prospect of Mr C's party. It looked to be just the medicine I needed.

WEDNESDAY, DECEMBER 18:
On Wednesday afternoon, the second day of Hanukkah, I loaded up Mr Conrad's present along with my music books and took it to my lessons.

"Now what have we here?" said Mr C as I walked in carrying the gift in a big, heavy duty bag. He brighten a bit at this surprise, just as I'd hoped.

"It's your Hanukkah present," I told him. Taking it into the livingroom, I set it down on the coffee table.

"Oh, really? Why, thank you, Janette. That's very sweet of you. May I open it now?"

"No, you may not. It can wait until after my lessons."

"But why?" Enjoying the tease, his eyes began to sparkle.

"Because there ought to be some suspense in getting a gift."

He came to look inside the bag but I pulled it shut. "Can't I just see the wrapping?"

"Well–all right."

He looked curiously at the gift as I lifted it from the bag. As I placed it in his arms, he felt the weight and looked even more puzzled.

"Well, one thing I can be sure of, it's not a tie." Then he put his ear to it. "I'm glad it's not ticking. What about the card? Can I open the card?"

"I'd rather we got on with my lessons, please."

"All right, then, go ahead and torture me. But remember, two can play at this game. And that reminds me. I'd like your help on Saturday. Could you come over around four thirty and help me lay out the hors d'oeuvres before the others get here?"

"Why? Is good maid service that hard to find?"

My comment was prompted by what Margo had told me about his party the year before with the people he'd hired to serve. Mr C looked at me with his lips parted in awe before a smile spread across his face and he began to laugh. I laughed, too, and had I been smarter, I'd have told him no. Instead I happily twittered, "Sure, I'd be glad to help out."

"Thank you," he said. "I pay by the hour."

Once lessons were done, I stayed to watch my man open his card and gift. It was good to see the smile on his face; his surprise and appreciation were genuine. As he put the items on the bar I asked to sample the brandy.

"Not without your parents being here," he said. "Which isn't a bad idea. I should invite them over. I haven't had a dinner party in quite some time."

"Oh, they would love that."

Knowing I shouldn't linger any longer, I excused myself from his presence with a reference to homework, then quickly gathered my music books and left. During the ride home, I considered the opportunity that had just been presented to me. The time I spent one on one with my teacher was always related to study, not allowing much in the way of intimate conversation. Even though the time before the caroling party would be short, I hoped to use it to learn more of him. Given all we'd been through together, it seemed I had a right to know.

SATURDAY, DECEMBER 21:

So like the chump that I was, on Saturday afternoon I made myself pretty and fragrant in a new outfit and went over to my favorite place to see my favorite man. Still I was careful not to accentuate too many of my positives. I arrived ten minutes early bundled up in my fringed buckskin jacket. Underneath I wore a long, loose fitting white beaded sweater over not too snug navy blue knee pants tucked into tall black boots. My black hair hung down about my shoulders and was topped with a tam that matched the sweater. Mr Conrad greeted me wearing a white apron over simple charcoal gray slacks topped by a black mock turtle neck sweater that lightly hugged his broad shoulders and nicely developed arms. He also wore my favorite cologne and a warm smile that was a clue to just how welcome I was.

"So what's cookin'?" I asked as he helped me off with my jacket.

"Come on in and see."

I followed him into the kitchen. All of the real preparation had been done and things only needed to be put on trays or just taken into the dining area. I was given my own apron and then we went to work. The mood stayed light for the first few minutes, but once we really got started, Mr C grew quiet and the light that had shown in his eyes disappeared. He became his old stoic self again.

"What's the matter?" I asked, reaching for a tray of finger sandwiches. "Feeling tired?"

"No. It's just that this has been such a rough semester and I'm coming down from that high level of stress. I sure do need this time off from school and I know you do, too. You've had as many perils as Pauline."

"Just about. But couldn't you come to our party and then leave town? You'll miss a real happenin' bash. My parents do it up big for Christmas."

"I'm sure it'll be lots of fun, Janette, but I really need to get away for a while; the sooner the better."

"So where are you going?"

"I'm not sure yet. I've received several invitations on both east and west coasts. I just need to make up my mind."

"Must be nice to have a problem like that. I'd head east–to New York."

"Really? You know, that's not a bad idea. It's been a while since I've seen Christmas in New York City."

"I'll bet it's fantastic."

"It can be."

"Will you do New Year's Eve there, too?"

"Probably."

I wanted to tell him to take me along, but I had the feeling that he'd do it if he could, so I said nothing and took my tray into the diningroom.

In just a few trips we'd brought everything out and set it in order. After that I took off my apron and stepped into the sunken living room. Mr Conrad followed. Stopping to stand in front of the fireplace, I looked up at the lovely Monet. Being no art expert, I was still somewhat familiar with the artist's work and had never seen this one in any books. My judgement said that it was from very early in his career. Suddenly a question flowed from my lips asking, "Who was she?"

"Huh? Who do you mean?"

"The friend who gave you the painting. Who was she?"

He was thoughtful. Then coming to stand next to me, he looked up at the canvas and said, "She was a retired actress and she was dying of cancer. She didn't have any family, so I helped her any way I could; this is one way in which she showed her gratitude. Her late husband bought the painting from the artist."

"What was her name?"

"Does it really matter?"

Disappointed, I turned to look at him and found him standing so close that my turning brought my face just a couple of inches from his chest. He wasn't looking at the painting anymore, but down at me. Immediately my body began to tremble slightly and to do other things, warning me that I'd better put some distance between us. But somehow I couldn't move–and he wouldn't move. Though it seemed like an age, we only stood there for about half a minute, saying nothing and doing nothing, until–

"I'm sorry, sweetheart," he said softly, raising his hands to gently brace my shoulders. "I believe you mean well, but–I just can't. . . ." He sighed and looked up at the painting for a moment. "At least not now. There are some memories that you don't want to live over again. Then there's the ones you hold onto, but you have to protect them because people don't understand. That's how this is, and for now you'll just have to accept it."

"All right." The trembling subsided and my inclination was to put my arms around him for comfort and understanding, but for propriety's sake, I remained as I was.

At that moment pain, frustration, longing, and sadness were reflected in his eyes and on his face. Then his features softened while his grip on my shoulders lessened and he slipped his arms around me. Pulling me close, he held me tenderly. But then the doorbell rang and disturbed the mood.

With a deep sigh, he released me and went to answer the door, leaving me with a spinning head and a heart beating hard and fast. Bob Johnson had arrived and it was now 5:15 p.m. Hearing his voice, I struggled into a happy, carefree facade while fruitlessly trying to clear my head and get back to normal. The other students arrived only minutes later, their presence demanding that my private thoughts be put aside. Still I was terribly distracted. Then at about 5:50 the group was complete and most of the food devoured. By 6:15 our voices were warmed up and we were on our way out.

Mr Johnson drove the small bus that Mr Conrad had hired, which carried most of us from place to place. Alan Haskell had tried to get me into the bus to sit with him, but Mr C saw to it that I was numbered with the few that rode in his car, which led the way to each stop. I managed to slip into the back seat so that we wouldn't seem like a couple.

Our visits were brief so that we could make all of our commitments before ten o'clock. Everyone was in high spirits, but it was tough for me to get back into a holiday mood, so I faked it. Between stops I was able to turn things over in my mind. Even though there was conversation, it was so trite that it wasn't obligatory for me to chime in at every instance. I limited my comments to brevities like "yeah" and "uh, huh," until I came to enough of a conclusion that would allow me to give it a rest and be more social.

David Conrad openly dated Vicky Marshall, a woman he could not be close to, and insists on being close to a woman he can't openly date–me. But he only gets so close. If he won't confide in me after all this time, it's just a one way street and it's all strictly for laughs–just like all the others. Maybe that's just the kind of man he is and no woman can really get close to him; after all, he's never been married. What makes a man like that?

I finally had my head together, or so I hoped. In spite of the way our relationship was getting into dangerous territory, there was just no closing the casebook on The Fox. It didn't matter that my limited resources held me back. Something deep within said that the problem he was hiding had to be rooted out and somehow resolved–for his sake and mine as well, since we'd become so deeply connected.

Though I would document the story behind the painting, it obviously held no link to the terror and tragedy alluded to by other things: guns, blackouts, screaming–any clue to that wouldn't be hanging over his fireplace. He wanted no reminders and had said so at the picnic. No. What I wanted was something he intended to keep buried forever. And Mr Johnson seemed bent on doing the same. So I had to kick back and bide my time. God was in control, and if he wanted me to get the job done, he'd have to make the arrangements. I only wanted to keep my sanity and self respect intact.

After caroling at six houses (one of which was Mrs MacGregor's), two nursing homes and the children's ward at the Methodist hospital, we headed toward our final destination where the party would be. Whereas last year's bash had been at Mr C's, this time his recently widowed aunt, Mildred Gross, had been gracious enough to open her home to us. And what a home! It was amongst the new ones then being built in the foothills on the east end of town. The rooms were spacious and elegantly decorated. Rich draperies hung from the satin papered walls, paintings and lovely antiques abounded. Best of all, the view of the city was magnificent from her windows.

A fabulous table had been spread for us in the basement where the decor was a bit homeier with its dark wood furniture, green and blue plaid sofa and chairs. Here a fire was burning in the red brick fire place to greet us as we came down. I rushed to its warmth as did several others before finding a place to sit. So large was the blaze that it didn't take long at all to lose the chill, but as I tried to move away, Alan Haskell blocked my exit.

"What it is!" he said, smiling. "And isn't this convenient?"

I gave him a dubious look, saying, "Do you mind? I'd like to get by."

Alan wouldn't budge. I tried to sidestep him but he mirrored my movements and raised his arms at each side to prevent my escape.

"Not just yet. I cannot pass up an opportunity like this." He glanced up as he spoke, and following his gaze I discovered a giant garland of mistletoe stretched out across the ceiling and hanging right over my head.

Alan grinned and moved even closer. The fire behind me was getting hotter, and those around me were enjoying the fun too much to let me pass. There seemed no other way out.

"All right," I said. "But don't make a major production out of it."

Which is exactly what he did. After dramatically pushing up both sleeves, Alan took me tenderly in his arms with a corny romantic flair that struck me terribly funny. I giggled, but he wasn't discouraged. He planted a flurry of kisses about my face and neck which was not only amusing, it tickled. Finally I laughed so hysterically that he gave up and let me go.

Now, this wasn't the only place where mistletoe was hung. The house was lousy with it. Large and small sprigs were found over doorways, over couches and chairs, hanging from chandeliers, and even above light switches. Until it was removed, Mr Conrad was slightly paranoid, giving me another excuse to chuckle. Unfortunately our kind hostess was very embarrassed when informed of the romantic herb's abundance. Her grandchildren, who were visiting for the holidays, were the culprits, and had to help take it down.

"Feeling better now?" I quietly asked Mr C as we both approached the punch bowl. "Too bad Helen isn't here. She'd have loved this."

His reply was a dirty look as he gave me the cup he had filled. "You keep it up and there'll be no Hanukkah present."

"What?"
"I will not repeat myself."
"But–"
He left the table and, for the moment, pretended to ignore me. Confidence in the way the man loved to spoil me kept me from taking his response seriously.

We all sang again after having eaten enough. Tired of Christmas songs, we chose ones we'd worked on that year and in past years. This prompted talk about what to do next spring and possibilities for the following year for those who would remain. Delighted at this turn in the conversation, Alan took advantage of the subject to promote his ideas for a show.

As the discussion continued and grew lively, our hostess quietly came to me, touched my arm and asked me to come with her. Without a word I arose and followed her up the stairs and down the hall to a dimly lit reading room where Mr Conrad was waiting.

"Happy Hanukkah, Janette." My teacher smiled warmly from where he stood next to a large ornate silver menorah with several colored abbreviated candles. It was on a small table in the middle of the room, and at its base was a box of matches.

"Oh! It's gorgeous. Is this my present?"
"No, but it's around here somewhere. Can you remember the prayers?"
"I only know the first one. You'll have to help me."
"Baruch atah Adonai Elohenu melech ha olam–" We prayed together. Then, nervous and excited, I picked up the matches and lit the *shamas* candle. Remembering the lovely song that accompanied the lighting of each candle, I started it quietly and was joined by Mr Conrad and his aunt who stood watching from the doorway as I lit each little taper. It made me so homesick for Alef Tav that I almost burst into tears.

"This was very lovely," said Aunt Mildred with a wistful smile. "Enjoy the rest while I get back to the party."

His mood much brighter, my teacher offered a mischievous smile as his aunt retreated down the hall. "And now for your first present," he said, and turning to a decorative wall shelf, he took from it a small box wrapped in silver paper and tied with blue ribbon. I knew it was a book before even getting it open, but had no idea what kind. Beneath the silver, inside a plain white box was a deep burgundy leather bound book. The title was in French. It was a Bible, and my name was engraved in gold on the cover. Inside he wrote, "To the loveliest angel I've ever known."

"Oh, Mr Conrad!" Now a tear did escape, and I could not let myself look at him or I'd have thrown my arms around him. "It's beautiful . . . and so very thoughtful."

"I'm glad you like it. Now, there's one more."
"More? Oh, but you've given me so much already."

He turned again to the shelf and brought down a small slender package that had the look of being another black velvet case. More rhinestones? My hands trembled as I undid the wrapping. It was jewelry, all right. A lovely diamond bracelet in white gold, quite a bit different from the others he'd given me. But then this wasn't costume jewelry.

"Oh! Oh! It's fabulous!" I lifted it from the case and held it before my eyes. The white stones glittered wonderfully in the candle light. "And the diamonds are–"

"Yes, Janette, the diamonds are real, so if anyone asks where you got it–"

"I won't tell a soul," I said softly, so overcome that I barely noticed the prohibitory tug of my conscience. "Not even Letty Johnson."

"I know I shouldn't give you something like this, so if you don't want to accept it, I'll certainly understand, but you deserve this and a whole lot more. Honey, you've helped me these past few months in ways that you don't even realize, and this is my way of saying thank you."

All manner of emotions flowed through my heart as he took my left hand and gently pushed the sleeve up my arm: joy, gratitude, excitement, and love. Love that ached to be expressed with a greater affection than was correct for our relationship. Not daring to let these desires find release, I began to shake all over as he took the bracelet from my fingers and laid it across my wrist. That and the warm, gentle touch of his hands which began to stir other feelings.

"You have such a tiny wrist," he said quietly as he fastened the bracelet. "So very delicate . . . and soft."

Mr Conrad did not let go of my wrist. He used it to pull me closer to him, as if to get what he had missed out on earlier at the apartment when Mr Johnson rang the bell. As he drew me to him, fear rose up within me. Fear of what I might say or do. Fear of something that I didn't dare give myself to. This fear was hot and made me start to swoon, made my knees want to buckle. Then as he touched my face and lifted my chin, it nearly made me wet my pants.

"We'd better get back to the others," was all he said as he looked down on me. "You go on back to the party and I'll clean up here. All right?"

"A-a-all right," I whispered, barely able to respond.

"Happy Hanukkah, Janette." Turning my face a little to the side, he then kissed me tenderly on the cheek, right near my temple, then planted another gentle kiss on my ear.

SUNDAY, DECEMBER 22:

No matter how I had sought to kill it, the memory of David Conrad's touch and little kisses played on and on in my head for the rest of that evening and then greeted me with the sunrise, pulling me down into a whirling pit of longing and desire. And I no longer wanted to struggle against it. I was back at that "follow him anywhere" stage where nothing else seemed to matter but having my Mr Conrad.

If only he had really kissed me. Why didn't he? I know he wanted more than that. These thoughts and my imagination took me in the direction of a sweet first kiss.

But he's always wanted more. So, what else is new?
With this last thought the whirling began to slow and with it the flow of sap to my brain. It allowed my mind to take a turn toward sensible thinking. It also kept me from going down the hall, bringing the phone into my room and dialing his number before he could catch his plane.

Last night was just a big slip in propriety for him, I reasoned, while also saying that I was better off with a diamond bracelet than a bastard child. Had he gone any further and kissed my mouth, I really could have been a lost soul. Now that the Christmas season was at hand, I saw the chance to regroup and maybe get over this love sickness. But I had to work hard to get my head really clear; still I managed. Had I been alone, I never would have made it. Having to face a family like mine at the breakfast table meant that I must force the romantic fog to lift or risk questions and comments about the literal daze I was in. Just the short time we were together helped me to find a more solid foothold in sanity and drag myself up toward common sense. By the time they left for Sunday school, I was able to get into my own routine for the day, all the time reasoning things out.

My head began to ache as it always did when I had to go over and over all the reasons it would be foolish to give myself to David Conrad; but I kept it up anyway, seeing it as the only way to handle my plight. The only other way would be for he and I to have one of those heart to heart talks. But what would we say, and what would it do to the rest of our time together? *What if he was in love with me? What if–?*

Stop it, Janette! You'll end up right back in the pit!

Figuratively slapping myself, I remembered that with him leaving town, there would be no chance to talk until school was back in session. So I decided that even if he wanted something extracurricular with me, his list of women was long enough already, and there was no need to add my name– even if it were at the top. Then I remembered that he'd torn up that list. But even so, had I given in to him during this last little break from propriety, it wouldn't be long before all I had left of the affair would be memories of lost virginity and the lifelong shame of having been so stupid, just like Lisa O.

Last of all, I found the presence of mind to look at myself and how I had tried to always be so attractive to him, like at the victory party. We'd been attracted to each other from day one, and why shouldn't he be interested? How could I fault him entirely for crossing the line when I was always so available and tempting? After all, how often had I declined his requests for my company, not to mention his gifts?

At last my feet were back on the ground, or at least somewhere in the vicinity. I forgave my Mr Conrad for being the promiscuous man that he was–or had been, and let my fears and angst subside. I also forgave myself and determined to be more circumspect and reserved in our relationship. Then, before leaving for The Rock, I placed the lovely French Bible on a shelf with my other Bibles, and buried the diamond bracelet along with the other jewelry. I then determined to keep a good grip on my own thoughts and desires and to not do anything that would further encourage his untoward attentions.

That evening I was delighted to have a strong enough distraction to further clear up my head. Not long after supper I ran back to church for the special meeting for the caroling party, getting there early as did quite a few others. It was always that way, people coming early and staying late. We were *mishpocheh*–family. And even though parts of the building were still under construction, it looked and felt very homey in a rustic, hippy sort of fashion not typical of church.

While looking over some of the work that had just been completed in our simple sanctuary, I noticed a couple of the brothers giving the grand tour to someone new. As we passed each other, they introduced me to the newcomer and we shook hands. His name was Ted.

Haut boy!

Now, there were some good looking single men at The Rock (none of which had ever given me a ripple), but there was something different about this one. The sight of him hit much more than my hormones. He had the face of an angel and a halo to match. His jaw was strong and his perfectly formed nose had a slight upturn. His hazel eyes had a pleasant sparkle in them and a dimple appeared on his right cheek as he smiled. Oh, and he was built just the way I like 'em! A young man (probably in his mid to early twenties), he stood about five foot six, was broad shouldered with a stocky, muscular build, and had a thick neck like a boxer's. That and the rough condition of his hands suggested that he was some sort of laborer; maybe a machinist or an auto mechanic, judging from the oil colored stains the soap had neglected to remove. His wavy blonde hair was cut red neck short, and his fair skin didn't seem to have seen much of central New Mexico's sunny climate; then as light as he was dressed (a flannel shirt and denim jacket) the winters must have been very cold wherever he was from. And the halo? All I knew was that the power of God on him was strong and bright, and it was something I felt compelled to explore.

After our brief introduction, they went the other way while I, resisting the temptation to follow along, went to get more hot chocolate from the kitchen before the meeting started.

The meeting's agenda included more than finishing plans for the caroling outreach. During this session the elders would better organize the street ministry. Once the meeting was underway, the basics of evangelism were covered. The desire was not to promote our church but our Lord, and to offer his love and truth to those willing to receive. The necessity of prayer in making our efforts effective was continually emphasized. Then the discussion went to mode of operation and safety, which went hand in hand. Arguments were to be avoided at all cost. No one would go out alone; females would always have a male present. Teams would be in twos, threes and never more than four; each would have a name for easy

ID and an assigned territory. Eventually a walkie talkie would be issued to each team and a communication base set up at the church for emergencies and other needs; teams would check in and out.

Even though nights had turned very cold, most regularly scheduled outreach would take place in the evening, Friday and Saturday nights in particular, even when services were going on. In Albuquerque the winters were usually mild, seldom bringing heavy snow and never getting below zero, so there would be no problem in finding people to reach, and the relatively low night life of the season would keep the less experienced in our ranks from being overwhelmed. The parts of town targeted, such as the area surrounding the University of New Mexico and the clusters of nightspots along Central, always had plenty of traffic no matter what the time of year.

After a short break, the topic was our caroling outreach. For that we would divide up into eight groups of six or more people and then meet at our last stop, which was St Basil's Catholic Church, a good distance away in the South Valley. There we would attend midnight mass as well as sing outside the church. At this point in the discussion, the man I'd met earlier, Ted Molloy, was introduced to the group. Some of our people had met him while out witnessing, and he was a parish priest at St Basil's.

A priest? A Catholic priest? Oh, God, don't do this to me.

"Uh, I h-h-h-have to admit that this k-kind of ch-church is way off the b-beaten path for me. . . . J-just a few y-years ago things were m-much different in m-my church, and I'd never h-have set foot in a P-Protestant church. But–God brought me here. I know it. He's g-got a lot of things he wants me t-to learn. I j–just hope you'll help me by p-praying for m-me and by b-being p-p-patient with me w-w-while I–learn. What I'm f-finding here l-looks like what I've b-b-been praying for–for a long time. Thank you."

Done with his bit, the priest took a seat and the meeting was brought to a close. All that was left was to choose partners and put our names on the list. To my dismay, I already had a strong impression in my spirit who was supposed to be mine. I looked around, though, just to be sure. Then when I saw him standing alone, I once again introduced myself to Ted Molloy.

"Hi. I'm Janette. We met just before the meeting." He only glanced at me and nodded his reply before turning to look around the room. "So are you joining the street ministry?"

"Yes." Molloy gave me a quick once over again with an expression that read, "You've got to be kidding," then looked away while saying, "I'll be with the pastor and his wife."

"Oh." *Hmmm, born again AND Catholic? I didn't know it was possible. Well, live and learn. And what happened to the stuttering? His problem must be speaking in front of crowds.*

From the way this man now behaved, I was having doubts about his salvation being genuine. We'd only just met and already there was something about me he didn't like. Was it my age, color or configuration?

I got the feeling that it was all of the above. Why God wanted me to waste my time on such a jerk was beyond me; and I was no longer interested in him, since his Catholicism and my Judaism would mix like garlic and chocolate ice cream. What could I say? Looking at him with spiritual eyes I searched to see if the "halo" was still there. To my surprise, it was.

Having done what I had been told to do, and not feeling sorry about his refusal, I was about to walk away. But there was a definite nudge in my spirit saying I should try again.

"You know," I said casually. "At first I thought about going in a trio, but it'll be much more fun if I can ride my Indian."

"What?" He did a double take and then looked dead at me. "You don't mean that beautiful old bike parked out back?"

"Yep. Turquoise blue and white with the silver and black conchos on the black saddle bags."

"And it's yours?" Incredulous, he looked me over again. His appraisal did not seem flattering. "How old are you?"

"Seventeen." Getting bored with this character, I reached into my back pocket for the item on one of the chains that I wore with my jeans: an old set of brass knuckles. I took them off the chain and fingered them while working to keep my voice and manner pleasant. "My old boyfriend fixed it up and gave it to me as a birthday present. Nice, huh?"

"Yeah, real nice . . . How does she run?"

"Perfect. I keep it well maintained."

"Yeah, my oldest brother used to ride one sort of like it. His was a black and red combo, but it may have been a later model. What year is yours?"

"1948."

"Are you sure that's a Scout? Looks more like a Chief."

"Well, it started out as one. At least, that's what he told me. He wanted it to look pretty for me and dressed it up. He worked from the manual, but I know he borrowed parts from a lot of bikes before he was done."

"Man! Those were great machines. And that Indian head was the coolest thing. When I saw your bike I–well, I was sure hoping to meet the owner to see if I could at least take it for a spin."

"Well, I kind of thought God wanted you on that bike for street ministry, but since you've made your choice, I'll have to find somebody else."

"Uh, I, uh–I don't have to go with Jim and Jo Ann, but–are you really seventeen?"

"You want to see my driver's licence?" By then the brass knuckles were on my right hand. He finally noticed them as I reached into my little shoulder bag and took out my wallet. I meant it to imply that I wasn't just a cute little girl to be condescended to.

"Okay," said Molloy. His hand trembled noticeably as he returned my licence. Looking at me again, his searching gaze was different, as if trying to see inside me. He took a deep breath and resignedly said, "Look, I'm really sorry. I never–what I mean is, if you'll have me, I'm yours."

"Swell." *Just what I've always wanted.*

Rubbing his chin, he laughed nervously and shook his head. "Man! This is all so–surreal! Don't get me wrong; I think it's wonderful, but sometimes it's so fantastic that it's just too much to take. It's like a trip to fairyland. And like Peter walking on the water, it's scares the hell out of me."

"And you're just getting started, aren't you? Well, use your prayer language more. That'll help you adjust."

"What? Oh, you mean the speaking in tongues? Oh, no. No, I–uh, got a taste of that when I came to your meeting the other night, with everybody praying or singing in tongues; now, the singing in tongues was rather nice. Anyway, we talked about it afterwards, and of course I know the Biblical basis for it, but–do I really have to go that far out?"

"Well, if you ever plan to get your boat out of the harbor, you might as well tank up here where nobody will put you down for it. Besides, you'll need it for street ministry."

"Oh, yeah? How's that?"

"Look, when it comes to the baptism of the Holy Spirit, don't get distracted by speaking in tongues or anything else. Just focus on the Holy Spirit himself because he's what's important. I mean, how much of Jesus you want in your life, a little bit or a lot?"

"As much as I can get."

"Well, the Holy Spirit is God's spirit, right? The Bible says that he's the one who teaches us and reveals God's truth so that we can genuinely come to know our Heavenly Father. So what needs to be considered is this: in a literal, Biblical sense, baptism is a complete immersion. Am I right?"

"Yes, that's correct."

"Therefore being baptized in the Holy Spirit is to be immersed in the Spirit of God. Anything wrong with that?"

"No, not at all. Keep talking."

"The main thing is to lay hold on the purpose for it. Most believers have their favorite Bible characters or saints that they want to be like, right? But without the baptism of the Holy Spirit, they'll never even come close. Why? Because that's where the power comes from. And I'm not just talking about all the gifts and miracles, but for holy and righteous living, and for that deep, satisfying relationship with God. Even if we could be a goodie two-shoes and keep our noses clean under our own power, what does the Bible say about that?"

"It says that our own righteousness is like filthy rags."

"Which means that the power has to come from God. Even Jesus said that he couldn't do anything without his father. Are we any better?"

"Of course not."

"Well, that's why we need the baptism of the Holy Spirit, because all that we need comes with it. It affords us an entrance into the same exact power Jesus had–only in a smaller dose, since we're not without sin. So the whole idea behind it is to get more of God so that we can be more like him."

"You make a very good point. As a matter of fact, what you've said happens to be exactly what I've been praying for. Exactly. Ever since I became aware–really aware of the Holy Spirit, I've been asking God for more. You see, it's like you said; I've always wanted that same power and the closeness to God that the saints had. So what do I do?"

"Let's get Jim or Jo Ann or maybe one of the other elders and we'll pray for you."

It only took a minute to round up Jim and Jo Ann Foster. Together we went to one of the prayer rooms to seek the Lord for the outpouring of God's Holy Spirit for Ted Molloy.

Only a few inaudible words of prayer were mumbled by Jim and Jo Ann before they both broke forth into singing. The young priest seemed inhibited, but with his head bowed in humility, it showed that his heart was open to receive from God. With our worship, the presence of God began to manifest; that's when Ted's hands went up, his body shook, and the heavenly language began to flow from his lips.

Molloy wasn't the only one getting a dose of the power. We must have been in that room at least twenty minutes. By the time we came out, most everyone else had gone. Some went to Hungry Harry's, the restaurant up the street, for a late bite and fellowship. Jim and Jo Ann decided to join them while Ted and I hung out a bit longer at the church.

My new partner wasn't saying much. Still tripping around in the heavenly realm, all he could do was laugh. Conversation wasn't possible with anyone in this state, as I well knew, but I wanted to talk and get acquainted with the man I'd be running the streets with. The laughter was wearing his body out and soon he couldn't take it any more. With his eyes he begged me for help.

"Just ask him to stop," I said.

He did so silently, and in a few seconds he was calm.

Resisting the temptation to get the man giggling again, I suggested we should go get coffee or something.

"Sure," he said. "Can we take the Indian?"

"Yeah, sure."

Out the back door we went. The small parking lot right behind the building is where I always parked.

"You know," said Ted. "I had plans to try and buy this bike from you."

"Oh, yeah? You like it that much?"

Rather than explain with words, he pointed to a car parked about thirty feet away. It was a 1956 Chevy four door hard top with wide white sidewall tires. Immediately chills went through me as I got the message. It was Ted's car, and the turquoise blue and white paint job matched mine exactly.

I looked for a long moment and then slowly turned to look at him. He wasn't smiling. "What's the interior like?"

"Same color blue with black trim."

"Hmm. . . . Let's go."

I mounted the bike and started up the engine. The priest climbed on behind me and we took off into the start of an adventure that would last us the rest of our lives.

It was good having someone on behind me again. It was a little work to compensate for the extra weight, but in the cold night air the added warmth was nice. We headed south on San Mateo and made a right on Central toward the University. After a few blocks I stopped at a light and let the priest take the helm. He was ecstatic, like a child with a brand new toy. Just watching him did something to me. His joy was contagious, and any aversion I had to him faded completely in the light of it.

On a hunch that Molloy hadn't seen too much of the area, I had him drive us out of town on Route 66 to a certain place in the road where one caught his first view of the city coming from the west. At night it was breathtaking. And just as I'd figured, he hadn't seen it before; so we stopped there for a few minutes to enjoy the view while I told him some historical details about the area, throwing in a few Indian legends for color. Then he got really tickled when I howled like a coyote and one howled back. He enjoyed this little tour so much that he made me promise to take him sightseeing.

Finally we headed back and stopped at an all night diner. I got an order of fries and a Bubble Up while Ted seemed to order half the menu.

"We're going to have a great time!" he said, sliding into the booth so fast that he hit the wall.

"You'd better believe it!" I happily slid in across from him and leaned back in the corner. "So what'll we call our team?"

"What? Oh, yeah. Our two man motorcycle team has to have a name. How about Pat and Mike?"

"Oh, no, please!" I laughed and shook my head. "I knew you were Irish."

"I sure am."

"And you're from Chicago."

"Yeah. Did I mention that?"

"No, you didn't. And you're also a boxer."

"Yes, and what else?"

"You're an auto mechanic."

"Anything more, Sherlock?"

"Look, I have family from Chicago, so I caught your accent. My dad was a boxer, so I recognized the traits. Back at the church you pointed out the car you were driving; it's more than ten years old, has a custom paint job and your hands look like you work on cars. Since you're a priest by occupation and you're not working in a factory–well, elemen'try."

"Say, that's pretty good. You know, kid, you're kind of different. I really like you. Yeah, we're gonna get along just fine. Pat and Mike?"

"I'd prefer Toody and Muldoon, but if you insist. So, who's Pat and who's Mike?"

"I'll be Mike."

"That gives me top billing. I'll go for that."

"And now that we've settled that, tell me something: Were you always into this kind of faith? I mean, this is all so new to me, but at the same time–"

"It's like you've known about it all your life."

"Yes!"

"I grew up in a dead, dry Methodist church. I've only been in touch with the real thing for–oh, almost two years now."

"Is that all? But you seem to know so much."

"Not compared to some. I have had some great teachers, though, and I stay in the Scriptures all the time. But I have to confess that some of what comes out of my mouth isn't me at all. It's the Lord–literally–and for that I'm very grateful, since I don't have all the answers."

"So tell me how you got into this."

"Well, I left home for a while and stumbled onto a ki–a–a commune of believers up in Colorado. They told me about the Lord, then I experienced him for myself. I gave my heart to the Lord the first night I was there."

"A Christian commune, huh? You know, I've heard that some of these communes aren't necessarily healthy places. You must have found a good one. What group was yours with? Was it that, uh–oh, what's that group I heard about. . . . Was it the Children of God?"

By this time I had finally had it with the lie I'd been living. Up to this point I had kept mum over things I saw and heard that I knew were wrong, and walked on eggs lest my beliefs be misunderstood and trampled on. But looking at this man who was so willing to take a gamble and break from tradition, I sensed the possibility for something that would be liberating for both of us. Something strange was obviously afoot with us being paired up, so I decided to take a chance myself and lay everything on the table.

"No," I replied. "This was an obscure group. And it wasn't exactly–well, what you'd call Christian. It was a kibbutz called Alef Tav, and the people there were Jewish."

"Huh? Now, wait just a minute." Ted's eyes narrowed and he looked at me sideways. "Would you say that again?"

"The commune was a kibbutz called Alef Tav, and the people there were Jewish."

"Jewish? You're telling me that you heard about this kind of religion from people calling themselves Jews? Now, I know that occasionally Jews will convert, but then they're not Jews anymore. How could you learn anything about the power of Christ from people still calling themselves Jews when those kind only acknowledge Jesus historically?"

"Let's just say that they're a throwback to an earlier time."

"What time is that?"

"Well, tell me, was Jesus a Christian? Was Luke or Peter or any of the others disciples, were they Christians?"

"We were first called Christians–"

"That was later on and by other people. Think about it. Historically, Jesus did not start a new religion, nor did his followers. From what I've learned, we weren't even called the Church until the Archbishop of Canterbury thought it was such a hot idea; the Greek word that church comes from isn't once mentioned in Scripture, and that's a fact. Come on! You know this stuff. You have to. The Apostle Paul talked plenty about his Jewish identity. There's the spiritual olive tree that we're all grafted into that represents Israel. The apostles talked of the Israel of God. The book of The Revelation refers to the twelve tribes of Israel and God's appointed feasts. *This* is the earlier time in our history that these people at Alef Tav are reaching back to–the time *before* we all became Christians and before we became known as the Church."

"Well, it's news to me, and I think it'd be new to a lot of people. To be honest, I've never met a person still calling himself a Jew that embraces the Gospel of Jesus Christ. In my experience, other than those that convert, Jews hate Jesus and want nothing to do with him. I've seen and heard it for myself one too many times, and in spite of what you're saying, it's something that goes back to when Christ walked the earth. Now, you know as well as I do that the Jews killed Jesus."

"Oh? And the gentiles didn't? You make it sound as if the Jews were the only ones involved."

"Well, sure the Romans had their part in it, but the whole idea to kill Jesus originated with the Jews."

"Oh, really? All of them? Did every last man, woman and child in Israel help to plan his crucifixion, or was it just a select few? Do you think Nicodemus was in the crowd yelling 'crucify him'?"

"All right, I get your drift." Molloy stopped a moment to sort things through. "And I have to admit that what you're saying does make sense, but–maybe it's just that I've never heard this before. It's always been–"

"The Jews were the bad guys."

"Yes."

"Which would include all of Jesus' family, by the way. But let's focus for a minute on the real bad guys, whoever they were, and then tell me one thing, okay? What was one of the last things Jesus said before he died on the cross? He mentioned something about forgiveness, didn't he?"

My words seemed to hit him like a fist. He went suddenly back against the red vinyl seat and sat with his mouth open. The astonishment on his face told me he got the message.

"He–he said, 'Father, forgive them; for they know not what they do.'"

"That's right. Now, don't you think his heavenly father forgave them, and don't you think we should, too?"

"You're right. You're absolutely right. Why couldn't I see this before?"

"Why, indeed. But the Holy Spirit has a way of opening up our eyes to lots of things we've never seen before, especially if one applies one's self to some serious Bible study. Then you might even discover that the idea to kill Jesus didn't come from the Jews at all."

"Huh? Oh, now, come on! Now you're pulling my leg!"

"No, I'm not. I can show you right from the Scriptures."

"Okay, so show me."

I pulled my little Bible from my bag and went to sit next to Ted so he could see for himself what I was reading. First was my favorite verse on the subject, which is found in the book of Acts. It's where Stephen is about to get stoned and he quotes from the Psalms and the prophets. This portion plainly answers the whodunit question when it comes to the crucifixion of Jesus Christ, placing the blame exactly where it belongs–on everybody, including God as the instigator. Then I showed him the words of Jesus about laying down his own life. Finally I added a couple of prophesies out of the Psalms and Isaiah to deal with any remaining doubt.

"So the whole idea of Messiah dying for us was God's from the very beginning," I said. "And all the nations of the world share in the guilt because, in one way or another, everyone had a hand in it. And if a Jewish person seems to hate Jesus, it's only because of all of the hatred that people have hurled at them in his name."

"Hmmm. . . . I, uh–Janette, you're going to have to forgive me, but I've had so much new stuff thrown at me in such a short time that–well, it's a bit overwhelming. I hope you don't mind, but I need to spend time in prayer and meditation on this and a few other things."

"Sure." I closed my Bible and went back to my place across the table. "I understand. I went through some serious culture shock and head trips myself up at Alef Tav."

"I'll bet. Now, these Jews that you met, did they keep both Christian and Jewish traditions? How did it work?"

It amazed me that he wanted to continue, since I could tell that the transition he was in was doing some heavy things inside his brain. But I freely answered, sharing my experiences with joy and tenderness as I explained about the community, its workings and its reason for being.

"You know, that sounds like fun." Molloy spoke wistfully when I was done satisfying his curiosity. "Do you think they'd let a–a bigoted jerk like me come in?"

"Don't be so hard on yourself, Ted. These day's we're all learning new stuff. And yes, they would welcome you without reservation. I felt as much at home with them as I ever did with my own family."

"Sounds like what monastic life ought to be. I think maybe I would like to see that place. Alef Tav, right?"

"Uh, huh."

"What's that mean? Do you know?"

"Try Alpha and Omega."

"Oh, really? Yes, I want to go there."

"Good. Just let me know when and I'll get you set up."

It was then that our order was ready. After giving thanks, we continued our conversation. Then as we began to eat, I decided to inquire of my partner what he had asked of me.

"Okay, Ted, now what about you? You heard about Rock of the Witness through the street ministry, right?"

"Yeah. You know, whoever said that God works in strange and mysterious ways sure knew what he was talking about. Wow! You with your Jews who believe in Jesus, and me, a Catholic priest moonlighting at a Protestant church." Molloy shuddered and shook his head. "Maybe someday I'll let you in on what this has all been doing to my head. Yes, I met Jim and Jo Ann along with some of the others when they were standing outside of Mahoney's singing hymns."

"Is that Mahoney's Bar and Grill on east Central?"

"Yes, and it's been about the only place in this beans and tortilla town to look anything like home. I can go there to relax and drink–I mean, think things over. You see, Janette, this isn't my archdiocese. I was transferred to New Mexico temporarily as–I don't know, sort of a punishment, I guess. . . . No, not a punishment. It just seems that way. The idea is for me to get a firsthand look at the Church from a different cultural angle so that I can break out of the mold I was brought up in. Anyway, when I first heard that I was coming here, I thought they were sending me to a third world country. Now, after a few months, I'm still not sure; so this really hasn't been a very pleasant experience. That is until I found you guys at The Rock."

"Well, did you get in trouble?"

"Not really, but my first two assignments were less than wonderful. Oh, there was some personality conflict, but that's not unusual. Then there were things that happened that it's tough to know how to deal with."

"Like what?"

"Like–dropping the host down the front of a lady's dress." I laughed freely, but Ted had yet to find any humor in it. "It was high mass on Easter Sunday. The woman was huge and her neckline was sort of low. What was I supposed to do, go fishing for it?"

"What did you do?"

"I didn't get the chance to do anything. The pastor took the situation out of my hands, but I sure got a down dressing later."

"So, how long are you in for?"

"Not sure. A year, maybe. I've already been here three months. Guess it depends on how long it takes to get done with the project they gave me. Or maybe when the archbishop thinks I've had enough."

"What's the project?"

"It's a study on Catholicism and the American Indian. I'm supposed to get some first hand experience on a reservation or two–or three. My parish is close to one, and I went down to check out the church there and talk to the priests. It's run by some of the strangest Franciscans I've ever met. I haven't been back lately, though. So far most of my research has been done at the public library. I figure that way I can pick certain tribes to study before I start traveling around the state.

"That was a very smart move. The last thing you want to do is go traipsing around alone on some of those places, especially at night."

"Yes, and especially since I'm white. But so many of them in this area are Catholic and I am a priest. Shouldn't that make a difference?"

"I wouldn't bet on it. Doing the tourist bit is one thing. Getting into their business is another. If I were you, I'd be real careful and always stay prayed up. You must be near the Isleta reservation."

"Right. St Augustine. Their's is one of the oldest missions in the U.S."

"Like I said, be careful. Watch your attitude. On reservation land the Indians are the law and you will be greatly out numbered, especially if you should get out of God's will."

"Thanks for the warning. I was told something like that when I first got here, but I needed to hear it again."

"So, what part of Chicago are you from, south side?"

"Yes, my family started out in Bridgeport but moved to Kenwood when I was around eight years old."

"That's next door to Hyde Park."

"Ah, so you've been there."

"A few times, but the visits were never for more than a week or two, so what I've seen of the city is limited."

"Well, you'll have to come and visit me when I go back; then I can show you the town. Funny, but I can't wait to get home, and yet I know God has a purpose for me here. I want to stay and find out what's in store; which gets me back to my story. See, the group from Rock of the Witness was standing outside just a few feet away from the door of Mahoney's and singing the most heavenly music I think I've ever heard. When I came out, the sound arrested me; the voices, the words and–and the harmonies were glorious! But it was more than hearing the music. There was a great sense of joy and love in it that just overwhelmed me; before I knew it I was balling like a baby. Then I was drawn to get closer to these people. It was an awful strong feeling, because when I got a good look at them and saw the long hair and beards on some of the men, the scene didn't look too inviting. But the feeling wouldn't let me alone, so I walked over. The next thing I knew they let me join their group. I'd say it was kind of like it was tonight when the Holy Spirit came and baptized me, only then I couldn't move once I got in with them. I just felt something happening; happening around me and inside me. I don't know how to describe it, really. Maybe you know already. Then Jim laid his hand on my head and began to speak to me saying how much God loved me, that my prayers had been heard, and how he'd called me to know him and serve him in ways I hadn't yet learned. And–oh, I can't remember it all, but I do know that he talked about me being made a true priest, one that God would delight in. 'A true servant of the Most High God,' and–oh, and 'not according to the ways of men.' He said that several times. As a matter of fact, that message was in there a lot, but worded differently each time. Anyway, he said so many things, and it was like he spoke to all the deepest desires of my heart, things nobody else could possibly know. Then the way he said it–the words and phrases he used let me know that this really was from God. That guy didn't know me from Adam, and since I wasn't wearing a collar, he couldn't possibly know that I was a priest, let alone all that other stuff. Amazing! It was God saying all those things to me. Me–Ted Molloy. I still have trouble believing it."

"Was it scary?"

"You'd better believe it. But not near as bad as the night I first came to The Rock. That was downright bizarre!"

"What happened?"

"Well, as you've probably noticed, I'm a bit paranoid about this whole business because, in spite of the fact that Catholics and Protestants are now allowed to mix and mingle, not everybody has jumped onto that boat and this could cause trouble for me. See, when I went to seminary things were one way; when I came out, they were another. I'm still adjusting and so are lots of people. Just imagine yourself in my shoes. I've been a good Catholic all my life. I'd never before set foot in a Protestant church for any reason whatsoever, and the first time I do, it has to be Rock of the Witness."

"Oy v'voy."

"Exactly. So with my background, I naturally wasn't too hot on the idea of going to The Rock, even though I felt I had to. Well, if God wanted it then so did I, so I worked up the nerve and drove up there on a Friday night and saw this–this thing that they call a church. Was I ever disappointed. I thought sure they had a little more sanctity than that. It looked more like a bar than what I came out of to meet these people. But I couldn't just drive away without giving it a chance. So I got out of my car, and as I walked toward the door I started to feel that same power and love I felt that night on the street, so I figured I was doing the right thing. Anyway, I had arrived pretty early and the service hadn't started yet. Only two or three people had come besides me and the band. Well, I was hoping that when I got inside maybe it would look a little more like a church, but it didn't. The crucifixion mural in the hall was just starting to get some paint on it, and the only religious article in the sanctuary was the wooden cross at the back of the stage. So I went in, sat down and waited. Then the longer I sat there, the more uncomfortable I felt about being there. Plus I didn't think much of the scenery. Rough hewn wood and cheap, Mexican style chandeliers with dimmers aren't exactly what you'd call inspiring. So I got up and left. At least that's what I thought I did. I'm certain I remember getting to my feet, going down the hall and seeing the light coming through from the front parking lot when I got to the foyer. Then the next thing I knew, I was seated right back in the sanctuary. Well, I was rather confused, so I thought about it for a moment and decided to try it again. Only this time I couldn't even get up. My legs didn't have any power in them. Scared me so bad I almost–well, anyway, I got the message. Then later on, after the service started, I had a much better attitude."

"Yeah, I'll bet."

"It was great, but at the same time–painful. This meeting was so far beyond anything I'd ever seen that it totally blew my mind. But the joy was so real–and so powerful! And with the Holy Spirit sitting on me like an elephant the whole time, he not only kept me right there in my seat, he was dealing with me about false piety and all the other lies I'd been living. I tell you, conviction of sin is mighty uncomfortable, but when the power of sin is broken–man! There's nothing in the world better than that."

As we talked, it became apparent that this was quite a different man from the one I'd met just a short while ago. Further deliverance had taken place with his receiving of the Holy Spirit's baptism. The curtness, reticence and fear he had displayed earlier had vanished. Other things were gone, too, although I didn't know exactly what. Now I felt perfectly at ease with him. He didn't seem at all like a Catholic priest. He didn't seem like a Ted, either. All the time we talked, it was in the back of my mind to call him Teddy. He looked like one to me, with his hazel eyes shining bright and eager, and there was a childlike quality to his demeanor. Somehow he seemed like too much fun to be simply 'Ted.'

"Pardon my saying so," I said. "But you don't seem like you'd be a priest. Would you mind if I called you Teddy?"

"No, not at all. It's what my family and old friends call me–well, they did before I was ordained, anyway. I kind of miss it sometimes even though Ted sounds more adult. Somehow 'Father Teddy' just wouldn't work."

"No, it wouldn't. So is it Edward or Theodore?"

"Theodore. Theodore Francis John-Joseph Molloy. So, what do you like to be called?"

"I don't really have a nick name. Sometimes my friends call me Jan, but mostly everybody calls me Janette. Just call me anything but Janet. I have reason to hate that name."

"Yeah? How come?"

"An ugly and obnoxious girl in my third grade class was named Janet, and the teacher used to get our names confused. Janet and I never got along, either. Nobody did."

Teddy cocked his head to one side and studied me for a moment. "I like Jenny. Yeah! Jenny's a good name for you, especially since you sing. I heard you the first night I came to The Rock. You have a wonderful voice."

"Thank you."

"You know, I'm glad you picked me out, and that you ride that Indian. I would never have picked you. Women always spell trouble, especially–"

"Especially for a guy in your racket."

"If you, uh, if you want to put it that way. You're not one o' them femme fatales, are ya?"

"Well–"

"Naw, you'd never make it; not in jeans and carrying brass knuckles. And the other thing is that you look so young. Every time I look at you I can't help thinking your licence is a phony. I never pegged you for seventeen."

This was quite understandable. My look of maturity and sophistication was generally reserved for school. If ever I wore makeup to services or happenings that involved Rock of the Witness, it was never much. With them I preferred to blend in with the hippie crowd as much as possible, plus I didn't care to leave a trail of lipstick or foundation on those I hugged. So this particular evening there was only a touch of color on my lips and a few strokes of mascara on my lashes. My shapely figure, which would have better betrayed my age, was obscured by a fringed buckskin poncho that hung past my hips. With my hair in a ponytail and under a hat, I'd have had no problem blending in with seventh or eighth graders.

"I turned seventeen last July."

"Oh, I believe you. And after listening to you talk, I'd say you were much older than that, but I'd have to close my eyes. I honestly thought maybe you were about thirteen or fourteen at first, partly because you're a small fry. I know that those Indian racers are light, but to handle it well with someone my size riding with you, you must have a little muscle."

"Oh, I don't know. I guess. Want to see for yourself?"

Teddy had a good laugh when I put my arm out on the table with my hand up for arm wrestling. "Oh, come on!" he said, but a second later he put his brawny arm out. I obviously couldn't beat him, but there were guys that I could, and I was proud of the strength I'd acquired from so much hard labor and exercise. We clasped our hands together on the table top and in a brief moment it was all over. But Teddy did have to use a touch of effort and was therefore properly impressed. "Hey! Not bad for a shrimp. Do you work out?"

"All the time. So tell me, how old are you?"

"Twenty eight."

"That's what I figured. That means you haven't been a priest very long."

"Right, just a couple of years. Fortunately my parish is far enough away so that no one will interfere. But I'm not going to think like that. Times have changed."

"Teddy, if God wants you involved at The Rock, you won't have any problems. Just relax and enjoy yourself."

"Oh, I know. It's just that I've had such a rough start. But speaking of enjoyment, I'm anxious to explore the different ministries you have and see how they function. I never imagined I'd feel this way, but it's exciting to see how a group like your little independent church does things. And I'm especially interested in the music. The Catholic liturgy is beautiful but there's so little good music. And there's certainly not a lot of variety. Things may be changing, but still. . . . I mean, the stuff your band plays would be a bit difficult for some people to digest. But you know what?"

"What?"

"That's just what I want for mass!"

"No kidding?"

"For the folk mass. All we have are acoustic guitars, a tambourine and bass. Without drums and all the other instruments it won't seem quite so—"

"Pentecostal?"

"Exactly. Oh, but I'd love it if we could have drums. I'd go out and get a trap set, if I thought it would go over. But it's tough enough as it is to get some people to accept the recent changes in the liturgy. It's sure been hard for me. Drums and electric guitars would definitely turn some people off."

"Oh, so you're a drummer, eh? Make sure you tell David Richardson. Sometimes we need a stand-in."

As our conversation went on into the night, we learned a lot about each other and discovered enough common ground for a fine relationship. We both had a great love for sailing and the sea; only he actually had some solid experience, while for me it was still in the realm of dreams to be realized. (Teddy promised to help me get my sea legs.) He'd even been to the same silent movie theater that I had, and so we talked about which films we'd seen. We grew so comfortable so quickly that, had it not already been so late, we might have talked until sunup. As it was, I didn't make it home till almost 2:00 a.m. After leaving the burger joint to go back to the church for Teddy's car, we stood around and talked some more.

After exchanging phone numbers and addresses, my new partner invited me to a roller skating party that the youth of his parish were having just before New Years. I was delighted to go.

We said goodbye with the customary Christian hug, but it was more than convention. I could sense his elevated joy and love for God as he held me tight, and the feeling was electric. As Teddy and I went our separate ways home, I took the feeling with me.

MONDAY, DECEMBER 23:

The eve of Christmas Eve was the traditional night for my family's annual holiday bash. Preparation had been going on for weeks. From top to bottom the house was made spick and span, valuables hidden away, and the whole place decorated for the season. Cooking and cleaning was my department while the detailed and sometimes difficult job of hanging decorations was done by those who cared about it. Ribbons and garlands, holly and blinking lights, frosted window panes, a giant Christmas tree topped with a gold star that touched the ceiling, and a jolly black faced Santa on the roof next to the chimney were a part of my family's traditions. Even the stone lions, Marvin and George, were decked with red ribbons. Luminarias lined the roof and walk way. For the backyard, Christmas lights and glowing candy canes were strung from house to garage, trees and fence.

In spite of the holiday hubbub, thoughts of David Conrad and the remembrance of our last encounter still dominated my thoughts. But now thoughts of my new partner floated along side, alternating in prominence. The question now was, could Teddy Molloy be the answer to prayer that I'd been waiting for? The way we'd finally hit it off made it a good possibility. But even if he were, I knew it would take time for the right relationship to develop. He would have to convert. But it was good to have someone else to think about. It softened the angst over The Fox. Even so, Ted Molloy would have to be quite a man to make me forget David Conrad.

That evening the sound of rhythm and blues and big band music from our stereo could be heard nearly half way down the block, but then the neighbors were all invited to the party as well, so no one complained. The lively and soulful strains of artists such as Louis Jordan, Elmore James, Sam Cook, and Bobbie "Blue" Bland, with songs such as "Dust My Broom", "Saturday Night Fish Fry", and "Merry Christmas, Mamma" spun around on records, usually at seventy-eight or forty-five revolutions per minute. Cars lined the street in front of our house as relatives, friends, select drug store customers and vendors came to the celebration. Many brought gifts along with liquor and more treats to add to the spread of soul food, Mexican American, American, and "kosher style" dishes that we put out. There were moments when we, the kids, had our hands full, running back and forth to the kitchen, keeping things in order as items came in. However, we did have help that allowed us to enjoy the party. It was generally the only time my parents hired people to serve so that we wouldn't have to.

Like the rest of the family, I looked forward to the party every year, but always with mixed emotions. The excitement of all the preparations and the festivities themselves made it a joyous occasion, but there were certain people that attended who put a damper on things, especially once they'd over imbibed. Why my parents refused to limit these people was beyond me. It seemed so unlike their usual common sense. When I had tended bar, refusing drinks or watering down the alcohol had to be done surreptitiously because Daddy didn't like it. "It's Christmas," he always explained, but I got the feeling, from the number of business people that always showed up, that it had just as much to do with the store. So we learned whom to avoid and looked out for ourselves as we moved through the crowded house, especially as the evening wore on and people did more drinking than eating. Usually my brothers and sisters escaped outside to the back yard with the other kids that came to the party. This year, being completely free from tending bar, I was able to join them for the entire evening.

My brainy and handsome brother Aaron was home for the holidays. It was good having him around, even though he got on my case for not helping more with the party. He brought out the stereo from his room and set it up way in the back so that the kids could groove to a more contemporary sound. For me the best part of the whole deal was having my friends from the ADG there. Most had been to the yearly party many times before, but this was only Billy Osborn's second time.

He was dressed better than I'd ever seen him, looking grown up and sophisticated in his best blue Sunday suit. Billy smelled of Aqua Velva and his hair was out of his eyes, neatly trimmed and Vitalisized so that it didn't blow around.

I could feel his eyes on me as I danced. Billy was drinking egg nog and talking about the Apollo 8 mission with Mr Fletcher and some of the other guys, all the while trying to get up the nerve to ask for his turn with me. A slow song came on, one of those dreamy numbers by Smokey Robinson. Before I could sit down, The Kid was up and taking me by the hand.

"Come on, Lady J," he said quietly. "Let's dance."

I didn't refuse. Giving him my hand, I let Billy put his arm around me and we tried to move together to the music. He was a country/western two-stepper, a bit unaccustomed to the smooth, soulful glide needed for this song, but I managed to follow his lead, and it didn't turn out too bad.

"You know, Janette," said Billy after a few measures, dropping his good ol' boy facade. "You have really changed. I didn't like it at first, but I guess I've been getting used to it. It's nice. Real nice."

"I'm glad you think so," I said sincerely.

"I just wish my daddy would, too. If it weren't for my mother and trying not to break her heart, I'd have left home a long time ago. Why do some people have to be so idiotic and foolish? I wish I was black or you were white or that the world was different. A girl as sweet, intelligent and pretty as you are isn't that easy to find."

"I can think of several, and some are members of the Guild. Billy Osborn, I think you just want something you know you can't have."

"Maybe. Oh, I know you're right, we shouldn't get involved, but–"

"No buts, Billy. I like you too much as a friend. Things need to stay as they are."

"Okay, but would you do me one favor?"

"What's that?"

The music stopped. Billy kept my hand in his and led me along the side of the house and away from the others. I was pretty sure I knew what he wanted.

"Look, Janette," he said. "If you do this one thing for me, I promise I'll leave you alone. Would you let me kiss you?"

Smiling, I thought it over for a moment. Would he really keep his promise if I did?

"Look, I mean it. I won't bother you anymore at all if you just kiss me this one time."

"Really?"

"Cross my heart and hope."

"Well–okay."

Knowing the chance might never come again, Billy made the most of it. He slipped his arms around my waist and pulled me close, holding me

with more tenderness than when we had danced. Then came the kiss. There was curiosity in the first brief moment that his lips touched mine, and then the passion followed. Or maybe I should say affection. Yes. The years of friendship between us had produced a genuine love and respect that kept it from getting too far into lust. And when it was over, he smiled and shook his head. We both laughed.
"Thanks, Janette. I won't forget this."
I won't either, Billy.

TUESDAY, DEC. 24 - THURSDAY, DEC. 27:
And so Christmas came and went. The Rock's caroling outreach on Christmas Eve was a big success with several new souls coming into the Kingdom. That and all the happenings since the start of vacation gave me so much to do, to think about and look forward to, that the happy bustle of Christmas Day paled in the light of it.

Even though life was more subdued with the passing of Christmas, there were year end events to look forward to. Mommy and Daddy always went out with friends on New Years Eve while the rest of us stayed home with Guy Lombardo or whoever else was on the tube. This year I had the option of joining my friends at The Rock to pray the new year in, but I had mixed feelings about that, given what I'd learned about the holiday. Still, before any of that, there was St Basil's skating party on the 27th. I had told Teddy that I would come to the parish, thinking it would work better that way. Though the rink was closer to my neighborhood, it would give me a better chance to get to know the folks at his church. I also wanted to get used to seeing Teddy in his natural habitat.

We met by the fellowship hall. There I was introduced to the other kids as well as the adults who would help with driving. Everyone was friendly and cordial. It was nice to know that I, being a stranger, would not be ignored. I even felt relaxed enough to separate myself from Teddy, but he made sure I rode in his car. He even placed me next to himself in the front seat. But there was one problem. It was a bit awkward with everyone else calling him "Father Molloy" or "Father Ted" while I wasn't about to call him "Father" anything. So I tried to use his name as little as possible or call him Ted, but he was still Teddy to me and I couldn't help but call him that when not thinking. It drew some curious looks and chuckles, but Teddy treated it as nothing so that the others would gradually learn to accept it.

The old rink, having recently had a face lift, was quite a bit different from the last time I skated there. Gone was the Wurlitzer organ, and in its place was a DJ booth where a man played recordings of top 40 music. The afternoon flew happily by as we played skating games, danced the Hokey Poky and rolled to the hits. Teddy was an excellent skater, not at all lacking in grace. He was so good that I refused to skate with him rather than be embarrassed, but he insisted. Then after three delightful hours, it was time to take off our wheels and head back to the South Valley. It seemed like no time at all before the skating party was just a memory.

Not in the mood to go home where I might not be so well occupied, I didn't want the good time to end. The problem was being afraid of the direction my thoughts were taking me. There were still several days left of vacation, and yet I looked forward with some anxiousness to going back to school. The reason why was upsetting me; so I took my time saying goodbye to everyone, making myself the last one to leave, in the hope that Teddy would hang with me for a while. Thank God, I wasn't disappointed.

"Say, I'm glad you didn't run off," he said when the others were gone. "I've been wanting to talk to you. Let's go into the rectory. We can use the office and talk there."

The rectory was a large, pale green two story brick house trimmed in white, with a simple peaked roof and lots of windows. Inside, it was a nice, clean, homey looking place, very masculine with its white walls, hard wood floors, blue-gray carpet, dark wood paneling and plain furnishings. There were the typical religious pictures and objects on the walls that I expected. A large wooden crucifix, a print of the last supper, a picture of the current pope and similar items decked the walls. I'd never been in such a place and would have liked to have seen more. Upstairs would be where the priests had their private rooms. But did they have their own televisions? Did they have a pool table or other fun things? With Teddy being my partner, I was sure I could get him to give me a tour or at least tell me about it.

The office was downstairs. This was one of two which he shared with the other priests. It was a fair sized room with two black leather trimmed chairs, a small black leather sofa against one wall and a matching easy chair in the adjacent corner. More dark wood, more pictures but pastoral scenes. Certificates, awards, and licensing also had their places on the walls. Rather than talk to me from behind the big oak desk, Teddy took the two upholstered hard back chairs and angled them toward each other.

"I've been thinking," he said after a bit of silence. "You know, I really could use your help here."

"Here?" I said, bewildered. "How? With what?"

"The music, mainly. I know you go to your own church on Sundays, but–well, I'd really like to have you help me work with the group that plays for guitar mass. Just for a while. Would you mind? You've already met some of the people."

"Yes, I noticed. No, I wouldn't mind at all, as long as they don't mind me horning in." *God! What am I saying? I already have enough to do. And play for mass? Shades of idolatry! What will I be doing next, kissing statues? What am I even doing here? How did I get suckered into this? God, get me out of this! Why'd you give me a priest for a partner in the first place?*

"Well, Janette, we can certainly pray for God to make things go smoothly. But the other thing is the youth group. I'm not really in charge of it; one of the laymen is. They do, however, like me to help out and try to encourage the kids in spiritual things. . . ."

This sounded almost like he wanted me to join the parish. *Oh, no you don't. Music is one thing, but I am not Catholic and I'm not going to pretend to be. Honest to Pete!* "Teddy, I'm not sure about that one. I've got enough irons in the fire as it is. Why don't we just play it by ear?"

There I go again! What is the matter with me? Don't I know how to just say 'no' and leave it at that?

"Fine, Jenny. Whatever's best for you. I don't want to overload you. I think maybe I'm getting a little too excited and need to slow down a bit."

"Sounds like a wise decision."

"Anyway, could you come to mass next Sunday? That'll give you a chance to hear the group play."

"Sure. What time is the service?"

"Ten o'clock."

"Okay, I'll be there."

He leaned back in his chair and laughed. "You know, mate, my feet have hardly touched the ground since Friday night. Sometimes it's hard to know what to do with myself."

"May I make a suggestion?"

"Sure."

"Let's take the Scout and go for a spin."

SUNDAY, DECEMBER 29:

Stand, sing, sit, kneel, sit, stand, sing. I'd been to mass for weddings and funerals, but not just for the sake of worship. I resigned myself to accepting my commitment to play for services, but now had to discern where to draw the line as far as entering in. I already knew that the rules of Rome prohibited me from taking communion with my Catholic friends, but that worked both ways because I wasn't interested in the "un-bloody sacrifice" of the mass. The Bible declared that Jesus was crucified only once and that being enough, making this concept of sacrificing him at every mass contrary and therefore undesirable. There were other things that were also taboo, like kneeling before a statue or offering prayers to anyone but HaShem, all clearly forbidden in the Scriptures. Still there were things that I wasn't sure of or didn't know about at all. But given my purpose for being at St Basil's, I figured that as long as I was ignorant of them that I'd be okay. Maybe even better off, since that would make it easier to minister to these people instead of looking at all the nonkosher things about their religion. After all, I knew it was God getting me into this. Further education could come later, but I wouldn't put it off too long.

I came early and sat toward the back, wanting to keep a low profile and observe without interruption. All the while I kept trying to picture my new partner in priestly habits and robes like he had been on Christmas Eve, mainly for the sake of fixing this blond beef cake in my mind as a priest. It wasn't long before the vision became reality and appeared at the back of the church. The mass had begun.

To me, Teddy's frame didn't look so hot in robes. With his stocky build, they made him look chunky. Of course, such things weren't meant to be flattering to the figure, but I still felt they ought to do something to make the wearer attractive. He was a happy celebrant, singing out loud and clear with his fine tenor voice. A few people in the tiny crowd that gathered for the service seemed to catch his enthusiasm, even clapping their hands during the songs as they were encouraged to do.

There were four people in the group that played for the folk or guitar mass. Two of the singers, a pretty blond teenage girl and an even prettier nun with big, brown Loretta Young eyes in a black habit, also played guitars. A stout, olive complected nun sang and banged a tambourine. A tall, gangly, dark-haired man, who looked to be about college age, played the standup bass. The nun on guitar led the singing, and was doing her best to be joyful, but something about it didn't seem quite natural. The others didn't even try; they just concentrated on the music and getting it right. Only Teddy's celebration seemed to flow freely from within.

When time came for the homily, Teddy gripped the top of the podium with both hands, filled his lungs with air and launched out into the deep. He had spoken very little up to this point, making use of lay people for such things as reading the Scriptures, so I'd forgotten how he stuttered, since he only displayed the handicap in front of crowds. Now, here again was the same Porky Pig routine, only not quite so bad. It broke my heart, but at the same time I admired his courage. Still he kept it very brief–less than five minutes–and reading his sermon helped keep his tongue in control. So he made it all the way through without too much difficulty, and what he said was very good and to the point.

After mass was the Catholic version of *oneg Shabbat*: coffee and donuts over in the fellowship hall. I hung out and talked to those who remembered me from the skating party and got better acquainted. Then before too long, Teddy came and took me aside.

"What do you think of the group," he asked in a low voice.

"Musically they're fine–you know, for what they do. I thought some of the songs were a little slow, but the singers have good voices and those who play instruments do fine."

"Yes, but there's so little joy in their presentation. They might as well be playing a funeral mass, Janette."

"Well, what else can you expect from people who don't know Jesus? These people may know their religion, but it doesn't mean that they know God. How could they possibly cut loose and praise him for real if they're not even saved?"

"Oh . . . well, that makes sense. Then we'll just have to get them saved. I'll take some time to talk to each one of them about it. If I can't get around to everybody, then we might even deal with it at the next rehearsal."

"Uh–well, okay, but–you really need to pray about that beforehand. They've got to be ready to receive it first."

"Oh, I intend to. I know how it works, and I'll certainly spend time praying for their salvation."

"So, when's rehearsal?"

"Thursday night at 7:30 in the sanctuary. Oh, but we skip next week because of the new year. That makes the next rehearsal January 9th."

"I'll be there. You know, aside from the group, it'd be great if you did some singing. I love your voice. Has a nice rich tone to it. What are you, second tenor?"

"That's about right. Not quite a baritone, but certainly not a first tenor."

"Think about this: it would really be effective for you to sing a song and then preach on the message in it."

"Hmmm, that does sound like a good idea. Sure, we can work that into the mass without any problem."

"Great. And that reminds me. You need to get prayer for that stuttering. Teddy, God's given you a call to preach and he wants that to go."

"Yeah, I know. Sure, Jenny, that's fine with me. I wanted us to spend some time in prayer anyway. But why don't you let me show you around first and get that out of the way."

I had meant to ask for a tour of this place and explanation of a few things, but then thought perhaps it might be best to remain ignorant. On the other hand, I didn't want to do anything stupid and offend somebody, so when he made the offer, I followed along and made mental notes.

Since another mass going on, we began with walking the grounds of the church plant. The buildings were made of a variety of materials including adobe, stucco, brass, aluminum, wood, and cinder block. I saw the little school, learned where the nuns lived, learned a little more about the rectory (two televisions but no pool table), and heard a little about the general activity of the place. The parish actually dated back to the early 1930's with much of the support for building and upkeep coming from wealthy ranchers. With lower attendance in recent years, that support was naturally not as plentiful as it once was, so St Basil's had fallen into a state of disrepair. One or two of the buildings had been replaced or modified down through the years, but otherwise, all was as it had first been. A dark mossy green, light gray and black were the main colors throughout. Only the church itself, a grand and interesting blend of art deco and traditional Spanish design purposely remained untouched by remodeling, except for necessities such as paint, new electrical wiring and heat. The brass accents on the church had turned a matching shade of green to the rest of it. Decorative bells on the facade graced the tower housing the larger bell which rang on Sundays. It could have used some cleaning up, but still it was lovely to look at. What I found of greater interest were the constant comparisons Teddy made to the grander churches and facilities in Chicago and the longing in his expression as he spoke of their bustling operations. It didn't take much to see why he saw his transfer as punishment.

By the time we made the rounds of the other buildings, the last service of the day had ended and the sanctuary was empty. Teddy then took me inside and up and down the aisles. The decor was not as ornate as some Catholic churches I had seen. The walls were a pale gray-green, and the trim was dark wood and brass. Here some of the brass was its true color with something of a shine to it. As we went along, my friend told me who the different saints were in the stained glass windows as well as the ones in statue form along the walls. These painted plaster and wooden images were on either side of the altar and nestled in alcoves along both sides of the sanctuary. The candles in red glass at their feet were a lovely contrast to the various shades of green. Also in front of these statues were padlocked money boxes. At the feet of Mary's benevolent image were also flowers that I suspected were an offering of some kind. Then reciting some of the prayers as examples of the ritual, Teddy explained the framed mosaic scenes placed evenly on either side of the main seating area. These were called the Twelve Stations of the Cross. I also learned about the fonts of holy water and confessionals. We went into one of the carved, brass trimmed wooden doors and gave me an example of what went on in there. Then we went through the doors behind the altar and into the sacristy. There Teddy showed me the different robes he wore and explained a few basic things about his part in the liturgy and the sacraments.

I could tell by the way he spoke with such detail and the intense look in his eye, how deeply this priest loved his religion. This made me think again about the dreamy ideas beginning to form in my mind. While the Roman Catholic priesthood meant absolutely nothing to me, it meant plenty to him. The more I saw of the depth to which his religion possessed him, the more apparent it became that a romance with Teddy Molloy–if it ever got off the ground–would become too complicated and simply mess up a good friendship and ministry. Common sense and logic told me that the vast differences currently between us would make it impractical and a great strain, and therefore foolish. The Holy Spirit within me seemed to agree, and that was enough for me to close the subject, though reluctantly.

Done with the tour, it was time for a quick phone call to let Mommy know I wouldn't be home for dinner. Then we headed back to the sanctuary for prayer. I would rather have gone some place else for that, but decided I'd better get used to the scenery and gave it over to Y'shua.

Even as we began our prayer session with worship, I silently addressed the subject of our relationship and included every area I could think of. Though I was still tempted to transfer my feelings for David Conrad onto this priestly Palooka, recalling what I'd just witnessed, I yielded to wisdom and sacrificed both heart and hormones on the altar right off the bat; then I threw in my strong aversion to Catholicism for good measure, before praying for the two of us openly in a fashion sensitive to my partner's feelings. Teddy also covered this territory aloud, and thus confirmed the wisdom in restraining any romantic notions. Though he had gone through some considerable changes, his commitment to the strict celibacy of the Catholic priesthood obviously remained intact.

In the process of praying for each other, important issues came to light. Last and seemingly most important was the problem at the root of Teddy's stuttering.

"Yeah, I guess I know when it started," he said in answer to my inquiry. "Mother was going to have another baby, but this time something was wrong. She went to the hospital and they kept her for days, and it was just before Christmas. Well, I was only about five years old, and for the first time, I had a part in the Christmas program at church. All they gave me was a couple of lines to say, and I memorized them–but that was before Mother got sick. By the time we did the play, I was so terrified of what might happen to my mother that all I could remember was the first three words, and I could barely get them out. I said them again and again, hoping the rest of it would come back to me, but it didn't. Everyone else thought it was pretty funny, but I couldn't handle it and ran off stage. From there on out . . . well, you've heard me."

"Oh, Theodore!" I joined him where he sat on the steps of the altar. Kneeling and laying hands on him as I felt I should, head first, then heart, we both prayed in the Spirit until we felt a release.

Teddy raised his head and shook it slightly. "Wow . . . something lifted."

"I know. Why don't you go up there and preach?"

He pulled away and got to his feet. Going to the same platform where he'd ministered that morning, Teddy said his homily again in a fraction of the time, without any hesitation.

"Thank you, Jesus!" he shouted, punching the air. "Praise God! Jenny, before this, even without people here I still would have stuttered some!"

"It's gone, Teddy, and it's gone for good. Now you can preach like God wants you to."

He danced around, so happy he didn't know what to do with himself. I was sure he'd have swung from the rafters, had he been able to reach them.

"Run!" I told him. And he did. All around the sanctuary, Teddy ran shouting and laughing until he'd released some of the joy he felt, and I laughed along with him.

Slowing down on the seventh lap, my partner stopped in front of me and said, "Look, mate, let's get out of here. I'm so hungry I could eat a horse."

"There's a pretty good hole-in-the-wall place down here, next to the Piggly Wiggley."

"Let's go."

It was indescribable then, just as it is now, but something uncanny and powerful transpired during the time we spent in that sanctuary. Something deeper and far more curious than any healing or new revelation. The glow of it followed us as we rode off in search of good food, riding on my motorcycle; and rather than fade, it would subtly and silently work its way into our very bones.

Chapter Five
The Brush Off

TUESDAY, JANUARY 14, 1969:

Seventy five, eighty, eighty five miles per hour. The strange beauty of the rugged desert landscape went by unnoticed as I opened up the throttle on my Indian Scout along the Mother Road toward Grants and Gallup. There was a bar in Gallup where I could get a good hot lunch and a toddy to go with it, no questions asked. Driven on by the twisted ache in my stomach and the anguish in my heart, the hope was that traveling the distance would act as a balm and a tonic for the wounds I had sustained since classes started again.

The day was clear and cold and perfect for ditching school. In my condition, studying was a waste of time . . . especially in a classroom with David Conrad. Running home and crying into my pillow to muffle the sobbing and wailing was getting old and embarrassing. I had to straighten up and there was no choice in the matter.

A change had taken place. A change that was perfectly understandable. School had been going again for just over a week, and though things should have picked up right where they'd left off, the morning of the first day, while sitting in my usual place waiting for Mr Conrad to come by, he never came, and yet his car was in the parking lot when I went to look. When I had asked about it later, he apologized for not calling me to say we couldn't meet for breakfast anymore. No reason was given other than that he now had "some very important things to do" during that time. Though he wasn't gruff with me, his avoidance of my eyes combined with a gut feeling told me I'd better not press for details.

So little Janette West was now a has been, just like all the others. She had been dumped off her pedestal and her heart severely broken in the fall. The toughest part was that she'd probably asked for it. The reason? It was likely that David Conrad was now playing it smart. After all, it did look as if the situation had gotten much too hot and needed cooling down.

My heart had been broken before, but never had I endured this kind of pain. My body literally felt crushed from the loss, and the sorrow was so deep that it was as if someone had died. As I drove into Grants, the sobbing started up again all on its own and I had to find a place to pull over. It took me about five minutes to gain control and keep heading west.

There was no figuring out to do, no searching for clues or trying various angles, except to decide whether or not I'd chased him off by not falling into his arms and letting him make love to me, or if he'd gotten scared and decided to line up with what was proper and safe by putting our relationship on ice. No matter what, I couldn't fault him for finally doing what he should have done months ago. But it sure hurt like crazy, and I had no recourse, no chance to talk it out and give or hear explanations. Suddenly the fun and laughter were over.

It was going on nine thirty when I passed the road to Church Rock. Having slowed down to a more reasonable speed while going through

Grants, I now moved even slower, knowing that things to do in Gallup were limited. They had some parks and a museum or two, but I enjoyed the souvenir and curio shops the best.

Being in another setting helped to put my head in a different place, and after about an hour of walking the streets and browsing the various storefronts, I was beginning to feel better. So around eleven thirty I stopped in at the Silver Spur Saloon for an early lunch.

At breakfast as at my other meals over the past few days, I'd had very little appetite. But now I was very hungry, and the hot roast beef sandwich on my plate disappeared in no time. But the drink I savored, thinking and putting my situation in its proper perspective between sips of blackberry brandy blended with champagne.

It didn't matter that David Conrad had become a part of me like nobody else ever had, there was still no way I could continue feeling such deep hurt over been discarded. It would begin to show in such a way as to invite inquiry, if people hadn't noticed already. That was something I couldn't afford, nor could he, especially since news of our estrangement was sure to travel fast. Facing up to the fact that the current situation was necessary, I determined to take my bitter and ugly medicine and try to go on as if nothing at all had happened. Almost. No matter how strong I was, I could never be chipper or enthusiastic like before in the classroom or at my lessons. It would be tough enough just to make myself practice.

Arriving home at slightly before my usual time of 3:20 p.m., I made a quiet entrance through the back door and dashed up to my room without being seen. I immediately got out of my leather chaps and other biker gear and dressed for the evening ahead. Since it was Tuesday night, I had a blessed distraction from the blues to look forward to.

That night was worship rehearsal. Instead of crowding into David Richardson's house, we now met at the church. With construction being days from completion, all major activities were held there except for a few weekly Bible studies. It was slightly different than the place Teddy Molloy had first seen, though still far from traditional. Large colorful banners now decorated the sanctuary to encourage and bless those who came to worship. Dark red carpet covered the stage and the wooden seats. Otherwise, it was still the same plain room. The wonderfully graphic crucifixion mural in the vestibule was now complete and would greet anyone coming into the sanctuary from the front door. The kitchen, classrooms, fellowship hall, prayer rooms, and offices were finished and usable except for a few minor details.

I wanted to get there as soon as possible so that I didn't lapse back into impromptu crying jags. On arrival I went through the church taking much needed hugs from this person and that before getting set up. Then as I got down to business I heard the voice of my new partner coming in through the back way. Was I ever glad to see him.

Teddy carried a large musical instrument in a hard brown case. This he hadn't told me about. He had brought a cello.

I waited anxiously until his arms were free, then dropped what I was doing and went to greet him. Teddy gave the most wonderful hugs. This time he even picked me up. It was just the medicine I needed.

"You didn't tell me about this," I said. Back on the ground I turned to run my hand over the cello case. "I thought you only played drums."

"Oh, well, I play piano, too," he said. "But as for this–well, it's my favorite and it's what I do best. Of course it's been a few years since I've really played, but this is something that will always stay with me. I rented this the other day so I could sit in with you guys and learn the music; the hymns in particular."

"Are you going to play with us for meetings?"

"Yeah. I thought it'd work best with slow and moderate tunes."

"Sure! We'll just put a mike on it. Does Richardson know?"

"I haven't told anybody."

"Well, get set up and tuned. I'm gonna talk to David."

David Richardson thought it was such a good idea that rehearsal began with work on the hymns and slow choruses. The results were extraordinary. Teddy played extremely well and God poured out an anointing through his music that blew us all away. Instead of getting out by nine or nine thirty we played and worshiped till almost midnight.

As we packed up and made ready to leave, something came to mind that I had thought of earlier. Once my gear was together, I went to Teddy and said, "Before I forget again, would you like to come to my house for dinner on Sunday?"

His eyes lit up. "Dinner? Did you say dinner?"

"Yeah. You want to come for dinner?"

"Sure! Whatcha gonna have?"

"Don't know yet. Whadda ya like?"

"Well, matey, right now I'll eat anything that doesn't have chili in it. I am sick to death of eating Mexican food every single solitary day. You know, when it comes to beans, Boston's got nothing on this town. For once, I would just like to have a good, home cooked American meal."

"That bad, huh? Well, the Lord has seen thy suffering and heard the cry of thine heart. There shall be no chili; neither shalt there be any pinto beans."

"Oh, bless you! What time do we eat?"

"One o'clock. One thirty or there abouts."

"Fine. I can hardly wait!"

WEDNESDAY, JANUARY 15:

So the following morning at breakfast I told my parents that I had a guest coming on Sunday and plans were made. I counted it a blessing that Teddy Molloy provided something else to occupy my thoughts and look forward to. All of the activities we were involved in together made the pain in my heart just a little easier to handle.

Still the hours at school drug by. It seemed as if I had to propel myself along mentally to make the minutes move faster, dodging every thought of Mr C. I dreaded my classes with him. Enjoyment was gone from every aspect. In Choir and Madrigals the music did nothing to move me, except to provoke melancholy. Fortunately, fellow students who noticed the absence of my smile had finally stopped asking what was wrong, no doubt due to my sour "leave me alone" expression. So far I'd been able to hide or withhold the flow of salt water, though I ached to let it out on almost anyone's shoulder. But this was something so very personal and embarrassing that I saw no choice but to suffer through it alone, except to pour it out to my cousin Georgia in letters.

For David Conrad, daily life was also strained. Although he had never been overly cheerful, he was now prone to scowling and being short tempered. Once word got around that he and I weren't together as usual, he was peppered with questions. His excuse? New and important work to do. Janette would only get in the way. But still people talked and comments were made either to him or in his presence about the absence of his little friend. Talk was that he and I had fallen out, even though he insisted that such wasn't the case. But to people like Mr Fletcher who knew me well and saw me on a regular basis, it was plain to see how miserable I was. Out of concern, Bill took me aside at lunch this particular day to ask if there was some kind of problem between me and my Mr Conrad.

We sat back in the morgue with the door closed while the rest of the ADG lunched and played cards.

"Janette–" Bill paused to choose his words carefully. "You've really been in the doldrums lately, and if I can I'd like to help. What's been happening?"

"I wish it didn't show so much. Sorry, Bill, but it's really not something I care to talk about."

"Mind if I take a guess?"

"Well–no. Go ahead."

"Is it you and Conrad?"

"How'd you know? Is there a lot of talk?"

"Some. I wouldn't have thought anything about it if I hadn't noticed how blue you've been. What is it?"

"I don't want to assume anything, Bill. We haven't argued, and I don't think I've done anything. Something changed over the holidays. When I tried to talk to him about it, he gave me the runaround. That isn't like him, so the only thing I could come up with is–well–"

"You know you can trust me, Janette. Please."

Not wanting to cause the man any trouble I only mentioned one side of it. "Well, it could be that he thinks I've developed a crush on him and now he wants to cool things off."

"Okay. Any truth to it?"

"I don't deny that I like him a lot, but I'm not the type to drool. I've gone all out to keep my feet on the ground since there wasn't any point in dreaming."

"Good girl. He hasn't put the make on you, has he?"

"No. It's been strictly friendship."

"I just wish there was something I could do." Fletcher shook his head and sighed. "I hate to see you getting hurt like this, especially if it's over nothing. And Dave had better be careful to straighten this up before Mrs Mac gets wind of it, if she hasn't already." He paused again, biting his lip in thought. "I can't sit still over this. He could be in trouble or something; maybe under duress."

I perked up at that comment. "You know, Bill, I always figured him to be the victim of something, but could never get a solid lead on it. Margo felt the same way."

"I'll put a tail on him for a bit and see what turns up."

"Thanks. Let me know if you find anything."

That ended that and we rejoined the others. Knowing someone else knew and cared about my woes lifted me a little. It was doubtful that Bill's suspicion of trouble was connected with my situation, but surveillance might expose something of Mr C's hidden past and the information would be welcome.

As the school day drew to a close and my lesson time approached, I started getting angry. Now people were talking and who knows what they were saying. Usually I didn't care about gossip, but this was uncalled for. And Mr Conrad was giving me more than just the brush off. It was the silent treatment. He avoided anything but the most necessary contact with me. I could understand him wanting to cool things off, but what had I done to deserve this? After all, the impropriety had been his and not mine. What he was putting me through was intentional and unnecessary. Why should I, being the innocent party, continue to have tender feelings for someone who would deal me such a low blow? So that afternoon I arrived for my lessons with jaw set, eyes clear and a definite chip on my shoulder. I was greeted with a quiet hello and a lethargic, "How are you?" I was very tempted to tell him, and in graphic detail, but made no reply at all.

With a little more presence of mind than the week before, I was able to sit down at the piano and apply myself to the notes on the page with grit and determination to get everything right and then accomplishing it, dynamics and all. Mr Conrad commented with a note of surprise in his voice that I did exceptionally well.

Then it was on to singing. This I expected would also go well, although circumstances prevented me from being quite as expressive as in the past. Back on a full classical regimen, first was the lively Handel piece, "Here Amid the Shady Woods", which was so easy that I wondered why he'd even assigned it. Schubert's "Du Bist Die Ruh" was a bit more work, since I had to deal with the German lyrics. But I made it through all right. It wasn't until I got to the Fauré number, "Rencontre" and began singing of sadness, pain and frustrated dreams of love, that I lost it. Somewhere around the second page, my voice cut out as all of my pain rose to the surface and decided to take over.

Mr Conrad stopped playing the accompaniment and was silent while I covered my face with my hands and turned away from him. Struggling to keep the sobs from escaping, my whole body shook with the effort until I had to brace myself on the piano. Finally the emotions won out and the tears flowed along with wailing.

"Janette, why don't you sit down for a little while?"

A glance in his direction showed me that he had gotten to his feet, but still he remained by the piano bench. Had things been as they once were, he would certainly have come close to comfort me. Now he kept his distance. I wailed louder.

"Janette–Janette, please sit down and–and let me bring you a cup of tea."

Yeah, that Earl Grey stuff that I like. A lot of good that'll do, but okay.

Without a word and still avoiding his eyes, I moved to the love seat and waited for my teacher to bring tea. With his exit to the kitchen, my dark feelings abated to the point that I could at least be quiet, though the tears continued a constant flow. I dug tissues out of my purse and did what I could to clean my face and clear my nose. Imagining what I must have looked like, the last thing I wanted to see was a mirror, but I thought it might be a good idea to run to the bathroom and throw some water on my face real quick while Mr Conrad was getting my refreshment. Then I remembered that he had one of those newfangled ovens that could boil a cup of water in a minute, so I used my compact to help me get all the mascara or anything else I might have missed. And sure enough, in two shakes he was back with hot tea just the way I like it, with milk and honey on the side.

Tea. Hmmph! Wish I could hit the bar instead.

He returned and set the tray before me, then sat in the closest chair. While tears continued to stream down my face, I prepared my tea with trembling hands. Then I sipped and thought of what I should say, if anything.

The tea actually was a bit refreshing. It felt good having something warm inside me, and I enjoyed its fragrance. The tears lessened as moments passed, but I just couldn't think of a proper way to broach the subject of our estrangement. Just as I emptied my cup and was about to say something– anything–to address the problem, Pirate jumped up beside me, purring loudly.

"Hello, Pirate." Turning all my attention to him, I stroked his fur and found the ability to smile for a few seconds as he rubbed against me and bumped me with his head. "You still love me, don't you? Huh? Yeah, you still love me."

Then as the old tabby pressed his strong paws on my leg and stepped onto my lap, his sweet affection provoked another upheaval of sobbing and tears. I hugged and petted the furry creature as much as I thought he would endure, keeping the wailing to a minimum while I watered him with my tears. To my surprise, Pirate stayed with me and eventually curled up into a ball.

Mr Conrad finally spoke when it seemed I might stop crying. "Janette?"

"What?"

"Would you like to tell me about it?"

"No. I think you should tell me about it. You're the one with such a big fat problem that you won't even give me the time of day."

"I guess it is that bad, isn't it?"

"Yes, it is."

"Then I apologize. Look, honey, it isn't anything you've done. It's just that–in some ways I've been a very foolish man, and–well, I'm going through an ordeal that I must work out by myself, and it's going to take everything I've got. That's why there's just no room for you right now. I don't know . . . ultimately, I want to protect you, not hurt you. If I had known what to say to you, believe me, I would have said it. It's just that right now I'm pretty desperate. Please forgive me."

"Okay, but why don't you trust me?"

"I do trust you, sweetheart. But this isn't about trust."

"Are you in some sort of trouble?"

"Yes and no. It's not anything that I can't handle, but that doesn't mean it's not difficult."

Was Fletcher right? No, I don't buy this. If there's a real problem, what's it got to do with breaking up him and me– unless it's about him and me? "Can I get you some more tea?"

"Yes. Please."

Mr C's explanation didn't make sense, but then again, maybe there was something heavy going down. Maybe another ex-girlfriends was making trouble. At least now we had talked and he had confirmed that the fault wasn't with me. So for the moment I could level off and try to accept the fact that we were going to remain distant for a while until he got through whatever it was. Hopefully life would then go back to normal.

After the second cup of tea, I went to the bathroom and washed my face in cold water. Then I gathered my things and left, deciding not to waste time trying to figure anything out or make an attempt to pry into something he didn't want to share. Instead I turned my thoughts to what explanation I would give my parents once they saw my red and puffy eyes.

A generalized excuse of not feeling well and expressing the desire to go to bed early got me off the hook at home where they had noticed anyway how low I had been lately. I even asked if we had any Geritol in the house. Daddy said he would bring some home from work the next day. In the meantime, Mommy suggested castor oil.

THURSDAY, JANUARY 16:

A decent night's sleep and a hearty breakfast the next morning made me think that a good pick-me-up really was in order. It brought to mind Holly Richardson's words back in October about staying on top of my physical health in order to stay in control emotionally. That reminded me of the other things she had said, like the part about Mr Conrad and I going through more trials. This was no doubt one of them. Then there was the part about not leaning to my own understanding. Mr Johnson had said the same thing. But without much understanding of this situation, it didn't seem likely that I could lean in the wrong direction if I wanted to.

With some semblance of progress in my painful circumstances, I faced the day with slightly less heaviness on my heart. This time the hours passed at a fairly normal rate of speed, in spite of a perpetual preoccupation with Mr Conrad. It was impossible to shut off. Even while I listened in class or worked on written assignments, or made attempts to focus on the pleasant events ahead of me, it was as if a portion of my brain kept going non-stop over the whole crummy business. Of course, the fact that I had to look at the man for most of the day didn't help at all.

After school, it was all I could do to keep my feet from taking me in the direction of Margo's house. Not that she wouldn't understand. Of all people, Margo understood this kind of pain. She would gladly hear my woes and let me cry rivers as she had once poured out her anguish over Mr Fletcher to me. But I wanted godly counsel and prayer, whereas she would hand me a bottle. In my weakened condition, the temptation to over imbibe was not what I needed. So I went home, and with no school work to do, napped untill it was time for dinner.

The closer it got to time for rehearsal at St Basil's, the quieter the noise in my head became. My spirit perked up as I threw my gear together and headed out the door. Pulling out of the driveway, I envisioned Teddy's face and smiled. Then I laughed. He was like a kid, so happy and excited over the new things in his spiritual life. Now, that was the kind of man I really wanted: a godly man and a good musician to boot. Why on earth did he have to be a priest? Celibacy for him was not what it was for me. All dating and romance was strictly taboo. It would be no trouble at all for me to provide just a tiny bit of temptation for him in that area, but what I feared most was that it would kill what was happening on a spiritual plane. I knew that if we were to have anything beyond friendship, he would first have to convert, and that made the spiritual aspects even more important. So I was stuck right where I was. For the moment, anyway. It might be no for now, but a little farther down the road, that could change. So I made sure that things between us remained brother-and-sisterly. At this point I figured that anything too tempting or forward in appearance would send him high-tailing it back to Illinois. Maintaining a childlike and tomboyish demeanor was certain to do the trick. And no perfume, either. That way our relationship was far more likely to remain uncomplicated by sensual distractions.

My first meeting with St Basil's worship band had been more of a get acquainted deal, even though we did work on music. Teddy had introduced me as a very special friend of his that he had stolen from another parish. Then he had let me talk to them about music and the spiritual value of what it was we were supposed to be doing. The group listened, but gave very little response. To see that this would change, Teddy had been true to his word about praying and taking what opportunity he could to talk to them individually about salvation, but progress was slow. I got there a little early and he told me the latest.

"Now, Sr Mary Catherine does know Jesus," he said, referring to the stout tambourine player. "I talked to her at length and we had a good time of prayer and fellowship. All she needs is the baptism of the Holy Spirit. But I don't get any witness in my spirit that Sr Mary John is really saved."

"How about the others? Have you seen any of them since last week?"

"Just Cindy. I talked to her Saturday, but I get the feeling she's into some sin that she enjoys too much. She never comes to me for confession, but I'm sure I know what it is. No, she doesn't want to get any closer to Jesus than she is right now."

"Well, I don't know how you want to work this, but we don't need all of the people we've got. As they begin to open their hearts to Jesus, let's move ahead. If certain ones don't, they can go do something else. Otherwise they'll hinder the flow of the Spirit."

"I agree."

We got set up and tuned, and once we were all together, we prayed and started work. Beginning with two simple songs from the repertoire of Rock of the Witness went well. Then we beefed up some of the songs they always did. At least we tried. Sr Mary John had difficulty with some of the rhythms, especially at such a lively pace. But they were learning, and as they loosened up, it was getting to be a lot of fun.

"Okay, you guys," I said toward the end of the first hour. "You're starting to enjoy yourselves and that's great, but it'll help you even more to inspire people to participate if you meditate on the words to these songs. So think about what you're singing. You can't put the message across to them if it doesn't mean anything to you."

"You make it sound like we're preaching the Gospel," remarked Cindy.

"That's exactly what you're doing," I told her. "Even if you're only playing the bass like Paul here, your ability to praise God and worship him from the heart is going to speak to somebody about the truth of Jesus Christ and what he can do for them. If you find that you can't, then it has to be that you're not hep to what he can do."

"You mean like what he did for Father Molloy," said Sr Mary Catherine. "It's wonderful that his stuttering is gone."

"But that's not the only thing he's done for me these past few weeks," said Teddy. "Haven't you noticed?"

"You're sure a whole lot happier," said Paul. "You're like a different person."

"Yes! He changed me and he healed me. When Jesus becomes real to you and a part of your everyday life, that's when miracles can happen."

"But how do I get Jesus to be real to me like he is to you?" asked Paul.

That did it. Not another note was played that evening, even though there was more music to work on. Before the night was over, everyone except Cindy got to experience just what Teddy and I had been talking about.

FRIDAY, JANUARY 17:
After the joy of Thursday night, I floated so high that I started off Friday morning with a smile that didn't fade until Stage Band rehearsal. Like Madrigals, this was still an extracurricular activity, even though ours was the best in the region; and it was because of its notoriety that the principal allowed students to be excused from classes for the occasional long rehearsal during school hours. Mr J usually planned these rehearsals for fourth period and let it run no less than thirty minutes into the lunch hour. So that day, instead of being in Choir with Mr C, I had the great pleasure of being with Bob Johnson. But the joy wasn't meant to last. Starting with our theme song, Route 66, I couldn't have been happier. We did several such songs with light themes, but it was the love songs that did me in. One after another, they wore away at my heart until I was not only back down to earth but sinking several feet beneath the figurative surface. For the final number I couldn't even get the words out: *Smile, though your heart is aching. Smile, even though it's breaking. . . .* No, not this time. Barely able to keep the tears back, I looked at Mr J and shook my head in the negative. Naturally he wouldn't just let me walk out of rehearsal when I asked to be excused. Since we were almost done, he told me to stick around.

As the band hurried to put their instruments away and take advantage of the last thirty minutes of lunch, Mr Johnson took me aside, put an arm around my shoulder and spoke quietly with concern.

"What's the matter, babe? Are you and Mr Conrad having a problem?"

"Uh, w-well–" I floundered at his pointed question. "Uh–yes and no."

"Then you two are still getting along okay? I know he hasn't been his self since he got back from New York, and I understand that he's kind of pushed you aside."

"Yes, he has."

"Do you know why?"

"He won't tell me. When I saw him at the caroling party, everything was just great. I finally asked him about it the other day and he said it wasn't anything that I've done."

"Okay. Maybe I'll have another talk with him. It scares me when he starts having problems. The kind of trouble he gets himself into is never small. You keep praying for him, okay?"

"I will."

"Do you want to cry?" I nodded. "Then you go right ahead."

He gave me his handkerchief and put his arms around me. With the white cloth pressed to my face, I leaned on his chest and let go for a short while.

The up and down, back and forth, happy and sad was starting to do strange things to my head. When I got home that afternoon my mind felt slightly fuzzy, and there were long periods that were blank as I performed tasks automatically. But it made time pass quickly and that was good.

There was a big temptation to find hope of restoration in Mr J's influence on Mr Conrad, but I preferred being a mindless space cadet to setting my heart on such a chance, even if it was a good one. Tonight, however, there was another option. The week had finally ended and so I raised my outlook and reached for the oasis found only in the Sabbath of the Lord and the happier side of my teenage existence known as spiritual fellowship.

The night sky was clear and the morning snowfall had long since melted, giving "Pat and Mike" another opportunity to take the message of Messiah to the streets. The Friday night meeting, which started at half past seven, was usually over shortly after nine, just as it was this evening. Afterward, Teddy and I quickly stashed our instruments away and headed out.

Our first stop was the park in front of UNM, at that time a popular hangout for dope heads and hippies in general. All it took was a walk through to have someone approach us for the purpose of buying or selling drugs or acquiring spare change. But with all the hippies and transients in this town, a simple walk down the street often got the same results. If things at the park were slow, we liked to pick one of the prime "sin spots" along Central or some of its cross streets in the vicinity of the University or the church. That's how this evening went.

"Look! Somebody's pulling out," said Teddy and turned the bike down a side street, taking a newly emptied parking space near the entrance of a bar called Lulu's Place. It also put us close to the parking lot. "Okay, Jenny. What do you know about this joint?"

"Well, it's obvious from the sound of the music that this is a country/western bar. It's as respectable as places like this go, which means no illegal activity and no frequent brawls. The owners can't afford to bring in live entertainment, but the jukebox is big and loud and they've got a good size dance floor, so it's fairly popular."

"And you've never been inside."

"Nope."

"Someday I want to hear more about that detective's club of yours. You must have had some real adventures."

The bar was one of Jacob Noonan's former hangouts; something that stirred old memories and that peculiar feeling of regret over his untimely death. Remembering how the whole business had been brought to a close and the caring and generosity of David Conrad, my composure began to go and I had to shut the thoughts out completely.

For the next hour or so, Teddy and I handed out tracts and talked to the customers going in or out of Lulu's. Most responded casually and were polite. Some were thankful when they took the time to look at what we were handing out. What always made it feel worthwhile, though, was when people stopped to talk. That night we got two different ones with stories of deeply troubled lives. Both gratefully allowed us to pray with them.

"You want to hang out some more or go get coffee?" Teddy turned and looked me over. He could tell by the way I was starting to shiver that it was about time to quit.

"Coffee," I said and hunched my shoulders. "I can't take this the way you can."

"That's fine. It just means you can teach me more stuff. I want to get a handle on the way you mark your Bible."

"Do you remember your Hebrew words for the week?"

"I sure do. I also have the alphabet memorized and I'm ready for more. How are you doing with your Greek?"

"Okay, but not as good as you are with the Hebrew."

It was then about a quarter to twelve. We hopped on the Scout and went to Hungry Harry's, the all-night restaurant usually frequented by people from Rock of the Witness. There were a few patrons scattered about in the black vinyl booths. Those who knew Teddy and me smiled and waved hello. We could have joined them and usually did, but this time my partner pulled me into a booth all our own.

To make communication easier as we studied, Teddy and I sat side by side. We shoved at each other with our elbows for a bit of fun and then looked around for the waitress.

"There she is," I said as the woman walked out from the kitchen with an order. She acknowledged our presence and said she'd be with us in a minute.

"Where's your Bible?" he asked and bounced in his seat.

"In a minute! Now, Teddy, tell me something. Didn't you study the Bible in seminary?"

"Sure, but not extensively. And certainly not like this, since the Bible isn't supposed to be of any private interpretation; we weren't allowed to think for ourselves. Instead of memorizing Scripture the way you guys do, I've had to memorize prayers, liturgy and all the other things pertaining to my priestly office. I could've learned more about the Bible, though, if I'd wanted to. It just wasn't required."

"Maybe it's good that you didn't. Some of what I hear they teach in those places isn't too right on."

"Oh, that wouldn't be the case where I went. But anyway, I did study New Testament Greek, and that's going to be very valuable to me now. Then I took one course on the New Testament and Bible history, which was pretty interesting. Later on they gave us philosophy, psychology, church history, and religion. Now, ask me about church history or any of the church fathers like Augustine and I'll tell you plenty."

"Some other time, if you don't mind. Teddy, how could you go through eight years of that? My brain gets fried just thinking about it. Especially since you were imprisoned there and you had all those lousy rules."

"It was tough, all right, but it loosened up toward the end, thank God.

A lot has changed since Vatican II. More than I ever imagined. And please don't judge every other priest by me. Seminaries and religious experiences vary quite a bit in the Catholic Church, as I'm sure it does with Protestants. It all depends on–say, here comes the waitress. Are you gonna eat?"

"I might have something sweet to go with the coffee."

"Well, I've been in the mood for a hot turkey sandwich."

After placing our order, study began. I explained to Teddy more of the things he'd asked me about, starting by putting the Hebrew words he'd learned into a phrase and showing him a couple more. He in turn worked with me on the Greek he'd given me to learn. Then we got down to my system of Bible study, and as the night stretched slowly into morning, I began to notice that Teddy was studying me more than the books. It only made me slightly uncomfortable. Finally I caught him at it and held his gaze with a questioning smile.

"What's the matter with you?" I gently chided. "Why do you keep looking at me?"

"I don't know," he replied casually.

"You do, too."

"Well, because–you're beautiful."

"Huh?"

"You're beautiful. You–you shine with the Spirit."

"I do?"

"Sure you do. I wouldn't say it if you didn't."

My cheeks grew warm with blushing as I thought about what he said.

"Does it bother you to have me look at you? I'm sorry if–"

"No, that's okay. Sometimes I see the same thing in you."

"Really?"

"Sure. I saw it the night we first met."

"Even then? Now, that's amazing."

"Well, yes and no. It took a little effort, but I figured it out. See, it's the Lord in us, on us, or whatever. I'm sure that he's just shining out, and he can do that whenever he wants. So it's not like we're such hot stuff."

"I can go with that. But Jenny, I don't see him on other people quite like I do you. I think you are special. As a matter of fact, I know you are."

"Well, Teddy, I could easily debate that, but it's getting late and I have chores tomorrow. I mean today. I think we ought to quit and go home."

"Yeah, it is late. But I'll see you on Sunday, anyway. Only this time I get to see how good a cook you are. Mmm–mph!"

SATURDAY, JANUARY 18:

All the way home and even as I fell asleep, I thought of what Teddy had said. In the morning before the day got too busy, I kept thinking about it. Special? Well, I certainly was different. No doubt about that at all. Still it was a blessing that he thought of me that way. Thinking of how he wanted my company and coveted my spiritual gifts brought a touch of healing to the wounds on my heart left by David Conrad. It was interesting that we both saw that special glow on each other. Like the night we first met, Teddy Molloy still had an angelic air about him that sometimes made me want to stare. But since he had yet to discover my many short comings and I his, the natural deduction was that the attraction we had for each other was simply the draw of God's Holy Spirit. But he had a good point. I'd seen it on others, but not to the same degree that I saw it on him. Something curious was afoot in the heavenly realm and the implications gave me goose bumps.

SUNDAY, JANUARY 19:

Right after mass on Sunday, I rushed home to get dinner ready. Even though I'd started preparations the day before, I wanted to be sure everything was perfect and that it would be done cooking by the time Teddy arrived. I had a ball in the kitchen, considering him in every culinary detail. Having seen how he could eat, I had prayed for God to make this meal extra special and then made plenty of it. On the menu was a huge roast beef cooked nice and slow, mashed potatoes and gravy, then corn on the cob and green beans fresh from the market. Home made apple pie and ice cream were for dessert.

When the family got home from their services, I was blessed with more hands to help with work such as setting the table, and putting the food into nice serving dishes.

"Janette, I think your new boyfriend's here," said Olivia, who was setting the table.

"Boyfriend?"

"Is that him?" my mother asked as she set out condiments.

Boyfriend? Honestly! Invite a friend over and just because he's a guy they've got to think....

Looking out the kitchen door and through the dining room window, I saw the turquoise blue and white Chevy out front. "That's him, all right."

"Well, I hope you're not going to greet him like that."

"Huh? Oh!"

To endure the heat of the kitchen I had put on an old summer night shirt and an apron over it. I tore upstairs to change into slacks and a nice blouse and came down just as my parents and Teddy were introducing themselves.

"There she is," my father said.

Teddy turned to face me with a happy grin that deeply blessed my soul. To my surprise my partner looked different, and even more attractive. Not wanting to draw attention to his priestly profession, he had left off wearing his Roman collar. Then for the sake of a good first impression upon my parents, he wore a white shirt and black tie along with dark brown slacks and tweed sport coat. In innocence he held his arms out to me and I practically jumped into them. In suspicion and surprise my parents exchanged glances.

"Are you ready to eat?" I asked him.

"You'd better believe it," he said. "Lead the way. It smells wonderful!"

Minutes later we were all seated around the table and the rest of the introductions were made. Daddy said grace and then we in turn said our Bible verses until it got to Teddy.

"Bible verse," prodded Gregory. "Say a Bible verse."

"Uh, let's see," Teddy said, then spouted off happily with John 3:16.

With my work all done, the others served and I got to watch Teddy chow down. He sat directly across from me in the place of my brother, Aaron, who was back in school.

"That's a nice car you drive, Ted," said Daddy. "Looks like it's in mint condition."

"I try to keep it that way," he said. "Got it a few years ago and fixed it up myself. Cars are a big hobby of mine."

"Do you go to Janette's church?" asked mother.

"Well, sort of."

Oh, no! They're going to grill him. They're thinking we're sweethearts and I haven't told them yet that he's a priest. I wish they would just hush up and let him eat!

"Uh, may I please have some more roast beef?" Teddy requested happily. He added other things to his plate as well. "Thank you. Oh, this meal is such an answer to prayer. Ever since I've been in New Mexico it's been chili morning, noon and night, unless I ate out. I can't remember when I've eaten food this good. Jenny, did you really cook all of this?"

"Yes, I did."

"That's right," said Mommy. "Janette cooked every bit of this meal all by herself; the dessert, too."

"Yeah, she's a great cook," said little Gregory. "So if you two ever decide to get married, you'll eat good all the time."

Teddy was dumbfounded. He turned a deep shade of scarlet and then turned his eyes on me. "You didn't tell them?"

"I'm sorry, Teddy. I forgot. Please forgive me."

"What didn't you tell us, Janette?" asked Daddy.

"Teddy is a Catholic priest."

My parents looked across the table at each other, stunned. "A what?!" They chorused.

"Yes," said Teddy, his smile gone and fork frozen in mid air. "I'm a Catholic priest."

"A *Roman* Catholic priest?" asked Mommy.

"Yes," he replied. "Roman Catholic."

Now all eyes turned to me.

"Hey, it's not my idea," I said. "Besides, he's just here for dinner, not nuptials. Look, Teddy and I are just friends."

Everyone seemed to relax and sat quietly while thinking it over, except for little Gregory who boldly asked, "What's a Catholic priest?"

"Well," said Mommy. "He a preacher kind of like at our church, but his church doesn't allow him to get married."

"It doesn't? Well, that's stupid."

"Gregory! That's not nice. Just hush if you can't be polite."

"Oh, that's all right," said Teddy. "It's not as if he doesn't have a point. There are plenty of Catholics that feel the same way, believe me. But on the other hand, celibacy actually does have benefits. There are some things you just can't do when you have a wife and kids."

"Well, now you don't have to ask what he does for a living," I said. "Teddy, save room for dessert. You're going to need it, 'cause it ain't Jell-O."

Still my parents wanted to know more about my Theodore, so after dinner, the four of us sat in the family room and talked. As soon as they found out that he was from my father's hometown, Daddy monopolized most of the conversation. There seemed to be something special about being from the south side of Chicago that still to this day escapes me. They had a good time finding out the things they had in common, such as a love for baseball and the White Sox. Since both were big boxing fans, they discussed that sport as well, and I got to hear about some of Teddy's pugilistic exploits. He even said he would teach me the art of boxing.

Just as it had been when I first met this man, my parents began to wonder the same thing about him that I did; only I had not yet asked the question. Finally, after a brief pause in the conversation, my mother was bold enough to say, "Teddy, whatever made you want to become a priest?"

"Well, I'm not really sure," he replied. "I guess it's just something I've always wanted to do. My sister Terry and I (I have a twin sister), we used to talk about it ever since we were tiny. It started out as a game, of course. We kids'd play mass and she liked to dress up as a nun, and naturally I was always the priest. Eventually that's what we became. Oh, I guess I've always been attracted to the religious life. It's certainly not something for everybody and you probably think that there are a lot of other things I could have done with my life; but a priest plays a very important part in the lives of people who are Roman Catholic, and I've always had a great deal of respect and admiration for the ones I've known growing up. I guess I just wanted to be like them."

"Now, how did you meet Janette?" asked Daddy.

"Oh, at the fellowship, Rock of the Witness. I learned about the place when the pastor and some of the others were out on the street ministering the Gospel. Now Janette and I are partners in the street ministry."

"Street ministry?" said Mommy with a frown. "Now, that's the one thing that bothers me. I would think that could get kind of dangerous."

"Not as long as she's with me," said Teddy. "And the Lord looks out for the both of us, besides."

"He's also joined the band," I interjected. "Teddy's a very good musician. He sings and plays the cello beautifully. You really should come hear him."

"But you're a Catholic priest," said Daddy. "Now, I've been to Janette's church, and I know what goes on there. Isn't that seriously off the beaten path for you? And isn't your going there against the rules of your religion?"

"Yes, it's definitely out of the ordinary for me. And as for worshiping at Protestant churches–well, my church has grown more acceptant of Protestant faiths, but what I'm doing still might be frowned upon."

"Then what are you doing there, if you don't mind my asking?"

"Well, Mr West, I guess you could say that God doesn't always play according to the rules of the Church. At least that's what I'm finding out. It's a bit difficult to explain because I'm still trying to understand it myself. When you've been brought up to think that your religion has cornered the market on God, only to find out that people in other churches are actually experiencing what you've only dreamed about, it's quite a shock, to say the least. Then again, everything God is doing has been happening so fast that I haven't had time to work it all out theologically. It's all I can do to keep up with what he brings me—like Janette, for instance. She's really been an answer to prayer."

"It's nice to hear somebody say that, as hard headed as she is. Be careful, though, she's a natural born trouble maker."

If I'd had something, I'd have thrown it, but instead I just gave Daddy a dirty look. Although he was partly right, he needn't have said so to Teddy.

"Oh, no," was Teddy's response. "Not Janette. She'll be one to keep me out of trouble. I think she's an angel."

"With horns and a tail," laughed Mommy. "At least she used to be. She's been behaving herself lately."

"Would you like some more dessert or something?" I asked Teddy. The subject needed changing.

"No, thanks. I really should go. It's getting late."

"Well, I've certainly enjoyed meeting you," said Daddy, and Mommy echoed the sentiment. "I hope you'll come back and see us again. Do you shoot pool?"

"Oh, yes, I love a good game of pool."

"We just got a new table at Christmas time. Come on back and we'll play some. Come back any time you like."

"Janette, why don't you give Teddy some of that food to take home," said Mommy. "And give him one of those pies, too."

I took Teddy into the kitchen and gave him whatever he wanted, bagged it and put it in a box to take home. Then we went outside to his car to say our goodbyes.

"You have a real nice family," said Teddy warmly. "Makes me feel a little home sick."

"My father meant what he said. You can come back any time you want. We'll even feed you."

"Thank you. Thank you very much. That's nice to know." Teddy stowed away his food in the front seat of his car, then turned again to me. "Jenny, thanks again for a wonderful meal and a very pleasant afternoon. I'd stay longer, but right now I need to go do something I haven't taken the time for lately, and that's to just be completely alone with the Lord for a while. If I don't I'm gonna bust."

"I know. I can feel it."

Teddy gathered me up in his arms and held me lovingly. Sensing that he prayed silently, I did the same. When he released me, there were tears on his face and his smile was a sober one. "I love you, Jenny. You really are an angel."

"Thanks, partner, I need to hear stuff like that."

With one more quick embrace and a peck on the lips, Teddy got into his Chevy and took off.

Offering pleasant comments and gentle warnings about romance, my parents chattered on about my friend during the commercial breaks as the family watched television. I did my best to respond, but my heart was bent on talking to the Lord about this unique man he'd brought into my life. For hours after he left, I could feel the warmth of his arms around me. Then he filled my thoughts and prayers as I drifted off to sleep. It wasn't until I got up to go to school the next morning that I realized just what a timely godsend he was. The hours I'd spent that weekend with Teddy Molloy had eclipsed all thought of David Conrad.

MONDAY, JANUARY 20-TUESDAY, JANUARY 21:

Back in school on Monday, the painful feelings rose once more to their place of prominence as rejection was again thrown in my face. Mr Conrad had never given me undue attention in class, but now it seemed I got none at all. When I thought about the anguish and humiliation ahead of me that week and endless days beyond, my heart felt sick, and an even heavier depression threatened to take hold. I never realized just how much I did love this man, since I'd spent so much time and effort trying to deny it. Then when I compared school with how happy I'd been over the weekend, I determined that the present situation would not continue.

Now it was a matter of survival. I had already experienced what deep depression could do and had no desire to end up in that pit again. Getting over this broken friendship while having it constantly in my face five days a week wasn't possible. The entire association had to be dissolved. But each time I thought of quitting private lessons, my main worry was always over my parents' reaction. But with no end in sight to this dilemma, my emotional health and well being became the priority, and that would just have to be the way this ugly cookie crumbled. They would have to be told the whole story, and there was no other way around it. With the new semester coming up, the timing couldn't be better. I would lose him for one class, anyway, which was Music Theory. But now, David Conrad would no longer be my teacher for anything.

These thoughts began to form in my weary head on Monday afternoon and I continued to refine them on Tuesday. It certainly seemed the best thing to do, and yet when I imagined severing all ties, a cry of "No!!" resounded from somewhere deep within me with such vehemence that it couldn't be ignored. That and having considered the results from all angles made me decide not to be too hasty. The repercussions would be very damaging to Mr Conrad if I dropped French and all my music classes. My parents wouldn't be the only ones to want to know what had happened. Mrs MacGregor would certainly take him to task, and the gossip mongers would have a heyday. My love for this man wasn't dead yet, so I wanted to make him aware of my plans and give him the opportunity to show what he was really made of. Whatever unpleasantness he was going through now, this would not make his life any easier.

The most opportune time for this talk would be after my lessons on Wednesday. I couldn't afford to wait any longer than that, and I believed it was best for him as well to have this resolved soon. So having prepared myself mentally and rehearsed what I would say, I set my heart to do it and found comfort enough to get me through another day.

WEDNESDAY, JANUARY 22:
My test in Music Theory went well, thanks to David Richardson. He had helped me study, explaining things in much simpler language than the text book or my teacher. Seconds after I handed in my paper, the bell rang. Before moving into the alto section for Choir, I reminded myself of plans for the afternoon and began going over what I would tell Mr Conrad. However, it seemed that he just might beat me to it, for as the classroom began to clear, he approached and asked if I would please stay in at noon for a few minutes so he could talk to me.

I had avoided his eyes in the practice I had taken up of being as cold to him as he was to me, but still caught something that looked like sympathy in his expression. Also, the tone of his voice had been soft, with what sounded like a touch of regret. Hope began to rise up in me as I puzzled over what he wanted, but I was too cautious to entertain it much. The let down would be too great. Besides, it could be about something related to school and not us at all. Maybe it had to do with my performance. In spite of reduced concentration during the past few weeks, I was reasonably sure my grades hadn't slipped that badly, if at all; but I might be wrong. Whatever it was, I had no intention of being made a fool of and would be on my guard.

When class was dismissed for lunch, I remained seated in the third row of the alto section and determined to make no effort to get closer to Mr Conrad for conversation's sake, even if he asked. Hardening my posture and my heart as well, I kept my eyes turned from him and waited.

There was no sound in the room except the light shuffling of paper and then footsteps as he ascended to the third level and sat down next to me. I turned enough to hear and see him but still refused to look directly at him.

"Janette, there are some things that a man just doesn't discuss with a young woman; especially one as young and as lovely as you. But what I can tell you is this: seeing you every day has only made me feel more and more ashamed of the way I've lived for so many years; it's been absolute torment, trying to work through and face up to certain things. It's not that I wanted to mistreat you, honey; I just–couldn't take it, that's all. And frankly, I still feel about an inch high when I'm around you. But I've been hurting you, and I don't want to go on that way. You mean the world to me, and I want it to be right between us. So would you please, please forgive me?"

It blew all my plans to bits and made it impossible to free myself of him, but how could I not forgive him? His being so honest and speaking with such tenderness destroyed all of my defenses. Now, I was right back where I was before Christmas–and worse. "Yes," I whispered. "Yes, I forgive you."

I turned my head in his direction but still refused to look at him, afraid that if I did I would loose the battle completely; afraid that my eyes would betray the very desire I had worked so hard to conceal.

"Janette?"

His hand touched my face, found the underside of my chin and lifted my countenance to his. By then the tears were starting to roll down my cheeks; any fight that was in me suddenly vanished, leaving me immobilized and unable to resist as he studied my face and looked into my eyes. I, helpless to do otherwise, looked back. Was it just my imagination or did his face move closer? His fingers, warm and gentle, brushed some of the tears aside and brushed back the hair from my face.

God! God! I can't do this. I can't–not love him. I'm so tired of crying. Y'shua, help me!

As the tears came flooding forth, Mr Conrad drew me to his shoulder.

THURSDAY JANUARY 23 - FRIDAY, JANUARY 24:

For days after Mr Conrad's apology, I indulged my heart and allowed myself to believe something of lasting value could actually happen between us. It was the only way I could turn off the tears. His sincere words, the warm touch of his hand and his arms around me had sent me back to that proverbial drawing board. The man was clearly penitent and his affection for me was also quite evident. He was no longer the proud peacock he'd been when he flirted with me that first day of school. But believing he felt more than friendship not only felt good, it felt too good, bringing me a warm glow of peace and a happy anticipation of something absolutely wonderful. But that battle with reason and logic still continued in the midst of it all, making the threat of tears never far away.

I almost didn't go to school on Thursday, afraid that I couldn't control myself. He started up the old breakfast routine almost as if it had never stopped. The constant battle inside me made the day seem much too long and Friday was a carbon copy. In between, however, was an oasis in St Basil's rehearsal on Thursday night. Then on Friday I had the sweetness of the Sabbath and the weekend to look forward to.

While getting up from the dinner table on Friday evening, I heard the sound of a car pulling up in the driveway. Not expecting it to be for me, I thought nothing of it and took my dishes into the kitchen. Seconds later my name was called.

"Janette," said Daddy. "Teddy's here."

"What?" I ran happily to greet my unexpected guest and was doubly surprised. As promised, Teddy had begun teaching me to box, giving me a brief lesson Tuesday night and a better one on Thursday. Now he stood at my front door, bringing me a punching bag. "Is this for real?"

"Where would you like it?" he asked with a grin.

"In the garage," I replied and turned to call for my father, but he was right behind me.

"Well, for Pete's sake!" Daddy shook his head and laughed. "You really are going to teach her to box, aren't you?"

"Sure, why not? It's just for fun."

"Yeah, that's what you think. Well, let's get it put away so we don't keep standing in this cold. Janette, when you get your coat get mine, too, would you, please?"

The three of us went around back to the garage. Daddy lifted the heavy wooden door and quickly cleared a space for the black, oblong bag.

"I'll hang it up for her tomorrow, I guess," said Daddy.

"Teddy, where on earth did you get this?" I asked.

"I was driving by and saw it hanging in the window of the Salvation Army Store. Something told me you might like it."

"It's great! Thank you."

"What's next, a pair of gloves?" said Daddy as he brought down the garage door. "If I knew where mine were, you could use them."

"Oh, I might be able to scare some up," said Teddy.

Once inside the house again, we sat down for a few minutes before time to go to rehearsal. I brought a cup of coffee and piece of cake to Teddy in the family room where he and Daddy sat talking, and then joined them.

"The bag isn't the only reason I stopped by." Teddy casually reached over and slapped me on the back of the head.

"Ow! You just wait, Molloy."

"I've been waiting. I'll be an old man by the time you lay a glove on me. Well, as I was saying, Mr West, I had another reason to stop by. There's a little snow storm coming in tonight. I figured Janette and I would just take my car."

"That was very thoughtful of you, Ted," said Daddy.

"I forgot to listen to the weather report like I usually do," I confessed. "Thanks, Teddy."

"Jenny, whenever the weather's bad, you call me and we'll ride together. As for Thursday nights, I'll even come get you, if necessary."

"That reminds me. Why don't you come by here and have dinner on Tuesdays before we go to rehearsal? Then we can go together."

"Sure, if it's all right with your folks."

"It's perfectly all right," said Daddy. You're welcome here any time, so don't be bashful."

"Thank you, Mr West. I certainly do appreciate your hospitality. Well, Jenny, are you ready? We need to go now."

"You're right. I'll get my stuff. It won't take but a minute."

Up the stairs and then down again I came with guitar and bag of music in hand. While I put my coat back on, Teddy took my things out to the car. After kissing Daddy goodbye, I followed him out.

"Thanks for the punching bag," I said as we pulled out into the street. "It's going to get a lot of use, I can tell you that."

"Good. I'm sure you'll have fun with it."

"You know, I've been meaning to ask you something. Teddy, when you were boxing, what did they call you? Did you have one of those catchy names?"

"Sure. I didn't particularly want one, though. My own name was good enough for me."

"Well, what did they call you?"

"The Wild Irish Rogue."

"Ohhhh, really? Oooo! I like that." The words struck a chord in my spirit that sent chills through me. "Yeah, Wild Irish Rogue. Sounds prophetic. Who named you that?"

Teddy laughed. "You won't believe it. My grandmother gave me that name."

"No kidding? Which grandmother."

"Why?"

"Humor me. I have a theory. Was it your mother's mother, the Baptist?"

"No, it was my father's mother. I think I was always a favorite of hers."

"Was she very religious?"

"No more than any of the rest of us, I don't think. But now that you mention it, she was different. Yeah. You know, she was from Ireland, and the Irish do have their superstitions; lots of them. She never cared for any of that, though, and she wasn't much for the blarney, either. She was a very strong, no nonsense kind of woman; wise and thrifty, but at the same time tender, caring and even generous. You know, Jenny, I think I see what you're getting at."

"There's a lot to be said for a godly heritage, Teddy, the praying mothers and grandmothers and all. I just figured with the way things have happened so powerfully for you in spiritual ways, that you must have had somebody somewhere in your life that knew the Lord and prayed seriously for you."

"You know, I think you're right."

Ten minutes later, Teddy and I were at the church and getting set up. Then it was time for prayer.

Albuquerque's weather can be very changeable. The day had started cloudy and then turned fair. Then the storm that Teddy spoke of rolled in around eight o'clock and dropped more than an inch of snow before it was through. That meant no street ministry, so after the meeting, my partner and I went to Hungry Harry's and continued our study where we'd left off the week before.

By midnight the storm had moved on, and there were stars showing through the clouds. It seemed like a good time to do something else. Tired of bending over the books, I was ready to pack up and go home. But home wasn't home for Teddy, and he was never in a hurry to return to St Basil's.

"You party pooper," he chided after I mentioned our busy day on Saturday. "It's a gorgeous night out. Wouldn't you like to go for a ride?"

"If it's just a little one."

Leaving the restaurant, we stopped at an all-night liquor store. We pulled up at the drive through window where Teddy got a couple of six packs of beer and a six pack of our favorite soda along with paper cups that were gratis. Then we took off going north, then east toward the mountains, meandering in an attempt to get as close to the foothills as possible.

"So what's so important about Saturday that you need your beauty rest so bad?"

"I've got a gig tomorrow with the stage band."

"You sing with your school band?"

"Yeah. I'd invite you out, but it's for some women's club social, so it's not open to the general public."

"I have confessions tomorrow and that'll include visitation. I couldn't make it anyway. So, you must be involved a lot with music at school. Do you sing in the choir?"

"That and then some."

"Well, tell me about it. Isn't it fun for you?"

"It used to be. I guess it still is, in a way. Look, do you mind if we don't talk about school right now? I'd just as soon not think about it, if it's not absolutely necessary."

"Okay. Sorry to hear that."

Up to that point I had been able to keep my thoughts clear of David Conrad. Now I could think of nothing else, though I still paid attention to Teddy. The longing and despair still overwhelmed me at moments, settling down gradually or striking me suddenly like an ocean wave and pulling me under in its current. I had just barely made it through this day without an embarrassing break down, and now I was fighting one again. It didn't take much to provoke a crying jag, but it took every ounce of determination I had to keep one down.

Suddenly I turned to look at the man behind the wheel and studied his fine Caucasian features in the pale intermittent street light: the pleasant mouth, the nose with its slight upturn, a strong, well formed chin and jaw line. Funny, how the face of this Irish American priest could be angelic and impish all at the same time. Looking at him brought to mind happier times and the realization that more were ahead. Comparing the commonalities of this new relationship to mine with Mr C showed quite a contrast. Musically speaking, Teddy and I were more relaxed, always having fun, even when we worked hard in rehearsals; also we could worship HaShem together, which added a dimension of delight that my teacher couldn't begin to approach, no matter how great his talent and knowledge was. Then, although there was some blessing in sharing from the Scriptures with Mr C, with Teddy there was often a mighty flow of the Holy Spirit that brought the thrill of new revelation for both of us during study. The longer I looked at the visage of this rebel priest, the better my outlook seemed. God had blessed me with a beautiful and unique friendship in which I could find a joy and fulfillment presently impossible with David Conrad.

"I guess I'd better get you home," said Teddy, turning to look at me while stopped at a light. "You're getting kind of quiet. Are you doing okay?"

"Yeah, I'm okay."

"Come here. Sit next to me."

More than happy to comply, I slid across the seat and let him put his arm around my neck in a teasing gesture, then drop it down around my shoulder. As we headed home through the deserted streets, it occurred to me that if this kept up (and there was no reason why it shouldn't) it just might be possible to get over my Mr Conrad.

SATURDAY, JANUARY 25:

The West Albuquerque Women's Club program was a luncheon that started at one o'clock in the afternoon. I had to be there no later than 12:15. Mommy would drop me off and Mr Johnson would bring me home. So for me, chores were suspended, and in the morning hours I got myself ready.

I was dropped off at the venue and was all ready to breeze right through the side door along with one of the boys in the band. Then a tall, dark-haired, middle-aged woman, who was rushing about, suddenly halted and turned in my direction. Stepping in front of me, she put out her hand to stop me from going in. Looking haughtily down her nose, she said disdainfully, "May I help you?"

"I'm with the band," I said flatly.

The woman, a Hispanic whose skin was nearly as dark as my own, suddenly smiled condescendingly and said, "Oh, you're the entertainment. Then by all means, go right in."

Just what I need.

Resisting the temptation to use the situation to vent other feelings, I gritted my teeth and kept going until I found where I was supposed to be. Behind the curtain, the band was set up on stage and ready to go, but Mr Johnson was off somewhere. I took a chair backstage in the wings and waited. A moment later I heard his voice. When he saw me in my dark blue, satin and lace off the shoulder dress and my mother's silver fox stole, he whistled.

"My goodness!" Mr Johnson laughed and shook his head. "I thought I was used to this, but I guess I'm not. Janette, you just don't look like the little girl I used to know."

I stood up to get my hug from him and received a kiss on the cheek as well. "That's because I'm not the little girl you used to know."

"You're right about that. Look, we'll be starting in about fifteen minutes. I took that last song, the Chaplin number, out of the program since it upset you. Are you feeling okay, now? I had a talk with Conrad the other day. He said he would apologize to you."

"He did. Thank you."

"He would have done it anyway. He told me he was upset by the way he'd hurt you. David's a good man. He just needs Jesus. So stay with him, okay? I'd sure appreciate it."

"I don't seem to have a choice. But don't worry. And if I can't get through to him, God will send somebody else."

"Maybe. But I have a feeling that you're the special one. Maybe even the last one. God set this up with you especially to draw him in. I just know it."

"I've felt that, too. Still we have to wait and see."

He was right in believing the Lord had set me up with Mr C. I had seen it from the beginning, only I hadn't thought about it lately. So, like it or not, I was stuck for the rest of the school year being his precious little shadow, because it was all in God's plan. Dandy. But it wasn't necessarily the Lord's fault that I had gone too far in the way I felt about the man–except that I had prayed about it quite a bit. That was one thing I still couldn't figure out, but there had to be an answer. And since God was perfect, it had to mean that I had missed it somewhere.

The stage band's presentation went well that afternoon, including my performance as vocalist. Finding an old family friend amongst the members of this hoity-toity sewing circle helped raise my spirits a bit and eclipse the incident that had happened when I first arrived. But once the excitement of the show was over and I was back home wearing blue jeans again, the longing and desire for the forbidden dominated my thoughts. That night I cried myself to sleep.

SUNDAY, JANUARY 26:

Our group for the ten o'clock folk mass had one less person come Sunday morning, leaving me more room to play. After a lengthy conversation with Cindy on Saturday, Teddy found it necessary to explain to her the reasons why she could no longer take part. Now she was nowhere to be seen. The rest of us, unrestricted by her reticence and inability to fully enter in, pulled tighter together in the Spirit. The results were a better performance and a greater anointing.

Just before the homily, Teddy sang a short solo while I accompanied him on guitar. He had wanted me to add my voice, but I had thought his alone would be better, for several reasons. After all, this was his ministry and he was the one people would look to for guidance. Being freshly ordained and a new kid on the block, he was still proving himself to these people and needed to be the outstanding one. This is what I felt the Lord telling me. And I, not being Catholic, much preferred to stay in the background, anyway.

The silence that followed the special song was broken only by the sound of someone's muffled weeping at the back of the sanctuary. Everyone else seemed awe struck, either staring into space or up at Teddy. Because of the mood, the silence was allowed to continue a few seconds for contemplation. When Teddy gave his homily, the people seemed to listen intently with the same look of wonder on many of their faces. Then when mass was ending, rather than the usual lively song, he had us play something with a moderate tempo for the recessional, to keep hearts turned in the same direction.

"This has to have been the most wonderful mass I've ever attended," said Sr Mary John, as she put away her guitar. "I was never so moved as I was during Father Molloy's song. And his homily was very thought provoking."

I barely caught her words, and only heard bits and pieces of the conversation that ensued as we packed up. It had been a big enough effort to concentrate on the mass. Even though I had done my part without a hitch and was able to stay in the flow of the Spirit, it had been a struggle to do so. For some reason I just couldn't pull myself far enough out of the gloom.

While the others went over to the fellowship hall or wherever, I went back to the sacristy where Teddy was changing out of his robes. With my thoughts still divided, I watched him hang up the garments and yet didn't see much of anything. Before I knew it, he stood in front of me wearing a blue plaid shirt of heavy cotton and his eyes appeared much the same color.

"You want to get donuts?" I asked.

"Naw. I'm not hungry. Besides, I'd rather they have the chance to talk about what happened at mass without me there. They might be a little more honest with themselves and less embarrassed. I heard enough comments at the door."

"So what do you want to do until dinner time? You are coming for dinner, aren't you?"

"Well, to be honest, I had something else in mind. It seems that a certain young lady promised to take me sight seeing."

"Huh?"

"Don't you remember? I've been here for months and I've hardly seen anything, not even the tramway. I've had one trip up to Santa Fe and that's been it. Come on, Jenny. You can't go back on your word."

"All right. But we can ride the tramway anytime. I'll show you some sights, all right. I'll even show you a ghost town."

"Really? Sounds good. The roads will be clear, so let's take the Indian."

As we walked out and into the sunshine, the details of our excursion were going through my head and I suddenly became concerned that the two of us taking off together might cause a problem. "Say, Molloy. You want to work this a little more discreetly? I don't want you to get into any trouble?"

"Trouble? What do you mean?"

"Well–"

"Oh, I get it; because you're a girl." He laughed. "Come on, you're just a kid. Nobody's gonna think anything."

"Yeah, I guess not. But look. Another thing is that I ought to stop by my house and leave a note so they won't expect us for dinner. Then we'll hop on the freeway."

"No, let's call them from the road. But while we're on the subject, I did tell Monsignor Mitchell and the other priests a little bit about you; enough that they know you're kind of special to me. What we do need to be careful about, though, is what we say around those guys. You know?"

"Sure, that goes without saying."

There were three other priests at St Basil's. Monsignor Mitchell, an elderly white man, was the pastor. Father Lucero, a middle-aged Hispanic originally from Mexico City, was his assistant. The other one, Father Lacy, was temporary and part time at the parish, much like Teddy was. Also a fairly young man and the most interesting of the three, he was a hospital chaplain who was soon headed for the armed forces and Viet Nam in order to minister to the Catholic soldiers.

"So that you'll know, Jenny, I didn't tell them you weren't Catholic. However I did mention that you were going to help me with the project I was sent here to do. I did ask you about that, didn't I?"

Project? Oh, Lord! What now? "You mean your assignment you got when they shipped you here?"

"Right."

"Yeah, I'll help you. Piece o' cake."

"You think so?"

"I'm an Indian, ain't I?"

"That's right, I forgot."

"See, you can start with me. Come on, let's go."

Leaving my gear at the rectory, we took off and headed northeast toward the little towns of Golden and Madrid. It was a perfect day for a ride: crisp and clear, with most of the snow being in the higher elevations. Sitting behind him, I spoke into Teddy's ear and told him about points of interest and local legend. Madrid (pronounced Mad-rid) was what I particularly wanted to show him, because it was a ghost town and had a museum. The little mining community had boomed big in the 1920's, then dwindled down to a handful of people after coal ceased to be an important fuel. It was now being taken over by hippies and Bohemian types moving into the old houses and fixing them up.

It was a brief tour to see the museum and coal mine, then we walked the tiny town itself, where tall, gaunt wooden houses stood weathered and bleached by the sun. Some were erect and others at angles in the likeness of timeworn grave markers. Then we rode back through Golden, which hardly seemed like a town at all, and stopped at the tavern for lunch.

So far I was enjoying the day, but the threat of depression was never far off. This time, in spite of my partner's good company, my mind drifted constantly toward David Conrad. As I sat in the rustic restaurant and bar eating a sandwich, my thoughts had me at the grand piano playing ragtime.

Teddy reached across the table and slapped me on the side of the head. "You haven't heard a word I've said," he complained. "What's the matter with you?"

I shrugged and said nothing, unsure if it would do to share this kind of thing. Not only was it embarrassing, I couldn't imagine he'd be much help, being celibate. But he wouldn't leave it alone. Frowning thoughtfully, he took a guess.

"Come on, is it school? Uhhh–" Suddenly a light went on. "Do you have a boyfriend? Yeah, that's it. Come on, tell me."

With a heavy sigh I finally said, "He's not my boyfriend. He was a very good friend until he started acting strange and ignoring me on purpose. Now all of a sudden he wants to be friends again."

"Didn't he apologize?"

"Yeah, a few days ago, but now I almost wish he hadn't."

"Look, tell me what happened. Maybe I can help."

"Well–" This had to be done carefully. I didn't want him to know it was my teacher that I was sappy over. So I omitted certain angles of the story to make it seem as if it were another student. It worked.

"Well, Jenny, if your friend was only going through some tough times, he could have told you up front. It sounds to me like maybe he took your friendship to be more than he wanted at the time. Could be he had a girl he was trying to impress and didn't want you around to mess things up."

"That–sounds plausible."

"I suppose you'd rather stop being friends because you think you might get hurt again. Am I right?"

"Yes." At that point the tears started up, and for the life of me I couldn't regain my composure.

"Look, Jenny, we're about done here. Why don't we leave now and take what's left to go."

Teddy paid the tab and we left. Then after riding a short distance down the road, he pulled off to the side where a group of boulders provided a good place to sit. There I was able to let it all out.

To me, being so upset was a waste of time and good company, especially with the day being so lovely. But I wept and wailed, clinging to Teddy who held me and prayed in his spiritual language. It seemed like an age before my soul finally vented enough of the pain and I could be quiet. But even though I felt better, Teddy was deeply concerned.

"Jenny–" He paused a few seconds before posing his question. "You're really in love with this guy, aren't you?"

I said nothing, but there was no denying it. I was very much in love with David Conrad.

Teddy sighed, and now he was the one to fall silent. After a moment or so he said, "Honey, you're still so very, very young. You have your whole life ahead of you, with dreams to fulfill and all sorts of worlds to explore. Sure, you're mature in some ways, but when it gets down to it, you're still just a kid–and so is he. You shouldn't expect him to have serious feelings of love at that age. Sure, it happens sometimes, but even if he did, you'd both be in for a real tough struggle if you married. So stop being heartbroken. Believe me, it's not worth it. He's not worthy of your affection anyhow, if he would treat you the way he did. Real love doesn't turn on and off for the sake of convenience, so you won't be losing much if you let him go. Besides, how can you go adventuring on the high seas when you're tied to some guy? Look, Jenny, God has something much better for you now than mooning over that character."

I agreed, and for the moment Teddy was that something better. It wasn't romance yet, but that might change. In the meanwhile it was a relationship I could put my whole heart into without fear. Suddenly The Fox in all his beauty was beginning to pale next to the bright angel whose arms were now around me.

The depression was starting to lift and I managed a smile.

"There you go!" said Teddy. "Now, that's how I like to see my girl's face. Ah! She's all ship shape and beautiful again."

Now I'm his girl and he says I'm beautiful. I like that.

Laughing, I gave him a big hug and a kiss on the cheek. "Theodore Francis John Joseph Molloy, I love you. And I wouldn't trade you for anything else in this world!"

In another minute or two we were off again. We headed back to the north and on through Santa Fe, up to Los Alamos, then west to Valle Grande. In our travels we had a snowball fight, and in a place where our voices echoed, we wrote a song. I also got another boxing lesson and a few bruises to go with it, as did my beloved Theodore. Then, just as the sun was setting, we rode through Jemez Springs where the walls of the canyon turn a glorious rainbow of hues in the late afternoon. It was a wonderful end to a very special day.

Chapter Six
Hearts and Flowers

MONDAY AFTERNOON, JANUARY 27:
Georgia was coming. The letter she sent that brought the news was waiting for me when I got home from school. Anxiously ripping open the pink rice paper envelope, I devoured the first two paragraphs before I even got to my room. Then inside with the door closed, I read and reread and danced a hora.

At last I'd have someone to whom I could unburden my whole soul and get prayer to boot. Gorgeous George, far more experienced than I in affairs of the heart, was exactly the person I needed to see. It wouldn't be for a few weeks yet, but at least I could look forward to her arrival. In the meantime I would write her a letter and tell her more of my plight.

She was headed for Albuquerque to escape, even though chances were good that her mother and sister would follow. Her mother, my Aunt Laura, was my father's half sister, and the eldest. Following in the footsteps of her late father, Aunt Laura had become a lawyer, then a judge. Along the way she married a prominent attorney who passed away from a heart attack in 1964. Georgia also had plans to become a lawyer but now had doubts and misgivings. Not happy with things at home or at school, she would take a few courses at UNM until deciding what she really wanted to do. If Aunt Laura found it convenient to follow her, it would only be for a visit, as she wanted the family to meet her future intended. This was the Englishman she'd met while vacationing in Europe: Jonathan Angrahm of the prestigious House of Angrahm Publishers.

Finding hope in this timely news did make my pathway seem brighter, but I still needed a stronger antidote for my pain. Nothing was going on that night, so I thought to call Teddy and see what he was up to. Once I was done practicing music, I took the phone into my room and made the call.

"Hello?" The voice was not Teddy's. From the southern accent, I knew it was Father Lacy, the new priest.

"Uh, hi," I said. "Is, uh, Father Molloy there?"

Using Teddy's title bothered me for doctrinal reasons, but the Lord had told me that if I didn't use it around his peers that they would get suspicious, and it would cause a problem.

"Father Molloy? Yes. Who's calling?"

"Janette West."

I held my breath while waiting for him to come to the phone. When he was on the line my spirits lifted immediately.

"Hi, sweetheart," he said. "How are you?"

"Okay, I guess."

"How was school today?"

"The same. No. It was worse, actually."

"Well, that's no good. Maybe I can suggest something to get your mind off of that problem."

"That would be nice."

"You know, it's a good thing you called. I wanted to ask you a couple of questions."

"Okay, shoot."

"I've been trying to dig up certain verses on the second coming, so I was looking in the book of The Revelation. I noticed the references to Jewish holy days and thought maybe you could help me make a little more sense out of it."

We spent the next five minutes or so discussing the last book of the Bible which contains John's apocalyptic message and vision. The topic of the return of Christ was currently popular with evangelical believers and referred to often, so Teddy was searching it out. Fortunately I had delved into it heavily and was able to help.

"You know," I finally said. "We could talk about this for hours. If you're not busy tonight, why don't we meet somewhere and really study."

"Okay. Your place or mine?"

"I'll come down there. I'd like to get out of the house. You want to wait till after dinner?"

"Uh, no, come now. We'll go down to Drake's and I'll treat you to burgers. And don't come here, just meet me at Drake's"

"Okay, great. I'll be there in a few minutes."

Since it was close to dinner time, Mommy needed to know that I was going out, but I had to find her first. I ran through the house looking and calling, until I found her at last on the back porch taking laundry out of the dryer. When I told her that Teddy wanted to buy me dinner and have Bible study, she smiled and chuckled.

"You be very careful, Janette," she said. "He's a nice man, but he's a man and much older than you. Bible study and church are fine, but you still need to be careful."

"Mommy, he thinks of me as a child," I replied. "So there's nothing to worry about. It may look different, but Teddy and I are just good friends."

"Well, that's the best way to start out, but I doubt if it'll stay that way. I've got eyes. So you be real careful, hear? I mean that, now."

"Yes, Mommy." *Romance. I wish!*

Trying my best to ignore Mother's well-meaning remarks, I ran back upstairs to freshen up a little and get my books. In just a few minutes, I was out the door.

I rolled into the parking lot of Drake's just as my partner was getting out of his Chevy with his bag of books. There was a spot next to his car, so I took it.

"Hi, babe." Teddy kissed my cheek and gave me a hand as I dismounted. "I'll grab your books."

"Thanks."

The once modern cinnamon, orange and white facade of Drake's on south Broadway was badly in need of paint and repair, but its looks didn't keep the customers away. Healthy portions of tasty green or red American style chili along with large beef patties on the burgers made for lots of repeat business. We walked inside and joined the hungry crowd waiting to order. Being the dinner hour, there was a long line at the register backed all the way up to the door. To make sure we got a good place to sit, I took a booth and sat with the books while Teddy stood in line.

While waiting, I got set up. When we did this sort of thing, it was very important to have plenty of napkins in order to keep food stains off the study materials. Finding our napkin holder almost empty on one side, I traded it with a fuller one at another table. Then I set out the books, the colored pencils and rulers used for marking and began reading through some of my notes on The Revelation.

"So what have you got?" Teddy had finally ordered our food and come to join me. "I could tell over the phone that you've studied this in depth."

"Yes, I have. So I can say with some authority that if you want to understand the last book of the Bible, you have to be firmly grounded in the Old Testament."

"That may be so, but I've found some interesting things in my Greek New Testament that are real eye openers. Besides, I'm just getting started, so it may be a good while before I get into the Pentateuch the way you do. But I enjoy Psalms, Proverbs, Isaiah, and lately Jeremiah. I really like Isaiah, though. It's got a lot of Jesus in it."

"Yes, but you see, all the Old Testament books do, if you know what to look for. And since you like Isaiah, we'll start there to study the second coming. Then we'll hit the gospels."

"But what about St John's Revelation?"

"Don't worry. We'll get to that eventually. We have to lay a foundation first."

Getting an early start had been a good idea. Juggling books with burgers and fries, we spent the whole evening pouring over the Scriptures. We had such a fruitful study that it was very difficult to put the books away.

"Well, the more you know, the more you find out you don't know," said Teddy as the eleven o'clock hour approached. He closed his Bible and pushed it aside. "No wonder that vision is so tough to decipher. But it makes a whole lot more sense now than before. You're right about the necessity of Old Testament studies. The cross references to the tabernacle and holy days make a world of difference. It actually simplifies interpretation. I've been playing it safe by staying mostly in the New Testament, but that has to change."

Hallelujah! Priest, your days a numbered.

"Janette—now I have a question to ask you. How did you get to be so—so old?"

I smiled and bit my bottom lip before answering, "I read a lot. I've been devouring books since I was four years old, and much of what I've read since the age of eight has been at an adult level."

"So you're a heavy duty bookworm, huh? Yeah, that figures. I just never thought of it. Come on, little sis, let's go."

We packed up our books and walked out into the night air. The parking lot was almost empty, now, and the avenues quiet except for an occasional passing vehicle. Teddy tossed his bag onto the seat of his car and waited while I tied mine on the back of the Scout. Then it was time to say goodbye.

As Teddy wrapped his strong arms around me and pulled me close to his chest, the warmth from his body felt better than a heating pad. Slipping my arms under his open jacket to return his embrace, I thought how I seemed to fit very well in his niches and curves, making it difficult to resist the temptation to stay there. It was so comfortable. So healing! And yet desire was strangely absent, as if a wall–a thin wall–was there to keep it out, unless it was invited in.

Standing there in the silence, a sweet peace settled upon us that neither of us wanted to disturb. Pulling ourselves apart at last, we looked at each other and smiled. I could still feel the magnetic energy of his spirit to mine as he touched my face.

"Is it supposed to be this way?" he asked, his eyes reflecting the same combination of joy and confusion I felt at that moment. "Sometimes I just don't get it and it scares me; even makes me feel guilty sometimes because it's so strong. Other times I understand it perfectly and it feels just like heaven itself. It really does."

"Of course, it does. That's what it is."

"Well, I hope so, because I like this. I like it a lot." Then with his hand on my cheek, he bent down and gently pressed his lips to mine before we parted.

TUESDAY JANUARY 28:
As long as possible, I hung on to the feeling of Monday night's study with Teddy. Especially the way it ended. Hoping that it would continue in my dreams, perhaps with an extra added dimension, I awoke Tuesday morning to find that it had not. Disappointed, I went on and got ready for school, all the while playing the tender scene in my head.

To avoid slipping into frustration and depression, I drifted in and out of that same reverie while trying to pay attention to Mr C at breakfast. I might have daydreamed intermittently all morning, had he not come up with a distraction wonderful and exciting enough to keep me in the present.

"I have a surprise for you," he said right after *ha motzi*.

"Oh? What's that?"

"Have you heard of the Anthony Vaughn Chorale?"

"Yes, of course."

"Well, Tony Vaughn is a very old friend of mine. He's going to be in town in a few weeks with his group, and I thought you'd like to hear them."

"Yes, I'd love to."

"Good. But there is a catch."

"I should have known. What is it?"

"I'd like Tony to hear you sing. Would you mind staying after the show and doing a song or two for him?"

"Would I mind? I'd love to sing for Anthony Vaughn."

"Good. I've already talked to him about you. Be sure and mark your calendar. The concert is February 14th. That's a Friday. I'll call your parents and make all the arrangements."

What a jolt. Suddenly visions of traveling the world with this famous choral group filled my head. But my imaginings were interrupted shortly by Mr Conrad with some other news.

"Oh, there's something else you need to know. Mr Johnson and I have finally worked out a program for the spring concert. I'm afraid it won't be quite what you and Alan had in mind, but there just isn't the time to do such an elaborate stage production. But I think you'll both be satisfied with what we've done."

"Really? I'm happy to hear that, and Alan will be, too."

"Good. We'll even have costumes. By the way, I'm sending off to L.A. for some period clothing for the girls to use in the show. You may not need any, but still you can have first pick, if you like."

"Thank you, and I would like to have first pick."

"Even though we're keeping the choreography limited, it'll still be plenty of work, which means after school rehearsals, but I think it'll be fun."

"I'm sure it will be, and I'm certainly glad you think so. But to be honest, I really don't want to dance in the show. Sure, it's fun and all, and I suppose I do okay, but I'm just not good enough. I've never taken lessons like Alan has. Besides, I really don't have the time to rehearse."

"Janette, this is highschool, not Broadway. Don't worry about your ability. You're good enough for what I've got planned. And what do you mean, you don't have time? Didn't I lighten up on the homework? What else keeps you so busy? Is it church activities?"

I smiled, and the smile became a grin as I thought of all the good times spent with Teddy Molloy, the night before in particular. "Busy? Oh, you said it! I'm running back and forth between two churches now."

"Oh, really?"

"Uh, huh. There's this new brother in the Lord that I've teamed up with for street ministry. He's Roman Catholic, of all things, and he moonlights at Rock of the Witness. Oh, he's as bad as you are when it comes to finding things for me to do. It's thanks to him that I now have two rehearsals a week. We're both in the worship band at The Rock on Friday nights, and he drafted me to help with the band at his church on Sundays. Then there's all the time we spend in Bible study. I don't know what time I got in last night." I suddenly thought about the knot tying and boxing lessons and laughed. "Oh, and he's teaching me about sailing and how to box."

"How to what?"

"Well, sailing and boxing. He knows a lot about sailing and he's an amateur boxer, or at least he used to be. He's giving me lessons. It's lots of fun! I've gotten a couple of bruises, though, but you should see what I did to him. Last time I got in a lucky punch and almost blacked his eye."

Mr Conrad didn't seem to know what to think about all of this. I might have told him more about my Theodore except that his mood became suddenly somber. It didn't make sense that he should turn so quickly from the happy mood of just seconds ago. I could even feel the change, and it wasn't a pleasant sensation.

"What's the matter?" I asked.

Preoccupied with his gloomy thoughts, his brief response of, "What?" was barely audible.

"Are you all right? You look upset."

"Uh, no, it's–it's just that, uh–I remembered something rather important." He was very distracted but seemed to push it aside quickly as he picked back up on the conversation by saying, "Well, it sounds to me as if you have a new sweetheart."

"My parents think that, too, but I don't." I shook my head and reached for my books to prepare for study. "Not at this stage of the game, anyway. It would complicate things too much if we went in that direction. After all, he's Catholic."

"I see. Well, it does pay to be careful."

Whatever had briefly drawn Mr Conrad into dark thoughts now seemed to be gone and we passed the rest of our time as usual–except that I had to struggle to keep my mind off of our upcoming date and my audition with Anthony Vaughn.

At home that evening, buttons were once more strained to the breaking point as I told my parents about the concert and my audition on Valentine's Day. I saved the news for the dinner table so that all the family could hear. Since Teddy was also present, he wouldn't have to wait for the story.

"That's wonderful!" Mommy squealed with excitement and bounced in her chair. "Absolutely wonderful!"

"My goodness!" said Daddy, smiling with delight. "This could be an opportunity for you to go places and meet people, Janette. Who knows where this might take you if you're accepted to join his group. Some of his soloists have gone on to do very well as popular recording artists."

"I know. I've thought about that. But if Mr Vaughn wants me, it'll mean postponing college for a while. I couldn't travel and go to school, too."

"Well, don't worry about that. We can work something out, I'm sure."

"Janette," said Mommy. "As soon as possible we're going to shop for a new dress for that concert."

"I don't think I need a new dress," I said.

"Janette in a dress?" Teddy joked. "I'd like to see that."

"Be careful, Molloy," I told him. "I've been working out on the speed bag that Daddy got me, and I'm getting good."

While we chattered about the details and the possibilities surrounding my audition, Teddy grew quiet and seemed to withdraw. When I finally noticed it, I was stunned and very disappointed that he wasn't happy for me like everyone else. After dinner, on our way to rehearsal, I asked him about it.

"Teddy, what's the matter with you? I get the feeling you don't think my audition is such a good thing."

"Well, I'm not sure that I do."

"But why?"

"Oh, a couple of reasons. For one, if you get accepted you'll be singing for Anthony Vaughn instead of using your voice to share the Gospel. Now, ministering in music is what you really want to do, and I happen to think it's what you should do. But the other reason I have is purely selfish."

"Oh, yeah?"

"When you started talking about traveling around the world, I realized that I wouldn't see you anymore, and I've gotten kind of used to having you around. We're like shipmates, you know."

"But I'll come home some time."

"Yes, but your home is here. Mine is in Chicago."

Even though I'd always known that Teddy would someday return to Illinois, this was the first time I considered what it would be like without him. He had become such a fixture in my world and my attachment to him was very strong. I didn't like the idea of being apart from him indefinitely, but then our lives were ultimately headed in different directions, since he was a priest. It wasn't pleasant to think that what we had now was only temporary, especially while our relationship felt eternal. But given the circumstances, our separation couldn't be helped. Unless he'd up and decide to leave the Church of Rome, it was something we'd both have to learn to live with.

On one hand, this concern made me want to latch on tighter to my priestly friend, while on the other hand it made me cautious. If his church should happen to ship him off to some remote corner of the world, then the best we could do would be to write letters, and how long would that last? But if he stayed in the Chicago area, there was always the chance that I could visit him. After all, I did have family there.

That evening, as I got ready for bed, I conveyed my thoughts and feelings to the Lord. His response almost made me wish I hadn't. With the pain I was already going through over David Conrad, I was prone to take the attitude of caution with Teddy. Instead I got hit with an outpouring of God's love for the man that would make it extremely difficult, if not impossible, to shut him out of my heart.

WEDNESDAY, JANUARY 29:

While preparing to face the day, I determined to enjoy both of my men. It was almost funny. The one I wanted was a man I probably could but shouldn't have–either as boyfriend or husband. The other man seemed much more available and desirable (in a practical sense) and yet wasn't really available at all. But accepting my peculiar circumstances brought peace, until I reached the campus and suddenly wanted to hide from my Mr Conrad. Then while I hesitated, I lost the opportunity.

From a few feet away came the sound of his footsteps. I turned to see my teacher approach carrying two pastry boxes tied with string. *"Bon jour, ma petite chérie,"* he said, smiling. "Let's study up in the room this morning."

I made no reply and simply followed along.

He'd brought a Thermos of hot coffee in his briefcase. The pastry boxes held an assortment of sopapillas, some with meat and cheese, while others were sugary.

"I hope you don't mind," he said as he laid things out on his desk. "I just wasn't in the mood to have other people around us this morning. I thought it would be nice for a change so that we could relax and say whatever we want however we want. Frankly, I'd prefer this every morning, but–well, people might make trouble if they found out."

"Did you bring cream?"

"Uh–there's powdered milk in the cabinet there, and sugar. I'll get it."

Once we were settled (I sat next to him at the table which extended his desk), we said virtually nothing to each other. Somehow there was comfort and warmth in the silence. Now I was glad we were together alone. I could look at him and enjoy him without concern for what anyone might think. He was right. And in the quiet and peace, all my anxiety faded and I found myself wondering why I'd ever felt that way.

"See? Isn't this nice? Here, baby, take another napkin."

"Yes, it is nice."

"And it's the closest thing to a date I've had in about two months. See? You've tamed me; made me behave."

"Me?"

"Sure. Who else? All I can say is that I'm glad that you did. I wasn't a very happy man. I still have a ways to go, but I am happier now."

"I'm glad of that."

"Are you happy, sweetheart?"

I didn't respond right away, a little afraid of my answer. Shortly, though, I smiled and said, "Yes. Yes, I'm happy."

"Good. That's what I want to hear, and it's what I want to see. You mean a lot to me."

As you can imagine, I was completely disarmed and nearly ready to throw my doubts away about loving him. And any minute I expected him to come kiss me and say that he loved me. Instead. . . .

"Janette–oh, no, maybe I shouldn't mention it."

"What?"

"Well–" He sighed and his smile faded. "This is going to sound rather silly coming from me, but I'm pretty desperate, so I was thinking you might talk to God for me."

"Okay." I reached for another pastry, took a bite and prepared to listen.

Mr C lowered his head for a moment, then looked at me with a plaintive expression. "Janette, there's a–a certain young woman that I've been interested in for quite some time, but the situation is very awkward. She's much younger than I am and she's deeply religious. I didn't dare come on strong and chase her off, so I've tried subtler ways to let her know how I feel. I'd like to be a little more direct in my approach, but I just can't seem to get up the nerve. I know that she has feelings for me, but I'm terrified that, even if she does care, she'll reject me. If she'd accept me, I'd ask her to marry me. So if you'll pray for me, maybe I'll get the miracle I need."

Out of his entire declaration, the only words that really registered were in the first sentence, and that was enough to shoot me down. Crushed was how I felt. Exactly as if I'd been flattened by a steamroller. One moment I was at the top of the world, my name the only one on his love list because all the others had been eliminated. I was the one he kept around. I was his "sweetheart," his "baby," and it looked like the dream might come true. But it just wasn't meant to be.

At first I was too stunned to cry, nor could I move. I sat expressionless while he spoke, working desperately to hold on to sobriety. It didn't work. The power for speech left me and I felt my head spinning slowly as emotions began to rise, threatening tears and sobbing. I gripped the edges of my chair and did my best, but at last the tears began to appear and flow down my cheeks. Finally I could move enough to lower my head and turn to the side away from him. Finding a napkin, I shoved my face into it.

"Janette? Honey, what–what's the matter?" With his hand on my shoulder, he turned me a little in his direction, though I resisted. "Are you crying?"

Stop it, Janette! Somebody could walk in on this scene. That did it. Seconds later the upheaval subsided and on the outside, at least, I was only a little shaky. "I-I, uh, I–"

"Honey?"

Don't call me that!!! The bite I'd taken now stuck in my throat, so I stood up and patted my chest.

"Did you swallow wrong or something?" He got to his feet, but when he reached for me I held up my hand. "Can you breathe?"

It took a moment, but I managed to calm down enough to swallow. "Uh, yeah. I'm–I'm okay now."

"Thank God." As we sat down again, he reached for my hand, gave it a gentle squeeze, then gave me his handkerchief. "Would you like to read a bit now?"

"Y-yes, I'd like to read." *Well, I guess he knows now. I don't see how he couldn't after seeing me cry. And there was no mistaking that.*

It was embarrassing, and yet it made life easier to think that I no longer had to hide my feelings for this man. The day went by with only a few tears shed at lunch time, while I sat in a lonely corner, sorting things out. Then at my lessons, my Mr Conrad cured the blues with ragtime and working on the song I would perform for Anthony Vaughn. He did his best to make me laugh, and that made me love him all the more.

He wanted to keep me past my lesson time, but I was a good girl, and before he could even explain himself, I beat it out of there with some trumped up excuse. Then, desperate as I was, when I got home I ran upstairs and called Teddy just to hear his voice. Then it wasn't enough. What I needed was to see him, so I reminded him of the pool table and asked if he was in the mood for a game.

"Sure, I'd love it," he said. "But I'm getting ready now to say mass at six o'clock. It won't last long, though, so I can be there around 7:30, if not before."

"That's fine. I'll fix you a plate so you can have dinner here. I'll tell my parents and we can team up against them."

Knowing well the way to this man's heart, I made sure there would be plenty of tasty snacks waiting when he came over. Right after dinner I threw together a batch of peanut butter cookies, some easy hors d'oeuvres and then popped some popcorn.

A warm hug and a peck on the lips was becoming standard with Teddy and I. And man! Did those arms ever feel good. I almost started to bawl again, but managed to maintain my composure so that no one else would see. Had it only been Teddy around, I would have let it all out.

"So, how are you?" Teddy looked me right in the eye.

"Better, now," I said, letting my eyes tell him what I didn't dare say in front of the others.

"Well, Mr Molloy," said Daddy, reaching out to shake Teddy's hand. "Have your dinner and then let's get started."

The rest of the family came in to watch the fun. My father was a very good player and hard to beat, but Teddy was no slouch, so the contests between us were a true challenge. For a couple of hours at least, I was able to have a real good time and lose my troubles. Looking at Teddy, I again regretted that he was a priest and that things couldn't be different with us; only there was no ardor to accompany this wishful thinking. To keep it that way, I didn't entertain the thought for long.

We called it quits somewhere around ten thirty, since we all had things to do the next day. But Teddy lingered with me a while when I walked him to his car.

"I'm glad I came tonight," he said. "For several reasons. I guess it's still pretty rough going for you with that young man of yours. What's his name again?"

"David. But we're getting along okay, now. It's just that it turns out, um, that he–" A sob interrupted my words as the tears began to flow. "Uh, there is another girl. . . . I f-found that out today and–it's been sort of painful to deal with."

"Come here, mate." He pulled me to his chest and held me with tenderness as I vented my anguish. While gently caressing me, he began praying in the Spirit.

What happened next was odd. First the tone of his prayer reflected comfort for my torment. He placed a hand on my head with an anointing so powerful that it went through my body like a bolt of lightening. Seconds later he began to laugh. And he kept on laughing. Raising my head, I demanded to know what the revelation was that changed his mood.

"I have absolutely no idea," he replied. "But while I prayed, this tremendous power came, and I got this–this huge dose of joy." He paused a second or two and prayed silently. "I don't know what's going to happen, Jenny, but God has a big, big blessing in store for you. And it'll be soon. Very soon."

"Really?"

"Yes, like in the next couple of weeks or so. Uh, huh. I feel like it's already happened."

THURSDAY, JANUARY 30:

Unless it had to do with my up coming audition on the fourteenth, I couldn't for the life of me imagine what was about to come down, so I quickly pigeonholed what Teddy had said. Then the next day, I slept later than usual and came into class the same time as everybody else. Fast approaching the end of my rope, I was in no mood for another morning of breakfast with Conrad. But it only served to make matters worse. Right after first period, my beloved teacher asked me to stay after class. When we were alone, he closed the door.

"Where were you this morning?" he asked, his tone quiet and even.

"I–I wasn't feeling up to coming in early," I said after a moment or two. "I have been staying out late quite a bit."

"Going to rehearsals and whatnot?"

"Yes."

"I see. Are you sure you're not angry with me?"

"Oh, no. I'm not–"

"Look at me."

Up to that point I'd been avoiding his gaze, but now I didn't dare. Literally gritting my teeth, I stiffened my spine and got a grip on my emotions before looking at him straight on. I nearly lost it, though, for the brief moment when he touched my hair and then my cheek.

"Janette, it upsets me to see you like this. If there's something troubling you or if you're not feeling well, then I wish you'd tell me. Call me at home if you like, but don't just disappear. Now, you stop this burning the candle at both ends and take care of yourself."

"I'll–I'll try."

"I hope so. I want you in good shape for your audition. Well, do you think I'll see you at breakfast tomorrow?"

"Yes." My weak reply was barely audible, but that made no difference to him.

"Good," he said as if he felt he'd persuaded me. "And I hope to see your lovely smile again. I miss it." He looked as if he wanted to say something more, but didn't. Instead he smiled lovingly down at me with a twinkle in his eye as if he knew something I didn't.

The tardy excuse for my next class had already been written out, so he just placed it in my hand. As I took it, our hands touched for a brief second, and I left feeling indescribably low. I fell into a stupor, and for the first time in years I was tempted to go out and get totally plastered.

Midway through second period, I got permission to go to the nurse. The way I looked, it didn't take much to convince anybody that I was sick. I went home and dug out a bottle of my mother's sleeping pills, took half of one and went to bed until time for dinner. The next day I stayed home from school all together.

I had to be in pretty bad shape not to care whether or not I saw Teddy, but I called and told him that I wasn't coming to rehearsal. When I hung up the phone I laughed sardonically. Hadn't Mr Conrad told me to stop staying out late? Well, it was what I had done. Instead I spent the evening wrapped up in a blanket watching television with the family for an hour or so and then crashing early to the tune of another sleeping pill.

FRIDAY, JANUARY 31:

And did I turn up happy and smiling for my man on Friday? Not on your life. I stayed home "sick" again and spent the time with some old friends known as record albums and books. Most of them had gone by the wayside because of my busy schedule, so I sat alone in my room and traveled the realm of imagination, escaping for the time being from my hopeless love for The Fox. After a few hours of soaking my psyche in suspense and good humor, I did feel a lot less blue. By lunch time my head was much clearer, and I was starting to feel I could face the situation for at least a little while longer. Maybe a little physical rest was just what I needed.

Still I didn't elude him entirely. Late that afternoon he called to check on me. Fortunately someone else got to the phone before I could, so he only spoke to my mother who gave him the news on my health. She was delighted to have him so concerned, but my feelings were mixed.

Teddy also called that afternoon to see how I was doing and if I'd be at services. I said that I would and promised to be in good spirits. Still it was tough going. Even though the Lord in his love and mercy was present to sustain me, it was as if he gave me just enough to keep my head above water. Not at all like the powerful outflow of his spirit last fall when those evil boys were after me. But it was better than nothing. Anxiety lessened with the lighting of my Sabbath candles and the time spent opening my heart to the Lord before going out. Then at church, the meeting and the time spent ministering on the street both lifted my spirits back up to joyful.

SUNDAY, FEBRUARY 2:
Then on Sunday I got something else for my heart and head to deal with. Teddy came for dinner and was intent on keeping me cheerful. First of all, he insisted on helping with the dishes. He washed, I rinsed and dried, while Charlotte also dried and put things away. No sooner had my mind started to drift into dangerous territory than Teddy began to sing.

"'This is my father's world,'" he began, then stopped. "Help me out, Jenny. I can't remember all the words."

It was one of my favorite hymns, and I joined in gladly. We soon split up into harmony and the effect made Charlotte stop working and just listen for a bit.

After the second verse of that song, we started on another hymn. Soon the rest of the family had come into the kitchen and diningroom to listen. They tried to give us requests, but Teddy only knew the ones he had learned for services at The Rock, so we stuck with what we could sing together.

When the dishes were done, Teddy and I went outside with the rest of the kids to enjoy the day and play some games.

"How about dolly head?" asked Gregory.

"What did you say?" asked Teddy.

"Dolly head," he repeated.

"Yeah, dolly head," said Olivia. "Go get it, Gregory."

"It's really just a game of tag," I explained. "What we do is use an old doll's head to hit each other with instead of our hands. When the hair's all gone and we can't use that any more, then the game becomes dolly arm or dolly leg or whatever we've got left–including the torso."

Teddy laughed. "Sounds like fun. A little warped, but fun."

To initiate Teddy, we made him be "it" first. But his feet were fast and his aim deadly. He got Charlotte in just a few minutes and then she had to take the head and run.

There were some pretty good places to hide in our back yard, such as the lilacs and other bushes growing along the fence and garage. The only problem was that if one picked the wrong part of the yard to hide in like Teddy did, Panqué, the neighbor's dog, would come bark at you and give you away.

Now I was it. The blue eyes went click-click in the old doll's head as I went running for a victim. Amelia dodged out of the way as the hairy plastic sphere went flying at her. She took off running before I could retrieve it, but the sound of a barking dog told me where I could find someone else.

"Gotcha!" Parting the branches of a bush, I tagged Teddy.

"Doggonit," he said and took hold of the matted blonde hair. "That stupid mutt gave me away."

"Panqué always does that," I remarked. "He also gets a real kick out of sneaking up on us and scaring us half to death."

"Well, I know a way to fix his wagon."

Teddy dropped the doll's head and went into the house. He came back in a few minutes with a table spoon from the kitchen with something on it.

"Here, doggie. Here, Panqué." Teddy leaned over the chain link fence and beckoned to the reddish-brown, short haired hunting dog.

"What's that on the spoon?" I asked.

"Peanut butter."

As the hound leaped and barked, Teddy pushed the creamy paste off the spoon and onto the dog's long pointed snout. He went for it.

"What's going on?" asked Daniel. He and Amelia came and joined us at the fence.

"Watch," said Teddy.

Panqué had a very difficult time ingesting the large glob of peanut butter. It stuck to the roof of his mouth and the results were hilarious. Before too long, the others came out of hiding and joined us. We laughed hysterically while watching the dog's efforts to dislodge the food.

"Come on, you guys," said Olivia after watching for a few minutes. "Let's play some more."

"Not me," said Teddy. "I've had enough."

"Aw, come on," said Gregory.

But Teddy begged off and I was going to quit with him. As it was, they decided on another pastime, one that took them to the sidewalk in front of the house.

"Come talk to me," said Teddy and led me around back of the garage. We sat down on the sparse grass underneath the giant fig tree that grew there. Here we were out of the wind and away from the others. He sat for a minute or so in silence, absentmindedly pulling at the grass while putting his thoughts together. Knowing it must be something rather important, I waited patiently and prayed quietly in the Spirit.

"Jenny, what do you think of us? You know, the way God has teamed us up and–and the way we get along so well?"

"I think it's wonderful. Miraculous, even."

"Do you think what we have is worth keeping?"

"I never thought of it, but sure."

"Well, so do I. The thing is, though, that I won't be settling down in Albuquerque. Oh, I'll be here at least until August, but then I'll have to go back to Chicago. Janette–I know it's a lot to ask, but when I do go back, I'd like to take you with me."

The world seemed to turn upside down and then rock back into place. My head grew light and my body strangely warm as Teddy's words echoed in my mind. My first assumption was that this was a marriage proposal, and yet somehow it didn't jive. Rather than try to respond right away, I thought it best to be quiet and give him a chance to explain further.

"Look," he went on. "I know you've got plans for college, and then there's that audition with Anthony Vaughn. But just listen to me for a minute and think about this. You know as well as I do that this–this partnership God has given us is something that's very, very out of the ordinary. It's not like anything you'd even dream about because you never imagined it could exist. It's a beautiful gift from God, Jenny, and I want to hang on to it. I believe we need to because we're not going to find this again. Look, if you go with me, then we can keep on with our ministry and do even more–including fun stuff, like sailing. The transition won't be easy because the setup will be different, and also because you're not Catholic. But if we work together on it, I'm sure we can pull it off. I was thinking that you could go to college in the Chicago area, since you've wanted to go out of state. But before school starts, what I'd like is for you to try a convent for a while, at least for the summer. My sister Theresa is in a very good one in the area; it's a progressive teaching order. I'm sure that something could be worked out for you to spend some time there and get the feel of the religious life. Maybe you'll find that you like the concept of being married only to Christ. The Church is changing; and it's changing for the better, mate. And if we take advantage of this season of transformation, a lot can be done to bring the message of salvation and the Holy Spirit to Catholics like me who've never understood it before. But whether you like the convent or not, if you come with me, I promise I'll take good care of you. If I can help it, you won't ever want for anything. Would you come with me? Please?"

Well, a marriage proposal it wasn't. Now I understood all those little hints he'd been dropping about my converting to Catholicism. But that wasn't about to happen, and I wouldn't dream of taking the veil. Maybe he felt the call to be eternally celibate, but HaShem had yet to speak to me along those lines. On the other hand, how could I not say yes? He was certainly right about what God had given us. It was not an everyday thing and not something I wanted to lose, either. Traveling the globe with Anthony Vaughn would be fun and maybe even lucrative; a big career in music could very well come out of it. But that wasn't a sure thing, especially if God didn't want it. Nor would it ever take me to the heights that ministering with Teddy did, and that was a sure thing. I loved this man, and I knew we could have a great time bringing people into God's kingdom. As long as he didn't really expect me to become a nun, why not go?

Further thought brought me to the realization that Teddy's proposition could be the answer to the whole problem with David Conrad, for the time being as well as in the future. As long as I was even in the same town with that man, I would be hard pressed to get free of my love for him. But living in Chicago with a whole new experience to deal with, plus having Teddy as my closest companion, it wouldn't take long at all. Then in the meantime, it would give me something else to think about, to plan for and to dream about that would eventually push David Conrad out of my heart–or at least take him down a peg or two.

Yes. I would go. Unless God showed me otherwise, or my parents raised a big stink over it, there was no reason why not. I could make tentative plans and start looking into what some of the universities in that area had to offer, pick the best one for my major and apply. This could be a wonderful adventure. I would be in a big city with so much more to see and do, and I'd have family nearby. Considering how much my parents liked Teddy, it was doubtful there would be much of a problem in getting them to agree to it.

He watched me and waited hopefully. In the fading sunlight of the afternoon, Teddy's hazel eyes had turned a soft and beautiful shade of blue. Those eyes looked intently into mine and seemed to peer inside my soul. That alone made it next to impossible to decline his offer. Looking back at him with an open heart, I gave him my answer.

"Teddy, I would love to go with you to Chicago."

"You–you mean it? You'd really go with me?"

"Sure, why not? There's nothing holding me here. The Anthony Vaughn thing may or may not pan out, but I'd much rather minister anyway. Of course I'll have to get my parents' approval, but if you can hang on here in Albuquerque at least until the end of June, maybe we can go together."

"Praise God!" He threw his arms around me and buried his face in my hair. "Oh, Jenny, thank you. Thank you so much! I promise you won't regret it. Oh, God! Oh, thank you Jesus!"

MONDAY, FEB. 3 -- THURSDAY, FEB. 6:

"Chicago!" As I said the word I tried to bring to mind all I'd seen and heard about the place as a child. But soon all of the images faded from my thoughts as I heard that familiar footfall and it was time for the old breakfast routine.

Happy and smiling: that's what my man had asked for and that's what he got. I had decided that the only way I could do it and avoid his prying into my emotional state was to simply indulge my feelings of love for him and imagine that he was in love with me. Of course, that didn't mean I gave him longing looks. Everything on the surface was to be back to normal. That, however, was only for the moments when it was just the two of us. Otherwise I drew my happiness from thoughts of Teddy and our adventures in ministry–especially the Chicago adventure. It was even on my heart to mention something of it to Mr C and ask if he knew a college in the area with a good music department. But feeling a check in my spirit, I decided to ask Mr Johnson instead. At lunch time I ducked into his room and told him, without mention of Teddy, that I would like to look at Illinois for higher learning, the Chicago area in particular. With some knowledge of that neck of the woods, he gave me the names of a couple of universities with excellent music programs.

So things overall were starting to go smoothly. It only got rough at my lesson on Wednesday. Mr Conrad just had to sit next to me on the piano bench and demonstrate a thing or two. Then he just had to make sure my posture was perfect when singing, and saw fit to make the adjustments personally! That took me a good while to recover from, but then thoughts of my beloved Theodore helped me bounce back.

The idea was for me to wait before mentioning anything to my parents about going to Chicago until our plans were well laid out, and until my family got to know Teddy a bit better. He came around even more now, which was a blessing and a delight. Having his company to look forward to is what got me through every school day. On Monday he'd shown up again in the afternoon, this time to give the sedan a tune up and oil change. Afterwards we played pool. Tuesday had, of course, been rehearsal at The Rock, but instead of being at my house just for dinner, he came an hour early and gave me another boxing lesson. Wednesday we went out to the ADG firing range where I taught him to use a handgun, which speeded up my recovery from what I'd endured that afternoon at my lessons. After that, we spent an hour or so in the Scriptures over at Drake's. Thursday night was, of course, rehearsal at St Basil's. I stayed afterward and we went out for a ride in the desert. There under the starry sky we had a nice long talk, mostly about Chicago and life in a convent. That was only a warm up for what would happen Friday night.

FRIDAY EVENING, FEBRUARY 7:
Even though the weather was good, things seemed slower than usual out on the streets. Teddy and I had only talked to a handful of people, compared to the usual numbers. It seemed odd to both of us, and a little frustrating.

"Mind if we check in early?" asked Teddy. "It's slow tonight, and I want to talk to you about some things, anyway."

"Sure, mate, go ahead," I replied.

After calling home base to tell them we were off for the evening, we went back to the church for the Chevy and then took off again for what was becoming our favorite spot: the vista point west of town.

The evening grew even colder, but that was nothing to my Chicago man. At our destination, he got out and stood in front of the car and looked down on the lights that spread as far south as Las Lunas. The light breeze caught his golden curls which hadn't seen a razor since mid December. I huddled near him, perched on the bumper and wrapped up in an old blanket which he kept in the back seat. I only pretended to look at the lights. It was Teddy I wanted to see. After a while he stopped watching them, too, looking past them as his thoughts carried him far away.

"Well, I've been putting this off all week," he finally said. "But I can't put it off any longer. Since you're going with me to Chicago, I might as well tell you what to expect concerning my family. You won't meet them right away, but you will eventually."

Though it appeared at first that his purpose was to provide information, before long I found myself in the role that Teddy held as a priest of Rome–the confessor. As he took me down the lane of his memories I heard about his beautiful and saintly mother, his bigoted and opinionated father, his boisterous brothers, and sweet and sour sisters. Along the way he related to me that his father and the poisons of the local culture had sullied his young soul in spite of his mother's efforts to instill within them all a higher sense of purpose. Fortunately her work wasn't entirely in vain, which was why Teddy was able to judge the evil in his own heart for what it was.

Sensing the depth of regret and repentance underlying his talk, I got up, wrapped my arms around him and hugged him a good one. While returning my affection Teddy felt how I shivered and rubbed some warmth into my back and shoulders.

"Let's go to the car," he said. "You might catch cold."

With a blanket on my legs and Teddy's arms to keep me warm, I leaned happily against him and heard even more of his confession. As he digressed further and I asked questions, I also became privy to details of the struggles of his seminary years at a place called Mundelein. There Teddy had nearly killed a man because of the rage built up inside him from disappointment and frustration over his inability to adjust to the peculiar life and disciplines necessary to becoming a priest. Terribly homesick and not finding the spiritual depth he had imagined his training would impart, it was reaching the end of himself that had caused him to cry out to God from the depths of his being. God's answer to that desperate prayer marked the beginning of his journey into the spiritual life he had always longed for. Not only did he find a great measure of inner peace that he'd never known before, it opened his eyes to God's method of dealing with his old ways of thinking by bringing answered prayer through distasteful means–such as the half breed Japanese man he met at Mundelein, street singing Jesus freaks from Rock of the Witness, and a certain young black girl with a vintage Indian motorcycle.

"You've been through a lot of changes," I said as it seemed he had reached the end of his stories.

"It felt like a hundred miles of bad road, but you have no idea how thankful I am. Looking back, I can see how my path was clearly marked, but on the way here, I couldn't see past my nose. God even used my foolishness as a benefit. If I hadn't gone through such hell with my first two assignments, not only would I not have come here, I'd probably still be so full of myself that I'd never have received what God had for me. I was sick with humiliation over having to come to this town. And just like I knew I would, I hated it here the first couple of months. The city, the culture, the diocese; this is like being in a third world country."

"It almost is in some respects. Why do you think I want out?"

"Well, stick with me, mate, and there'll be ports of call a plenty; I'll see to that. Oh, Albuquerque isn't so bad now, especially since I found The Rock and you, but I have to admit that I'm anxious to get back to Illinois and get something happening on a larger scale. I'm not quite sure how it'll work, but I really get excited about you going back with me. God has given the two of us something so amazing, babe. I don't know how, but it needs to be shared with other people."

I wasn't so sure about that. What was developing between us was like nothing I'd ever heard of, and the more time we spent together, the stronger–and the stranger–it got. Too often did we finish each other's thoughts or begin singing the same song at the same time in the same key. But what really shook me up were the things that were starting to happen in our dreams, not to mention when we were awake. If we couldn't understand it, how on earth could it be explained to anybody else? While Teddy was hot to trot, I was more than willing to keep it as our business and nobody else's.

SATURDAY, FEBRUARY 8:

Saturday morning I awoke from a series of peculiar and troubling dreams. Although Chicago and the Molloy clan had been the subject in my thoughts when I climbed into bed, none of those things figured into the rambling sequence of stories that ran through my head once I slept. Instead David Conrad was the focal point, and this theme continued the entire night. Because I preferred not to have my waking hours filled with thoughts of my teacher, I ignored the desire to consider what significance the dreams might have. Then when he chased me and wooed me again on Saturday night and into Sunday morning, I began to wonder if God was trying to tell me something. But with mass at St Basil's and Teddy's company to enjoy, on Sunday morning I shoved the dreams aside for a love that was far less painful to ponder.

SUNDAY, FEBRUARY 9:

"Do it again! Do it again!"

Teddy stood in front of the garage with one sleeve ripped open while the kids yelled for more. Lifting the other arm, he repeated his performance, flexing his muscles until the blue cotton fabric ripped.

"Wanna see more?" he asked.

"Yeah! More! More!" the children cried.

This time he pumped up all the muscles in his torso and the shirt ripped wide open both front and back.

"Wow! That's neat!" said Adrian. "Wish I could do that."

"Eat all your vegetables and maybe you will someday." Teddy pulled the remains of the shirt from his body. He threw it at Adrian and it covered the boy's head.

Now all that clothed Teddy's hairless chest was his athletic shirt. The kids oooh'd and ah'd at his well-defined muscles, so he flexed and posed for them, then let the smaller ones dangle from his arms. It made me wish I were younger.

"Me next," I said.

Teddy scowled. "Aw, get outta here. You're too big."

"Not for a big, strong muscle man like you. Please?"

"No! Now cut it out."

Soon Teddy put on another shirt and we went on with other things. A few of the neighborhood kids had joined us that afternoon and we played our usual games. Some had a marble game going, while the rest jumped rope a short distance away.

The outer screen door of the covered back porch opened, and Daddy stood there for a while watching us play. After several moments passed, he beckoned to Teddy and the two men went inside the house. I didn't think much about it and went on playing. But when Teddy didn't come back after a reasonable amount of time, I began to wonder why.

At last it was getting dark and a cold wind was blowing. Time to go inside and Teddy still hadn't returned. As soon as I got in the house, I went to find him. He and Daddy were just coming out of the family room as I went there to seek him out.

Teddy's expression was sober and pensive. He gave half a smile upon seeing me, then looked somewhat bewildered.

"What were you two talking about?" I asked in a soft voice, while Daddy headed upstairs.

Hesitating, he rubbed his chin and said, "Let's go out front and talk."

I grabbed a jacket from the hall closet and we went to sit on the front porch. There in the dim yellow light, I listened to a strange tale.

My parents were convinced that he and I were very much in love. The talk this afternoon happened because Daddy had wanted to know just what Teddy's intentions were. He had tried his best to convince Daddy that there was no romance between us, but without success. After all, he and I were together almost every day, we were very affectionate and often kissed each other; then there was that joy and happiness that often showed in our eyes when we looked at each other. All of the signs were there, Daddy had said, and whether we knew it or not, or whether or not we were willing to admit it, Teddy and I were in love.

Since Teddy had not been willing to fess up to our amour, Daddy went on and tried to sell him on the good points of the two of us getting married. Teddy then countered with the obstacles involved in his being a priest, of the problems of dealing with his family, *etc.,* which were some of the reasons why he had no desire to have a wife right now, if ever. Daddy then insisted that there were ways of handling those problems if enough time and effort were taken to work things out. He, of course, was more than willing to help in any way possible, if Teddy should decide to change his mind and marry me. On that note the discussion had ended.

"Oh, Theodore!" I cried, taking his hand. "I'm so sorry. Somehow I never dreamed this kind of thing would happen."

"Well, mate, it's really flattering in a way," he said. "Your father's a fine man, and for him to think well enough of me to want me to marry his daughter–well, I have to say that I feel honored. Now, Jenny, I don't want to say anything to hurt you, but even as strong as my feelings are for you–"

"Look, it's okay. Besides, I'm not in love with you, either."

"Thanks, mate. I just wish your father could understand. I'd have taken the opportunity to mention you going to Chicago with me, except that I was afraid he'd see that as the perfect reason for us getting hitched. It'd cause much more trouble than I'm able to handle right now. Besides, I like things just the way they are. It's like being a kid all over again, and a love affair would only spoil it. It'd spoil the–the purity and innocence and bring in all kinds of problems and fear and worry. But–even if I wanted to marry you, as deeply as I've come to love you, it still wouldn't be an easy situation: struggling along to build a ministry with the possibility of having a family, too. . . . Just thinking about it for too long ties my stomach in knots. And what if I never could see my mother and father again? If I got married and left the priesthood, they'd be ashamed of me. The whole family would. And it would bring shame on them. I couldn't do that. Celibacy is the only way."

"Look, don't let this bother you. It's really not that serious. So what if my folks don't understand what God is doing with us. At least they're not trying to keep us apart."

"Yeah, you're right about that."

"Besides, what would I want to marry you for?"

"And what's wrong with me?"

"Well, first of all, you haven't got much money, so how could you support me? I have expensive tastes, you know."

"Okay."

"And we would probably clash quite a bit over religion."

"That's possible."

"But the main thing is that I just don't think I could handle having kids as funny looking as you are."

"Why you little–"

"Ow!" Teddy's reaction was to slap me on the side of my head and shove me off the bench. I lay there glaring up at him in mock anger. "Wife beater," I growled.

"And you know what else?" Teddy got up and stood over me. "It just so happens that I've got a fair amount of cash set aside. But if you want fancy things, you can earn the money for them yourself like my mother did."

"Well, knowing you, you'll want to keep on being a priest and hide our marriage in the closet. Why don't you go out and get a real job, you deadbeat!" I grabbed his legs and yanked them out from under him. Teddy sat down awfully hard on the porch. He didn't cry out very loud but the face he made told me that he was not a happy man. "Oh! Teddy, I'm so sorry! I didn't mean to hurt you. Are you okay?"

"No, I'm not okay. That hurt!"

I scrambled to my feet and offered him a hand up. He got a firm grip and then yanked me down. Pulling me crosswise over him, Teddy held me down and spanked my bottom. It hurt like the dickens.

"Ow! Let me go!" Squirming with all my might did not set me free, and my arms were in such a position that I could not hit back. "Stop! Ow!"

"I'm surprised you can even feel it with all the padding you've got. Call me a deadbeat, will ya?" He paused for a moment and just held me down. "Say uncle."

"I will not!"

"Better say it." He hit me again, harder.

"Ow! Okay. Uncle!" He released me, but I took my time getting up. "Now I sure ain't gonna marry you."

"Well, that's all right by me."

"You wanna go watch TV?" Again I offered him a hand up, knowing the fooling was over.

"Sure." Teddy pulled himself up and then looked at his watch. "Ed Sullivan ought to be on about now."

As we all sat around the big TV, my thoughts were divided. This thing about Teddy and me getting married had been under my skin even before Daddy had called him on the carpet. Again I asked myself if I was falling in love with him. The answer was still no. Teddy was a wonderful man, but not quite the man I was looking for–yet. That he could become that man, I had no doubt, but it would certainly take a while. But the more I thought of going to Chicago and the more concrete my plans became, I couldn't get away from the feeling that if I made the trip, eventually it would happen. I would fall hopelessly in love with a man that didn't want to get married.

Going through the possibilities in my mind made me realize the direction things would naturally go. Once Mr C was out of the picture, how could I be strong enough to keep my love for Teddy from turning into something deeper? So much about him was attractive. Unless I stayed with family, once I was far away from home, there wouldn't be anyone else but him for good times and intimate conversations. He would be the center of my social life. How would I be able to resist the desire for more than friendship with such a strong affection between us, especially after the void left by David Conrad?

This was not a happy prospect. Sure, men like Teddy didn't come along every day, but he didn't want me, at least not now. And in light of what he had just told me, chances weren't good for him falling in love with me at all. It could be just as agonizing as what I was going through over The Fox, and I wasn't about to go through that again. So maybe going to Chicago wasn't such a hot idea after all. It would break Teddy's heart if I didn't go, but that would just be too bad. Unless something could be worked out so that I wouldn't have such a dilemma, that's the way it would have to be.

That night, after Teddy was gone and everyone else was in bed, there was only one conclusion I could come to. If I was going to Chicago to stay, then I'd better plan on changing his mind about marriage. That meant working to make myself more attractive to him in order to give myself the edge and the confidence that he'd want me as much as I would come to want him. Then once the relationship was on a more intimate level, waiting on him to learn certain things wouldn't be a problem. I could wait years, as long as I knew that he loved and wanted me. That was, of course, if I stayed beyond the summer months. Remembering what God had said from the beginning about hands off with any romance made me think that to do so wouldn't be kosher. It was possible that even going for the summer might prove dangerous in that regard. A lot could happen in just a few months. A lot already had.

So I had an idea of what to expect if I went, and I knew that it probably wasn't smart, even short term. But then I thought about not going. What would I do if I didn't? I wasn't about to stay in Albuquerque as long as David Conrad was there. I just had to go away to school. Then I thought about not seeing Teddy anymore. Already he was so much a part of me that it felt strange to think of being without him. What we had was a rarity and to throw it away would be foolish. Just the thought of being apart from him for who only knows how long gnawed painfully at my insides.

As I lay in the dark, weeping over this tortuous puzzle, I began to think that maybe the reason why romance was off limits with Teddy was just to give him time to get grounded in spiritual things without the complications of a love affair. Perhaps there would be no problem if it were to happen at a later date when he was more stable and mature. Maybe he was even God's provision for what I couldn't have with The Fox. He might even be the man HaShem had picked out for me to match up with that list I'd made. He did come frighteningly close, and in my estimation, only a little time was needed to make us more suitable for each other.

I let myself imagine what it would be like in the clinches with Teddy, which was easy to do, given the affection we already shared. But when compared to David Conrad, my strong and handsome priest didn't turn me on to the same degree. But he was better than nothing, and better than a lot of men, I was sure. Certainly I could learn to love him as much as I did my reformed playboy. (That is, if he truly was reformed.) Also, a permanent relationship with Teddy seemed more attainable. It might take some doing but it could be done.

It was time my parents knew about the Chicago plans, and time I had a little talk with my mother to get some womanly wisdom from her. After all, dealing with grown men was still new territory for me. Then in the meantime I would pull a few things from my own bag of feminine mystique to see what would happen. Subtly and gradually I would change to see how Teddy would react, starting with Tuesday night rehearsal. If he got wise to what I was doing, he'd probably be gone in a heartbeat. The heat had to be turned up slowly so that he didn't notice the temperature change. Then I'd find out just how badly this priest wanted to stay celibate.

WEDNESDAY, FEBRUARY 12:
"You'll do fine on Friday." Mr Conrad turned to me from where he sat on the piano bench at the end of my lesson hour. "You know, I didn't realize it, but with that being Valentine's Day, I must be keeping you from a hot date with one of your boyfriends."

"Oh, no, it's nothing. Alan asked me out, but I'd have said no anyway. I don't want to encourage him."

"Come here. Let me see your hands." When I did as he asked, he looked them over, then took hold of them, pulled me a bit closer and gently rubbed my fingers. "Can you find the time to get a manicure before Friday?"

"Uh–uh, s-sure. Tomorrow . . . after school."

"Good. Well, that's all for today. I'll see you tomorrow."

Once he'd let go, I slowly collected everything but myself and somehow made it out the door, still feeling the warmth of his touch and wondering why he had to be so affectionate and yet hadn't gone a step further. Now the prospect of Teddy Molloy seemed flat as a warm soda without the fizz.

And speaking of which, things had gone well Tuesday night with my plans to undermine my partner's priestly vows. Although I now had no interest, I knew the feeling might pass, so I took the opportunity to talk to my parents that Wednesday night while Teddy wasn't around. My mother wasn't feeling well due to a queasy stomach, so we had to gather in their bedroom. When I told them about him wanting me to go with him to Chicago, they both laughed out loud.

"Say what?" Mommy said with a puzzled smile. "And he says he's not sweet on you!"

"Well, if he'd just marry you," said Daddy. "He could take you to Chicago or any place else he wants you to go. But he shouldn't expect you to follow him around just on G.P. Maybe you think you've got a platonic relationship now, but how long would that last? Especially the way you two are always hanging on each other. Janette, you can do what you want, I guess, since you'll be eighteen soon, but it wouldn't be wise to go off with him like that and not get married first."

"I feel the same way," said Mommy. "I'm sure Teddy means well, and he's nice and very religious, but–I don't know. Why don't you let your Daddy and me think about this for a little while, okay? Maybe there's a way to work things out to make sure they go in your favor."

FRIDAY, FEBRUARY 14:
Valentine's Day–at last. I'd only had plans for my audition, but romance showed up anyway. I read the card for the umpteenth time and laid it down again. Thank God, no one else had seen it. The delivery came

just as I got home from school, so all that anyone knew was that I had received an anonymous bouquet. "To the joy of my life," was printed in gold on the card's crimson cover. Inside was hand written, "Janette, for me there is no flower more beautiful or more fragrant than you, the woman I love." It pierced my soul each time I read it. There was no signature and the handwriting was not familiar enough to place. The scent of the roses it came with was intoxicating: two dozen and deepest red.

But flowers are not complete without candy. Yes, there were chocolates in a gold box, but the box was not made of paper. It was a gold music box filled with tiny heart shaped chocolates wrapped in bright red foil. Dark chocolate–my favorite!

Not knowing the identity of the sender was driving me nuts. I had done my best to trace the origin of this exquisite offering, considering how little time there was to do it in. The few phone calls I was able to make were all dead ends. Mommy and Daddy were naturally certain that Teddy had sent them. Fat chance. Even though he was warming to my little changes, I knew better than to think that. My choice had been Billy Osborn, but he wouldn't confess to it. Since there wasn't much time to pursue it, I photographed the items together and separately to preserve the memory. Then I just enjoyed the fragrance and prepared for the evening ahead.

Though I was tempted to adorn myself with my man in mind, I dressed to make a favorable impression on Anthony Vaughn. Wanting to be taken seriously, I wore just a hint of my favorite fragrance, and for a mature look, selected a simple dark green silk dress with a bateau neckline interrupted by a two inch slit; cut kind of low in the back, it had cuffed 3/4 length sleeves, tastefully hugged my curves, and the straight skirt was about 3" below the knee. My shoes were lovely black beaded pumps, and as usual, my stockings were seamed. I chose the rhinestone set Mr C had given me, which was the only thing I did with him in mind. Then my hair was pulled back from my face and into a plain French roll, with simple waves and curls atop my head. I then made a small corsage from the bouquet and added a few of the tiny buds to my hair as well. Last was a stunning champagne mink sling cape that was sent to me in January by Lydia Katzman from Aleph Tav.

We met at the UNM auditorium about twenty minutes before the show. Feeling nervous, I stood back behind my parents, while they greeted each other and chit chatted. Then my teacher drew me out.

"Janette, are you hiding from me?" he asked.

"No, here I am," I said, stepping into view.

"My! Is that you?" He looked at me with pleasant surprise.

"You were expecting Joan of Arc?"

"Not in that armor. Anthony Vaughn won't stand a chance." My parents laughed heartily over that one. "Oh, and I think I hear some knees knocking. Are you nervous?"

"I sure am."

"Then we'll have to do something about that. You sit right next to me.

I know a wonderful cure for stage fright."

We went inside the auditorium and found our seats. I settled myself between Mommy and Mr Conrad and held my breath for a moment. It was difficult to keep from trembling. I closed the fur around me to hide the shakes and tried to imagine what Conrad's cure for the jitters could be.

At last the curtain went up and the program started. The show held my attention and so I began to relax. Then at the end of the first number, Mr Conrad leaned over and whispered a silly joke in my ear. It was very funny and particularly absurd, but I didn't dare laugh out loud since the applause had died down and the next number was coming up. He did this intermittently throughout the entire first half of the show, even saying humorous things about Mr Vaughn. It did help my nerves a great deal, on both counts.

At intermission we got up to stretch our legs and make use of the facilities. In the ladies room I saw to my needs quickly and took time to warm up my voice a little while waiting for my slow moving mother who hadn't quite recovered from the stomach flu or whatever had plagued her that week. Standing near the exit, I flinched when I heard the sound of retching coming from one of the stalls. She was sick again.

It looked like the rest of the evening was ruined. Her illness meant we would have to go home. She had been more excited over this concert and audition than me, and so had Daddy; it was really a shame that it had to turn out this way.

As soon as she came out of the stall, I helped mother clean up and arrange herself neatly before going out to join the men, all the while trying to accept the fact that I wouldn't be singing for Mr Vaughn. Her sickly pallor and the discomfort in her expression confirmed the worst. Maybe this was God's way of answering the question about traveling with the Anthony Vaughn Chorale. I paused a moment to let the idea sink in and to check Mommy's dress and hair one more time. Then with one hand on her arm and the other around her waist, I let her lean on me while helping her out the door.

When Daddy saw us coming with me supporting his ailing wife, he sighed deeply and shook his head. "I knew you should have stayed home," he gently chided her as he stepped up and took her from me. Then turning to Mr Conrad, he said, "My wife hasn't been feeling well the past couple of days. I'd better get her home. If you don't mind taking Janette home afterwards, she can stay for her audition."

"I'd be more than happy to," said Mr Conrad. "I'm so sorry this happened. I do hope she'll be better soon."

"I'll take care of her," said Daddy. "I'm sure she'll be fine in a few days. She just didn't stay in bed long enough."

In a matter of minutes my parents were gone, and I was back in my seat watching the curtain rise. Pleased at being able to audition after all, I should have been happier. But left alone with Mr Conrad, that fear-inspired palsy started up in my legs again and threatened to spread to the rest of my body. With just the two of us, it wasn't so easy to lose myself in the music. The change seemed to affect my teacher as well because there weren't any more jokes, only an occasional comment. We were both rather quiet until the program was over.

"Are you ready?" he asked as the house lights went up.

"I was earlier, but–hic–I'm not too sure now. Hic! Oh, no!"

I hiccupped again and again. Holding my breath, I looked helplessly at Mr C who only sighed and looked exasperated.

"Come on," he said, rising from his seat. "We'll get you some water."

We made it to the lobby as quickly as possible and found a drinking fountain. Sipping slowly, I made every effort to calm myself. *Ah, there! Now they're g–hic!* Highly chagrined, anxiously I looked again to Mr Conrad. Sensing the degree of my distress, he quickly put his own frustrations aside and thought of a solution.

"Don't worry. We'll fix it," he said. "Come on."

Taking my hand, he pulled me along through the dispersing crowd, making me feel like a little girl as I followed his brisk footsteps. Soon we came to a door that led backstage. Turning the knob, he pushed it wide and we stepped into darkness.

With my small, trembling hands in both of his, Mr Conrad made us to stand facing each other. "Now just be still and relax," he said softly.

Just the coolness and the obscurity of the place were enough to sooth me; but in the quiet, that awful sound caused by the upheaval in my chest seemed magnified, threatening to renew panic. As my eyes adjusted to the deep shadows, I found myself staring into Mr Conrad's neck tie. The tiny point of light that was his stickpin became the focal point I used to help my concentration. Knowing I didn't dare regress, I struggled desperately to hold the little ground of calm that I had gained so far.

"Now, let's get rid of those hiccups." Mr Conrad released my hands, and reaching up, slipped his hands under my cape to rest on my shoulders. "Close your eyes, Janette. Relax."

In the split second that anxiety began a fresh upsurge, I felt his strong hands, soft and warm upon my neck and shoulders, kneading and caressing in a gentle massage. The initial shock did the trick. The annoying spasms stopped immediately. But that touch was more than I could handle, and only the urgency of the moment kept me from giving way to the usual fears and misgivings. Instead I allowed myself the pleasure of his caress and the joy of being so close to him. That killed the bad case of nerves and replaced apprehension with desire. For a split second I even started to reach for him, but the sound of his voice checked my advances.

"Janette, I want you to listen to me very carefully. I'm going to tell you something, and I want you to hear every word I say. Look at me."

Now his hands firmly braced my shoulders. I opened my eyes and fixed them on his face.

"Honey, this is only an audition. This is not going to make your career. It's not even a stepping stone. I didn't tell you this before, but Tony is not looking for any new voices for the choir right now, nor will he be any time soon. The only reason he's going to hear you sing tonight is because I asked him to, and that's all. That's it. And it's only going to last for a few lousy minutes and then it will all be over. Over and done. Do you understand what I'm saying?"

His words sobered me up considerably, and I let them sink in before I answered with, "I understand."

"Good. Now I want you to go do it and get it over with. You're very good and you know it. You have every reason to be confident. All right?"

"All right."

"Good. Now, this is for luck."

The moment I had once dreaded and yet desperately desired came at last. Slipping his arms around me, he drew me close while pressing his lips to mine in a simple, yet tender, kiss. But the two or three seconds that it lasted allowed little time for me to contemplate, respond to or even enjoy the feel of it or the warmth of his embrace. Except for evidence provided by the racing of my pulse and the spinning of my head, the moment passed so quickly that it hardly seemed real. The next thing I knew, my teacher had me by the hand and was pulling me along through the maze of backstage curtains and whatnot, until we came out onto the lighted stage where Mr Anthony Vaughn was waiting.

"Ah! There you are," said Vaughn, smiling as he arose from his chair near the piano. "I was beginning to wonder."

Tony Vaughn was a tall, heavy set, dark haired man with a beautiful beard that sported streaks of white hair running through on either side. The sight of this famous choirmaster helped me work hard to overcome the shock of having been kissed by my teacher. Within seconds I stopped gaping, though I couldn't quite stop trembling. Then as the two old friends greeted each other with a warm handshake and embrace, I found the presence of mind to cloak my discombobulation in a pleasant smile, squared shoulders and a slightly lifted chin.

"So is this the young lady you were telling me about?" Mr Vaughn turned to me and flashed a charming smile.

"Tony, meet Janette West," said Mr C. "Janette, this is my good friend Anthony Vaughn."

Though it was still an incredible struggle, I upheld my false composure as we exchanged amenities; the effort payed off in actually bringing me the calm that I needed. Then after Vaughn inquired about my parents and all was explained, we got down to the business of my audition.

My chosen piece was "Love Nest." George Burns and Gracie Allen had used the chorus from it as their theme song, but the words and the verse which I would include had fallen into obscurity. Remembering what Mr Conrad had said, I quickly put a rising fear back in its place and got started. And as he had coached me during my lessons, I avoided looking directly at Mr Vaughn and simply lost myself in this beautiful song that I adored.

When I'd finished, from somewhere offstage came the sound of applause, but Tony Vaughn just sat staring at me with a befuddled look. "How old are you, young lady?"

"Seventeen," I replied.

"Yes, seventeen," he said to himself. "David, did you, uh–"

"The interpretation is all hers, Tony." said Mr C.

"Seventeen, eh?" After a moment of thought, Mr Vaughn said, "Young lady, if you were eighteen, I'd ask you to start next week. Budget be damned, your kind of talent doesn't come along everyday. But you'd better finish school first. We can talk things over once you've had the chance to talk it over with your parents."

Stunned, I turned to my teacher, who winked at me and smiled.

"And now, David," said Vaughn. "Is it request time?"

"Yes, Tony, it's request time." said Mr C and played a few jazz chords. "Anything you'd like to hear. Janette?"

"Yes?"

"Sing whatever Mr Vaughn wants to hear."

"Huh?"

"You know, just like you did for me that time with Mr Johnson. You remember."

What in the–

Suddenly Tony Vaughn was naming popular tunes from twenty and thirty years ago for me to sing. Too angry at my teacher to be nervous about it, I simply came up with the lyrics, tried to get into the music and enjoy myself. After two songs he nudged Mr C off of the piano bench and played the accompaniment himself to speed things up.

A few people from the chorale began to come out from the wings to listen. My audition was turning into a concert! Some songs we did as abbreviated versions, thank God. We finally stopped at song number eight.

Mr Vaughn thanked me for being such a good sport, and I received a round of applause that I still cherish to this day. Then the others who had come out left us, all except a pretty and petite woman with ash blond hair and brown eyes. I recognized her as one of the soloists. She didn't look that much older than me; mid to late twenties at the most. Her name was Andrea, and she was introduced to us as Tony Vaughn's wife.

"Dave," said Mr Vaughn. "Time to go get something to eat at that restaurant you were telling me about."

"All right." Mr Conrad glanced over at me. "But I'll have to take Janette home first."

"What for? Doesn't she eat? Come on, we'll all go."

"I'll just call my parents," I said. "There's a pay phone in the lobby. It'll just take a minute and I'm sure it'll be fine if I go along."

"I'll go with you just in case," said Mr Conrad.

Out in the lobby, we found the phone and I made the call.

"Daddy? Hi, it's me. How's Mommy?"

"She's a little better. She went to bed as soon as we got in. I've just been waiting for you to get home. How did it go?"

"Fantastic! Mr Vaughn really liked me, but I'll tell you all about it later. He wants me and Mr Conrad to go with him and his wife to have something to eat. Is that okay?"

"Sure. That sounds nice. Sure, Janette, go ahead and have a good time. Do you mind if I don't wait up for you?"

"You don't have to wait up for me. I'll be fine."

"All right. But I'll leave a light on downstairs."

When I hung up the phone, I was so elated that I squealed and gave Mr Conrad a hug. "Let's go," I told him, grabbed his hand and took off to get back with the Vaughns.

Conversation was general but lively as we rode along, until Tony Vaughn asked a few questions about me. In answer Mr Conrad told bits of our story while including comments on what a fine songwriter I was. That prompted Vaughn to ask for the chance to hear some of my music, which gave me an unexpected rush to add to the beautiful high I was already on.

Our destination was Militi's, an Italian restaurant and bar in the northeast heights. With the dinner crowd having thinned out, it was only a moment or so before we were seated in a booth with menus in our hands.

"So, what did you think of the concert?" asked Vaughn after we ordered.

"I thought it was great," I said. "You included songs by some of my favorite composers."

"Oh, I enjoyed it, too," said Mr Conrad. "But I'd say you could use better arrangements for your pop songs."

"I know," said Vaughn. "So why don't you do some for me. You've nothing better to do."

"You only say that because you've never taught school."

"Well, don't give the little beggars so much home work. Then you won't have so many papers to correct."

"You can say that again," was my remark.

"You know what?" Mr Conrad responded after a moment of thought. "Next fall I just may be able to find the time, that is if everything happens the way I hope it will. If so, I just might be teaching part time, if at all."

"Okay," said Vaughn. "You let me know, because I want to take you up on that. I'm serious."

"All right, I'll let you know in a couple of months."

Conversation paused briefly when the waiter brought our cocktails. Taking a sip of a virgin Mai Tai, I twirled the little umbrella and silently reveled in the pleasure of the moment. Could all this lead to a career for me? Maybe not, but it was sure fun to think about. Then, looking across the table at the Vaughns made it seem like a double date. They sat close to each other, his arm around her shoulder most of the time. Her youthfulness was an interesting contrast to his maturity: the steaks of gray in his hair and neatly trimmed beard, the facial lines that come with age;

he was older than Mr Conrad and yet the years between Vaughn and his wife didn't seem to make a bit of difference to them. May and September, Ruth and Boaz, Jane Eyre and Mr Rochester. *If things were only different.* But they weren't. As far as I knew, David Conrad still planned to marry someone else and I was just a side dish. So with that realization, I ended a deadly train of thought and set my heart to just enjoy the evening.

The Vaughn's romance and recent marriage was the next topic, which was, thankfully, cut short by dinner being served. Then talk changed briefly to items more privy to Mr C and Tony Vaughn, *i.e.,* catching up on old friends, *etc.* Then it was swapping stories; something we all got in on in one way or another. Although such things as the Noonan case came up, mostly we laughed at the funny stories we each had to share.

Time seemed to slow its pace until it barely moved at all. Long after the last bite of dinner was taken, we sat and talked and laughed and drank. Everyone had a delightful time, and for me it could have gone on all night. But the restaurant had to close, and so at last we had to go home.

On the way to the parking lot, I remembered something that had come to mind earlier and even mentioned to Mr Conrad somewhat in jest.

"Well," I said to Mr C. "Do I get to drive or don't I?"

"I haven't had that much to drink," he protested.

"Oh, yes you have," I told him. "And I haven't even had so much as a glass of wine, thank you very much. Now, all I want is to make it home in one piece. Do you mind?"

Mr Conrad looked over at Mr Vaughn.

"She's right," Vaughn told him. "Let her have the keys."

"All right." Mr Conrad opened the door and gave me the keys to his Jaguar. Inwardly I squealed as I slipped into the driver's seat and acquainted myself with the dashboard. This was going to be a real treat to drive.

We dropped the Vaughns off at their hotel and then drove to my house. The ride home was full of happy talk about the evening. I had very much enjoyed Mr Conrad's friends and their stories, and we laughed about them some more. As I pulled the car into the driveway, I was reluctant to let the evening end.

"Now may I have my keys?" Mr Conrad held the door open for me and helped me out of the car.

"No," I said emphatically and kept them from his grasp. "Not until you've had some coffee. Come on in and I'll fix you a cup."

"Okay, you're the boss."

What had happened backstage had been mostly eclipsed by the audition and dinner, but not anymore. As we came into the dimly lit house and Mr Conrad helped me off with my fur, the scene and what led up to it ran through my head. 'Luck' my eye. Just an excuse for something he'd wanted to do since the day we'd met. So I didn't dwell on it. Since he'd always been a good boy and never gotten out of hand, I did my best to overlook it. Besides, I didn't care to spoil a happy mood over an incident that might never repeat itself. Pushing it aside once again, I determined to enjoy what was left of the evening.

With my teacher seated in the living room, I went off to the kitchen. Oddly enough I began to feel tired and started to lag a bit. Accustomed to staying out much later than this, I figured that all the excitement must have done me in. Pulling myself together, I concentrated on fixing a small pot of coffee and getting out a nice cup and saucer. Once the pot was on the stove I went back in to join Mr Conrad.

There was still something of a glow in the fire place. I stirred the ashes, added some kindling and a small log before taking a seat in the chair nearest Mr C where he sat on the couch. A lively little blaze was now on the hearth.

"I'm so sorry your parents missed out on tonight," he said, turning to look at me. "I hope your mother is feeling better."

"Daddy said she was. I'm sorry, too, but it might not have been as much fun for me if they'd been there. I had such a good time. Thank you for a very special evening."

"You're more than welcome." Something came to his mind that made him laugh. The sight and sound of it was a great pleasure for me. I always enjoyed seeing him happy instead of stoic and business-like. "One of these days," he said, peering at me over his glasses. "One of these days you are going to kill me for something I've done."

"What? What did you do?"

He laughed again. "I wish I could tell you now, but I'd like to make it home in one piece, too."

I gave him a dubious look and tried to imagine what it could possibly be. "Okay, Mr Cat, cough up the canary. This has something to do with tonight, doesn't it?"

"Oh, it might, and then again it might not. You'll find out soon enough. I'll tell you when I think it's safe."

"That may be never. I'm ready to kill you now for what you pulled at my audition. Just you wait."

"Did I scare you?"

"You most certainly did. As if I wasn't nervous enough."

"Oh. Well, I am not sorry. It went over very well. Tony and everybody else loved it. You really are quite good."

I excused myself to go check the coffee. It was just starting to perk. As I picked up the empty cup, it clattered against the saucer, giving away my fatigue. I set it down and decided both pot and cup should go on a tray so that Mr Conrad could have as much as he wanted.

"Thank you," he said as I set the tray before him. When I went to resume my seat in the chair he patted the place beside him on the couch and said, "No, come sit next to me."

Once again remembering that backstage kiss, I didn't want to put myself in a vulnerable position with this man who did find me attractive, and who had also been drinking. And yet I didn't want to put a damper on the evening by refusing him. Figuring that the odds were against getting attacked in my own house with my parents asleep upstairs, I went to join him and kept a few inches of safety between us.

Suddenly I couldn't think of a thing to say. I watched as he sipped his coffee quietly, thoughtfully. He stared into the fire and the blaze reflected in his glasses, all but obscuring his eyes. I grew a bit uneasy as I watched him, and suddenly wished that the evening was over. It was a relief when he at last emptied his cup.

"Would you like me to pour you another?" I asked.

"No, thank you." He put his cup on the tray and turned to me. I turned to look at the fire, trembling even more, and not from fatigue. "Did you like the flowers and candy I sent?"

An indescribable feeling came over me when I heard his question. It was shock and amazement that spread through my entire being. Now I did look at him. "It was you! You sent the flowers and. . . ."

"Yes and the music box with the little chocolates. Did you like them?"

Remembering the note, my powers of speech suddenly deserted me. Finally I said, "Yes, they–they're love–ly."

Reaching up, he gently touched my hair. "Are these some of the roses?"

"Yes," I whispered.

"I meant what I said in the card. Every word of it. I love you, Janette. And there isn't anyone else. There never will be."

Mr Conrad spoke the words softly but quite clearly, so there was no mistaking what he said. The room spun round and reason and logic deserted me. All grew fuzzy and then my thought processes came to a halt.

For months I had fantasized love scenes just such as this between myself and my man, and now that it was happening, I didn't know what to do. More than afraid, I was terrified. Of course, it wasn't supposed to happen quite this way. And always in the back of my mind had been what Mrs Mac had told me of her marriage. But here he was, still an unbeliever and offering his love to me. Was there a proper response for this? If so, I didn't know what it was. I didn't know much of anything at the moment. My breathing became erratic and my heart was beating in double time. I closed my eyes and tried to compose myself but doubt, suspicion and fear kept me in a panic. I shook like an old washing machine.

David Conrad, the man of my dreams and the desire of so many women and teenaged girls, gave my cheek a gentle kiss and then slipped an arm around my shoulder, pulling me close. I made a feeble attempt to resist, but he wouldn't allow it. So I leaned on him and tried desperately not to hyperventilate.

"Don't be afraid, honey," he said, kissing my hair.

Tell the fire not to burn, while you're at it, I thought, angry at myself for losing my grip. From the way he held me and touched me, I knew he was trying to calm me down, but it wasn't working. Was he for real? His nearness just made me more upset and that served to embarrass me, which added more to my anxiety. Incapable of approaching the situation in a calm, straight forward manner, it showed me up as being a little girl unable to deal with the advances of an older man.

"You're like a scared rabbit." Gently stroking the hair at my temple, he kissed the spot twice and said, "I'm not going to hurt you, honey. I love you too much for that."

There it is again–he loves me. Me. So I'm the woman he wants to marry. Woman? Ha! If I were a real woman, I wouldn't be so doggone petrified. I don't want to scare him off or make him change his mind. Y'shua!!!

I tried to be even angrier at myself in hopes of quieting my other emotions, but it did little good. Finally I had enough sense to pray in the Spirit. That's when things began to change. As I lay against him with my eyes closed, praying silently and sometimes under my breath, the fear began to lessen, and with it my trembling. Then I could enjoy his touch and warm to his nearness. I wanted him to kiss me.

The grandfather clock in the hall struck the half hour. The crystal clock over the fireplace instantly joined it in harmony. It was half past one. The pounding in my chest was still going, but not quite as loud. My trembling was hardly noticeable.

A deep sigh came from his chest. "I'd better leave. I don't want anyone upstairs to wake up and find us like this."

He was reluctant to let me go. Poor man. I was sure he'd planned on getting a much different reaction than the one I'd given him. The ache in his heart was quite visible on his face as he pulled away and got to his feet.

Oh, HaShem, he's leaving. Why can't I say something? Why can't I do something? I forced my body up and took a step toward him. "David–"

He was putting on his overcoat. Letting it settle onto his shoulders, he turned to look at me. His pain seem to lessen after hearing the sound of his first name on my lips. "Yes?"

"I–I just need a little time, okay?"

"All right."

I wanted to say more, to tell him how I felt. It was what he wanted to hear and I knew it, but I just couldn't bring myself to say it. Like I hoped he would, he came and took me in his arms again. This time I returned his embrace and pressed myself to him. It was the best I could do and he seemed to get the message.

"I'd better go," he said and released me, except to take my hand as we walked to the door. "Would you do something for me?" Seeming more hopeful, he turned to me again before stepping out the door.

"I'll try."

"Call me tomorrow night around eight. Please? I just want to hear your voice."

"I will."

He touched my face and leaned down as if to kiss me, but thinking better of it, simply said goodnight and went to his car.

SATURDAY, FEBRUARY 15:
   The state of my nerves did not improve with the sunrise. I awoke the next morning and remembered everything that happened, except that it didn't seem real. But I knew very well the reality of it all. David Conrad loved me and wanted me for his wife. I loved him, too–and desperately. But would our marriage work? That desire to follow him anywhere was back in spades, and all I wanted was for him to touch me and kiss me like there was no tomorrow. But common sense was too strong to leave me there. I had to think things through.
   Now it all made sense. It would have made sense much sooner, had I not been so afraid and in such denial. "When you have eliminated the impossible, whatever remains, however improbable, must be the truth," said Sherlock Holmes in one of the Conan Doyle stories, and these were words I'd lived by as a detective–until David Conrad came along and turned me into mush. Now it was all obvious: the flirtation, the constant attention and activity, the gifts, the tender words. And it was plain as the sun at noonday that I was the subject of his recent prayer request. Still it didn't change the question of what to do. Even though he loved me, what did love mean to a man like that? He was a man with a decadent past who was twice my age and who still hadn't embraced Y'shua.
   This was not a decision I could make alone. I didn't trust myself and had to have counsel and confirmation for the direction I was wanting to go. The Holisters were coming to dinner Monday night, so I could wait to talk and pray with Georgia. If I was going to marry David Conrad, I had to be sure I wasn't getting into something I would regret later.
   My family gave the expected happy and excited response to my news when I shared with them the results of my audition at the breakfast table. I somehow managed to bring myself up out of my troubled state so that I wouldn't have other questions to answer. This helped but didn't cure me by a long shot. Then that evening, a few minutes before eight, I sat in my room with drink in hand and pondered the telephone: rum and RC Cola. I had always wondered why booze was called liquid courage. Now I understood.
   Y'shua, tell me what to say to this man. One more sip and my glass was empty. I felt a little ashamed, but filled it again, picked up the receiver and dialed.
   "Hello?"
   Just the sound of his voice made me start to come unglued. That deep, rich baritone quality had a different effect now that real romance had entered the picture.
   "Hi," I finally said. "It's–it's me."
   "Well, hello 'me.' How are you?"
   "I don't know. Okay, I guess."
   "How's your mother doing?"
   "Much better. She was up this afternoon, but she's still taking it easy. Daddy won't let her do much."

"That's good. I spoke with your father earlier when she was still in bed. I'm so glad she's improved. Oh, uh, are you ready for the test on Monday?"

"What test–oh! In French. No, I haven't had time to study."

"I thought that might be the case. You've been pretty busy. I can postpone it, if you like."

"Oh, would you, please? I'd really appreciate it."

"Sure. Consider it done."

He kept the conversation going and kept it light. He said he had some more ragtime for me to play. We only talked a few minutes, and not once did David refer our romance. I was relieved, and somehow it made him even more dear to me. He cared enough not to pressure me. When I hung up the phone, I thought about how much I loved him and asked myself again if I should marry him.

Except as a fanciful someday thing, marriage had never been anywhere in my plans. Even recent developments with Teddy Molloy hadn't seemed this serious. Now the idea as concrete reality was set before me in the form of David Conrad. Marriage generally meant being a wife and mother, housekeeping, babies, etc. I'd hoped to see something of the world first, not to mention college, but how could I pass up an offer like this? Rejecting him seemed utterly foolish, not to mention painful; but at the same time, there was so much about him that I didn't know. And the thought that he didn't want me to know more struck a fearful chord.

SUNDAY, FEBRUARY 16:

Sunday morning, I slept late and then went out alone on my bike. I had called Teddy the night before and told him I was feeling lousy and not up to playing for mass. He didn't press for details, assuming I was ill.

I had to be alone, to clear my head and not think about anything. One of my favorite places to find peace and quiet was the big cemetery on south Broadway. Guarded by a high wall and wrought iron gates, it was very old and full of vines, shrubs and tall trees that were too plentiful to tame. Finding solitude was no problem there. I loved to read the stones and enjoy the quiet, so that morning I sought it out as a pleasant escape. But after a short while, thoughts of my man flooded in again, and I knew I needed a much stronger distraction. Reluctantly I got on my Indian and headed further south.

God, if only he wasn't a non-believer. I know there are exceptions to the rule but–well, you know. And I can't figure out what else is going on here. Is this where I'm not supposed to lean on my own understanding?

Bingo!

That revelation made a difference, but I was still incredibly overwhelmed, wondering how to handle a love affair with a grown man of his age and experience. It was obvious to anyone what he was accustomed to getting. How could I follow in the footsteps of those he knew before me?

This was not the way I had planned to get a husband. I needed the other pieces of this puzzle and the inability to go forward with a decision was dragging me down into that old pit of depression. But this dilemma was sure to reach some sort of resolution when Georgia arrived, and that was the following evening. So determined to let the whole business rest until then, I turned my thoughts to the next diversion.

Only a small twinge of guilt went through me as I passed St Basil's. This wasn't something Teddy could help me with, and I didn't dare see him and give myself away. I had a different destination in mind: a complete departure from current events. There might be a wait of ten minutes, but the Halsteds would soon be home from church and I could drop in to see them.

As I drove past the big ranch with its vast sea of black and white cows, they were just pulling into the driveway. Deciding not to wait for them to get settled in, I turned around and pulled in behind them.

"Well, hey there, Janette," said Mama Halsted as she got out of the car. A short, sweet faced, heavyset woman with green eyes and gray hair died a reddish brown, she looked just as I remembered. "How y'all doin'? What brings you down here t' see us? You ain't heard from Petey, have you?"

"Hello, Janette," grumbled Papa Halsted, a tall, wiry, white haired man whose shoulders were finally beginning to droop with age. He turned his piercing gray eyes to me and nodded as he said, "How y'all doin'?"

"Just fine," I replied. "Hope you all are doin' well."

"Cain't complain," sighed Mama Halsted. "Come on in and set a while. You can have dinner with us, if ya like."

"Why, thank you. Don't mind if I do."

They always entered their house from the back door while the front door was for special occasions. I followed them in and took a seat at the kitchen table.

"So what d'you hear from Petey?" asked Papa.

"Ain't heard from him but once since I got back from Colorado," I said. "Thought maybe y'all 'd heard from him."

"He don't write like he used to," said Mama. "'Course we got a card 'n' letter from him at Christmas time, but he ain't wrote but once since then."

"Last time I heard from him was a week after the new year. But he sounded like he was doin' okay; just workin' hard."

The longer I stayed around the Halsteds or anyone else with an accent, the more I began to sound like them. Usually I had to make a conscious effort to speak normally, as with Mrs MacGregor. But with the Halsteds it had done more for our relationship if I blended in.

And speaking of blending in.

Papa opened the refrigerator door, pulled out a couple of beers and handed one to me before joining me at the table.

"Sometimes I really wish he'd come home," said Mama. "But when I think about them sendin' him off to Viet Nam and us losin' another boy–"

"What?!"
"They sent a telegram last month that said Troy was missin' in action."
"Oh, my goodness! Well, how's Jesse doin' over there?"
"All right, I guess, but he's changed. Still writes us regular, though. Good thing is we can expect him to be home before too long. And supposedly he'll be home for good."
"Where's Frank and Joey?"
"Oh, they always hang out with their friends for a while after services. They'll be home as soon as it's time t'eat."

Papa Halsted never talked about his boys and the war. It was a tough issue for him, having fought in two wars and yet knowing his own sons might never make it home from a place where it seemed our country had no business. He was not a demonstrative man when it came to showing love, at least not in the typical sense, but he loved his sons and would stand silently by them, whether they wanted to go into the armed forces or not. So he didn't care much if Peter was in Canada.

Frank and Joey did make it home just in time to eat. I joined the family for dinner and spent the rest of the afternoon catching up on things, watching TV and drinking that ghastly beer. It was like a time machine that allowed me to escape into the past, only some of the faces were missing.

The sun was just setting as I got home. Even though it was still early, I fixed myself a snack and took it up to my room, not wanting anyone to pry into my moodiness. Before I could slip down into depression I went to bed, letting the memories of the afternoon put me to sleep instead of a pill.

MONDAY, FEBRUARY 17:

The sky was dark with gray clouds and rain on Monday morning, a complement to the way I felt. A deeper depression came over me as the day drew on. With my nerves worn to a frazzle, I skipped the morning breakfast routine and then went through the motions of living out the day. I only lived for the moment I could talk with Georgia. It was just a matter of a few hours before I would see her. Mr Conrad wasn't doing too good, either. He seemed upset and distracted. Whenever my eyes met his, I thought I saw pain behind them. That added guilt to the load I already carried.

So the day drug by. Minutes passed the way they do at a lackluster revival. There were moments when I was ready to chuck it all and tell David Conrad exactly what he wanted to hear. It seemed to be killing us both for me to keep resisting. He looked positively miserable, as if he'd had a very rough night. I had to do something to make him feel better.

When it was time for Choir, I ran to get there as soon as possible just to be near him. Maybe it would do some good to talk with him for a bit, even if it was just about the weather. I felt I should comfort him somehow, but at the same time didn't want to give him false hope.

Just a few more hours. . . .
Mr Conrad stopped me as I came through the door.
"Janette," he said, cool and matter of fact. "I need to see you after class, just for a couple of minutes."
"Sure." *Good. I'll be alone with him.*
For the second time that school year, Choir was dismissed early for lunch. If anything, we usually got out late. I stayed behind and waited by my teacher's desk. As the last student stepped over the threshold, he spoke.
"I just wanted to tell you that your costumes for the spring concert have arrived. They came on Saturday. I'd have told you about it on the phone, but I wanted to look at them first and see what kind of condition they were in. Could you come with me after school to get them?"
"Sure. I don't see why not."
"Good. Meet me out on the parking lot after school."
I wanted to say something else. Anything to give him a clue to the way I felt, and that I didn't want to hurt him. Instead I just stood there. "Uh–"
"Yes, Janette?"
Just saying I was sorry wasn't the right thing. What I needed to say was that I loved him, but I couldn't find the courage. What finally came out was, "I can't stay long this afternoon. We're having a dinner party tonight."
"Don't worry, I won't keep you long. Go on to lunch, now. I'll see you this afternoon."
With no appetite, I fasted through lunch as I had through breakfast. Finding a place out of the cold and wind and away from other people, I tried to pray but it didn't work. All I could think of was David Conrad and what I'd be throwing away by saying no to him. Memories of what it was like when he held me, touched me, the way he looked at me, played in my head no matter how I tried to drive them away.
The sky grew darker. That afternoon it rained hard and heavy for an hour or so. When school was out, it lessened to a soft, gentle, steady rain–the kind I loved to walk in for peace and inspiration. At that moment, however, its charm was lost on me.
I was prompt in meeting Mr Conrad after school. We met at the exit and walked to his car, sharing his large black umbrella. It was an effort to remain calm, knowing the position I was putting myself in. But he had said he would give me time to think things over and I believed him. Leaving that worry alone, I closed my eyes for a moment and relaxed as best as I could against the cool leather seats as we rolled out of the parking lot.
We rode along in silence. It rained hard again as we made our way through the city streets. The sound was comforting and I was glad for it.
At the apartment, a large theatrical trunk, a medium sized trunk, and a footlocker sat in the middle of the living room floor. They were old and well traveled, but their sturdy metal and leather construction had kept them in fair condition. The hand truck that moved them about was close

by.

"Those are the costumes?" I asked as Mr C helped me off with my coat.

"Right. Go ahead and open them up and tell me what you think. While you're doing that, I'll fix us something to drink. What would you like? Tea? Cocoa maybe?"

"Cocoa sounds good."

He disappeared into the kitchen while I went to explore.

The first trunk I opened was the medium one. Packed to the brim, it had everyday sort of things. Cute but nothing like what I had in mind, until I got near the middle and found several after five dresses in a variety of colors and fabrics. I held a navy moiré silk number up to see how it would fit. Not bad. Only a tad too roomy, and the hem would need raising a bit.

"Certain ones might be a little long in the skirt." Mr C came in with two steaming mugs. "But they ought to fit you pretty good otherwise. See anything you like?"

"Yeah, plenty." I was now going through the large trunk, finding some very lovely evening clothes. "Some look as if they'll fit better than others. See this one?" I held up a pale pink satin ball gown with spaghetti straps.

"You want to try it on?"

"I'd better not. I'm getting a bit carried away as it is."

"Have you tried any of the shoes?"

"Not yet. Haven't seen too many."

"Try the footlocker."

"Cute."

This trunk was full of shoes, belts and other accessories. Surprisingly enough, some of the shoes fit. I minced around in a pair of red and white high heels while looking for the dress I'd seen earlier that matched them. "No!" I said aloud to myself, stopping short of finding the dress. "I'd better quit now or I'll be late getting home."

I took a few sips of my cocoa and started putting things away. Mr Conrad helped. When we finished and the trunks were closed, I discovered that I still wore the red shoes.

"Wait a minute," I said. "I've got to take these off."

Mr Conrad supported me on one arm to keep me from falling while I kicked off the shoes. Getting rid of the last one threw me off balance, and I would have fallen had he not held on to me. After steadying myself, I tried to bend down to get the shoes, but my man wouldn't let me.

"That can wait," he said, pulling me to him. "There's some other business I'd like to take care of."

Suddenly filled with terror, I tried to pull away but he held me fast. Unable to find my voice, I pleaded with my eyes for him to let me go. Instead his arms went around me and his embrace became gentle as it brought me to him.

I trembled like crazy all over again. This time, though, still weak from fasting, the conflict inside me was impossible to control. Unable to cope, I simply fainted.

When I came to, my weak little body lay stretched out on the sofa with a light blanket over me. Mr Conrad had put a bit of ammonia under my nose to revive me and now sat beside me, perched on the edge of the couch. His concerned gaze fixed intently on my face was the first thing I saw as my eyes fluttered open. Knowing I would be wary of his touch, he was a good boy and kept his hands to himself.

"How do you feel?" he asked.

"I'm–I'm okay," I replied while trying unsuccessfully to raise myself. I hadn't near enough strength for the effort.

"Don't." He put a gentle hand on my shoulder to keep me from doing any more. "Whatever you do, don't get up. Just lie still for a bit. When was the last time you had anything to eat?"

"Yesterday."

Anger flashed in his eyes but he said nothing. Instead, he got up and went to the kitchen. He returned quickly with two pieces of cold fried chicken, some cookies and a glass of apple juice on a tray. Putting it down on the coffee table, he set about gathering some throw pillows. Then he raised me up and put the pillows behind me for support. He sat in silent concern while I ate. I finished all the chicken, a couple of cookies and half the juice before giving up the tray.

"Now, how do you feel?" he asked.

"Much better. Thank you."

Showing the truth of my words, I sat up straight and managed a smile. Then I looked at my watch, not wanting time to slip by. But before I could even read the numbers, he covered the face with his hand and sternly said, "No, Janette. You're not going anywhere just yet."

"But–"

The look on his face silenced me. His jaw was set with determination while his eyes looked desperately wild with pain and anguish. As he realized I would no longer resist, his expression softened. He seemed on the verge of tears as he took my little brown hand in his and prepared to speak.

"Honey, I know I agreed to give you some time, but–this is more than I can stand. Look, I'm not going to drag you off to bed, if that's what you're afraid of. That's not what this is about." He paused and in exasperation tightened his grip on my hand and cried, "Stop torturing me, Janette! I can't take it any more! Baby, I am on the level, I swear it. The life I used to live is over and the man I used to be is gone. Can't you see that? It's all because I want a new life, and I want that life with you. Come on, you must have figured it out by now: you're the woman I want to marry, and all this time I've been courting you. Maybe I didn't do it right, but I did my best to show how much you mean to me and that I want to make you happy. Look, if–if you'll just give me a chance; if you'll stop running from me–whatever we need to work out, we can do it. Try having some faith for us and try to see God's part in all this. You once said yourself that he brought us together. Maybe I couldn't see it then, but I sure believe it now. I'm beginning to believe in a lot of things I lost faith in, God included, because of you and because I know you're in love with me. If his name happens to be Jesus or Y'shua, then it's all right by me. Anybody who could send someone like you to love me certainly has my vote. If I could only hear you say what you really feel. Please, Janette, I just need to hear it."

At last he had given me what I needed. The depth of David Conrad's sincerity plus his willingness to open his heart to Y'shua made all the difference in the world. Even as he spoke, the Holy Spirit confirmed the truth of his words and told me other things that he didn't say. Peace soon replaced the fear and turmoil inside of me as it became clear that HaShem had arranged for this love to grow between us. Now I could say without reservation what my man wanted to hear.

I was still a little shaky, and the fear that came naturally with my lack of experience made me hesitate. But I loved this man and wanted him, and that gave me the courage I needed. Since words weren't enough, I reached up and slipped my arms around his neck. Gently pulling his head down to my level I kissed his cheek and spoke softly in his ear, "Oh, David, I do love you. I love you with all my heart."

"You do?" His hands slipped around my waist and caressed me. "Say it again, baby. I need to hear it. Please tell me you want me."

I brushed my lips against his ear and said that there wasn't another man in this world that I could ever want. Warm tears dropped from his face and onto my shoulder as he sighed deeply. It was a great release for me as well.

The clock on the wall gently tolled the half hour. It was 4:30. Knowing I dared not be any later getting home, I slowly pulled away. "David, I really should go now."

"In a minute." He laid me back against the pillows, leaned over me and expressed his happiness in unrestrained kisses.

It was twenty minutes to six when we finally walked in the door to my house. My head was in such a thick romantic haze that I still can't remember the entire explanation Mr Conrad gave my mother, and neither can he. I do know for sure that it wasn't the truth. He began with something about the spring concert and went on to make our late arrival all my fault, saying I had insisted on first chance at the costumes. All the while there was an edge in his voice as he pretended to be put out with me. Being lightheaded, I had an overwhelming desire to laugh out loud at this charade. When I did slip once and a chuckle escaped, my teacher feigned anger and shock at my flippancy. I stood there astounded at his acting ability as he said it wasn't funny, and that it was the last time he would let me take advantage of him. My mouth flew open with amazement at his choice of words and I could have shrieked! But the anger on my mother's face told me I wouldn't have long to live if I did. So I stifled the laugh, feigned penitence, then apologized to Mommy and Mr Conrad, and escaped upstairs to my room.

Chapter Seven
Intimacies

MONDAY EVENING, FEBRUARY 17:
Mommy had gone all out for dinner preparations. Seldom did we use the good dishes or put on our Sunday clothes for guests on a week night. But with Aunt Laura bringing in her English boyfriend, it was an extra special occasion.

It seemed Aunt Laura had picked a winner. Being a man of average height with a healthy physique, the distinguished looking Jonathan Angrahm first appeared to be as reserved and austere as a character out of Dickens. His head was topped with jet black curls barely touched by gray, his cheeks sported long sideburns that were approaching the size of mutton chops. The nose was long but nicely formed, with only a slight hook; his chin appeared firm and strong. The man's most noticeable feature, however, was a unique set of eyes. Large and dark, they were topped by heavy black brows, and had the fierceness and piercing quality of a young Billy Graham. But as appearances are often deceiving, so it was in this case.

I couldn't have asked for a better distraction for all the emotional changes I'd been going through than this Englishman. He wanted us all to call him Johnny, saying that he had long been in a very stuffy business with very stuffy people and did not like having a stuffy name. The prestigious House of Angrahm Publishers had been his family's business for three generations. The high quality of its publications was known all over Great Britain and on the Continent as well. Johnny happily confessed to us that he was the black sheep of his family, for he cared very little for their way of doing things. It was one reason he planned to leave England all together. Too often and for too long, he and certain family members had rubbed each other the wrong way. Johnny felt that the change was years overdue and meeting Aunt Laura had prompted him to at last do something about it. He only hoped his son would make the move with him. But even more, this man who seemed so upper crusty while indeed being terribly rich, and not too terribly handsome, was terribly, terribly funny. He had what seemed an endless repertoire of interesting and hilarious stories that had us in stitches, and he claimed that every single one of them was true. And it wasn't just the stories themselves but the way he had of telling them. At times the man seemed down right insane, often adding gestures and sound effects to his narrative; the way he played to the younger children, it was obvious that this was for their benefit. But as an expert story teller, Johnny also put us on the edge of our seats and made us teary eyed. Having been a fighter pilot in World War II, he had seen a great deal of action. He gave us the exciting details of how he survived the famous Battle of Britain, and how some of his friends had not. He told of later getting wounded when shot down over the English channel, and how it saved his life by keeping him from being transferred to the Middle East with his squadron, the 602. Torpedoed by a German submarine, their transport never reached its destination. But the story that gripped us the most was one of the worst moments in his flying career. While shepherding home a damaged B17 bomber, himself and his faithful wing man, Pilot Officer Archer, were jumped by a large group of FW190's of JG26, the top German squadron in the Luftwaffe. His wing man was shot down and the B17 was also lost. Johnny's plane, badly shot up, limped back to England with a damaged engine after managing to disengage from combat–by flying under a railway bridge! He then crash landed his Spitfire at an emergency American airfield on the coast of Britain. But as much as he loved to tell his stories, Johnny refused to brag. Aunt Laura was the one to fill in with information about him being one of England's top aces and all the medals he had won.

Now, what about Georgia? As soon as she was in the door, I hugged her, pulled her aside to say we had to talk, then asked if she could spend the night. She answered yes, and so all that remained was for our guests to go home so I could tell her what had happened between me my teacher.

Had I not been having such a good time, I would have been a bit peeved at having our guests stay so long, and on a week night to boot. We all laughed and talked, and even did some singing until almost midnight. The younger kids were, of course, sent to bed much earlier, but Charlotte, Olivia and I were allowed to stay up until they finally called it a night.

"All right," said Georgia, once we were in my room with the door closed. "What is up with you? I can't remember when I've seen you this giddy without a drink in your hand."

"Does it show that much?" I asked.

"Well, I don't think anybody else paid it much attention, but you gave me a clue right away with that glazed look in your eyes and your desperate need to talk. Girl, you look positively slap happy. You must be in love with somebody. Who with?"

"That's only half of it, George. The best part is that he's in love with me."

"Is it that good looking priest?"

"No. It's the teacher."

"The teacher? Haut boy!"

"Shhh! Not so loud. Here, have a night gown." I threw Georgia one of my long flannel numbers and then got one for myself. "Look, let's either whisper or talk in code."

"I hate talking in code."

"Then talk low and speak French at least some of the time. I've gotten pretty good this past year."

So with that, the balance of our conversation was mostly in French. But as always, I won't make you wade through it.

"Now, when did this happen with the teacher?"

"This afternoon. No. No, it was Friday night, actually. It was this afternoon that we came to an understanding."

"Well! Tell me all the juicy little details. Did he kiss you?"

"I'll say he did."
"French kiss?"
"Oh, is there another kind?"
"Janette! I'm surprised at you! 'Is there another kind?' Honestly! You sound like me."
"I do, don't I?"
"Yes, and you ought to be ashamed. I have to reform you, girl."
"Over my dead body."
"Ooo! This *is* serious."
"You're right about that. He wants to marry me, George."
"Praise God! He really told you that?"
"He sure did."
"I want to know everything. Everything!"

Georgia sat enthralled while I told her the rest of what had happened with my Mr Conrad. Picking up where I'd left off in my last letter, I brought her up to the minute with all the intimate details of the afternoon.

"Incredible!" she said when I'd finished. "I love it. Man, oh, man! I wish I were in your shoes. Are those the roses over there on your dresser?"

"Yes." I turned to look at the bouquet, which had bloomed fully but was starting to die. Some of the flowers were already pressed in a book. "And there's the musical box of chocolates in the drawer of my night stand."

Georgia went to get the gold box and placed it on top of the night stand. Opening the lid, she pulled out a piece of candy and listened to the tune while pulling off the wrapper. "I don't recognize the melody."

"I don't either, but it's very pretty."

"Mmmm! This chocolate is excellent." Closing the lid, Georgia picked up the box to examine it better. "This is heavy." She turned the box over and peered closely at the bottom. "I was right. This is real gold–18 karat."

"What? Real gold?"

Georgia handed me the music box so I could see for myself. I found the stamp on the bottom and stared at it.

"Does your David have any single brothers? If so, I'd like to meet each and every one. I might even settle for a cousin."

"Georgia, this is going to take a while to get used to. This is so unreal!"

"So, tell me again what he looks like. Aren't there pictures in his file?"

"Sure."

Opening the closet door, I reached back to unlock my files and got out my Mr Conrad. Georgia licked her lips and whistled as she looked at the photos, which Margo had finally just given me, plus the more recent ones.

"Mama mia, pizzeria! Girl, you have hit the jackpot!"

"Read the Personal Information sheet."

She separated it from the rest of the pile and fanned the pages. "Say! This has to be longest P.I. sheet I've ever seen."

"Muggsy started it, but I've added some things."

I waited anxiously while Georgia read quickly. Certain things prompted little utterances or made her eyes get big. But when finished she looked at me with a knitted brow and shook her head. "I really hate to say this, kiddo, but something's definitely wrong here." Georgia flipped the pages with her thumb before setting them down, and then went on to explain herself. "Sure, it happens, but you know as well as I do that, on the average, men like this don't get serious with teeny boppers. You even said so yourself. A decent man his age with this kind of looks, talent and money should have already been happily involved with someone who was at least in their mid to late twenties. After all, he can travel anywhere. So with the whole world to choose from, is a good woman that hard to find?"

"Yes, I know. Margo tagged him a mystery man, too, as you've seen in her notes. Another girl pointed out how deeply he had buried himself in his work and said she thought he was trying to forget someone."

"She's probably right. If that's all there is to it, though, you shouldn't have too much to worry about."

"But what else could there be?"

"Who knows? People have all sorts of problems and neurosis. Wish there was some better clues in his file. That one trail you've been following about guns and nightmares doesn't go far enough."

"In spite of the way he flipped out at Lisa Overton's place, he seems to be very well adjusted. I've spent a lot of time with him and been close enough to see what kind of man he is. It's the reason why I fell in love with him, George. I seriously doubt if there's anything sinister there. Just read Margo's P.O. When I first told her Conrad was my teacher, she raved about how wonderful he was."

"Muggsy is good with her Personal Observations. She got even better when Fletcher started helping her do interviews."

"Well?" I asked when Georgia had finished with the P.O.

"Yeah, I see what you mean. Your boyfriend looks like a real swell character, especially since he dropped the playboy lifestyle. Hmmm, I don't know, Jan. Maybe he doesn't have long to live or something. Who knows what it could be? The most logical conclusion is that he's hiding a previous marriage, and his troubles could be connected with it. But as long as it's buried deep enough or was brief enough that you won't have to deal with an ex-wife, former in-laws or kids that are close to your age, then don't worry about it. One part of me says not to look this lovely gilt-edged gift horse in the mouth. The other part of me is naturally suspicious. That other part and common sense both say that you should be certain you know exactly what you're getting into, especially if you think you might be spending the rest of your life with this guy."

"Well, the fact that David Conrad is hiding something is old news. But up to now I've been riding on my doubts and suspicions, and it hasn't done a thing but make me miserable. From all that's happened these last few days, I'm learning that this is God's setup and I've just got to trust him to work out the details. Don't worry, I'm not going to walk into this blindfolded. I have every intention of getting all of those important little facts. But it's not like I just met this man yesterday; I do know him fairly well. Now I simply need to wait on God to bring whatever it is to light and work it out."

"Then that's what you should do. As long as you know God is in this–and I get a definite witness of that in my spirit, then just take it as it comes and listen to what the Lord says to do."

"Okay. That's just what I needed to hear."

"Good. So have you thought much about–? No, you can't have thought any about your wedding at this stage."

"Georgia! He's not even saved yet."

"Shh! So what? At this rate he will be. It's just that as I'm sitting here, I'm getting this strong picture of you coming down the aisle in white. I don't know what timing the Lord has in mind anymore than you do, but I do know from experience that whether it's next month or next year, you need to start making your plans as soon as possible. Do you have any idea how hard it is to plan a wedding at the last minute? It's tough enough to bring it off when you plan in advance."

"What if he wants to elope?"

"No. That doesn't sound right. You'd better let me help you. I've been maid of honor twice, remember? Listen to the voice of experience."

"All right, if you say so."

We talked into the wee hours of the morning, but I was still bright eyed and chipper the next day. That morning she dropped me off at school and made me promise to introduce me very soon to my future intended.

TUESDAY, FEBRUARY 18:

Next morning, rather than sit in the cafeteria, David and I went upstairs to the classroom. Along with coffee, he brought fresh empanadas and a few donuts. This time when he kissed me I was much more at ease. Even though the trembling started up again, it was more from excitement than fear. I wanted his arms around me. I was beginning to see just how much we did belong together.

"So when does my indoctrination begin?" he asked, smiling down at me.

"Your what?"

"You need to teach me more about the Jewish Jesus, remember? I think we ought to get started."

"Oh, you do? Okay."

"But not right this instant."

I started to slip away but David held me for one more kiss before letting go. Then he opened the door of the room to make things proper.

"Well, when you are ready," I said, opening the box of pastries. "You'll need a good study Bible. We'll have to go do some shopping."

"Okay. After school?"

"Sure. Give me time to go home and change and I'll come to your place."

"Why don't we just go from here?"

I gave him a knowing look.

"Oh, yeah, I suppose we should be careful. But we're together so much already that everyone's used to it. Besides, all I have to do is let people know you're converting me."

"Converting? You won't stop being Jewish, David, but still it's not a bad idea. Just be careful how you say it. They need to know you're sincere. Still, we can't be seen together all the time. I've got a better idea. I'll give you directions to the store and we can meet there after school."

"Fine. Then can I see you tonight? We really need to talk things over."

"Tonight? I have rehearsal tonight."

"Rehearsal for what?"

"Church band."

"Can't you get out of it? You have before."

"Well, sure. . . . I guess."

"Just pretend you're going to rehearsal and come to my place instead."

"No, wait, I can't." I'd completely forgotten about Teddy. That would be too hard to work with on such short notice. "I can't because there's a friend who comes for dinner and then we go to rehearsal together."

"Tomorrow night, then?"

"Sure, that'll work fine."

"Good. It'll be nice to spend a few hours alone where we can just relax."

As it began to get close to class time, I suggested to David that we begin speaking French and going over yesterday's lesson, not only for appearance sake, but also because of what my emotional state the day before had caused me to miss. Shortly after we started, the other students began to show up and join in on the review.

Shopping that afternoon was more fun than I'd anticipated. We hit two bookstores, first the Christian one and then the Jewish one just a few doors down. Before we even walked in, I knew what we would get for David, so that didn't take long. But when he saw my excitement over certain reference books and other things, he turned sugar daddy and bought me any old thing my heart desired. Of course, I could only take home a few items without drawing unwanted attention. David took the rest home with him where I could get them later.

I resisted the temptation to follow my man to his abode, knowing that, if I did, I'd never make it home before dinner. So we said goodbye at the last store with nothing more than a brief hug and went our separate ways.

Teddy was there when I got home. He was in the driveway fixing something under the hood of the station wagon. I parked around back and called hello before running upstairs to take my things in. Then with my stuff stowed away, I made sure I appeared plain, childlike and tomboyish before going back down to see what was happening and get a hug.

"Hi, sweetheart." Teddy wiped his hands and gave me the strong embrace I had hoped for. "How ya doin'? Feeling all better now?"

"Huh? Oh, yeah, I'm fine."

"Good. I was hoping you'd get back on your feet soon. I sure missed you on Sunday. I tried calling you yesterday, but you weren't home."

"You did? Oh. Well, we had company last night, so that's probably why I didn't get your message."

It was odd, but ages seemed to have passed since the weekend. I'd forgotten telling Teddy that I hadn't felt good.

"How'd your audition go?"

"It was great. Anthony Vaughn wants me but I'm not old enough, so I'll have to wait . . . if it's what God wants for me."

"Well, God has already led you in another direction, so we have that answer already. Anyway, I'm glad that it went well."

"Thanks. So what's up with the wagon?"

"Carburetor problems," he said. "Your dad told me about it when I was down to the drug store yesterday. I said I'd take care of it for him. I'm just now done and was about to take it for a test drive. Come go with me."

"Okay."

It as then that my commitment to go to Chicago came to mind. With the change in my relationship with David Conrad, there was no way I would go unless it was just for the summer. Except that David would likely throw a fit over it.

Until that realization came, I had been dying to tell Teddy something of how things had worked out with my man. Now I wondered if it would be wise. There was even the temptation to tell him the complete story, but it would have been foolish to expect him to accept what I had nearly rejected myself. Over all, the surprise would be much too fantastic and painful. That it would break his heart was inevitable, but I couldn't do it all at once. It would have to be done a little bit at a time.

I decided to say nothing about it that afternoon, but then the exhilaration from having David's love betrayed me. It shined on my face and would not dissipate in spite of the monkey wrench in our Chicago plans. As we went out on the test drive, Teddy made a comment.

"What are you in such high spirits about?" He turned and looked at me curiously while at a boulevard stop. "Is it the audition or did something special happen at school today?"

"Well–yes." I just couldn't hold back. He had to hear some of it, at least. "Something did happen today, and yesterday, and will again tomorrow."

"Oh, really? What's that?"

"Remember that guy who was giving me so much grief?"

"Yeah?"

"Well, we're, uh, not having problems anymore." I gave him a bright-eyed look that I hoped would deliver the message.

"Oh, so you've, uh, really patched things up." He gave me a sideways glance. "So, are you and David going steady now?"

"But definitely."

"Oh. Well, that's good, I suppose. At least now you won't be so down in the dumps. Jenny, I'm glad for you."

"You don't sound like it, but thanks anyway. Now, please, whatever you do, don't say a word to my family. I don't even want them to know he exists until the right time. Charlotte would just love to mess things up for me."

"All right, mum's the word. I won't tell a soul."

"Thanks. You're a pal."

The car ran just fine during our test drive, so when we got back to the house, I helped Teddy put things away. Then we went inside and washed up for dinner.

My thoughts were lost in David all during dinner. Every now and then, though, I'd look up at Teddy to find him looking back. He would smile, yet somehow didn't seem happy, while I was so wrapped up in bliss that I barely noticed. But by the time we were ready to go, I had learned to keep my facial muscles from breaking into a grin. I also determined to focus my thoughts in the present. As Teddy held the door for me to stash my gear away in the backseat of the Chevy, I was all set for a good rehearsal.

"Well, shipmate," said Teddy as we rode along. "I say we start you out on a small yacht. I'll talk to my brother Collin about you working at his boating business while you get your sea legs. It'll give you spending money while you learn."

"That'd be great." I replied with mixed feelings. He knew that it was one of my favorite dreams, and this was just another way of saying I should unload the boyfriend and keep my commitment to follow along behind him.

"Learn what you can now, babe, like those knots I showed you. Just because Lake Michigan is a called a lake, don't let that fool you. There's real adventure out on the water there. And once you're ready, I'll see that you get out on the lake regular enough to make a real sailor out of you. Okay, mate?"

"Fantastic!" As he spoke I could almost feel the deck rise and fall beneath me. This idea really lit my fire. "I've never seen any kind of ocean before. Once I even considered joining the Navy, but they don't let the women do any of the fun stuff. Oh, Teddy I'd love it."

"Well, that's for sure. And if my brother Paddy's around, I'm sure he'd be glad to sign on as part of the crew."

"Isn't Paddy your baby brother, and he's in the Navy?"

"Right. I just know you'll like him. He's a bit of a rascal, but he's loads of fun. We look a lot alike."

Teddy went on talking about the coming summer until we reached the church, even though I'd tried a couple of times to change the subject. From what I could see, and from what I felt inside, it was going to take a miracle for me to keep that commitment. Thinking the discussion was over, I put aside thoughts about Chicago because it really was a wait and see situation. Until I knew how it would pan out with David embracing the covenant, I wouldn't make any change in my summertime plans with Theodore.

So concentrating on music was easy for me at rehearsal. Unfortunately, Teddy was upset by the prospect of losing out. His mistakes and grumpiness throughout the evening and the sober expression whenever he looked at me made it clear that it was still uppermost in his thoughts.

A feeling of guilt began to nag me while tearing down and anticipating the ride home. Hurting Teddy was the last thing I wanted, yet I couldn't possibly explain what was going on. After loading our instruments and music into the car, we climbed in and he started the engine. While the car warmed up, he turned to me with what was on his heart.

"I guess you probably know I'm a little upset."

"Yes, I noticed."

"Look, honey, I know you love this guy, but have you really stopped to consider what you're doing? What kind of boy is he? Is he saved?"

"No. Not yet, but we've talked about it."

"Somehow I didn't think he was. What if he doesn't get saved? Then what?"

"I'm not sure."

"Well, you should be. Jenny, I hate to say this, but I really don't think you should see this guy at all. For one thing, you'll probably end up getting hurt even more than before, but especially because he's not a Christian. You know as well as I do what the Bible says about being unequally yoked with unbelievers, and there's good reason for that. Already I can see that he's pulling you away from things of the Spirit because you're having second thoughts about going to Chicago. Sure. You're thinking to stick around here so you two can sit and hold hands. But babe, you're only in highschool and this–this romance with David is all going to be over before you know it. Honey, don't let a temporary love affair rob you of things that are eternal. Don't put carnal things above the things of God. When you do, that's when you backslide and get into trouble. I don't want that to happen to you. I love you, Jenny. You're like flesh and blood to me. And I know that God has great plans for you; I can't let you throw them away. Couldn't you try to give up this thing with this guy?"

"I tried that for months, Teddy; it hasn't worked and there's a very good reason why. He's opening up his heart to Y'shua. Before I came home this afternoon we went shopping to get him a study Bible and some reference books. As for going to Chicago, it's not that I don't want to go; it's just that I anticipate him not wanting me to. As far as I'm concerned, it's all in God's hands to work out. I haven't changed my plans for the summer yet. So don't worry about this, okay? It may not seem like it to you, but I'm not just following my flesh."

"All right. But please promise me you'll be very, very careful. And promise me you'll think about what I've said. You have a high calling on your life. I know it like I know my own name. I wish you'd think more about that than going on dates and all that other stuff. God's kingdom is far more important than that."

"Don't worry. I'll be careful."

Putting the car in gear, Teddy took us out of the parking lot, his thoughts still running as he turned to watch for traffic. Sensing that he wasn't done with the topic, I braced myself for whatever was coming next.

"Look–oh, I don't know if I should tell you this now or later." Teddy glanced at his watch. It was twenty after ten. "I'll tell you about it some other time, since it's late. But the Lord has been giving me some very interesting dreams and even some visions. Most of them concern you."

"Yeah? Clue me in."

"I will, but not right now. Jenny–" Teddy's outlook had improved, but he was still a little troubled as he took my hand and said, "You're my mate and I need you. Please don't back out on me with this. If all you want is a boyfriend, you'll have more fellas than you can shake a stick at when you're getting your sea legs. So don't desert me. We're such a great team."

"Oh, Theodore." Sliding to the middle of the bench seat I gave him both my hands to hold. "I need you, too, and I don't want to disappoint you. But when it really gets down to it, the decision isn't mine to make. You knew that from the start. When I said I'd go with you, it was a decision I made on my own. It came from my heart, but I can't honestly say that I got direction from the Lord on it. So don't think I've forgotten that my life belongs to Y'shua. It does, and whatever his Holy Spirit says for me to do, I'll do. So if God wants me to go with you this summer, you can believe I will, and nothing and nobody will keep me away. Okay?"

"Okay."

What I said I meant sincerely, and I did my best to show it. Teddy responded with a smile. Hope shone in his eyes as he reached out to pull me close and yet as I returned his embrace and pressed my face to his neck, I knew his hope was in vain.

WEDNESDAY, FEBRUARY 19:

Where Teddy and I were concerned, the department of dreams and visions was not to be taken lightly, so his words made me a little unsure of what HaShem was indeed doing with the two of us. Still, it was something that would simply have to play itself out, so I prayed about the trip to Chicago and let it go. Besides, once in school, thoughts of my man obscured practically everything else.

My academic life suddenly had a different aura about it. Never had I been so happy and love sick. It was tough getting used to my feet being off the ground. All I could think about was David, whether we were together or apart, and that made me feel a little bit guilty. The last thing I wanted to do was school work. To sit and daydream threatened to become my primary occupation. Whether or not anyone else noticed the state I was in, David's change in mood was obvious to everyone and was becoming a hot topic with the gossip mongers on the faculty.

"Oh! I know what it is," Bonnie Smith declared with a snap of fingers. "I'll bet our Miss West has finally got him."

"Huh? What do you mean?" asked Donna Gilbert around a bite of lunch.

"You know! What we were just talking about. David Conrad! Haven't you seen how cheerful he's been?"

"I even heard him whistling in the hallway this morning," said Linda Armijo, Math teacher. "Yeah, I was thinking the same thing yesterday because I heard him laughing and joking after the faculty meeting. Never heard that before. I'll bet Janette's finally turned him into a Jesus freak."

"Well, I just now figured it out," said Smith. "I should have known, as religious as those two have been with all that Bible reading. I'd even go so far as to say he was asking for it and that it was only a matter of time."

"Well, so what?" said Bill Fletcher. "What difference does it make to you? After all, if it makes the man happy there's certainly nothing wrong with that."

"Yeah, but what about poor Vicky?" said Armijo. "From what I've heard, the very reason he quit her was because of Janette and her religion, and she's still pretty upset about it."

"Well, maybe Dave just came to his senses," said Bill.

"That's not a nice thing to say," said Gilbert. "Vicky is a very sweet girl and not at all like some people think. Just because she's not some holier-than-thou fanatic like Janette West, it doesn't mean she's not a nice girl."

Fletcher sat quiet and lightly pounded his fists on the table.

"Oh! There he is," said Armijo. She looked at David Conrad and sighed. "Somebody get him over here."

"What for?" said Gilbert. "So he can preach to us?"

"No. So we can ask him whether or not he got saved. That way we'll know for sure."

"Excellent idea," said Smith. She called out to David and waved her hand. Juggling brief case and a cafeteria tray, he reluctantly came over.

"Good afternoon, everyone," said David, trying to suppress the love light glowing in his blue-gray eyes.

Smith wore her best smile which always meant she wanted something. "Would you care to join us?"

"Pardon me if I don't, but I have some reading to do."

"But we want to ask you what you've been so happy about lately. You've been walking around like you won the Irish sweepstakes. We've been hearing that you've caught the same religious bug as Janette West. Is it true?"

"Well–not just yet, although I am looking at it a lot closer these days." He paused and seemed to be having second thoughts. "I think I will join you–for a moment." He took a seat across from Bonnie Smith and continued. "It's strange. It really has been uplifting since I decided to look more seriously at Janette's religion. I haven't taken the plunge yet, and it may take a while because there's a lot I still don't understand. To be honest, there are some things about it that are kind of frightening. Anyway, I was the one that made the decision. I like what it's done for Janette, and I figured it couldn't hurt to at least look into it. So I told her how I felt and she suggested I get a study Bible and some other books, and do some reading on my own. We actually went shopping the other day and she picked some books out for me. She'll be helping me, of course, whenever I need it. I just wish we could spend more time on it, given what she knows."

"Have you been to her church yet?" asked Mr Fletcher.

"No, not yet. That's one of the scary parts. Have you ever been to a Pentecostal church?"

"Nope, never have."

"Well, when the Spirit gets to really moving in one of those places, it can scare the pants off of you. I went to one once when I was a kid and wasn't too sure if I'd ever make it out alive. Janette says her church is a bit different than that, but it's still Pentecostal, so I'll have to work up to that."

"I don't blame you," said Gilbert. "I've heard a few stories myself."

"What I'd really like to do," said David. "Is to visit that kibbutz where she got started in all this. She's told me about it and it sounds more my speed. Maybe I'll take off some weekend and go for a short visit. I'm far more interested in the Jewish side of this thing than the Christianity. I'll feel better with traditions I'm already familiar with."

"I can understand that," said Fletcher. "I'm sure I'd feel the same way."

"Well, if you'll excuse me," said David, getting to his feet. "I'll go tackle that reading."

They waited until he was out of earshot before making any comment.

"Like I said," remarked Bonnie Smith. "It's only a matter of time."

"What a shame," said Donna Gilbert. "And he's so good looking. Poor Vicky."

"I don't know," said Linda Armijo. "He smiles more and that makes him even better looking to me. Maybe Bill is right. If it makes him happy, what's wrong with that? Hey, if it works for him, I might check it out for myself."

"It certainly works for me," said Fletcher as he got up and left the table.

This day was hardly worth remembering for me, except for the moments with my sweetheart. Music didn't interest me when I got to his place that afternoon; I only wanted to hold him. Because he felt the same way, our starting time was postponed when he joined me on the piano bench and steamed up my head even more. The part of my brain programmed for reason and logic warned me that somehow I had to snap out of the euphoria. But I wasn't sure if I could. This high was too vaulted and rapturous to come down from.

"I suppose I should give you your lesson," said David after the third kiss. "After all, your parents are paying for your time with me."

"As long as we're making music of some kind," I said. "Does it really matter?"

"Maybe not. You know, there are other things I'd like to teach you."

"Uh, oh." That frightened me enough to put my feet closer to the ground. Suddenly thinking with some sobriety, I gently pulled away.

"Honey, no," he said, drawing me back. "I was just kidding. Please, don't be afraid of me. I was only kidding."

"Okay." I relaxed and let him hold me again. "I don't know. Maybe I should have my lesson. We really shouldn't get into the habit of making love all the time."

"I know you're right, and I promise to behave so that we don't get ourselves into trouble. But can't today's lessons wait until next week? I'll send your folks a refund later for all the times we skip one. Right now, the only thing I want is to keep my arms around you."

"Me, too. Maybe that's why we need a chaperon."

"Chaperon? Don't you trust me?"

"It is a good safety precaution, but there's more to it than that. It'll be an advantage when it comes to seeing each other. You'll see. It's one of the things we can talk about tonight."

"But who could we get that we could trust? Margo?"

"No, my cousin Georgia. She already knows about us and we've already discussed it."

"You've already what?!"

"Now, honey, don't get upset. Everything's fine. George and I have been best friends since we were tiny; and she's nineteen, so that means she's legally an adult. She's also a founding member of the Amateur Detectives Guild, so if anybody can be trusted she can. Besides, she knew about you from the start. I had to tell her the rest of the story."

"Well, all right. I guess having a chaperon is a good idea. But not all the time, okay?"

"Okay."

"Now, let's do your lessons. After all, you are coming over tonight."

After coming home from David's, I was floating on cottony clouds again, though not quite as high as before. Still it made concentrating on homework almost impossible. It took twice as long as it normally did, since I had to read the same material several times before anything registered. Even when it was done, I couldn't be sure if it was right and had to remember to check it again later.

Wednesday was not one of my usual nights to go out, but I wasn't expecting anyone to challenge my leaving because I was gone so often. I didn't plan an excuse to give my parents for leaving the house, since they knew all of my usual haunts and had all the phone numbers in case of emergency; with five others at home to keep track of, they did not insist that I account for every hour of the day as they did when I was younger. I needed my freedom now more than ever, so I appreciated having parents that were beginning to see me more as a responsible adult than a child.

It was my turn to help do the dishes. Olivia would dry while I washed. I got started as soon as I was done eating and moved a little faster than usual because David was expecting me at seven o'clock. Finishing in record time, I then went upstairs to get ready. But as I was heading out the door, the unexpected happened.

"Janette," called my father's voice from the top of the stairs. "Where are you off to tonight? Are you going to David's by any chance?"

Fear sent a chill through me and I stopped in my tracks. He of course meant David Richardson.

"David's? Yeah," I said casually. "Yeah, I'm going over to David's."

"Good. Ask him if he's got another copy of his last album. I know somebody else who wants one."

"Okay."

Had I not been caught off guard, I probably could have come up with something more truthful and yet not given myself away. But I didn't let it bother me. I just hoped he didn't think it odd that I was going there without my guitar.

I was a few minutes early. My man greeted me with a warm embrace and tender kiss and ushered me into the living room.

We sat down on the couch and wrapped ourselves around each other. For a while my sweetheart and I sat in silence, content just to be so close. With my head against his chest I could hear his heart beat and feel his breathing. Closing my eyes, the steady rhythm helped me relax. I refused to give place to thoughts of fear and doubt. That was over, and I would not let those things rob me of the man I loved.

"Can I get you anything?" he asked.

"No, thanks, I'm fine."

"How long can you stay?"

I decided to set my own curfew. "Till ten."

"Good. Are you okay? You seem to be trembling a little."

"I am? I didn't notice."

"Still afraid?"

"I don't think so. I'm sure it's just because this is all so new and different. I don't know if I'll ever get used to this."

"You will. I'll make sure of that. A girl like you shouldn't be so uptight anyway. You must have had plenty of attention, not to mention other boyfriends."

"I've had some attention since my make over, but only a couple of boyfriends."

"So few, as pretty as you are?"

"I wasn't always this pretty. Besides, most guys are too afraid to cross the color line, so there's not a lot to choose from out here."

"How about Cowboy? Didn't you date him a long time?"

"I guess. It seemed we were just friends for most of the time. Then when he did get around to romance, we had to keep it hush-hush because he was white and I was too young for steady dating. Cowboy was nice, but he was awful shy. I was the first girl he'd ever kissed, so you can imagine how awkward that was, especially in the beginning."

"Yes, I can imagine. Well, there must have been someone else since him. How about up at Alef Tav? Oh, and what about Alan Haskell? I'll bet he's kissed you a few times."

"Yeah, but I didn't want it to be anymore than that."

"Oh, really? What didn't you like?"

"His kissing wasn't the problem. We failed to see eye to eye on some very important issues, so I didn't want things between us to go any further."

"I'm sure glad of that. What couldn't you agree on?"

"Religion and romance. Alan's a preacher's kid and his dad is an absolute phony, so he doesn't take God seriously. Then he came on too strong in his display of 'affection.' He was too grabby. Takes after his father, I'm sure."

"Okay, I'll buy that."

"As for the kibbutz, none of the guys dug me or I probably wouldn't be here. But there was this one very cute Israeli that I sort of liked."

"Oh?"

"Like I said, he didn't dig me, so it never turned into anything, which has been the story of my life until now. That's been a big part of my trouble with you. I never dreamed you'd pick me to get serious about."

"Don't I know it. You sure have given me a run for my money."

"But whatever made you want me in the first place?"

"Everything."

"No, be specific."

"I am. When I first saw you–" David stopped and smiled as he thought back. "Maybe I'd better explain something first. You see, I've always had a particular liking for–chocolate."

"Oh, really?"

"Just ask Bob Johnson. I had a huge crush on his oldest sister when I was a kid. Anyway, so here you come and I just couldn't believe my eyes. At first I thought you were a new faculty member or teacher's aid and I said to myself, 'Well, it's about time.' But when you didn't seem to be lost trying to find your classroom, I though maybe Bob sent you over as a practical joke. You were just too perfect: your hair, your perfume, your eyes and that beautiful smile, your figure and the classy way it was draped–the whole package. And you weren't just beautiful, baby, you were radiant! The sight of you that morning was almost like–like sunrise over the Grand Canyon. And I was all set to move right in on you when you slapped me down by letting me know you were a student. Then you really crushed me when you told me who you were. I didn't recover from that for weeks."

"That's understandable. So what else made you want me?"

"Well, to be honest, I'd have to say it was curiosity that helped kill this cat's solitary existence. From that first day, I thought about you every other minute. After all, I had you for three classes, which was enough to frighten any man. But at the same time, I was intrigued by all the things I'd heard about you and how incongruous they were with what I saw. I had to find out what the story was. It reminded me of people that go to horror movies, being fascinated and terrified all at the same time. For all I knew, you just might have up and decided to eat me for breakfast one morning. I thought it'd be wise to do something to prevent that. After all, you had friends on the faculty; why couldn't I be one of them? That's why I offered you lessons right away and tried to keep you in French class.

"So that's how it started out, but added to that is the fact that you gave me something nice to think about and look forward to that wasn't routine or ordinary. And somehow that first impression of you just would not go away. It haunted me, even in my dreams. You were so different, not just from the other students, but from all the other women I knew. It was captivating the way you always seemed to glow; the way you were always so happy and– well, peaceful–all those things were especially attractive. But to pinpoint a particular thing, place or time that meant falling in love is kind of tough. It was gradual, even though it happened fast. I was still afraid of you, so I had mixed feelings for the first few weeks. Then again, I couldn't let myself get too interested because of your age. But then we had brunch and got better acquainted–that was a big turning point." He laughed and shook his head. "First of all, you showed up looking so good that it was all I could do to keep from grabbing you and taking you home with me. But when you told me I was more than just another pretty face–that really did it. Not only wasn't I afraid of you any more, what you said tickled me for days. After that I was determined to hang onto you and real tight. I needed someone who could make me laugh and who was interesting to talk to. Common sense told me I was just infatuated and I tried to listen to it, but it lied. There were times I told myself you were just a novelty and that I had no real intention of getting involved, but–when I looked closely at all the things you were, I realized that, except for your age, you were exactly what I'd been looking for. And it felt so good after all these years of not feeling the flame that I decided against my better judgment to let it burn for a little while, only to find I couldn't put it out. Before I knew it I was a goner."

"So, how did you feel when I got kidnaped?"

"Are you kidding me? I was nearly a candidate for the funny farm. If it hadn't been for Margo, I'm sure I'd have lost it completely. No joke, honey. This may sound peculiar, but you know, that Noonan case is what really cinched it. Before that, I was still trying to ignore what I was beginning to feel and just focus on staying on your good side while finding out what you were about. But when you told me about that evil joker, it helped me see just what you were doing to me. Just the thought that he might hurt you kept me awake nights even before anything happened; I felt helpless because I didn't know how to protect you. Then when he actually had you, I didn't dare let myself think of the possibilities. That situation made it real clear what it was doing for me just to be near you–especially in the ambulance when you let me hold your hand and gave me that look of love. Oh, honey, if we'd been alone, I'd have kissed you right then and there. That night sealed my fate for sure. Oh, I still had occasional doubts after that, but I was bound and determined to ignore them."

I smiled at having hit my mark so well, but said nothing.

"Yes, brunch and the Noonan case were the final nails in my bachelor's coffin."

"Right! After we met for brunch was when you stopped wearing those ugly horn rimmed glasses at my lessons."

"Yes, I did. And you know what? To show you just how you messed up my head from the start, I didn't even consider that giving you so much attention might cause you to have a crush on me. Normally I avoid situations like that completely. When I did realize what I was doing, I wouldn't quit because I liked the idea–a lot. It started me daydreaming about what I would do if you did fall for me."

"Oh, really? Haut boy! I want to hear about that."

"Well–I'll tell you my daydreams if you tell me yours about me."

"Oh, never mind. Just go on."

"I thought you might feel that way. Anyway, that's pretty much it. We both know how much we have in common, which also has been a mind blower. I even got a kick out of your religion, although at the time I couldn't see God the same way you did. No, you weren't the monster they had told me about. You were a little angel sent from heaven. It's no wonder I got hooked and couldn't get loose."

"Oh, but you did make quite an effort."

"Sure, but only because you were such a tough customer. When I remembered how you had the nerve to tell me to my face that you weren't the least bit interested, I figured the mind set you had against me was stronger than anything else and I was just making a big mistake."

"Oh. I guess I did say that, didn't I? I sure didn't mean it. But if you had just said something sooner, I would have responded favorably to that."

"Ha! In a pig's eye. But don't think for a minute I wasn't dying to. I came close to it a few times, but courting you was such a delicate situation that I was afraid to mess it up. You know, when that look of love you had for me in the ambulance and at the victory party disappeared, I couldn't figure out what happened and I got pretty desperate, thinking I had to start all over again. I'd never seen a woman so determined to control her feelings and wasn't too sure what to do. But I did know that I had to convince you that I wanted you for more than just sex. The Noonan affair made me especially conscious of that issue. But then you told me yourself just what I was up against when we were dealing with Helen's crush on me. You and your damned logic. I could have strangled you! What you said to her let me know that I'd blow it for sure if I came on to you too strong or too soon. Then you told me you'd never consider marrying someone like me who didn't yet believe. So I worked on that and did all

I could to make you love me just as much as I loved you before I dared say or do anything. I figured you would fight me if I made an obvious move, and the last thing I wanted was for our first romantic encounter to be a big struggle. So I did little things, but I did a lot of little things that would tell you how I felt. Then that thing with Lisa Overton knocked all the wind out of my sails. I was so ashamed to have you see into that part of my life, and I didn't think you'd ever want me after that. But you seemed so understanding and forgiving that I took a chance the day of the caroling party and put my arms around you. Later I wanted to go a little farther when I gave you the bracelet. I'd have kissed you like I did the other night. But as soon as you picked up on what I was about to do, you almost flipped out. The look on your face told me I'd better change my plans. Oh, no. I wasn't about to have you start screaming bloody murder or give me a shiner like you did Alan Haskell, so I settled for less. And after seeing how terrified you were of my affection, I just gave up. I wasn't sure I'd ever get past the barriers you were putting up. So the next day after the caroling party, I hopped a plane to New York City to be with friends for the holidays and did what I could to put out the fire. I went to one party after another and half the shows on Broadway, but I still couldn't get you out of my system. And yet there was nothing I could do if you didn't want me. So when school started I kept my distance, rather than continue making a fool of myself. But when I saw how much it upset you for us to be apart, I had to make up with you and try again."

"I sure am glad you did."

"I am, too. It's more than a cliché when I say I've never felt quite this way about anyone else before. I don't know. You're pretty wonderful, but maybe it's also because I've been so long without the happiness I've always wanted."

"But why have you never married?"

He sighed heavily and thought for a moment. "Someday I'll tell you all about it. But for now, let's just say that I've been a very, very unlucky man. Right now, though, I'd say my luck is changing."

"This isn't luck. Luck is fickle; it changes in an instant."

"You've got that right. Only God could do something like this. I just wish he'd done it sooner."

"But David, I had to grow up first."

"Oh, come on! You're saying God made you just for me?"

"Well, it's possible. I sure wouldn't put it past him."

"That's interesting. I'll have to think about that one. Hmmm." He smiled over the thought and nodded. "That's a very nice concept. Yes, I like that."

"I just hope I've been worth the wait."

David turned and surveyed me hungrily. "That's a tough one, baby. You don't know what I've been through. But I guess I can say that having you now does make it much easier to forget the past. I don't know. Maybe if I'd had more faith years ago, God would have sent you along sooner.

Right now I'm just glad that he did. Whether God made you special for me or not, he sure knew what he was doing when he put us together. You are absolute perfection."

"I know I couldn't have picked anyone better than you. I may have resisted, honey, but it was never easy. Especially once we started getting better acquainted and you wouldn't let me alone."

"I didn't want to leave you alone and I didn't dare if I was going to make you love me. It was obvious from the start that it wouldn't be easy, even though I didn't count on the fight you put up. I expected trouble with you for another reason. See, I've already had some experience with your kind."

"With my kind? What's that supposed to mean?"

"Once upon a time there were these Christian women that I dated steadily (at separate times) who were very devout and talked, well–kind of like you do. Each was very attractive and I had hopes for something serious. But as soon as things started to get that way, they called it quits for no good reason. Each woman gave me the same line about not being 'unequally yoked' with an unbeliever."

"Oh. That's from a verse in the New Testament."

"Is that so? Well, wherever it comes from, I don't like it. I didn't like it then and I don't like it now. After a while I felt pretty sure you were thinking along those same lines, and eventually you confirmed it. There were times it made me mad enough to take that Bible of yours and rip it in two. But Janette, I was desperate, and I knew that if God was real, I could never beat him at his game. With those other women I secretly sneered at their religion and considered it childish. Maybe that's why nothing ever happened with them. So instead of letting myself get angry, this time I tried believing a little stronger; both you and Bob helped me a lot with that, not to mention Helen Bombardner and seeing the change in her life. That was a miracle for sure. Then I made efforts to pray and began going to temple more regularly."

"And you dumped all your girlfriends?"

"Yes, and for several reasons. First of all, I just wasn't interested in their company anymore. But also, I figured that where God was concerned he'd be much happier if I dropped them. Then again I figured that with them out of the picture, you'd have a better opinion of me. Except that it backfired when Lisa Overton became a jealous nutcase."

"Well, when Vicky collared me about your breakup, I was impressed with the reason you unloaded her. But you're right. That thing with Lisa didn't help things any. I knew you must have had other girlfriends, but it was different seeing up close how you can operate."

"So you knew? How?"

"Oh, element'ry! Why shouldn't there be others? I sure thought that teacher over at Jackson Elementary was awful cute. What was her name?"

"Okay, what clued you in?"

"There is a certain look in a woman's eye."

"And it's the same look I wanted to see in yours; but you kept it under wraps so that I'd only get a glimpse of it now and then, and never long enough for it to be encouraging."

"But it's good that I was able to hide it. If you could see it then so could others."

"That's a good point, but still it was pure agony to watch how you refused to let yourself go. I figured you were ready to stop fighting me the day I apologized, but you just kept it up. Ah, but the day we had breakfast in the classroom and I accidentally made you cry–I knew I had you."

"But once you were sure about the way I felt, why did it take you so long to approach me? You could have done it very easily at one of my lessons."

"I would have after your next lesson, but you rushed out when I asked you to stay. Of course, I could have tried making a date with you for another time, but you're so all-fired busy these days that I thought I'd just pour it on a bit heavy in advance of the setup I already had for Valentines Day. If it hadn't worked out like it did the night of the concert, I'd have hit on you at the next lesson for sure."

"Oh, boy!"

"I'm sure glad you feel that way. You did like the presents I sent you?"

"Oh, yes! I've never seen a larger or lovelier bouquet of roses. And your concept of a box of chocolates was the most!"

"That's a real gold box, you know."

"Yes. Georgia pointed that out to me and I almost didn't believe it. 18 karat gold! David, you overwhelmed me."

"Was it 18 karat? I can't remember, since I looked at so many. Did anybody else comment?"

"I'll say they did, but only about the roses. Thankfully, I was there when the delivery was made, so no one but Georgia has seen the card and the music box."

"Good. It's what I was hoping for. I paid extra to make sure the delivery was timed for when you got home from school and that the delivery guy gave it only to you. And, honey, there's plenty more where that came from. Whatever it takes to keep you next to me, it doesn't matter; and I've never said that to any other woman. I sure love you, baby."

"David, keep the money for now; it's novel but it doesn't really interest me. You're what interests me. If I'd had any idea how you really felt, I'd have given in to you a long time ago."

"Fat chance. Look, what I did for you any other girl would have flipped over–and they'd have gotten the message, too. But not you. That's why I had to start believing in miracles, because nothing short of divine intervention was going to bring you around. That's the truth. I told God that if he was real and loved me like everyone was telling me, then to make you fall hopelessly in love with me and I'd do anything he wanted for as long as I lived."

"Well, mister, you got what you asked for. I'm a pretty hopeless case.

And looking back, I was probably at that point long before you even started praying. The problem was that I just didn't want to admit it."

"Really? That soon?"

"Well, if not, I was sure on my way. Remember when I told you to have breakfast with Miss Marshall instead of me? Well–"

"I don't remember that."

"That was when we had laughed at her country music and you got in trouble with her. Remember? You said I was dangerous to be around."

"Oh, all right. I remember."

"Well, you don't know just how glad I was that you didn't stop asking me to breakfast then. I couldn't believe I'd said anything so incredibly stupid. By that time I was getting to be pretty well addicted to you."

"No kiddin'?"

"Oh, I'm sure. Like I said, I didn't want to admit it. Aside from the fact that I'd had more than my fill of one sided relationships, it was pride in my ability to control my emotions plus that good old common sense that told me such an affair would be pointless. I saw how you found me attractive, but I felt that even if something should happen, that it wouldn't last. So I could accept the fact that I loved you as a friend, but not that I was catching the same amorous ailment as all those other females. Oh, I was way above that sort of thing. Getting a crush on a teacher was for all those frilly little chumps that still have ruffles on their panties. But you did so many wonderful things and we were together so much that I honestly couldn't help myself. Still I had to stay in control so that you wouldn't get the wrong idea, or get scared and dump me if you saw that dreamy look again. I was playing it safe."

"You knew I wouldn't dump you. You just didn't think my intentions were honorable."

"Well, what was I supposed to think?"

"That in all of the time we spent together alone, I never once put the make on you. If I'd wanted to, I could have pushed your little buttons every other minute until you were seducing me. You're looking at an expert."

"I know."

"Sweetheart, I wanted to play it straight, for you and for myself. I didn't want anything cheap and dirty. I've had enough of that."

"That's something I needed to hear."

"I know, and every word of it is true. Now, I'd like to hear the story from your angle. What made me so hard to resist?"

"Well, my looks got your attention, and yours got mine."

"Thank you. That restores my ego, since you so rudely crushed it."

"Was it really that bad?"

"Yes. Not that I didn't have it coming. But still, once it's been deflated like that, you have to build it up again. Tell me what you liked about me."

"Oh, I don't know. There were the obvious things that got to my attention right away, but in order to feel anything beyond basic titillation,

I had to get to know you first."

"What did you like at first?"

"Well, you were very handsome, well dressed, intelligent, and you had plenty of dough."

He smiled. "You noticed my money right away?"

"Of course. In New Mexico wealth and class like yours sticks out like a glazed ham at an Orthodox bar mitzvah."

"Okay. So, what else did you like about me?"

"I liked the way you liked me, the way you couldn't stop looking at me that first day of school. That did nice things for my ego. Oh, and I loved your voice from the moment you first spoke. Then later on it really got to me when you sang. That took a long time to get used to."

"Good. I was hoping for that."

"You were? You stinker! You ought to be ashamed of yourself, trying to make a little girl swoon."

"I'm not sorry in the least. A man's got to do what a man's got to do." David deepened the tone of his voice. "Is this how my voice sounded when you first heard me speak?"

"You mean you did that on purpose?"

"I sure did. But what about you, with that deadly rose sent that you wear? What's that about, as if I didn't know?"

"It's simply how I like to smell. It's my trade mark."

"I'll say it is. That stuff put some powerful ideas in my head, especially when you wore it at your lessons. I couldn't think of flowers without being reminded of you. So what else did you like about me?"

"Nothing. At least not for a few days. And I was determined not to let those obvious, outward things turn my head. Especially your good looks."

"Right. What was that you said to Helen? It was something about there being good looking men on death row. Yeah, you really know how to encourage a fella."

"Will you stop that? David, what did impress me the most was far more important and you know it. What captured my heart was the way you tried to know me for yourself and accept me as the person I am rather than believe all of the bad things you'd heard. To be honest, I felt kind of sorry for you since you couldn't know whether or not I'd come after you someday, and it was obvious that we needed to get along. So I prayed for God to give us a good relationship, and did he ever! I'd never gotten so much help and attention before, all the way from private lessons up to working on my new songs. Then you were always so patient when I had problems with French; I certainly appreciated that. Now, it did bother me when you wouldn't let me drop the class, but later on I was glad. I don't know many teachers who would have taken the time with me that you did; I really thought it was wonderful."

"I thought it was wonderful, too, until Helen butted in."

"Were you doing that just to get next to me?"

"No, I'd have done it for anyone I felt would have applied themselves, but it was still in the back of my mind. Now go on. What else?"

"Let's see. Well, there was your courage and ingenuity in handling Jacob Noonan, not to mention the way you stayed with me through that whole ordeal. As a matter of fact, that was my point of no return. You saw how I was that night and then at the barbeque. You swept me off my feet. Before the Noonan incident, I liked you a lot and I could feel the love of God for you really strong at times; but afterward, I just out and out loved you, even though I did my best to control it. And then the things you did with music– at my lessons, with the choir and the madrigal group, plus your wonderful arrangements–but especially what you did with my music. That opened up my heart to you in a way that made you impossible to resist, even when I thought I wanted to. Oh, David, everything you did for me I liked. You've always been kind, thoughtful and generous, not only with me but with others. That let me know it was something real in you and that you weren't being nice to me just to save your own skin. Also, I've appreciated your ability to be open, honest and tactful all at the same time, especially when we've discussed religion. Qualities like that are what did me in and got me to dream of something more with you, not your looks or your money."

"Well, that is good to know. But tell me a little more. How'd you feel when I started coming on to you?"

"Confused at times. Afraid. Even though I wanted your affection, I didn't think you could want anything from me that you weren't getting from your girlfriends. I thought that it was just a hormonal attraction that came and went as you decided to entertain it, and then only for fun; so I ignored anything that appeared to be flirtation. Other times I was in agony because I was in love with a man who didn't love God and yet God wasn't helping me get free of it. I even got a dose of prayer and counseling about it from one of the sisters in the congregation, and it didn't do one bit of good. At least not the way I thought it should. So, yes, I was like those Christian women you dated. I guess I didn't get off as easy as they did."

"Hey!"

"You know I don't mean that. I'm just glad that I wised up to what was going on and didn't blow it by trying to do what I believed was the right thing. And now that I've stopped leaning to my own limited understanding of the way God works, I'm inclined to believe that he planned this before I was even born."

"What makes you say that?"

"Too many coincidences–which means that they aren't just coincidences. For one thing, with all the evangelism going on here through ministries like Rock of the Witness, I could have gotten saved right here in Albuquerque. Instead God sent me up to Colorado to some Jewish people. Then look at the make over I got up there and the clothes. God wanted you to see me as a woman instead of a little girl. He planned your first impression of me because he wanted it to stick. And what about all the things we have in common? You just happen to teach French and music which are my favorite subjects."

"You even wore my favorite color the first time I saw you. I see what you mean."

"Yes. As time goes on, I'm sure I'll see other things as well. It's funny. From our standpoint, God's sense of timing can be terribly slow, but he has the tendency to make things happen precisely when they need to. I get the feeling this is one of those that he's been piecing together for decades."

"So God was on my side after all?"

"You'd better believe he was. Sure, there's enough between us for a mutual attraction, but the Lord arranged for us to meet and mingle. He wanted us to love each other this way, and that's why neither one of us could shake the feelings we had. I just wish I'd known that then instead of finding it out now. I could have saved myself some bad headaches. But on the other hand, you had to come to that place of putting your trust in God, which might not have happened if I'd given in to you so soon. So I'd say that it came out about right."

"Well, I'm glad you can say that. It seems to me that it took a life time to get to where we are now. But that struggle is over, thank God. Now all I want is to hold you for the rest of my life. Janette, will you marry me?"

"Yes."

"You will?"

"Yes, David. I will."

In reply, he pulled me up tight against his chest, kissing my neck, my cheek and then my mouth, pushing my lips apart and sending his breath through my nostrils. Would I ever get used to the thrill? My head steamed up, and even with my eyes closed it was like the room was spinning. My heart was beating like crazy by the time he took his lips away.

Yes, I consented to marry David Conrad, but I didn't say when. I had not given up my hope of marrying a godly man, but I couldn't exactly lay down the law and give him an ultimatum. However long it took for him to receive Messiah's salvation, I would wait.

"I'd marry you tomorrow, if I could," he said. "But we'll probably have to wait until July when you're eighteen."

"Probably."

"I want kids, you know."

"How many?"

"I don't care. Not too many, though. I want to enjoy my wife."

"Do you want kids right away? What about my going to college?"

"Oh, you can still go to college, that is, if you don't mind going pregnant. College will be good for you. All you have to do is have the babies. I'll take care of them."

"You mean you want to do the diaper and bottle routine?"

"Sure, why not? Why go out and work if I don't have to? That way I can enjoy my kids as they grow up; get to know them instead of being a stranger like so many fathers are. If it turns out to be more than I can handle, then I'll hire a nanny. We'll get a housekeeper to do the other work so we can both enjoy life."

"Oh, and what about Anthony Vaughn?"

"I'm not sure. I honestly hadn't thought he'd want to take you because of his finances, but maybe you can travel with him during the summer months. Let me give it some more thought and we can talk about it later."

"Sounds good to me. Oh, David, this is so incredible.."

"It is for me, too, honey. Maybe–" He sighed and chewed his lip for a moment. "Maybe one of these days I'll tell you some of the things about me that you don't know. Then you'll understand just how much you mean to me. But not now."

"All right." This time I kissed him. I refused to be afraid any more. He was the man I was going to marry, and I wanted to give just as good as I got. David responded with passion and a blissful grin.

"Baby, you do just fine for a girl with so little experience. Are you sure you're telling me everything?"

"Yes, I'm sure."

"I don't know. I'm beginning to think the chaperon is actually going to protect me."

"Stop it. You're embarrassing me." I pinched him on the arm.

"Ow! You little beast. One of these days, so help me, I'm going to give you the spanking you deserve."

"Love me?"

"I sure do. Even when you're mean to me. You know, I hadn't planned on asking you to marry me tonight or I'd have had a ring for you."

"Oh, but David, I couldn't wear it anyway. People would ask questions."

"That's true. But you could wear it around your neck on a chain or just keep it in the box to look at. Anyway, I'm going to give you something else until I get your ring. It'll be a lot less conspicuous." David left me for a brief moment and went into his bedroom. He returned holding out an ordinary key ring with a single key on it. "This is for you," he said, then placed it in my hand and closed my fingers around it.

"The key to your heart?"

"You already have that. This is the key to my apartment. Now, don't take this wrong, baby. I'm not asking you to use it. But since you'll be living here someday, you ought to get used to the idea. This will be a reminder."

Propriety immediately said to give it back. The detective in me said to keep it for when it comes in handy. Then all of that was pushed aside as the reality of what he had just said hit me. Looking at the key and then the surroundings, a strange feeling went through me as I considered the eventuality of this commitment. Except for Alef Tav, I'd lived in one house all of my life, and now I was faced with taking up permanent residence with my Mr Conrad. I almost blew a fuse.

"I don't–know what to say." I finally told him.

David turned my wide eyed face toward his and studied me with concern. "I'm sorry, baby. It's not really appropriate to give you a spare apartment key, but it's only symbolic, to show that I'm giving up my independence to share my life with the woman I love. If it makes you uncomfortable, you don't have to accept it."

This was a nice sentiment which made the idea more palatable, but still I felt unsure. Then again, the whole business felt strange, and just being alone with this man wasn't the most proper thing for a young girl like me. At the same time, though, God had set it all up. Go figure.

"Well, Janette, do you want it?"

It wasn't as if he'd asked for the key to my place as in a situation where I lived alone, nor had he suggested I bring some of my things over. Believing David was on the level with the reasons he had presented, the detective in me won out. I closed my fingers around the little ring and said, "Just you try and get this away from me."

He sighed with relief and smiled again. "Good. Look, I'm a little hungry. Why don't we both go into the kitchen and see what's there?"

"Sure. I'm ready for something myself."

I dropped the key into my purse and followed David into the kitchen.

"Any TV dinners in there?" I asked, looking past him into the ice box.

"No. Do you like those things?"

"Yeah. That's how I cook."

"It is not. . . . Is it?"

"No, I'm teasing."

"It doesn't matter. I can be the chef or hire one. Want a sandwich? I've got some good cold cuts from the butcher."

"No, I'm kind of in the mood for something sweet."

"Okay. Check the cabinet above the spice rack."

David fixed himself half a sandwich and a beer while I had Scottish shortbread and a cup of tea. We sat down at the dining room table and talked some more.

"Now, tell me about this cousin of yours," said David. "What's her name again?"

"Georgia. Georgia Holister. She helped Margo and I start the Guild. Her code name is Gorgeous George."

"And is she?"

"Yes."

"Oh."

"Anyway, her family lives in one of the suburbs of Chicago, but she wants to stay here in Albuquerque and go to UNM for a while. She'll be getting a part time job and her own apartment, see. Once she gets her own place, all I have to do is say I'm going over to Georgia's and we can meet there any time we want."

"That sounds like a pretty good idea."

"Yes. And if we need to be out in public together, she can come along and make it look proper. That way it won't be just you and me and people will have nothing to talk about. With Georgia in on things, we can spend more time together than we ever could without her. We've even worked out a little code so we can talk about ourselves in front of other people. I'll be Lizzy and Georgia is Olga, and your code name is Joe. But there's more to the code than having different names. For instance, if you need to call me at home–which you probably shouldn't do unless it's important–you may want to disguise your voice at times and speak to me like you do at breakfast. Also there will be times when we talk about ourselves in the third person. But don't worry, I'll write it all out for you."

"Fine. Now, does Georgia speak French or Hebrew?"

"I'm glad you asked. She does speak French."

"Excellent! I think I'm going to like having a chaperon."

"Good. I thought you might see it that way."

"How close does she want to live to the campus? If she doesn't mind driving a couple of miles, I could get her a good deal on a real nice apartment."

"That's right! You can."

"Sure. Have her give me a call . . . Lizzy, old girl. Why no fancy name for me? Why just Joe?"

"Because I've heard that's what happiness is called."

David's expression turned to awe and pleasant surprise, and then his eyes grew moist as he said, "Baby, you are absolutely, positively the best ever."

"I'm sure glad you think so."

"Come here, you."

Refreshment was forgotten for the few moments that David wrapped his arms around me and showered me with tender affection. Also forgotten were the questions still floating in the back of my mind about my mystery man, all of which would have to wait for a more opportune time.

THURSDAY, FEBRUARY 20:

At school, while David was smiling and whistling happy tunes, I bounced back and forth between a mild state of shock and slap happy euphoria. Though now more alert, I still wasn't much good for anything. All I could think about was our commitment to marry, carrying the apartment key around in my hand and looking at it to remind myself that it was real. In this state of mind I had no business doing anything, especially crossing the street. Going home from school, I was oblivious to traffic and all else around me, until I heard my name being called and the repeated honking of a horn. Stopping in the middle of the street, I turned to see who it was that wanted me. Screeching tires and the honking of more horns told me to get out of the way, so I went on to the curb and shouted a reply across the way.

It looked like Johnny. Georgia had obviously sent him, but still it seemed odd to have him come for me. He was sitting in her little red sports car, parked a few feet from the gate I'd just come out of. As soon as it was safe to cross, I hurried over.

"Hullo!" he shouted. "Georgia sent me to get you."

"Great!" It was just as I had believed, so I climbed in without a second thought. A talk with Georgia was just what I needed.

"I wasn't sure I'd be able to find you," he said. "I don't know this city at all. Always quite an experience driving in this country."

"I would imagine so," I said, working to hold on to my American accent.

"By the by, I should introduce myself. My name is Noel."

That jolted me awake. I turned to look at the stranger behind the wheel to see why I had mistaken him for Johnny. There was an obvious age difference, since Noel wasn't much older than me; and this man's features were somewhat softer than his father's, making him much better looking. His mouth was slightly fuller than Johnny's; also his nose wasn't quite as long and had no hook. But both had the same jet black curly hair, long sideburns, and large, dark, piercing eyes topped with the same thick, black eyebrows.

"I feel as if I already know you," he went on, while starting the engine. "Georgia's told me so much about you," he said over his shoulder while waiting for a break in traffic.

"Well, she's certainly given you the advantage. She's said almost nothing about you."

"Yes, but then I've been with her more than you have lately. Letters can only say so much, you know."

"That's true."

"But to be perfectly honest, she wanted to surprise you. You know, since I was coming in later and all. Ah, now we go." With a break in the passing traffic, Noel pulled the car away from the curb and took a slow pace through the streets as we talked. "You see, Janette, people who don't know me often mistake me for my father at first, and occasionally my father is mistaken for me. Mostly it's the eyes that do the trick. Otherwise, we really don't look that much alike."

"I ought to strangle her."

"Just for having a bit of fun? Come now. You certainly don't mean it."

"Oh, yes I do. But I'll wait till she's no longer of any use to me. Then I'll get her."

"You're as funny as she is. Mind if I smoke?"

"Not really. Just crack the window."

"Thanks."

"You're an artist, I hear. You illustrate children's books?"

"Right. And book jackets sometimes. Ever since the family discovered I had artistic abilities they've been putting me to work. But painting's what I really like. You know, that awful modern stuff. I'm really quite good, even if I do say so myself. You're a bit of an artist, too, I understand."

"Sort of. I've got the talent but I've never done much to develop it.

George is much better than I am when it comes to that. My thing is music."

"I certainly do wish it were mine. I love music and I'm not without some talent, but for some reason my family has always discouraged me from taking lessons and pushed art instead. Which reminds me; Georgia's told me about your detective business. The–uh, what is it called?"

"The Amateur Detectives' Guild. It's just a club. What made you think of that?"

"Like I said, they've always done their best to keep me out of music, and it wasn't until recently that I discovered why and quite by accident. You see, my mother was in the music business; a singer. They never speak of her. I don't even know what she looked like except for a general description. About all I know is that she died when I was very young and that she was an American. Georgia promised she'd help me find out more about her. Since you're in that detective's whatever, I suppose she'll enlist your help as well."

"It doesn't sound like you have too many clues to go on. Do you think maybe she was famous?"

"I doubt it, or else I'm sure I'd know more. No, I'm afraid she must have been rather obscure; otherwise the servants or the locals wouldn't have been able to keep their mouths shut. From what I gather, no one in my household, either servants or relations, thought very highly of her, which means that she must have been quite wonderful. She didn't stay in England long because she couldn't get on with the family. Not many people can, so that's not exactly a black mark against her."

"Do you know her name?"

"Rebecca Anne. Childers was her maiden name. I wouldn't have known that if I hadn't at long last seen my birth certificate. Father's always taken care of things, you know."

"Have you got that with you?"

"Yes."

"Well, your little bit of information is a start, but I'd be willing to bet money that Rebecca Anne Childers had a stage name, which means don't get your hopes up. Still, we can give it a shot. I have a couple of friends from California who know a lot about show business and might be able to at least tell me some places to look for clues."

"If you can discover anything at all, I swear I'll be forever in your debt. Do you think perhaps–I'm sorry, but may I correctly assume that you're into Jesus just as Georgia is?"

"Oh, yes, very much so."

"Since you seem to agree with Georgia that I don't have any hope other than prayer, perhaps if you'll add you prayers to hers on my behalf, something will turn up. I find this whole Jesus People movement most interesting. At first I couldn't see what all the bother was, but having met Georgia and heard what she's had to say, I'd like to know more. Never cared much for religion personally; so stodgy and all, even though I'm sure it does someone some good somewhere. Now there's all these Jesus groups springing up all over and seeming quite fanatical, but in a pleasant sort of way, I think. Could it be just a fad, something that will be here today and gone tomorrow?"

"It's called revival and that's what comes and goes. It usually happens at least once in a generation, and it varies in how far it spreads. But the effects of it are always lasting. Real revival always brings with it tremendous change that will affect the area it touches for decades."

"Is that so? Revival. . . . Well, perhaps you and Georgia can show me some of this revival business so I can better understand it. Oh, and another thing entirely on a different note, but I've just remembered it. I'd like to know the best spots for soaking up local color. You know: cowboys, Indian reservations and all that sort of thing. Nothing touristy or artificial, you understand; I want the real thing so that I can paint and take photographs. I expect you'd be best to show me what I want."

That's all I need, another man hanging on to me. I never thought I'd say this, but I've got plenty of men to deal with and I don't need anymore. Let somebody else have this one. "Look, Noel, if it were possible, I'd love to show you around, but I don't have a lot of time to spare. This is my senior year of highschool, and that makes my schedule full of activities. Then again I'm involved with two different churches. I'll do what I can to help out, but don't expect too much, if anything. Georgia lived here for a while and knows quite a bit of New Mexico, so she can help; or once you meet them, you could ask one of my sisters. Charlotte might show you around."

"Charlotte. Is she older or younger than you?"

"Younger. I'm seventeen. How old are you?"

"I turned twenty just before Christmas."

"That's why your name is Noel."

"Yes, that's right. Now, here's our hotel. Is this where I make the turn for parking or have I missed it?"

"No, this is it coming up at the light."

"Thank you."

Johnny and Aunt Laura had rented one of the suites used by traveling dignitaries who come with an entourage. It gave them plenty of room for privacy, since the two were not yet married, yet it allowed them to communicate easily and have their meals together. Once inside I had no chance to talk with Georgia about David. Not only was Noel with us, but her mother, little sister Veronica and Johnny were there wanting to chat. Being with the Holister-Angrahm clan did bring a little more order to my thought processes, and I had a good time. Noel did two sketches of Georgia and I together, and we were each given one. But in spite of good company, there was still a deep need to talk about what I was going through. As soon as possible, I whispered to Georgia that I had to tell her the latest, but our chance to talk would be a while. I ended up staying for dinner. After that it was time to go home and get ready for rehearsal at St Basil's.

The chance to talk did come as Georgia drove me home. I gave her details of the past couple of days of being with David and she enjoyed every word.

"Oh, wow! I can't wait to meet this guy," she said, shaking her long brown curls. "Be sure to give me his number and I'll call him tomorrow about that apartment–and then some. I want to make sure he's for real."

"Oh, yeah? Well, you be careful. You mess anything up for me, dearie, and you'll be sorry."

"Now, come on, Jan, you know me. I guarantee he'll get the kid glove treatment. But this is for your well being, kiddo. Somebody's got to check him out with some objectivity."

"Okay, but I warn you, he's an expert at sidestepping areas he doesn't want to go into."

"We'll see about that. Oh, and that reminds me. I wanted to talk to you about this business with Noel's mother. Look, why don't you let me take you to this rehearsal, and then we can talk on the way?"

"Okay. Then you can meet Teddy."

"The priest? Okay, great."

Georgia pulled the car into the driveway and we both went into the house. About ten minutes later we were out on the street again and headed toward St Basil's.

"So what'll you do with the priest now, dump him?"

"Dump him? Whatever for?"

"I just figured you'd want to lose him so that David won't get jealous."

Before I could even mull it over, I had my answer. "Nope. My relationship with him is a different ball game. It wouldn't be right to give it up because we minister together."

"But I thought you had a thing for him as well. You said he was very affectionate and really good looking."

"Yes, he is, and while I have found him somewhat attractive, I've never had a real passion for him. I guess I could have, but the Lord said nix, and it turned out to be a good thing, too. He's got plenty to offer but he's not yet ready to give it away. Oh, but Mommy and Daddy think he and I are sweet on each other. Poor guy. They want us to get married."

"Seriously? Well! He must really be all right. Say, Jan, if you don't want him, can I have him?"

"Georgia! He's a Catholic priest."

"That's okay. I love a man in a uniform. You said he's born again and filled with the Holy Spirit, right?"

"Yeah."

"Then maybe he's ready to break with some more of his religion. He might even leave that church all together."

"Don't bet on it. Look, I know this guy. I know him real well, and he's Catholic to the bone. Leave him alone, George. That day may come, but I'm not holding my breath for it."

"Oh, I was just kidding. To be honest, I've been letting God straighten out that part of my life ever since I got saved, and I know it's something that's still in the works. I shouldn't even be joking about it because it really isn't funny. I'm not going to go back to the way I used to be for nothing or nobody. Did you know I only had one date in the last fourteen months?"

"Really? You've only been in the Kingdom for–let's see, sixteen months. That's amazing!"

"You've got that right. But I'm getting to the place where I prefer it because of what I'm learning by letting Jesus fill that part of my life. I know that eventually the Lord will allow me to marry, but I'm in no hurry. Oh, which reminds me, watch out for Noel. He's just as much of a lady killer as Johnny."

"Johnny is a lady killer?"

"Why not? He's got both money and personality. You've seen how charming he can be. Well, Noel's a bit of a charmer, too, only he has a more subtle approach. I told him where I stood right off the bat and he's behaved himself since then, but I get the feeling he might come after you. Not that you'd have any problem with him; I just thought I'd let you know."

"Thanks. Now about this business with his mother; why doesn't he just go to Los Angeles and hire a private eye? He'd get much better results and a lot quicker."

"He doesn't want Johnny to know what he's doing. If he went running off to California, Johnny would instantly know why. This thing about his mother has been kind of a sore spot between them for years. Now that Noel is old enough and has some real money of his own, he wants to do what he can to discover his past and yet keep the peace with his father."

"Poor Noel. I can't imagine why the big secret, but I think he's old enough to know about it now, whatever it is. He told me that he's twenty years old."

"That's right. It's kind of hard to remember, though, because he tends to act a lot younger than his age. He's led kind of a sheltered life, and he lives in sort of a dream world."

"I suspect that Johnny may, too, to some degree. Are you sure your mom ought to marry this guy?"

"I know what you mean. But she likes him, and I think he's nice enough. That's another thing. Noel says that this is the first time he's ever known his dad to get engaged. Johnny has never remarried or been this serious about anyone that he was aware of."

"Sounds interesting. Well, I'll talk to Helen Bombardner and see what she can tell me as to where to look for this woman. That's her home town."

"Why not ask your sweetheart? He'd know a lot more than Helen."

"If I think it's necessary, I will. Whatever happened to him in Hollywood hurt him pretty bad, so I'd like to take my time on that subject and wait for an open door."

"That's understandable. Now, where is this church again? You didn't give me very good directions."

"Just drive. It's almost to Isleta and it's right along the highway. We still have a ways to go. Which reminds me, I can't baby sit Noel, so somebody else'll have to. He asked me to take him around and show him some cowboys and Indians."

"Well, you are the one best suited for the job, but I'll see what I can do. I may know the places, but you know all the people, and that makes a big difference. Besides, you got turned into a bit of a cowgirl yourself when you were hanging out with Petey. Noel and Johnny both would be tickled pink to have you do some rope tricks and whatnot."

"What'd be fun would be to take them down and let them visit the Halsteds, but I haven't got the time to entertain Englishmen. I find them just as charming as the next person, but I've got a couple of other men that keep me heap plenty busy. Otherwise I'd be glad to."

"You know, I can see plainly why God put you in such a situation with your beautiful men. You've got enough control to keep things kosher. If I were in your shoes I'd blow it in a minute. As it is, I'm almost afraid to meet this priest of yours, if he's as wonderful as you say he is."

"He's pretty wonderful, all right; an honest to goodness angel. You'll see. And it's not just his looks, either; it's the power of God in his life. I sensed it when we first met. And since he's gotten baptised with the Spirit and deep into the Word–girl, he is really, really something. You should see the way the people are around him. They love him to pieces. Attendance at his mass has more than tripled just since I've been going there, and he tells me that now he has the longest line at the confessional on Saturdays."

"Praise God! But it sounds like he could be headed for some trouble. If he's drawing people that were going to the other priests, then they'll get uptight about his popularity."

"I know, and that's not the half of it. You should hear what he preaches. It's really right on. The pastor has already called him on the carpet for some of the things he's doing. But fortunately he's also drawing in a lot of new people and ones that had just quit coming to church altogether. He even goes out and gets them. The pastor sends him to make the rounds to members of their parish, so he's been knocking on their doors and everybody else's. If he meets somebody who's Protestant, he just says that Jesus Christ knows no denomination and talks to them anyway. Plus he's getting a lot of teenagers coming to his services. More people also means more money, though, so I don't think they're quite ready to make him stop altogether or ship him back to Chicago."

"Can they do that?"

"I'm sure they could arrange it. He'll be going back there eventually, but he's still got a project he's supposed to complete before that happens."

A few minutes more and we were pulling into the church parking lot. For the first time I was late, but only by a couple of minutes. Georgia helped me carry my gear in and kept in my shadow as I led the way. Rehearsal was in the sanctuary.

"There you are," said Teddy as I walked in. "I was beginning to—" His eyes looked behind me to Georgia. Curiosity colored his features for a moment before the smile he wore faded.

"I brought a friend," I said, smiling even though I could sense something wrong. "Teddy, this is my cousin Georgia. Georgia, this is Teddy Molloy."

She stepped up alongside me and gave a shy smile, which was rather uncharacteristic of her. Georgia had always been a real live one and her beauty had helped her get away with it. Her high yellow complexion was fair and flawless; her brown eyes were big and had beautiful long dark lashes above them. Long, wavy dark brown hair hung nearly as far as her waist. Her lovely figure was to be envied: 36"-22" 34".

Teddy looked at Georgia a moment more before putting on another smile and offering her his hand to shake.

"Pleased to meet you," he said. "Janette has told me a lot about you."

"I hope she didn't say too much. I've heard an awful lot about you, though. Can't wait to hear you preach."

Now Teddy genuinely smiled. "Why, thank you. Would you like to join us tonight? You didn't bring your flute by any chance?"

"No, I didn't," she said. "But I wouldn't mind singing just for tonight."

Whatever had caused the tension with Teddy seemed to be gone and was forgotten for the moment. I for one just enjoyed having Georgia sing with us and was glad that Teddy had asked her. It felt like old times, only better as we shared music and a microphone.

After going through the congregational songs, it was time to work on what we dubbed the sermon prelude, the song Teddy did just before the homily. Usually I played the accompaniment while he sang solo, but this time I was adding harmony on the chorus and Paul was playing bass.

With the prelude being done well a couple of times through, it was time to quit. Seldom did I stick around on Thursday nights, so as soon as I had my gear together, Georgia and I took off.

"I see what you mean," said Georgia, as she pulled the car out onto the road. "The anointing on him about bowls you over. He's got a beautiful voice, too, but at the beginning I got the feeling he didn't like me."

"I noticed that, too. But whatever it was, he seemed to get over it. I think maybe you reminded him of somebody."

"That could be. But anyway, I was talking to the Lord about him because he sounds so perfect, just like the kind of guy I'd like to have. I got a big fat no. He said he's got somebody else for me and that Teddy and I wouldn't really suit each other."

"That's like I figured, but still it would have been nice if you two could have gotten together; then you could get him to jump ship. I guess that's not what the Lord wants."

"I guess not. Oh, and I was also told that there's already somebody picked out for Teddy."

"Oh, really! I'm glad to hear that somebody else sees that. So are you coming to services tomorrow night?"

"Sure. I need to get back into fellowship. Noel wants to come, too, which means that Veronica will tag along. She won't want to be left out."

"Really? Praise God!"

"Yeah. I was a bit put out at first that Mom wanted to follow me out here, but then I figured God had his reasons, and that getting people saved was part of it. You know, if Noel gets zapped then Johnny will be dying of curiosity and we might get him there, too. Otherwise, he's not the least bit interested in anything that smacks of religion."

FRIDAY, FEBRUARY 21:
As the week ended and I looked forward to another Sabbath, I did so with a heart overflowing with thanksgiving to God. It was difficult to discipline myself and not lose track of time and space. My whole being was centered on praising HaShem, so with my spirit floating on such a high plane, this was one evening when I would rather have danced than played my guitar. But I packed it up anyway and took off for the Friday night service at a higher rate of speed than the law allowed. It was as if the bike was a part of me and felt the same heavenly euphoria. It moved effortlessly through evening traffic, the lanes opening up as I sped along. Yielding to the timelessness of the moment I found that the passing street scenes took on a strange beauty while at the same time seeming farther away. All that I saw and felt is now even harder to put into words than it was then, but the trip was amazing and unforgettable. According to my watch, it took me less than three minutes to get to Rock of the Witness.

"Hey, you're sure early," said Teddy who was in the process of setting up when I walked in.

"A little bit," I said, beaming as I took a short hop up onto the stage. "Guess what? My cousin Georgia's coming tonight and bringing her sister and an unsaved friend."

It was as if I hadn't said a thing. Watching my approach, Teddy's smile became slightly twisted and his eyes grew wide. When I stepped up to him for my hug he backed away.

"What's the matter?" I asked, disappointed.

"Man! There's sure a glow about you." His smile faded and fear flashed in his eyes. "What have you been doing?"

"Praising the Lord."

"You've been doing more than that."

I took another step in his direction and again he backed up, this time with an attitude of cowering as he tried not to look at me. Finally Teddy dropped to one knee and bowed his head. Assuming he wanted prayer, I went and laid my hands on his head. The next second he fell over on the stage and was out under the Power.

The anointing was unusually strong that evening, while at the same time

I could feel a restraint, as if it would blow us or some individual to pieces if God didn't hold back on what he was pouring out. As the Holy Spirit swept powerfully through the sanctuary fifteen minutes or so into the service, his presence filled the air with a golden mist, making it rather difficult for most of us to stay on our feet. Though brief, the ministry from the Scriptures was meaty, flowing in the same direction as the worship, with an emphasis on receiving the love of God. Then the Holy Spirit had us worship some more, in silence and in song.

Surprisingly enough the meeting let out close to the usual time, about 9:30. Teddy and I quickly threw our stuff together and prepared to go share Jesus with those out looking for a good time on the streets of Albuquerque.

"I don't see Georgia," I said as I shut my guitar case. "I wanted to talk to her before we split."

"Maybe she's in one of the prayer rooms," said Teddy. "You want to stick around and find out?"

"Naw, let's go. I can talk to her later. Otherwise we might not make it out of here."

In a few minutes we were out on the street and heading toward our territory near the University of New Mexico. Traffic differed depending on the time of month and whether or not people had just gotten paid. We always listened carefully to the Lord's direction on whether to ride the streets on the bike and talk to the people in cars, or do a bit of walking and standing. Tonight it was walking and standing.

Following our usual routine, Teddy and I stood next to the Scout and waited for junkies, drug dealers or anyone else to come by. Sometimes my vintage motorcycle attracted people, so we did get a variety. Within the first half hour we had four different men approach us in the attempt to buy or peddle drugs. "We've got a better high than that," we would tell them and they'd naturally want to score a hit of whatever we had. When we'd tell them our high was Jesus some would poke fun, argue or walk away while others listened in earnest. It was an interested party we were talking to that night when suddenly the man went into convulsions. While Teddy prayed and tried to keep him from hurting himself, I radioed for assistance.

Help arrived in less than five minutes. Another team from our territory came to our aid, one of them being a doctor. They took over the situation with the man who was going through withdrawals from his drug habit. We then went our way.

"That was scary," said Teddy. "I've never seen anything like that before. I've only heard about it."

"Same here. What a drag."

"Come on. Let's hit the other side of the street."

Across the street we went, taking the bike with us, but the feeling in my spirit said we were done for the night. As we repositioned ourselves under a street lamp, I made the decision to ask Teddy about his strange behavior regarding my cousin.

"So what was your problem with Georgia the other night?"

"Huh? Problem? Oh, uh, well for one thing, you don't look related. She looks almost like a white girl."

"Her mother's father was white. He was a judge. Georgia's dad was from a mixed background, too."

"Yeah, well I realized she was mixed. Guess I just wasn't expecting it."

There's a romantic story in this so I'll let you in on it. Aunt Laura's mother, Margaret Jackson, was a milliner, one of the most popular on Chicago's south side. Judge Albert Keegan, a man in his late forties, began buying her hats for his wife who wouldn't venture into the black neighborhood to shop. This was how they became acquainted. Over the years they developed a rapport and a strong affection for each other. Her personality was such a delightful contrast to his wife's that he fell in love with her. Judge Keegan confided in Margaret, even discussing his cases with her and asking her opinion. At one point in time he tried to get something more intimate started, but Margaret refused him because he was married. Even when his wife passed away, leaving him free to marry, race was the main issue and she resisted still. But he truly cared for her and kept up the pursuit. Being an older man who had already gained success in his career, he was very wealthy and could simply retire, making it easier to give up his social standing for her. Convincing Margaret that they would have a good life together, she gave her consent and they married. Although his family, friends and associates disowned him, the couple found lots of support from her family and social circle. The couple was very happy for the few years they were together before the judge died. Afterward she met and married my dad's father.

"So what else was it about Georgia? Did she remind you of somebody?"

"Yes. As a matter of fact, she reminds me of somebody I met in highschool."

"Somebody you didn't like?"

"Yeah, and in a big way. But don't worry about it. I won't transfer any bad feelings to Georgia. It's just something I'll have to get used to."

"Wait a minute." I paused to see what my spirit was picking up. "You're not going to have an easy time of it."

"Well, I've already been praying about it. I mean, she's your best friend and all, so I want to get along with her; plus I hate feeling this way about anybody, especially someone who's my sister in Christ. I want to keep my heart at peace."

Pausing again, I sought for more understanding. "You're going to need help. Whatever it is, you can't just pray yourself out of it. It goes too deep, kind of like the stuttering thing."

He bit his lip and said nothing.

"Teddy, look, if you don't want to tell me about it, that's fine. All I know is that you need some help with it."

"You probably know what it is already."

We had spent so much time together that Teddy and I were learning to read each other in a phenomenal way. It was getting more and more difficult to keep anything a secret.

"I'm sure I could find out if I wanted to, but I'd rather you told me."

"Look, Jenny, I really hadn't planned on talking about this tonight. Can't it wait?"

"That's up to you. Or rather, what does the Lord want?"

"Well–he's not going to send us anymore action; I knew that before we crossed the street. Why don't we go back to the church and check in?"

"Fine with me."

We did just that, then found an empty prayer room where we made ourselves comfortable on the thickly carpeted floor.

This time, talking didn't come easy for Teddy. I could feel his inner turmoil as he recalled events in his mind and prepared to relate them to me. He grew downcast and fidgety. I gave him my hand for comfort and he smiled for a moment.

"You know that I've wanted to be a priest for a long time. I didn't get pushed into it with any pressure from my family like some guys do. But girls have always liked me, even better than my older brothers. The only thing is that I've never been any good in the romance department."

"Really? But you're so affectionate."

"Well, with you I can be, 'cause you're like a little sister. And now that I think about it, you may be the first girl I'm not related to that I could put my arms around for any length of time without having my palms sweat. See, Jenny, I could never get much further than that. It's not as if I don't know the mechanics of how it works between the sexes, it's—"

"It's the process of getting there."

"Yes. See, I did date some in junior high and highschool, but anytime it got past the hand holding stage, it turned into a big disappointment. First of all, I never learned how to sweet talk a girl. Even if I did know what I wanted to say, I'd get all flustered and tongue tied. You remember how I used to stutter. That happened any time I was nervous, and not just on stage; so imagine me in a parked car with a girl."

"Now, wait a minute. Why'd you even park with a girl if you planned on being a priest?"

"Well—someone else was always in the driver's seat. See, I was too timid to go out alone on a date, so I'd double date or go in a group. With others to talk with, it made me feel more at ease. I also figured there was safety in numbers. Well, it wasn't always so safe, especially not after I was in highschool. Generally I'd ask a buddy to come along with his date, someone who I thought knew enough about girls so that, if I had any problems, he could help me out. Also, in the beginning, I didn't have a car, so I'd try to pick a guy that did. So he'd pick us up and sometimes at the end of an evening we'd wind up at some spot where the couples go to neck; there I'd be, stuck in the back seat with my date and the other couple making out up front. Now, the first girl I was parked with was kind of special. She was in my parish and seemed very nice. And very cute. I wanted to kiss her and she wanted to kiss me, too, so I did. Well, it was fine at first, but after a while she kept trying to stick her tongue in my mouth and I didn't go for that at all. It was pretty obvious that she was embarrassed and disappointed; so was I, so I didn't go out with her anymore. The last incident was much different, though. It was my second year in public highschool and I hardly knew the girl. She was a cheerleader and she looked a lot like Georgia. A guy on the wrestling team introduced us. She was a real knockout, and she seemed nice enough. Also, I was told she was a good Catholic."

"Why weren't you still in parochial school?"

"Couldn't afford it. The younger kids had to have their turn so we older kids spent our highschool years in public school."

"Oh. Go on."

"So we double dated with my 'pal' from the wrestling team. Now, I don't know whether or not the other parking incidents were planned, but this one definitely was. See, by then everybody knew that I wanted to be a priest, so some of the kids thought it'd be real funny if I lost my virginity before I went to seminary. They used to do things like put girly pictures in my locker or in my text books until I caught a guy doing it and beat the tar out of him. So anyway, they set me up with this girl that was loose and fast. Now, by this time I did have a car and had planned on driving, but my friend insisted on taking his car. That should have tipped me off, but we'd been good friends and I had no reason to distrust him. Anyway, this time when we parked it was in some out of the way, secluded place that looked like we were out in the country. We were supposed to be looking for someone's house and conveniently got lost. When we got to the place they had picked out, the other couple got out of the car, got a blanket from the trunk and ran off somewhere, leaving me alone with my date. Well, I was in no mood to swap spit with a strange girl, but didn't want to hurt her feelings; so I was about to offer to kiss her once, then suddenly changed my mind and announced that I was going to look for the others so we could get out of there. Then she grabbed my jacket and held onto me, begging me not to leave her alone. She handed me a lot of flattery and some stuff about there being nothing wrong with me having a nice time with a pretty girl. When she saw that I wasn't buying it, Jenny, the girl climbed on my lap and—and pulled off her sweater! As soon as I saw what she was doing I shut my eyes, but then I had to sit there for an eternity with her on my lap, teasing and tormenting me. And boy! Did she ever have a good time. When she saw how serious I really was, she laughed and started making crude jokes. When I couldn't take it anymore, I opened the car door and dumped her out on the ground. Then I went looking for the other couple, but when I found them they were involved over in the bushes. So I went back to the car, hot wired it and took off without my date. I drove back to civilization and parked it in a tow away zone with the lights on. Then I walked the rest of the way home."

"Wow. Were you still friends after that?"

"Not on your life. And what's more, later on I beat him mercilessly in a wrestling match. We've hated each other ever since."

"Tell me, was your date's sweater still in the car?"

"Oh, yeah, I forgot about that." He laughed heartily. "Yeah, it was."

"Well, Teddy, you gave them their comeuppance, and with their sin I'm sure they've reaped a lot more besides. Let it go if it now and get healed."

"It's not that easy, because it does go pretty deep. You know, when your dad tried to get me to marry you, I knew it'd be one way to keep us together, but aside from your being too young, I–well, I just don't think I could keep you happy. You'd end up bored and frustrated like all those other girls."

This was the part where I wished he'd been talking to a man. To me it was obvious that Teddy instinctively had what it would take to woo a woman–the right woman–successfully. After all, he'd come kind of close to snagging me.

"That's not true, and you know it. Teddy–" I touched his face and a tear rolled down upon my hand. "One thing is for certain, those girls didn't really care about you. Don't judge your ability or inability for expressing love on girls who were as selfish and insensitive as they were. Real love is patient, and it would never take advantage of or make fun. Look, you're kind, caring and very affectionate. That's the most important part. The rest–well, HaShem can teach you anything you need to know. You have all your equipment, don't you?"

"Yeah, sure."

"Then when God brings you the one he wants you to have, he'll show you what to do for both courtship and marriage. Don't underestimate him—and don't underestimate yourself, either. I hope you know by now that you're not called to remain celibate all your life."

"Oh, I think about that now and then. I'd like to know what it's like to have my own kids and a wife to come home to, but I no longer have that option. I'm a priest. It's my calling. It's what I've wanted all my life; and besides, the Holy Spirit said so when the guys spoke to me on the street."

"But that was conditional. The Lord said that it was to be according to his will and not the will of man, remember? It's not the will of God to force celibacy on a man or woman just because they want to serve him with a full heart. Besides, long before you took the vows of priesthood, you made a promise to God to do whatever it is he wanted. No, Teddy, you've been bought with a price and the choice isn't yours to make. Listen to me. What you're doing now is only for a season; and the desire you have in your heart for a wife and kids isn't only natural, those are things God wants for you."

He didn't confirm or deny what I said but was silent for a good little while. When he had put his thoughts together he replied, "No, Jenny I don't think so. But don't be concerned about me. God has already brought me some healing from what I've been through over this business of women."

"That's good, but the job isn't finished. When it is, then I'm sure you'll see your celibacy different."

"I doubt it. But you're right about the job not being finished, but this has helped some just talking about it."

"Good. So we'll pray about it and ask HaShem to heal your heart."

He submitted to my laying on of hands, but not seeing the need for having a good woman in his life, he wasn't quite as willing as when I'd prayed for him at other times.

"Thanks, Jenny. I know God brought this up for a reason, but it's not for me to get a wife, so it's not such a big deal. Besides, I've got you."

Yes, but for how long?

"Sure, you're thinking about how tough I've had it with being alone, and you're right—especially when you look at how close knit my family is. Family is what I missed the most in seminary. There we couldn't even talk to anybody except during certain hours, and they discouraged close relationships. You'd get in trouble if somebody even thought you were getting too friendly. And now that I'm a priest–man! Even my family looks at me differently. It wasn't until I met you and started coming here to The Rock that I rediscovered just how starved I am for affection. It feels good to put my arms around a girl without the fear of it turning into something sexual or being accused of getting out of bounds. I like being able to embrace a man as my brother. That sort of thing just doesn't happen in the communities of nuns and priests, and that's another reason why you mean so much to me. I get to hug and kiss you all I want, and you don't complain or ask me for something I can't give. The, uh, the only problem is–"

"I'm going to someone else to get it."

"Which is what I had really wanted to talk about tonight. Janette, I've been getting some very interesting dreams and visions, especially during prayer, and they concern the two of us. They come with a powerful anointing, so I know it's not just my wishful thinking. The first vision almost knocked me flat because it was so three dimensional. Scared me half to death! It showed us ministering to hundreds, maybe thousands of people. Then there's a reoccurring dream that's absolutely wonderful. We sing together, preach and teach together, and go all kinds of places. Then there are some others that are symbolic that I can't quite figure out. That's why I think you should come with me to Chicago and plan to stay. It's pretty obvious to me, and it should be to you, that Jesus wants us to keep ministering as a team. You know as well as I do that he didn't bring us together just for kicks. Look what's happened in just a couple of months."

He had a very good point, but then why was he the only one having these spectacular dreams and visions? My partner figured significantly in my dreams as well, but differently.

I took my time pondering this one. It was apparent from the beginning that God did have long range plans in mind when he teamed us up, but I had never bothered about what they were. Had my preoccupation with David Conrad stopped me from seeing what Teddy saw? No. My relationship with David was just as God-ordained as mine with Teddy. There had to be a time and place for both.

Some of what he envisioned were things that I, too, had thought about in passing daydreams, but not heavily and not necessarily with him. Still it didn't mean that they weren't valid. But now when I considered going to Chicago to stay, something deep within me said absolutely not. As I took a few moments to question HaShem about it, one verse of Scripture in particular came to mind. "Teddy, 'The vision is yet for an appointed time . . . though it tarry, wait for it; because it will surely come. . . .'"

"Say that again?"

I reached for my Bible and turned to the little book of Habakkuk, reading the full verse from the second chapter.

"So, you're saying that what the Lord's been showing me is for sometime in the distant future?"

"I don't know how distant, but what's happening with us now and anything else we see this year is simply foundational. In other words, don't hold your breath for a manifestation that is even close to what you're seeing. And when I think about it, that's how it has to be."

"But why?"

He would have to ask that question. It wasn't just because of my marrying David; aside from the fact that things take time to develop, I knew that there were certain ordeals that Teddy had to go through without me. Sins that he didn't see the need to let go of now, he would later learn to hate. Out of a natural desire to protect him, I would only get in the way of the process God had to take him through to get to that point. However, telling him this would be awkward and probably pointless. But before I could come up with a safe answer, Teddy gave me his interpretation.

"I think you're telling me that because you're afraid of what you'd have to give up. Jenny, as Christians we're called to a life of sacrifice. They don't preach much of that at The Rock, but it's something Catholics understand very well. My life of celibacy is a sacrifice to God so that I can live only for him. It would be more of a sacrifice for you because you were never taught it like I was, but I believe it's a sacrifice God wants you to make. With other celibates you'd have support, which is why you should spend time in the convent. Now, have you mentioned going with me to your parents yet?"

"Yes, I did. They haven't said no yet, but they don't think it'd be wise for us to go off together and not be married."

"Did you tell them you might live in a convent?"

"No."

"Then tell them. I think that would make a difference."

Had I wanted to I could have ripped his little sacrifice of celibacy argument to shreds, but that would only serve to put a rip in our relationship. That wasn't what we needed.

Seldom had our differences in doctrine posed a very big problem, so I was not at all comfortable with this situation. I felt myself pulling away from him, putting up walls to protect us from each other. I didn't want to hurt him or be pushed into saying something I didn't mean in order to placate him, but I had to say something.

"Teddy–a few weeks ago you shared things about yourself you thought I should know. Well, now it's my turn. It's not much, but there are things you don't know about me that have a bearing on this subject. There are some very important reasons why I could never be a nun."

"Oh. Are you not a virgin?"

"That's not it. And yes, I am a virgin."

"Okay, go on. I'm sorry, I won't interrupt again."

"Remember how you said that you didn't want anything to do with me when we first met? Well, I wasn't exactly thrilled about you, either, but for different reasons. Once they said you were a priest, I only talked to you because God was nudging me to. Teddy, I don't know what it's like to be Catholic but I'm learning, and I'm not as hard nosed about it as before we met. However, you haven't a clue about where my head is at. Haven't you wondered why I won't take communion when you've offered it to me?"

"Yes, I have."

"The reason is that the Catholic brand of communion is not Biblical, and for me to receive it would be sin. To put it mildly, I have a very strong dislike for the traditions your church has added to the word of God. I'm not exactly tickled with what most Protestants have done, either, so don't think it's bigotry. And I don't want to get caught up into an us verses them, I'm right/you're wrong trip, because that's darkness and bondage, too. All I want is to walk in a greater revelation of God's truth, and I can't do that by putting myself into something I know I'm not called to, especially when that something exalts itself above the Bible like Catholicism does.

"Look, if there was any doubt in my mind, I'd say let's seek the Lord about this right now. But I have no problem seeing the direction God wants me to go, and it isn't into a life of celibacy or the Roman Catholic Church. So you need to rethink your outlook and your interpretation, because there's college, a husband and a family in my future."

As Teddy listened I could see his hope waning and feel the slow death of his dreams. His gaze fell and he looked as if his life was beginning to fade in the face of improbability.

"Oh, Theodore! No! Don't despair. I believe your dreams and visions. I do! It's only a matter of when and how, not if. Your interpretation is in the context of your church and the way it functions, not to mention the way things are going now. That's not the correct interpretation and now you know why. HaShem will do it his way and in his time, so don't hold your breath for it and stop getting in the way. If you don't stop trying to make it happen your way, you'll cause a delay in it coming to pass. So just let it go and have faith. It will happen. Just be patient!"

"But–I don't understand. Why not now? To me the timing seems so perfect."

"If you saw it from God's angle, you'd change your mind."

"Yeah, if. . . . I had no idea you felt that way." He gave me a hard and unpleasant look. "No, I take that back. I had a feeling about it, but I hoped it would change." Teddy got to his feet and paced the floor. "Jenny, this is nuts! I just don't get it. Is God a tease? Why would he put something right in my grasp and then say I can't have it? What am I missing here?"

"I can't say for sure, but I gather that before we see those visions come to pass that there will be some things we need to learn or things that have to happen."

"Yeah, I guess. . . . Probably both."

I got to my feet and joined him. Addressing him now with a completely open heart, I grabbed his arm to stop his pacing.

"Teddy, look at me." He stood still but only glanced at me. Pulling gently on his arm, I managed to get him to sit down again, then stood in front of him and smoothed his hair. "Mate, I love you very much. Don't ever think that I don't. I would never have said I would go with you to Chicago if I didn't want to. You've gotten to be such a part of me that losing you would be like ripping out a piece of my heart."

"If–if I were–" He wouldn't complete his sentence. Turning away, he closed his eyes and tears started down his cheeks.

Wiping away the salty drops, I kissed him several times, trying to get him to look at me again. When he didn't, I pulled his head to my chest and cradled him in my arms. After a long moment he returned my embrace and we remained that way in silence for a while.

"I feel like a fool," said Teddy finally, pulling gently back and wiping his face. "In a whole lot more ways than one."

"What do you mean?"

I started to probe his heart for the answer, but he blocked me. Shaking his head, Teddy replied, "Maybe some other time. I still need to work this out. In the meantime, though–"

"What?"

"I don't know. Nothing."

"Please tell me. Please?"

"Well, the other thing I wanted to discuss was St Patrick's Day. Since I'm not at home in Chicago, it won't be quite the same. And to be honest, I'm glad that it won't be."

"Yeah, how come? I hear that they have a nice big parade and everything's dressed in green, including the river."

"Oh, that part's okay. It's the stuff like heavy drinking and fist fights."

"Fist fights?" I had to smile at that one. "Oh, yeah, you said you used to brawl. So it was part of holiday fun?"

"I'm afraid so. Not every year, but if we were lucky. . . . It's almost a family tradition, and not just for holidays. Ever since I can remember my dad and his brothers, and then my older brothers and I would, on occasion, just go out and start a Brannigan. One of our specialties was going into Protestant bars, especially if they catered to other races. We'd sit at the bar making unkind remarks. It's not something I'm particularly proud of."

"I can imagine. Well, I'd say the solution is simple. We'll have corned beef and cabbage at my place, dress the house in green, and Daddy'll get you all the green beer you can drink."

"But that really isn't what I want."

"It's not?"

"No. What I want is to try and break with some of the old traditions. That stuff's okay, I guess; there's certainly nothing wrong with the food, but the silliness and carousing don't honor the saint in a fashion he'd be pleased with. He brought the good news of Christ to Ireland and taught about the trinity. All the green beer and foolishness are so much a part of who I used to be that for now I'd prefer to do something different."

"Well, if we do it at my house, chances are very good that you're going to get all the typical Irish American trappings. Since Daddy's from Chicago, he knows what you guys do and my family won't understand if we try to get spiritual. Don't you want to turn the Rio Grande green? It's never been done that I know of."

"Nope, not interested . . . although that would be pretty funny. I wonder how much food coloring—? No, don't get me started. I'd rather you and I had a nice quiet traditional dinner and maybe sing some hymns. The problem is where."

"That's for sure. Well, with God all things are possible. Let's pray about it and see what he comes up with."

All would go back to normal between Teddy and I, but somehow I didn't expect him to make anymore suggestions about me taking the veil. I could only hope that if the time came to tell him I wouldn't go to Chicago at all, he could accept it without so much pain to his heart.

Chapter Eight
Torn Between

SATURDAY, FEBRUARY 22:
At first they talked by telephone. Late Friday afternoon, Georgia called David for apartment information and to give him a subtle third degree that uncovered nothing we didn't know already. I could have been with her when they talked, but didn't want to listen in. Being sneaky and having to know everything was a habit I had to get out of. I wanted to trust my man and have him know that I put my confidence in him. But I would be with her on Saturday when they met in person to look at apartments.

Before that, though, Georgia and I needed to catch up on what went down Friday night during and after the service. I got a delightful ear full when I went to meet her at the hotel on Saturday afternoon.

"Both their minds were totally blown," she told me as we got into her car. "This was the first time they'd seen God move with that kind of power. Oh, it was great! They both freaked out, especially Veronica. She started to cry and shake and then ended up on her knees like most everybody else. I couldn't believe it. All I had to do was sit and watch God do his thing. She's a different little girl, now."

"Fantastic! What about Noel?"

"He took a little longer, but Jesus got him, too. He sat through most of the service with his mouth hanging open. Then when the Spirit began to move on people for repentance, did he ever squirm. We finally went to one of the prayer rooms with one of the brothers because he had such a tough struggle with it. But he finally came in. And that's not all. Afterward we went to that all-night restaurant down the street where you said everybody goes and had a long talk about the meaning of what they'd done. I made sure they knew that church isn't the focal point but that knowing Jesus is. I threw out some questions and let them ask some, so I'm confident that they understand the importance of spending time in God's presence and reading the Bible. We also talked about what they could expect from Mama and Johnny and how to deal with that."

"Oh, yeah? How'd that go?"

"Pretty good. Naturally Veronica knows something of what I went through when I got saved, but said she doesn't care what Mama says or does. Noel wants more than anything to tell his father about Jesus so that he, too, can get saved, but he's reluctant to declare his faith openly on the home front, and with good reason. Johnny would only pick it apart and ridicule him. So rather than deal with that, Noel has a more subtle approach, and it's a scream. If we all help him, he believes he can get Johnny to come to The Rock. And if that happens, look out! With the power of God that moves through that place, he'll either get saved or turn tail and run."

"That's for sure. So what time did you get in last night?"

"Around 1:30. Still I had trouble getting to sleep because I was so high on the Lord. It must have been close to three before I finally dozed off.

When I woke up, everybody was already gone up to Santa Fe."

"By the way, how long are they going to be here?"

"Well, you heard what Johnny said the other night about doing his own thing in the publishing business. He may not stay in New Mexico, but he's not leaving the States. He's going to be looking even closer into what it would take to get something going here and decide where he wants to put down roots. He and my mother have decided to get married right away, so they've both got some big decisions to make. They're going to hang out in Albuquerque for a while until they work things out, so they're renting a four bedroom house and some cheap furniture to save on the hotel bills."

"What? Shacking up?"

"Yes and no. It'll be like at the hotel, only in a house. Mama and Johnny don't sleep together at all. She's too smart for that. They'll have separate rooms at opposite ends until they tie the knot. That'll be in a week or two."

Once we'd reached the vicinity of the apartment, we turned our attention to finding its location. Though close to a main drag, the entrance was on a quiet side street where there were mostly houses. The neighborhood seemed a rather nice one.

"That's it," I said, pointing to the complex on the west side of the street. "And there's David's car."

David had just gotten there himself and was waiting for us in the inner courtyard.

"Hi, honey," I greeted him, not quite sure how to act with my new boyfriend in public. I wanted to run and throw my arms about him but held back. Instead I gave him my hand.

"Well, don't I get a kiss?" he asked, looking at me forlornly as he caressed my fingers.

"In this town it's too easy to run into people you know, so it's better to be careful; but I'll make up for it later. David, this is Georgia."

"*Enchanté, mademoiselle.*" He turned to her and offered her his hand.

"I still don't believe it." Georgia shook his hand and her head as well while looking him over. "Things like this just don't happen to Janette."

"Hey!" I gave her a little push. "You'd better watch it."

"I'm sorry," she said. "It's just so utterly fantastic. My, but you sure are handsome."

"David, in case you haven't noticed, Georgia's rather outspoken. It's from having so many attorneys in the family."

"If anyone's used to outspoken women, it's me," he said. "Come on. Let's go take a look at the first apartment."

The pale yellow, two story building was old but in very good condition. The carpet was fairly new and so were the appliances. The rooms were large and the walls were thick, making it a great place to get studying done.

"This one looks fine," said Georgia. "I'll take it."

"Are you sure?" said David. "I really should have shown you the one upstairs first; that's the one I prefer. You'll get something of a view and you'll have a nice balcony."

Georgia chose the upstairs apartment. Once the paperwork was done, we all went out for coffee, where she got another chance to brush up on her French. Beginning with the subject of chaperoning, we made plans to have David's Bible study at her place on Wednesday nights once she moved in.

"Now, what about other evenings when you two want to get together?"

"You mean like on the weekends?" asked David.

"Right."

"Well, to be honest, there are some times when I'd like it to be just the two of us. But when she and I want to be out in public, we'll need to have you along."

"Okay. Is that what you want, Janette?"

"I think that'll be okay."

"Then it's fine with me. There's only one thing that's really bothering me about this. Before I got saved, I'd have thought nothing of telling any kind of believable lie to keep your affair a secret, but now what am I supposed to do if your mother calls and asks if I know where you are? If I happen to know that you're with him, I'll feel kind of funny telling a fib."

"Then just tell her the truth."

"What?!" David was incredulous.

"Sure," I said. "Tell anybody from my house who calls that I'm over at David's. If you don't get specific, they'll just think I'm over at David Richardson's place. I used to go there all the time when band rehearsals were at his house, but not so much anymore. But even without rehearsals, his house is a very lively place with people always coming in and out for fellowship. Even he might think I'm there somewhere if they should want to call him up. It's a pretty big house."

"But that's only with your family. Does anybody in the ADG know about you two?"

"No. You're the only one this side of heaven that knows—"

"What's the matter?"

"I just realized something. Holly Richardson knew about this even before I did. By the Spirit she saw it coming when I went to her for prayer and counseling last year."

"Really?"

"How did that happen?" asked David.

"Well, when you were pouring on the attention and I was having trouble with it, I told Holly what was happening and asked her for help. She must have picked up on what you were doing because at first she wanted me to back away from our friendship completely. Then the Lord must have shown her his plan for us because she changed her tune after she went down under the power of the Holy Spirit. She wouldn't tell me about it and I couldn't figure it out, but I sure understand it now."

"That's just too much," Georgia laughed.

David didn't have a comment, only a worried look. Holly could have blown the whistle on him and changed everything.

"But that doesn't mean we let her in on this now," I said. "The fewer people that know about it, the better."

Our afternoon together was pleasant, and would have been perfect had Georgia not opened her big mouth about David and I getting married real soon. It was difficult for me to say it ought to wait without giving a good reason why. David thought I was just fearful, which wasn't entirely untrue.

Later when Georgia took me back to her hotel to get my bike, I didn't go up to the suite. For me it was home for dinner and then right back out again. David wanted to get a head start on his Bible study, so I went to his apartment and we got out the books.

"I like your cousin, honey." David sat with his back on the arm of the sofa so he could see me. "I think Georgia will make the perfect chaperon."

"Good. I'm glad you approve."

"Also, I happen to agree with her about you and I getting married soon. I'd like to get married this summer."

"I know. As soon as I turn eighteen?"

"Sooner than that, if we're to have a decent honeymoon. I just don't relish the idea of asking your parent's permission. Oy vey."

"Oy vey? Oy gevault! You haven't seen—no, never mind. I don't want you anymore apprehensive than you are now."

"It's too late."

"I'm sorry. Forget I said anything because I was making an assumption and not considering God's hand in this. Y'shua put us together, remember? There's nothing to worry about."

"Well, I hope that's the case. And speaking of Y'shua, let's go ahead and get started on our study. I said I wanted to do it and I meant it. You know, I've been digging through some of the books you bought for yourself and I found one that's really quite interesting."

"Which one is that?"

"That exposé on the paganism in Christian worship, *The Two Babylons*."

"Oh, that one. Well, good, because you do need to read it. So do I, but I don't have time; plus it's cause problems in my present situation."

"What situation?"

"On Sundays I've been going to a Catholic church and playing for their folk mass. I already know a good number of things about Catholicism that clash with Torah, but I don't want to know everything just yet. I'm sure it would affect my ability to minister there, and right now being able to minister is the important thing."

"How'd you get into doing that?"

"A friend of mine at The Rock roped me into it. It's his church on other days of the week. He asked me to help him by working with the musicians."

"Oh . . . yeah. You mentioned something about that before. Well, after reading parts of that book, I can better understand why you'd rather be Jewish. If false worship upsets God like you say it does, then he must be pretty angry over all the pagan stuff in Christianity."

"Yes, but he's also very patient and merciful, which is why people don't get toasted for it. He knows that most of them are ignorant of what they do, so he shows up to bless people anyway. Still there are consequences."

"Shall we do our work here or at the dining room table?"

"It'll be more conducive to study in the dining room."

"All right. I'll go get my books."

As I took my things into the dining room and began setting up, I was reminded of Teddy and our studies together. Smiling at first, I then remembered our conversation on Friday night and experienced a touch of melancholy. Poor man. It broke my heart to know how deeply disappointed he was and would be when he got the final blow to his summer plans.

"Here we go." David broke into my reverie as he brought his Bible and reference books and set them on the table. "Now where should we start?"

"With prayer. Always start with prayer."

"Sounds good to me."

He sat beside me and together we honored God and asked his blessing on our time of study. Then it was down to cases.

"Okay," I said. "Let's get your Bible and we'll start you on a marking system so that as you read, you'll build up some good study notes. See? Look at mine."

"Yes, I remember. That's quite a bit of work you've done." David leafed through the pages of my reference Bible. "I've always wondered about that. You've got notes and then all these colors and symbols."

"That's my marking system. It helps me keep track of all the different subjects in the Bible. It ties them all together and makes it much easier to use and understand."

"Well, that's enough to sell me on it. Anything that'll make it easy to understand goes a long way with me. Will I need to take it to church?"

"You want to go to church?"

"I guess. Aren't I supposed to?"

"I–don't know about that. Actually, I'm surprised you'd even want to."

"Well, I don't, really. I just thought it was part of the package."

"To be honest, church shouldn't be the place for unbelievers. It's for those who already embrace the covenant to enter into God's presence, hear the Scriptures and be strengthened and encouraged through testimony and fellowship. Now, lots of people get saved at our services, but then there are the ones like you–the ones who'd rather get up and run or else sit through it and scoff because they're too afraid to believe. And with the way God moves in our services sometimes, I thought maybe you'd still find it too bizarre. But that's not the only reason I hesitate to invite you.

Like I've said, the place is wonderful, even amazing as churches go, but it's still church and very goyish. Just like other Christians, they have Babylonian and anti-Semitic traditions mixed in with truth, and out of ignorance they quote the Bible to support it. I'd rather you had a solid foundation first so you don't swallow some of that *bobbe-myseh* and get confused."

"Whatever you say, honey. You're the boss."

"Since there's no synagogue here where they preach Y'shua, there will come a time for church, but right now I don't think this is it. What's important is that you understand the basics in a biblical context. And since you're so willing to learn, it ought to be fun."

"Anything I get to do with you is fun."

The look he gave me melted my heart. A kiss was how I rewarded him. Then I forced myself back to the business at hand.

SUNDAY, FEBRUARY 23:

Even though Georgia had planned to go with me on Sunday to hear Teddy, she felt it was far more important to accompany Noel and Veronica to services at Rock of the Witness, and I agreed. So it was business as usual, and I got the impression my partner preferred it that way.

After mass I hung out in the sacristy, perched on top of a counter watching Father Molloy once again become plain old Teddy. His mood was much better than I had imagined it would be after our intense conversation, but then Saturday had been a very fruitful day for him. As he put away his robe and donned a dark red shirt, he chattered on and on about the blessings and miracles: who got saved, who got healed, who was delivered from drugs or alcohol, etc. Then with the last button in place, he turned and smiled happily at me. "Jenny, one of these days–" he said, love and renewed hope twinkling in his eyes. "Maybe not soon, but—you'll see. I know it."

"Have another dream?"

"I sure did. Wrote it down, too. But I'll not say anything more than that."

Two steps and Teddy was standing in front of me, ready to lift me down. We looked at each other for a long moment until it seemed the room was fading and the planet shifting.

Theodore Francis Molloy, I love you.

I know, babe. I know.

As he reached for my waist to help me down, I slipped my arms around his neck and gently pressed my mouth to his before dropping to the floor.

Teddy followed me home for dinner and we shared another wonderful afternoon getting dirty and sweaty while playing tackle football. We even had the pleasure of having Tony Gutierrez and Billy Osborn show up and join the fun for an hour or so. But along towards evening, Aunt Laura, Johnny and the kids dropped in. That's when Ireland and England had a few interesting moments together.

I could sense that Teddy took an instant dislike to Johnny, even though the man had done nothing more than say hello and shake his hand. Outwardly my partner showed no problem, but I knew his inner ticking. Immediately I began to pray in the Spirit. I also nudged Georgia and gave her the high sign for possible trouble. She didn't yet know Teddy well, but she knew Johnny and that was enough.

Some Englishmen have a very polite way of being extremely nasty, and at that Johnny was an expert. Having guessed Teddy's heritage (he was not introduced as being Catholic or Irish), he started in with a few 'concerned' comments about politics in England and worked his way from that into the problems in Northern Ireland and the IRA. But rather than be drawn into it, Teddy used the subject as a pivot point to talk about the subject of his homily that morning: the choice between heaven and hell.

"Now, mister, you've got a choice," said Teddy to end his commentary. "You can embrace the love of God on faith and find out that he's for real, or you can hold on to your hate and anger and let it carry you to the grave you've got that's waiting for you. But you don't have to take my word for any of this. You'll find out sooner or later." He paused for a thoughtful moment and then, speaking by the Spirit, looked Johnny straight in the eye. "And if you're not careful, it'll be a lot sooner than you think."

Johnny swallowed hard and looked surprised. Everyone at the table grew quiet. By then, all but Johnny, Laura and their brood had some idea of the power of God in Teddy's life. Even the youngest in my family had a healthy respect for it. It was fairly evident that the words he had just spoken were not to be taken lightly.

Aunt Laura was frightened and getting upset, but before she could come to Johnny's defense, my mother spoke up and said, "Why don't we have some music? Janette, go and get your guitar, would you, please? We can sing like we used to."

"Do you still have your old classical guitar?" asked Georgia.

"Sure," I said. "You want to play it?"

"Yeah. Bring it down, too."

So we tuned up the guitars and started with the old blues and folk songs that Georgia and I always used to play. It lightened the atmosphere quite a bit, and soon we were given requests. With country music being popular in England, Johnny knew and requested some of the songs I had learned from hanging with the Halsteds. I'd grown so used to singing them with a country twang that I could sing them no other way, and that got a lot of laughs.

A half hour or so into the music, I noticed Teddy was checking his watch. He would be leaving soon, even though he usually stayed longer. But before going, he requested I play a hymn. It was a children's song called "When He Cometh," and a mutual favorite of ours.

We sang all the verses and harmonized. Georgia put her guitar aside and sang a third part. Others joined in on the parts they knew, including Aunt Laura who had not heard the song since she was much younger.

> *Little children, little children, who love their Redeemer*
> *are the jewels, precious jewels, his loved and his own.*

Then we sang the first verse again, repeating the chorus without the guitar:

> *Like the stars of the morning, his bright crown adorning,*
> *they shall shine in their beauty, bright gems for his crown.*

With that and the sweet silence which followed, Teddy excused himself to go home. About twenty minutes later, the Holister-Angrahm clan made their exit as well.

MONDAY, FEBRUARY 24:
Monday marked the beginning of work on the spring concert. New music was handed out in choir, and after school would be the first dance rehearsal.

For dance I came only as an observer. Even though David would not work with me for a few weeks, some of the numbers he would rehearse with the others did concern me and I needed to know what was happening. So I came bringing my homework and sat several rows from the front.

The energy from Alan Haskell's excitement was so strong that it seemed to light up the stage. It was catching, too, and I could see the fervor spread as the dancers began to gather on stage to warm up. Dressed in more comfortable clothes–some girls wearing leotards and tights under a skirt, many of the boys in old slacks or blue jeans–they were very animated as they contorted and chattered away about the show. That is until Mr Conrad lined them up and began the rehearsal.

Suddenly the others seemed to fade into the background. When my sweetheart appeared in black comfortable slacks and a black, short sleeved cotton knit shirt that pleasantly accented his manly physique, that was the only thing my eyes wanted to see. As he began work on the first routine, the movements of his graceful body fascinated me.

Homework would have to wait until later, since my concentration had been spoiled. Other things could not, however. If I didn't have music of my own to be practiced as well as St Patrick's Day to prepare for, I would have stayed the whole time. I had to be circumspect about getting the items needed for the holiday; also it was just possible that I might get a lesson on Wednesday. After all, I still had college to look forward to, and I needed to be prepared.

Over the months, David and I had put together a package to send along with college applications. So far I'd been accepted at two schools in the Midwest, one with a full scholarship, and other applications were pending. But after all that, it looked as if my parents would get their wish anyway.

David had no desire to leave Albuquerque, at least not for a while, so my first and perhaps only year, would be at the UNM. Also, it was the most practical thing to spend the first year of our marriage in New Mexico so we could have two months out of the summer for a nice honeymoon without the worry of moving across country after we got back. So much for going to college out of state. The letdown was minor, though. The whole point of going away to school had been to get away from home, to travel and explore worlds beyond the one I'd known all my life. But now, because of David, I would have the opportunity to visit places I would otherwise only dream about. This made the compromise much easier to handle.

Anyway, once home from school, I practiced voice and piano. Then after dinner and doing dishes, I went into the family room to tell Mommy and Daddy about my plans with Teddy for St Patrick's Day so I could hit them up for the cash I needed. I already knew what they were going to think about our having a quiet dinner alone, so I just went ahead and let them think it.

"Well, well," said Daddy. "Maybe he's finally coming around. How much do you need?"

"I'm not sure, but it'll be a lot. I'd like to buy him a leather jacket and have his boxing name put on it."

"That's a lovely idea," Mommy remarked. "Why not have some sweat shirts printed up, too, or maybe some T shirts?"

"Good idea," said Daddy. "You know, Janette, you might have a better chance of winning Teddy over if you dressed a little less like a tomboy when he comes here. You can go upstairs and change into a pretty blouse and some slacks after you get home from church. And wear a nice fragrance, too."

"Well, I've never wanted people–you know, like people at his church–to get any ideas about us. That's why I dress different around him. Besides, he likes to roughhouse a lot and I don't want to do that in my good clothes. But don't worry. He's hugged me enough to know what I've got."

"That's true," said Daddy. "But those people from his church don't come to our house, and we can always buy you some more clothes; so wear something pretty when he's here. Since men like to look at women, it's also important for the man to see what you have."

"Yes, Daddy."

"He's such a nice young man," said Mommy. "I wish all you girls could find someone as good and decent as Teddy. Whatever you do, Janette, don't let him get away."

"Yes, Mommy."

Daddy reached for his wallet. I almost gasped when he pulled out one of his credit cards and said, "Here, Janette. Use this to do your shopping. Just be careful with it and keep track of what you buy. And if you need anything else, just let us know and we'll help you with it."

My goodness, but these people are anxious to become grandparents.

Well, they won't be entirely disappointed.

TUESDAY, FEBRUARY 25:

On Tuesday I began shopping. Even though I'd wanted to help Georgia move into her apartment, there wasn't that much to do, since her rental furniture was delivered by professionals. All she had was clothing, books and a few other personal items. Billy Osborne helped, as did Noel and Veronica, so there was nothing left to be done. But with so little time before St Patrick's Day, I didn't have the time, anyway.

After school I went downtown to the leather shop and ordered the jacket. I had surreptitiously taken Teddy's measurements on Sunday so that I could be sure to get the correct size. Once that was done, I stopped in at Fielding's to see what I could find in the way of Irish hymns and other music. The T-shirts and sweats could wait until Thursday.

WEDNESDAY, FEBRUARY 26:

Having David's first Bible study at Georgia's would have to wait until the following week. Georgia felt the Lord pressing her to entertain her sister and future step brother that evening, so I went to David's instead to begin our first in-depth study of the Scriptures. He caught on fast to many of the things I taught him, and this time–even though he still had doubts–his heart was willing. The evening was very fruitful and our concentration so intense that there was no time for making out afterwards.

FRIDAY, FEBRUARY 28:

With the week being such a busy one, it flew by, and soon I was lighting Sabbath candles again. With a heart so full of thanksgiving to God I was ready for another walk in the clouds. I had never been happier in all my life.

I thought of David all the way to church, marveling that such a thing could happen to me. Then when I arrived at The Rock and began setting up for the service, my wonderment broadened to include Teddy who still had yet to arrive. God had the strangest, most delightful sense of humor. What on earth was next?

Somehow I'd arrived a bit early. By the time I was set up and tuned, the others were just starting to come in. Catching a glimpse of one of my co-workers from the children's Sunday school as she came in to reserve a seat, I was just about to hop off the stage to go talk to her when suddenly Teddy came up behind me. He grabbed me up in his powerful arms and swung me around as if I didn't weigh an ounce.

"You stinker!" I laughed and took a backward swing at him. "You put me down this instant."

"Make me," he answered. Lowering me to the ground he turned me around to face him. Teddy's eyes appeared a soft gray-green for the moment as he looked adoringly at me. Then he pulled me to his chest for a big, long hug and a peck on the lips before letting me go to reach for his cello.

"You know that young couple I told you about the other day?" he said excitedly. "We talked for over an hour this afternoon and we prayed together. They both got saved."

"Praise God! Keep it up and you'll win the whole parish."

"I intend to."

Teddy then focused on setting up while I looked around, only to find that the woman was gone that I had wanted to see. As my eyes searched the darkened seating area, I happened to see a very familiar form by the front entrance. It was David.

Dread instantly arose in me. Why had he decided to show up all of a sudden? This was not good, but I wasn't sure why. Going to meet him, I didn't even get to say hello. Being very upset, David grabbed my arm and pulled me down the hall and all the way out into the little foyer.

"Who the hell is that?" he asked, his voice an angry whisper as he gestured toward the sanctuary.

"What?"

"You heard me. And keep your voice down."

"That–that's Teddy."

"Oh, so that's Teddy, huh? Is this the guy you spend so much time with having fun?"

My mouth gaped but I said nothing. I had forgotten even mentioning Teddy to David.

"Well, is it?"

"Yes."

"I thought so. Well, you two looked very cozy together. No wonder you didn't want me to come to church. What's the matter, can't you choose between us?"

"David, it's not like that. Teddy and I are just friends. He's like a brother."

"Oh, don't give me that! I know what I saw and how you looked at each other. That goes a whole lot deeper than that brother-sister stuff."

"It's not like that. Honest, honey! He's a Catholic priest."

"What? He's a what?"

"He's a Catholic priest."

That gave David something to think about. He shook his head as if to clear it. "A Catholic priest. And is that supposed to make a difference? Ha! Well, send him back to his Catholic church, because he doesn't belong here. And look, I don't care if he's the damned pope! He is still a man and he's going to act like a man, no matter how much religion he's got. Janette, if you want me like you say you do then you break things off with this guy, do you hear me? And you break it off tonight!"

David let go of me and walked quickly out the front door. I ran after him. "Where are you going?" I asked.

"I don't know," he said tersely. "But I'll be home later. Call me when you get out of church."

He got into his car and I watched him drive away, my forearm lightly bruised from his grip and my head in a whirl over this sudden rift in our happiness. Slowly I turned and walked back inside, stunned by the impact of David's angry words. I had only gone a few steps before literally running into Teddy who had come looking for me.

"Come on," he said. "It's almost time to get started."

Without a word, I followed him back inside.

With my head wildly reeling and my stomach in knots, I was in no condition to minister. As we stood in a circle to pray, all I could think of was David and how I needed to fix this new and awful situation.

As everyone broke the prayer circle and picked up their instruments, I took my guitar off its stand and put it in the case. David Richardson gave me a questioning look to which I shook my head; then I stepped off the stage and ran off to a prayer room.

After shutting the door behind me in the sound proof chamber and sitting down on the crimson carpeted altar/bench, I was able to allow anguish and fear to take their natural place. Trembling from the sudden and violent assault on my emotions, I sobbed and wailed until I couldn't take it anymore and then it was time to sober up and do some thinking.

Because I loved him so much, I began with the intention of granting David his demand, while also trying to invent a plausible excuse to give Teddy for not seeing him anymore; but even the thought of severing that friendship wrenched my soul to the point of torment. It was a pain so deep and fierce that it amazed me. Obviously our spiritual bond made it out of the question. But making David understand seemed even more impossible, and yet I couldn't give up David. With two options that weren't options at all, there seemed to be no resolution. David and Teddy would always be at odds and I would be caught in the middle. But logic dictated that, if God had set this up, there had to be a solution somewhere. I just couldn't figure out what it was–and the present situation called for an immediate remedy.

Overwhelmed, anxious and unable to keep still, I got up and prayed out my anguish in my spiritual language and pounded the carpet with my fists until I felt something had changed and I felt a lightness that made me feel close to normal. Still, with much of the aguish having subsided, I was no closer to knowing what to do. While the pulsating pain in my head grew less and less, I grabbed tissue to clean my face, prayed for wisdom and soberly worked on possibilities for handling David's jealousy. When I finally had enough to work with, it was time to make a phone call and put it to the test.

After cleaning up my used tissues and stuffing fresh ones in my pocket, I dug around in my jeans for change. Finding the right amount, I opened the door only to find Teddy on the floor waiting for me. He was parked against the wall right in front of the door, and I almost fell over his feet coming out.

"Hi, babe," he said casually. "How ya doin'?"

"Not too good, I guess. Look, I can't go out tonight. I've got some important business to take care of."

"You mean that guy who was here earlier?"

Oh, no! Did he hear what happened? My whole body filled with dread as Teddy quickly got up from the floor. "Look, just let me go make a quick phone call," I said. "I'll be right back."

There were a couple of pay phones near the kitchen. I hurried off to use one to call David. To my annoyance, Teddy followed right behind. As soon as I put my dime in the slot, Teddy's hand came down on the cradle.

"Janette, we need to talk." he said. There was a little smile on his face but it was not a happy one. "That man you were arguing with, you called him David. He's your boyfriend, isn't he?" My eyes betrayed the truth, but still I would not confess. Teddy's anger was growing by the second and he struggled to stay in control as he said, "Yes, he's your boyfriend. I didn't want to believe it, even though I heard enough of your conversation to know for sure. Do your parents know about your relationship with this man?"

"No," I replied meekly.

"Let's go somewhere so we can talk. And I don't mean a prayer room."

"Can't we talk later? I just need to–"

"Oh, no you don't. Call him and–and tell him you've got to talk to me first. After all, you do have to get rid of me, right? That's going to take some time and effort, you know. I don't go away that easy. Tell him whatever you want, Jenny, but if you go over there now, your parents will find out about this tonight. So why don't you and I go have a nice long discussion first."

"Oh. Okay."

He removed his hand and let me make the call. It rang three times before David answered. I could barely even respond to his hello.

"Uh, hi, David."

Teddy moved his head close to the receiver so that he could hear both sides of the conversation.

"Well, did you tell him?"

"No, not yet. We're going to talk now. I just wanted to let you know."

"Then why don't you come see me when you're done?"

Teddy shook his head, then covered the mouth piece and said, "Tell him it'll take a while and you can't stay out that late."

"I don't know, David. I don't think I'll be able to. I–I'm sure it'll take a while. I don't even know what to say yet."

"Well, I've got a few suggestions, but I don't think either of you would like them. All right, whatever it takes. But if it's not too late–no, even if it is late, call me. Call me as soon as you get home."

"All right. I will."

We hung up without saying goodbye.

"Let's go," said Teddy. "I've already put our stuff away."

We took the Chevy and headed east toward the foothills, riding in silence with his anger providing the atmosphere. Finding a large vacant lot, Teddy pulled in and parked.

"This is incredible," he mumbled to himself, enraged and deeply disappointed in my seemingly untoward behavior. Having reached the boiling point, Teddy looked out the window instead of at me. Pounding his fist on the door, he roared, "My God!!! Janette–you have absolutely no business carrying on with a grown man! It's disgusting!! I don't care if you are in highschool, you're still just a child!"

"I'm not a–"

"You have not stopped growing yet, you're not old enough to vote and you still live with your parents!!! Don't argue with me, Janette! What you're doing has to stop and I'm going to see to it that it does."

"It's not that simple. It can't and shouldn't be stopped."

He looked at me with horror and in anguish said, "You mean it's already gone that far?"

"No, it hasn't!" As I shouted my answer, its volume was choked by emotion and a fresh flow of tears. Still I continued, with sobs for added punctuation. "That's not what I meant. Will you–just listen for a minute–so I can tell you?"

"Listen to what? You've been lying to me all this time. You had me believing this guy was some school boy you were dating while the man is old enough to be your father!"

"It wasn't that I lied; I just couldn't tell the whole truth."

"All right, then let's have it, and make sure you don't leave anything out. Jesus, Mary and Joseph! How on earth did you get involved with this man?"

"How did I get involved with you?"

That arrested his tirade and made him think just a bit differently. He got the point, and though still upset, he calmed down considerably. "All right," Teddy said quietly. "I'm ready to listen."

Only in retrospect could something like this be funny. Both my men had the same worry about losing me completely to the other man, and both were wrong. But even in a grim sort of way, I found an appreciation of the irony that helped me to collect myself; so I sobered up enough to be intelligible and launched my tale.

He listened intently, and for the most part, did not interrupt. I made every effort to point out all the workings of the Lord with David and I, determining to make plain every single why and wherefore so Teddy would see that God had orchestrated the whole series of events that caused my teacher to fall in love with me and I with him. Beginning with the first day of school, my story met with immediate resistance. The idea that David first thought of me as an adult prompted the most incredulous stare. As Teddy listened to my explanation, he looked me over and grimaced, which was commentary enough. Still I did my best, giving each important detail and including the concept that God must have had David in mind when he brought me into his kingdom through a Jewish ministry, when he could have done it just as easily through Rock of the Witness. In between all the facts, I shared my inward struggles, prayers and reasoning over the whole business, so that my partner would know I wasn't being foolish or careless in any regard, if I could at all help it. That brought me to telling him about what happened when I went to Holly Richardson for help.

When I had finally brought the story up to the present day, Teddy's anger seemed to have lessened a great deal. Still it was there. He was just silent, and that kept me a little on the shaky side. Not having seen him so volatile, I longed for all of this to pass and for things between us to be as they once were.

Suddenly Teddy reached for the door handle. "I'll be back," he said and got out of the car.

He needed to walk off his rage and get his head as clear as possible in order to judge the situation correctly. He also had some deep pain and disappointment to work through. It would not be easy. Not only was he too emotionally involved, Teddy had too much to lose. He'd already lost plenty because my love affair had messed up his plans, and he had to know by now that we wouldn't spend summer together in Chicago. But if he wasn't careful, he could lose me altogether. Nor would he want to find himself opposing God if what I'd said was true.

While Teddy was gone to sort things out, I reached into the back seat and found the blanket, wrapped myself in it and tried to get a cat nap. All the crying I did earlier had taken a toll on my body and I felt wasted. At first my thoughts were still too active to let me drop off, but then the next thing I knew, Teddy woke me up as he was climbing back in and settling himself behind the wheel.

"Well...." Not yet ready to look at me, he sighed deeply and took a moment longer before finally giving his response. "That was quite a story. I'd rather not believe it, but I know you're not making it up. I even remember reading about your kidnaping in the paper, not to mention that grisly stuff on TV about the other girls." He paused again, mumbled something to himself and thought some more. Finally he turned to me with a look of frustration on his face. Slamming his fist against the dash he said, "I'm sorry, Jenny, but I just don't like it. I don't like him. He's way too old for you and in my book he's a jerk. But that's how I feel personally. Look, it's not that I can't see God's hand in what you've told me. In spite of the sickening way I feel about this, I listened to God while you spoke, so I can discern that he did put you together with this guy. I just–I just.... (Jesus, help me!) I wish to God that he was a believer. Maybe he really is beginning to open up to the Lord, but the fact remains that it's only so he can have you, and that's no good. He may even think he's sincere right now, but–you know, guys will say and do almost anything in order to win a girl, but once they get what they want, Jenny, they are as good as politicians at changing their tune. You know, I really should tell your parents about this. That way there wouldn't be the chance for anything bad happening because they wouldn't let this affair with your teacher go on. You're too young and too inexperienced for this kind of thing, and just one little mistake could ruin the rest of your life. Do you realize that? Do you know what I'm talking about?"

"Yes, I do."

"Good. I believe it. But there are two reasons why I won't. One is that you and David should be the ones to do it, and I think highly enough of you, Janette, to think you're going to take care of that. The second reason is that I sense the Lord telling me to wait a while. Now, I want to point out to you that he didn't tell me no. He just said to wait. So I will, and I'll do my best to trust God to handle the situation in the meantime."

"You–you will?" He responded with a curt nod. "Wow. . . . Thanks, Teddy. I promise, you will not be disappointed."

"Don't thank me, thank God. If it were up to me, I'd be at your house in ten minutes telling your folks the whole story."

"Well, thanks for being obedient to the Lord. And I will take care of business as soon as possible."

My partner sighed heavily and turned fully toward me with love, forgiveness and the weariness of despair in his eyes. He swallowed hard and gently said, "I believe you, honey. Even though it's hard for me to think of you as almost grown, I know you're a very sensible girl who's very strong in the Spirit. I'm sure that's why you and I are together and why God put you in that man's life for his salvation."

"Thank you."

"Now, I–I know you said that you intend to wait until David gets saved to marry him, but–" He paused to grimace at me again. "That just turns my stomach! I swear–I cannot imagine a little thing like you with a man like that. So help me, I'd like to–oh, would I ever . . . but I won't. It would only make matters worse. God must know what he's doing, so I'm inclined to believe this whole business with you two is to get him saved and for no other reason. Anyway, even though you plan to postpone marriage until he gives his life to Jesus, I still want to caution you not to compromise at all when it comes to that. It could just be my feelings, but I don't think so. Let Georgia do whatever she wants to get ready because there is wisdom in that, but I feel like you shouldn't make any concrete wedding plans until he gets genuinely saved and filled with the Holy Spirit. That means you make sure there's real evidence that he's a new man. Don't short change yourself, okay?"

"Okay."

"Good. Say, it's kind of stuffy in here."

The windows were all steamed up. Teddy turned to roll his window down and I did the same on my side of the car.

"So how old is this guy, anyway?"

"I don't know. I've never asked him."

"My guess is he's about thirty five, maybe a bit older."

"Really?"

"Yeah. It's only a hunch, but just to be on the safe side, let's say he's thirty five. And you're–what, sixteen? I can never remember."

"Seventeen. Eighteen in July."

"Right. Anyway, when you're twenty seven, he'll be forty five. Then when you're thirty seven he'll be fifty five. When you're forty seven he'll be sixty five. I guess that's not–too bad. But if he's forty or older, which I doubt, I strongly suggest you think long and hard before you marry that man. To put it discreetly, Jenny, older men don't always function the same as younger men, and before you know it you could be more of a nursemaid than a wife. You get the picture?"

"Yeah, I get it."

"So you honestly love this guy?"

"Yes. It's been as if I don't have a choice in the matter. But even so, he's well worth it. You just saw him when he was out of sorts. I know enough to see that he's truly a good man."

"Well, I sure hope so. Do you want me to get out of the way so that he won't be so jealous?"

"No."

"I was hoping you'd say that. I wouldn't do it anyway. I can be pretty stubborn when I want to be. There's no way in this world I'd give you up and leave you at the mercy of an older man, saved or unsaved. But we need to do something to take care of his jealousy." Teddy rolled his eyes and shook his head. "I can't believe I'm saying this. If it were up to me–"

"If it were up to you, you'd end up in jail."

He smiled wistfully at my accurate reading of his thoughts. "I certainly would. And your daddy would thank me by bailing me out. Now, that's a comforting thought." And it actually did help him feel better. From that point on he didn't look so tortured. I let him enjoy the concept a few seconds longer before reminding him with my elbow to get back to business. "Oh, now, what was I saying?" Teddy worked for a bit to recapture his thoughts. "I remember. We can't have your guy running around in a jealous rage. Under normal circumstances, he'd be right to have some concern over you and me, but God knows these circumstances are far from normal."

"Yes, they're paranormal. The problem is how to convince him of that. But you know, you can't really say that he doesn't have good reason to be jealous. Even though you and I aren't romantically involved, we stick awfully close. And don't forget, I've seen you get jealous of him, too. You'd just love to whisk me away to Chicago and wall me up in a convent, and he's been spoiling your plans."

"Jenny, come on! I wish you wouldn't say it that way. You–you make it sound like the Church is still in the Dark Ages. And you make it sound like torture."

"I'd comment on that, but we'd be getting off the subject. The point is, I have two men that I love very much that don't like each other–and with good reason. I don't want to lose either of you, Teddy, not ever. So somehow you two are going to have to learn to accept each other and be friends. If not–"

"Yeah, I know, I know. I've already figured that one out. Well, God is in the miracle working business, as they say, and we sure do need one for this. But I want you to know that I'm willing to do what I can to make things work, okay? As much as I detest this affair of yours, I understand that God is doing something significant in it, and I don't want to get in the way, if I can help it. This sort of stuff would have happened at some time or other, whether it was him or somebody else. No matter who you decide to marry, I'd still like to keep our friendship, if at all possible. After all, God put us together, too, and I just don't believe he wants us to split up."

"Me neither. Thinking about it grieves my spirit something fierce, so God must have a solution."

"I agree. Let's roll these windows back up and pray."

Holding hands wasn't enough. As I slid over to sit next to my Chicago man, he was reaching out to pull me closer. With his arm snugly around my shoulders, we began praying heavily in the Spirit until we both felt a release of the heaviness. Then letting the difficulties rest, we stayed close and chatted about other things on the way back to the church. Things like St Patrick's Day, which I was looking forward to now as much as Teddy. But as we said our goodbyes out on the parking lot, my partner hesitated a bit before taking off. There was one thing he hadn't told me.

"Jenny," he said, eyes a serious steel gray in the dim light, his smile fading. "I want to say one last thing about you and David. You know that I love you very much. You really are like a sister to me, so I'm going to tell you this, and if you want to tell him, too, you can. If that man ever does anything to take advantage of you, he's going to have to answer to me. And you won't have to tell me about it. I'll already know."

On that sobering note, we took our last hug and peck and headed home.

I would have taken a detour, but Teddy's route was mine, too, up to a point. So I went home, quietly dropped off my things, then went back out and over to David's. He answered the door in PJs and a robe and carrying a drink in his hand.

"I thought you might still come by," he said as I walked past and took a seat on the couch. "Can I get you anything?"

"No, thanks. I'm fine."

He came and sat beside me, took a sip from his glass and set it down. "So how'd it go?"

"Well–it was different. Much different than I thought it would be."

"Oh? Why? What happened?"

"Teddy overheard our argument in the foyer. He knows all about us now."

"Oh. . . . That's not good. But who would he tell?"

"My parents."

"Oy, oy, oy! Does he know them very well?"

"I'll say he does. But he said he wouldn't, even though he's itching to."

"Great. How'd you get him to clam up?"

"I told him everything about us, from the very beginning and right up to the minute. Teddy's not exactly keen on my dating an older man, but because he's able to see the Lord in this, he's willing to keep mum about it."

"Is he willing to step out of the picture?"

"No."

"Then just stop seeing him. Just see him in church or at rehearsals."

"Honey, it's not that simple. He's more than just a friend; Teddy is part of my family. I don't even have to be home for him to drop by and hang out. He shoots pool with my dad, eats us out of house and home and plays with my brothers and sisters. He's even works on our cars. They love him and he loves them. And frankly, what God is doing with my family by him being there is an answer to prayer for me. He's able to reach them with the Gospel in a way that I can't. Thanks to him, my family is slowly being transformed before my eyes. So, it's more than just telling him that I can't see him again."

"Yes, I guess it is pretty complicated. So you don't want to let go of him at all. Are you in love with this man?"

"No, of course not. But I do love him very much–as a good, close friend. David, I'm sure that under normal—" I paused before repeating what Teddy had said as something more detailed came to mind. "Honey, the problem here is that what we're dealing with just isn't an everyday sort of thing, either with you or with Teddy. It's paranormal. It's the hand of God. The setup for my relationship with you was arranged by God, and my friendship with Teddy was, too. But God not only made the relationship possible, he's made it something highly uncommon. That's why he and I can be so attached to each other and not have it get out of hand. It's the love of God that Teddy and I have for each other. That's what you saw tonight, and that's what everybody sees, only they don't always understand it. My parents think the same thing you do because they don't understand. David, please believe me, this business with me and Teddy is a whole different ball game. The usual rules don't apply. We are strictly brother and sister. Frankly, I like it that way. He likes it that way."

"Why? Is it your age, your skin color? Is he queer?"

"Oh, he likes women, but as a priest he has to deny certain aspects of his manhood, and he's powerfully dedicated to his vocation. Romantic involvement would complicate his life in ways he absolutely doesn't want to deal with. But the other aspect is my age. When I first met him, he didn't think I was old enough to drive. Remember when you and I first met? You thought I was an adult, didn't you?"

"I sure did."

"Okay, so look at me now. That's not how I look, is it?"

"Well, no, but–"

"David, sometimes the man can't remember I'm seventeen because I'm little and have this baby face. He's never seen me in a dress or make up, and I've done this intentionally because of religious complications–on both sides of the fence. So Teddy doesn't see me the way you do. In his eyes I'm a cute little baby sister and a tomboy. Since I keep my figure hidden in loose fitting clothes, he may not know I've got one."

"He knows. Believe me. If he's any kind of a man–"

"Well, he's certainly not paying it any attention. Trust me, honey. It really is innocent. Teddy already has six sisters back home in Illinois; I'm just one more, and we sure act like it. There are times when we knock each other around like The Three Stooges. It's not romantic in the least."

David reached for his drink and downed the rest of it. He held the empty glass and turned it about in his hands while mulling things over. When ready to speak, he sighed deeply and set it gently down again.

"I don't know what to say. Maybe I can believe all this, or at least I believe that you believe it, but do you have any idea how I feel? You probably don't remember, but I can't forget the look on your face the first time you told me about this guy. I knew then and there that if I didn't make a move on you that I'd lose any chance at all that I had with you. And tonight what I saw wasn't the two of you being silly. What I saw was love and affection. That man was holding you; not just a quick hug like I've seen with your other friends, but holding you very close for a good little bit, then on top of that he kissed you. Sweetheart, maybe what you say is true, but it's just a little too much for me to handle right now. I won't insist that you stop seeing him because the situation is too complicated, but don't expect me to go along with it other than that. I just can't help the way I feel. You're my miracle, my answer to prayer. Janette, you're everything I've ever wanted in a woman, and the last thing I need to see is you in another man's arms –especially a man like Teddy!"

It was hard to take the tortured look of fear on David's face. He seemed ready to cry any second. Such emotions don't respond well to logic, but I felt had to say something more to ease his suffering and calm his fears. He had no idea how glad I was to have my heart wrapped up in someone who sincerely loved me. Then I realized that warmth and affection was the best balm for his wounds.

"David, look at me." I moved closer and with a tender touch turned his face to me, then I let my hand slide down his neck and rest beneath his open collar. "I am very, very much in love with you and I like being teacher's pet. You should know by all that's happened between us that I could never love anyone else the way I love you. Believe me, Teddy couldn't take me away from you in a million years. He wouldn't even know how, being a priest. And besides, he's been too busy trying to turn me into a nun."

"Seriously? He wants you to be a nun?"

"Yes. Teddy's not just Catholic. He's Irish Catholic and a bit zealous. There's nothing he'd like better than to convert me so I could join his bunch. He's been pretty persistent about this nun business, though sometimes in a sneaky kind of way. He's dying to put me in a convent with his twin sister."

"Oh, really? Ha! Over my dead body."

"So, honey, do you really think you should worry about a Catholic priest being your competition? Honestly, how could a man like that even begin to compete with you? After all, you know I want more than just a good looking man. And kissing my brother can't give me the kind of jolt I get from you. The way you touch me and hold me tells a much different story and that's something I need. As a matter of fact, I could sure use some of that right now. That is, if you don't mind."

The tender look in his eyes told me that my words had hit the mark. Slipping his arm around my waist he said, "That has to be the best idea I've heard all day. Come sit on my lap."

SATURDAY, MARCH 1:
Since David needed so much reassurance of my love for him, it was a while before I could climb down from his lap and go home. (A tough job, but–well, you know.) Then with his jealousy being so sharp, continued affirmation seemed absolutely necessary. So after chores on Saturday, I went down to Little Pueblo and got a few items to put together into something I thought would help. When Monday came I would put my plan into action. In the meantime, however, my presence was required over at the hotel.

Aunt Laura and Johnny had rented the fourth largest suite that the Broadmore Hotel had to offer. Elegantly decorated in a theme of amber and ivory, the warm colors, wide windows, and crystal chandelier gave it a cheerful look. That evening the weather was a bit nasty, and so they were dining in and taking advantage of the fireplace, keeping the blaze lively. Noel, it seemed, had been the one that especially wanted me there. Why, I had no idea.

When I arrived, all were present except for Johnny. Aunt Laura sat by a window and occupied herself with needlepoint. I joined the others who were involved in a board game.

"I want to hear more about that fellow that was at your house last Sunday," Noel said to me as I took my seat. "He certainly put my father in his place. Is he really a Catholic priest? I could have sworn I saw him playing cello at Rock of the Witness on Friday night."

As I began telling Noel and the girls about Teddy Molloy, it struck me that I was finally cured of the tendency to take on the accents of others without thinking. The timing was most appropriate since Brits were to become part of my family. Smiling to myself and thanking God, I went on touting my priestly friend's good points for about ten minutes. Then Johnny came out of his room, up from an afternoon nap. As soon as he appeared, all conversation stopped.

"What, talking secrets again?" said Johnny. "Or am I the topic of your conversation."

"Oh, no, Father," said Noel. "It's just that we don't want to bother you with what we chat about. We simply don't want to have an argument."

"What sort of talk is it?"

"Well, remember, you did ask. You see, lately we've been going to this fantastic church."

"Bah! Religion: biggest waste of time, unless you happen to be poor. Even then you've got to be poor enough that you've no money left for them to take. You're not getting sucked into that, I hope?"

"Well, it's difficult not to at this particular church."

"They're pretty much all the same, if you ask me, and don't think I haven't been to a few. I don't care what name is on the front, they bore you to distraction and then expect you to pay for it. How is this new church any different?"

"Lots of ways. It's not easy to grasp, Father. I'm sure it'd be quite over your head. It certainly is mine. They actually open their Bibles and read from them. And all this time I thought they were only for record keeping and decoration."

"You mean everyone reads from the Bible? In what fashion? And do they understand it?"

"They certainly appear to. Everyone brings their own volume and they read together silently whilst the vicar–preacher or whatever–reads aloud. Then sometimes one or two congregants will stand up and read a verse or two that they found significant. Usually they tell how it applies to their circumstances or something they believe God did for them, but the comments can be most profound. You really wouldn't think they were that intelligent to look at some of them, but they certainly are confident."

"Well, what is the singing like? Do they sing the standard hymns?"

"I didn't recognize any. No, wait. They did sing something I thought sounded familiar. There's such a variety of music, and I must say that it's all quite good. They don't limit themselves to an organ or piano like most churches. They've a band of sorts; an interesting hodgepodge of instruments that changes slightly from week to week. Can't imagine how they make it work, but they do, and when they play their music it creates a most wonderful change in the atmosphere."

"Such as?"

"Difficult to say. For one thing, I've never seen anything like it in my life. Then again, the move of the Spirit, as they call it, seems to have slight variations at each service. But no matter. I know you don't care for church, so there's no use trying to explain it." Noel immediately turned to Georgia and asked her about her job prospects as a legal secretary. Johnny stood there for a moment with an odd look on his face as he pondered just what sort of church his son was going to.

Later on that evening we all joined in playing games and had a delightful time. From watching Johnny, it was certain that he noticed a change in his son, in attitude and vocabulary. Noel was genuinely happy. Gone were the acute sarcasm, swear words and the temper that had prompted them; a cheery, yet peaceful demeanor and occasional praises to God were in their place. Even the cigarettes were gone; no small thing, since Noel had smoked from the age of thirteen. It seemed only a matter of time before Jonathan Angrahm's curiosity got the better of him and he found himself at Rock of the Witness.

SUNDAY, MARCH 2:
 After what had passed between Teddy and Johnny the week before, Noel was anxious to hear Teddy preach, so he came along with Georgia and Veronica to mass the next day. By this time the crowd of worshipers at the folk mass had increased to well over two hundred. The first one I had attended drew only around sixty. Still, many of the newcomers were visitors from other parishes, and even some were the Protestants on whose doors Teddy had knocked. Some came to worship while others came out of curiosity. Then in accordance with his assignment, which he was finally doing some serious work on, he was even drawing people from Isleta.
 The service went better than usual, even though I was still feeling some of the effects of Friday night. Having Georgia and company helped to boost my spirits. The five of us went out after mass to a nice restaurant instead of going to my house; then we went riding in Teddy's car and we had a marvelous afternoon. And was there any tension between Teddy and Georgia? None whatsoever. They could see each other by the Spirit and accept what God had shown them. So with Teddy there was no fear, and with Georgia there was no temptation. But poor Veronica. She was developing a great big crush on my Wild Irish Rogue.

MONDAY, MARCH 3:
 Having talked so little with David since Friday night (I had managed a short phone call on Saturday), I could only hope that he still maintained a halfway positive attitude about me and Teddy. It troubled me to think of him being eaten up with jealousy, so with hope, prayer and stealth, I began an ongoing plan to remind my lover just how much I wanted him.
 Just as David reached for the door to the cafeteria, I slipped a small package of chocolate kisses into his pocket without notice and hoped he wouldn't find them too soon. He seemed in a good mood and so I relaxed, looking forward to a pleasant morning. But as we sat down together with our coffee and whatnot, David brought up Teddy first thing.
 "So this priest friend of yours knows all about me, huh?"
 "What? Oh, well–yeah, pretty much."
 "Then it's only right that I should know all about him. So tell me, what's he got that I haven't got?"
 "Oh, come on!"
 "No, no. I have a right. Now, tell me about this character. Where's he from? What's he like?"
 "Okay, since you insist. His name is Theodore Francis Molloy and he's born and raised in Chicago . . . Illinois."
 "That's cute."

"His family is middle class with ten kids."

"Is he the oldest?"

"No. He has a twin sister and they were born somewhere in the middle. Uh, let's see . . . he's always wanted to be a priest and his twin is a nun. Both his parents are Irish American so he's into that Irish heritage bag."

"What kind of car does he drive?"

"A 1956 Chevy with a custom paint job. He's also an auto mechanic, so he restored the car himself."

"Didn't you say something about him being a musician?"

"Right. He has a nice, strong second tenor voice, plus he plays drums and the cello."

"Cello, huh? Is he any good?"

"I'd say so."

"How long have you known this guy? Where'd you meet him? Did he just show up at church one day?"

"We met last December, the day after your caroling party. He came to Rock of the Witness to get involved in the street ministry and the Lord told me to pick him for a partner."

"Oh! So you picked him out."

"Not exactly. And be careful, you're drawing attention. Look, I knew what he was, and personally I'd never have picked him. He sure didn't want me, either."

"Oh? And why not?"

"Not only was I the wrong age and sex, like his father before him, Teddy Molloy was brought up to think Negroes are inferior. Then he met me and God did a number on him. I'm the first such friend he's ever had."

"No kidding? Well, he sure is making up for lost time. Now, he plays with you in band, and he's your partner for street ministry, right?"

"Right."

"You also said that he comes over to your house a lot, so he knows your family. What else do you do together?"

"Well, I told you about playing for mass, so we rehearse Thursday nights. Sunday afternoons and evenings he spends at my house. A couple of times we've gone to the firing range to shoot, and I taught him how. He teaches me to box because he used to be a boxer and I said I wanted to learn. He teaches me about sailing, too. Then sometimes we get into the Scriptures and have some pretty intense study time."

"So you're with him just as much as you are with me."

"I suppose so."

"More, really, since we spend most of our time together in a classroom. It's not like when it's just the two of us or with Georgia, so it doesn't count the same. I feel cheated."

"Da–Mr Conrad, please soften your tone. You know, maybe we should talk about this some other time. This really doesn't look good. People will think you're angry at me."

"I don't give a–I don't care what they think. They're not fluent enough to understand us anyway."

"They won't have to be if you don't calm down and use more Hebrew."

"All right. Now, all I have is one more question."

"Okay. Let's have it."

"What is it you like most about him? What is it that makes you want to be with him all the time?"

"That's two questions."

"Not really, and stop picking nits. It upsets me even more."

"I'm sorry. I was just trying a little humor. This is upsetting me, too."

"I'm sorry. I didn't mean for it to be this way, but I can't help it. I just don't want you with that man."

"I thought we had settled all of this."

"All I'm asking is that you answer a few questions. Is it wrong for me to want to know what goes on between you two? I sure don't think so."

"It's not the questions so much as the way you ask them. You might as well have a bright light and a black jack."

"I'm sorry." He sighed heavily, took off his glasses for a few seconds and rubbed his eyes. "I'm so sorry, sweetheart. I really didn't mean to do it this way. Please forgive me?"

"All right. I forgive you."

"Too bad we're not alone so I could really apologize."

"You can say that again. I could use some of that."

"Are you busy this afternoon?"

"No. But don't you have a dance rehearsal?"

"Uh, uh. We're going to see how much we can accomplish during choir and the noon hour for now. We'll have more rehearsals after school the closer it gets to show time. And I got rid of my other private students on week days, remember?"

"Yes you did. Then we can spend more time together."

"As long as you want to."

"I would love to. Now, do you still need me to answer your question?"

"Well– "

"All right, I will. What I like most about him is his love for God. Teddy is so desperate for a deeper spiritual life that he changes from one day to the next because he's growing so fast. He gets excited over prayer and worship and reading the Bible. And because his heart is so open to the Holy Spirit, Teddy just radiates the love of God. That's why I like being with him, and that's why we look at each other the way we do. It's not sensual at all, honey, it's a spiritual connection. Okay?"

"All right, if you say so."

For the moment David seemed appeased, and hopefully it would last a while before the next flare up. Maybe spending more time with him would help, but somehow I didn't think it would be enough.

The note on his desk said, "Check your pocket." I had casually placed it there while turning in my homework. It had no signature, but he glanced at me anyway after reading it, shuffled it under some paper and then began fishing around in his pockets. The look on his face told me that he got the message right away. David was careful not to let anyone see the chocolate kisses wrapped in clear cellophane and tied with a red ribbon; also inside was a love note. But all could see the smile on his face as he quickly shoved the package back into his pocket, then struggled to continue with class.

As soon as school was out, I rushed home to change and was in and out of the house before anyone even knew I was there. Then as agreed upon earlier, when I got to David's I let myself in. It was something I wanted to get accustomed to and he liked the idea. Since there was no one in the other apartment on his floor, there was no one to see me, a minor, coming and going with my own key.

David was making iced tea when I walked in. He poured two glasses but added spiced rum to his. "Hi, baby." he bent down and kissed me, then handed me my drink. "Thanks for the candy kisses. Was that your idea or Helen Bombardner's?"

"What? Oh, does it remind you of the apples?"

"A little."

"All right. Both the apples and the candy were my idea. Are you satisfied?"

"Kiss me again and I will be."

"I will if I can have a little of that rum in my tea."

"Well, all right. Just a little."

"Thank you."

"How long can you stay?"

"Well, it's Monday and I don't have home work. I can stay until five."

"Is that all? Maybe you should have come by this evening."

After he doctored my drink, I gave him the promised kiss and then wandered away down the hall to look at the photos on the wall. David followed. I stood in front of a wedding portrait of his parents for a moment and then moved on to others that had yet to be explained.

"That's my sister Judy with her husband and kids," he said. "That one's my brother Stephen and his family."

"I like this one," I said of a black and white portrait of a boy of about nine or ten years in short pants and a girl about twelve years old in a taffeta dress holding the hand of a toddler in a sailor suit. "Who are they?"

"That's me and my sister. The baby is my brother."

"Really? How cute." I studied that photo and then the one next to it of a slightly younger David on a Shetland pony. By then I was afraid to look any closer because I didn't want to accept what these old photographs revealed now that I had names for the faces. But it was too late. The clothes they wore appeared to be circa 1930. An auto in the background of the pony picture confirmed my suspicions. Remembering what Teddy had said about our age difference, a feeling of awe came over me. Now I was dying to ask David his age, but felt it was likely to upset him. However, the question wasn't necessary. Now I could make a pretty good guess. So I held my tongue and decided to wait until his jealousy had been assuaged a bit more.

Turning to David I smiled and took his arm. "You'll have to show me more sometime. I know you must have photo albums." *Not to mention the stuff around the corner.*

"I will . . . sometime. But for now, why don't we go sit outside? The day is still kind of nice."

Out on the balcony we sat close to each other on a white cushioned wrought iron bench set in the shelter of the walls; a matching table with a frosted glass top was at our feet. With a view of the city, mountains and mesas spread before us, we held hands and talked of where to go on our honeymoon. In spite of the topic, it was quite an effort to keep my mind on the conversation. My thoughts kept returning to the photographs and the fact that instead of the youthful early to mid thirties that Margo and I had believed him to be, the man that I had promised to marry was actually somewhere in his forties.

It didn't make me feel any less loving toward him. If anything, I wanted to draw nearer out of pity for his long years of loneliness. More than ever I wanted to give my love and assure him of my devotion. And more than ever I wanted to know what lay hidden in his past.

I would have stayed with my lover into the evening, had it not been impractical. I managed to tear myself away and headed home so that it wouldn't seem like I was irresponsible by being gone all the time. I'd heard that lecture a few times down through the years and wanted to play it safe.

Unable to keep my feelings inside, I needed Georgia's ear to bend. After dinner I took the phone into my room, got her on the line and poured out my heart. She listened with very little comment, which was just the therapy I needed to get back to normal. She did, however, voice her opinion and concluded as I had that whatever David went through in his past had to be terribly tragic for him to have come to this age and not married as it seemed he so obviously wanted to do. We both got the impression that the tragic circumstances surrounded his love life, but we both thought it better to pray rather than speculate, with so little to go on. God knew exactly what it was and would bring it out into the open when the time was right.

Chapter Nine
The Passion Ploy

WEDNESDAY, MARCH 5:
Hmmm, two aces and a king. I took two cards, not expecting anything big, and received another king. *Praise God!* Gradually raising the stakes to a hundred dollars in play money, I finally showed my winning hand. With that being my third one, Tommy McMichaels brought out a fresh deck.

I needed a good card game; something fun to take my mind off of worries. Even with David behaving himself, it was tough not to wonder if his jealousy would flare up again and cause another argument. So at lunch on Wednesday, I hurried over to the Journalism room to join the gang.

"Janette," Fletcher came up behind me and put his hand on my shoulder. "I won't take you out of the game, but I did want to ask you something."

"What's up?"

"I've been telling my pastor about you and he'd like you to come to our church and play some of your songs for the morning service. I don't suppose you're free on Sundays?"

"Well, no. But I'm not tied down either. What time is your service?"

"Eleven o'clock."

"Hmmm . . . your church is downtown, isn't it?"

"Yes. First Cumberland Presbyterian on Central. Reverend Franklin was hoping you'd come two weeks from this Sunday. That's the twenty-third. Oh, and you will get an honorarium."

"Let me check my schedule and I'll try to let you know by tomorrow."

I liked the idea of ministering at Mr Fletcher's church, but breaking from my Sunday routine bugged me. Not only did I like being at St Basil's, I was obligated to support Teddy. As much as he relied on me, and the more I thought about it, the more I wished I had just said no. But a talk with Teddy would settle it. That meant squeezing in a phone call somewhere in between music lessons and Bible study that evening. So that I wouldn't forget, I wrote myself a big note.

By the end of the day I was beginning to sense in my spirit that playing at Bills church was something I should do. Still it bothered me, so I talked to God about Teddy and how I always supported him with prayer during the mass, especially while he preached. It didn't seem right to leave the man hanging. I even considered doing the first half hour of mass and then taking off to go to First Cumberland by 11:00, only I needed setup time.

Another difficulty that came to mind while I considered this gig was whether or not I'd have to wear a dress. Though times were changing, generally at traditional churches, even nice pants were frowned upon for women. Another inconvenience. Again it made me wonder if this was something I ought to do.

Switch with Teddy. Let him have the Scout and take his car.

Yeah, that's a good idea. Father, is this important? If so, I won't complain anymore.

With that decided, my mind was settled enough to put the subject aside for later. I had music lessons to go to.

My finger was about to press the buzzer when I suddenly remembered the key and decided to let myself into my future home. As I walked in, he was at the piano playing and singing one of his comic renditions, "Dear Hearts and Gentile People." That meant he was in an especially good mood.

"I wondered if you were going to use your key," David said as he rose to greet me. "How's my sweetheart?"

"Fine, now that I'm here."

We embraced, kissed a couple of times and then it was down to business. Not an easy discipline, but we knew it was important to keep the lessons going. I couldn't stay too long afterwards, so we quit five minutes early because teacher had something special for me.

We went down into the sunken living room and sat next to each other on the couch. On the coffee table I saw a flat brown volume that looked like a receipt book, but I ignored it and turned my attention to David.

"Since we're going to be married soon," he said, reaching for the brown book. "You're going to have a lot of shopping to do, which means you'll need some money."

"Oh, but honey–"

"Don't you 'but honey' me. You need to be practical about this. Now listen, I know your parents are fairly well off and will want to pay for everything–that is if they give their consent–but they're not exactly wealthy. The point is, I want you to be able to get anything you want for our wedding and honeymoon. So if they can't afford the dress you want or whatever, you'll be able to do as you please. And if this isn't enough, then you just ask for more."

I watched as David opened his brown checkbook and began to write. It felt strange and exciting. More of the fairytale was coming true. Having a sugar daddy was something I'd always joked about with girlfriends, but never would I have dreamed of one day having or pursuing a man who could fill that roll.

He tore off the check and held it out to me. I made myself take it and then read aloud the figure that I saw. "Five hundred fifty dollars. That's great. Thank you, honey."

"No, dear, look at it again."

"F–five th–thousand five hundred? That's a lot of lettuce! David, I'll never spend all of this."

"I knew you'd say something like that. But honey, I want you to have your own bank account starting now. You'll be surprised how much some things cost and how fast this kind of money can go. You should have more jewelry that isn't made with rhinestones, you know, and although this won't buy much, you can at least put some items on lay-away. In the meantime, you should get a good set of luggage for the honeymoon and any other traveling we do. You'll need a lot of other things as well. You'll see. It's not just for the wedding, but for our life together."

"This is going to take some getting used to. I generally pinch pennies till they scream. Mommy and Daddy can be very generous, but they've also taught us the value of a dollar."

"Good. Then maybe you won't get out of control and put us in the poor house. But still, there's a whole lot more where that came from and I want you to have it."

This was scary. I looked again at this wonderful dream come true that wanted to share his fortune with me. Suddenly I began to wonder where all of his money did come from. There was so much about him that I didn't know. Was it wrong to want such knowledge? Not if we were going to be married. But would he get upset if I asked? Maybe. Maybe not. After all, he had said he'd talk about his past when the time was right. If he put if off too long, then I would ask. I just had to plan the right approach.

"Now, take another look at the check. Who issued it?"

"DBC Enterprises, Inc. Those are your initials."

"That's right. And what does the memo say?"

"'Education.'"

"Yes, because I'm going to teach you to be my wife."

"And so that no one will get suspicious. Baby, you're beginning to think like me. I must be rubbing off on you."

"You sure are. Now that check may take a little time to clear. Until it does, you can play with this."

From the back of the checkbook, David pulled a small fat envelope and placed it in my hand. I knew it was cash and I really didn't want it.

"Oh, David, this is too much. I–I'm not sure–"

"It's only a couple of hundred in small bills so you can open your bank account. Then you can deposit the check later without any fanfare."

"Oh, I see."

A minute or so later, I was out the door. Once home, I stashed the money in a safe place until I could get to the bank. Then seeing the note written to myself, I put in a call to Theodore and told him the news about the Sunday church gig.

"Well, Jenny," he responded slowly. "You can be sure I don't like the idea. Maybe I'm just being selfish, but we're partners, and it'll feel mighty strange up there without you." He sighed and thought some more. "I've never told you this, but I can really feel it when you're praying for me and it makes a big difference. Sometimes I get pretty scared, especially just before my homily. You know the battle I've been having with Fr Mitchell and Fr Lucero over what I preach. It doesn't matter how I justify it or how much the people like it, they keep telling me I'm going too far. But I guess the prayers of the nuns will have to be enough for that Sunday, if that's where the Lord wants you to be."

The other priests of St Basil's parish still couldn't grasp what was happening at Teddy's services. Not only was most of their information second hand, they didn't know the depth of his sincerity. Sometimes

Teddy's masses ran a little long, usually because he got carried away with his preaching. Also his homilies excited the people until practically the whole parish talked of little else. Believing that he was trying to make a name for himself by indulging in theatrics in the pattern of Bishop Sheen, or even worse, Oral Roberts or Billy Graham, they wanted him to shorten and tone down his sermons. They also didn't appreciate his quoting so much from the Bible. It didn't matter that Teddy constantly preached from the words of Jesus and stayed within the confines of Catholic orthodoxy; they felt that he was getting into dangerous territory.

"Look, Teddy, I tell you what. Why don't we get together the Saturday night before– "

"I may be busy that evening. If not, then that'll be fine. Otherwise we could trade vehicles Friday night. I can get the car back on Monday night, since that's St Patrick's Day."

"That'll work. You know, I think the Friday night switch might be best."

With those details taken care of, I would then talk to Mr Fletcher the following day and let him know my decision. In the meantime I could turn my thoughts to other things, such as preparing for Bible study that evening.

This time David and I met over at Georgia's. The three of us started with prayer and then Georgia excused herself to do some studying of her own.

The week before, David and I had covered the need for salvation and what Scripture taught regarding atonement, beginning with Torah and the Prophets. Tonight was more of the same but with emphasis on Messiah as the atonement. We went over many of the prophesies in the T'nach (Old Testament) that pointed to the death of Messiah for the sins of Israel and the world. David concluded, without suggestion from me, that the passages clearly described Y'shua, and the realization had a sobering effect.

I had hoped that from all of this that my man would be ready right then and there to embrace the Messianic covenant, but when I asked if he would like to receive Y'shua as his atonement, he was quiet.

"What's the matter, honey?" I asked. "Still don't believe or are you just not ready yet?"

"Well–I can understand and accept this far more than I used to, and right now I'd have to say that it's plain to see that Y'shua is the one the prophets wrote about. It'd be plain to anybody who'd take the time to study this with an open mind. The problem with me, honey, is that I don't know if I've got enough faith to make the same kind of commitment you have. I really don't. But don't worry. It'll happen. I just have to work through on my own."

David still had a few doubts nagging him from his old way of looking at religion. But what troubled him most was that deep sense of shame from the way he'd lived for so long.

THURSDAY, MARCH 13:
 But another distraction was the thought of me with Teddy. David cloaked this obsession very well because he didn't have a choice. Still it gnawed at him, so he had to do something. Knowing I was soon to see my partner in ministry, he called me at home on Thursday evening and timed it just as I was getting myself ready to go.
 "Hi, honey, are you busy?" he said, an impish smile in his voice.
 "You know good and well I am," I said quietly, a bit angry but smiling from love of him over his little ploy. "You ought to be ashamed. I'm surprised that you'd even call me. Be careful. No one would purposely eavesdrop, but anyone could pick up an extension if they don't know I'm on the phone."
 Switching to French, he said, "Now, I was a good boy. I did just like you said to do and disguised my voice and gave my name as Joe. But we can do our phone conversations the way we talk at school. So I guess you're going to see your other boyfriend tonight?"
 "Will you stop with that?"
 "I'm just teasing. But what's wrong with reminding you who your main squeeze is?"
 "You don't have to remind me."
 "But I want to. You should be here with me instead of him. I love you, baby, and this place is so empty without you. I'm not just jealous of that priest but anything that keeps us apart."
 "Really?"
 "Sure, I am. Look, what are you doing Saturday night?"
 "Well–nothing that I know of."
 "Then have dinner with me at my place. You'll get to see what kind of husband you're getting. I'm a pretty good cook, you know."
 "Uh, oh. Should I eat before I come?"
 "Not if you know what's good for you. Please say yes?"
 "I'll come. What time?"
 "Seven. And look as pretty as you can on that bike of yours, okay?"
 "I will. Now, I have to go or I'll be late."
 "All right, I'll let you go. But when you get to your rehearsal, you tell that musclebound leprechaun to keep his hands to his self."
 "What?" I laughed out loud. "Musclebound leprechaun? Oh, that's a good one. Ooo! I can't wait to use that."
 "Seriously?"
 "Oh, yeah. The next time I get a boxing lesson, maybe, or when we're playing games. Oh, sure."
 "Well, I'm glad I thought of it. Use it as much as you like."
 Fortunately, David's call didn't last long enough to make me late, but I did have to pick up my pace a little to get to St Basil's on time. After rehearsal, Teddy and I talked about my playing at First Cumberland Pres and exchanging vehicles. He stood leaning on the car door of the Chevy

at the driver's side while I sat behind the wheel and adjusted the seat.

"How's that?" he asked, looking doubtful.

"Better, but still not good enough. Look, as long as I can have a pillow to sit on, I'll be okay. I've driven the station wagon, you know. This feels like a sports car compared to that big old boat."

"I just want you to feel confident. Are you?"

"Yes."

"Are you sure you'll have to wear a dress?"

"Yes. Now, will you stop worrying? It's a piece o' cake. Believe me, I'll take good care of your baby."

"Well, all right. Now put the seat back and move over."

"Hungry?"

"A little."

"Ha! That'll be the day."

For that remark Teddy slapped the back of my head.

"Wait, Jenny. On second thought, why don't you drive? I'll get the blanket and you can sit on that." Teddy got the blanket from the back seat and we folded it to accommodate my height. Then he got in on the other side. "You know my favorite place. Let's go."

In a few minutes we were at the local Drake's hamburger stand without incident. I had no problem at all handling the Chevy, making Teddy more at ease with loaning me his car.

As we sat down in an orange vinyl booth together, I set myself to quietly enjoy my friend's company and watch him eat. Unlike me, though, Teddy was in the mood to talk.

"So how's what's his name?"

"David is fine."

"Still jealous of me?"

"Of course. He called tonight and said a few things because he knew we'd be together. But it was okay. Actually, he's handling it pretty well. Some guys'd keep on throwing fits and wouldn't care if the whole world knew what was going on."

Teddy shook his head. "Jenny, I have thought this thing through over and over again, and I'm sorry, but if it wasn't for the Holy Spirit telling me not to, I'd fix it so you'd never see that man again. It can't be anything more than infatuation on his part. Now, what kind of a man is he that he has to put his attentions on a child? A child!"

I couldn't believe what I was hearing. "Teddy, keep your voice down and stop calling me a child—or so help me Bob–"

"Okay, I'll stop. But would you just tell me what's wrong with this guy that he can't find a woman his own age? The whole thing just blows my mind, and it tears at my gut when I think of you with–with him! Oy v'voy!" He paused to try and control his angst. Then leaning toward me, he lowered his voice to say, "Jenny, why can't you just find a nice teenaged boy to go out and have fun with?"

"Can we change the subject? I don't want to keep arguing about this. I'll give him up on the day you get bar mitzvahed."

"Well, that'll never happen."

"And I have no plans to settle for less than what I've got. David is a kind, generous, and loving man who is wonderfully talented, highly intelligent and extremely handsome. He also happens to be stinking rich. His talents and interests are akin to mine, so that once he's saved and we're married, we can minister together doing what we enjoy most–music. And because he's Jewish, we'll have no problems when it comes to worship in our home, especially at holidays."

"Yeah. I don't get why you can't be a Christian like everybody else."

"Oh, yes you do. You're just afraid of it. You don't want to catch my zeal for the whole truth and end up being even more of a misfit. But we can talk about that later. The most important thing is whether or not I can be happy with David. I have no doubt at all that I will be. Now, if you know where I can find a younger man who's just as capable of giving me what he can, then you might have a case."

"Sweetheart, I do want you to be happy. I just–all right, I'll back off. But at the first sign that anything is wrong, you let me know, okay? I'm serious. You mean the world to me."

"Oh, Theodore. . . ." I wanted to put my arms around Teddy and kiss him; instead I reached out and took his hand. In return he gave my fingers a little squeeze, and as he did a tear rolled down his cheek. "Eat your food before it gets cold. Then let's get out of here."

He looked down at what remained of the double green chili cheese burger and chili cheese fries and seemed to have lost interest. Raising his eyes to me again he said, "Jenny, if you could just wait a couple of years, then–then maybe–" He didn't complete his sentence but then he didn't have to. The thought came to me as loudly as if he had spoken it.

"That's not a good idea. We love each other a lot, but I'm not too sure marriage would work for us. Not at this stage of the game. We'd have to wait more than just a couple of years."

Another tear rolled down his cheek, then another. "I can't eat anymore," he said. "Let's get out of here."

We didn't go back to the parish. Teddy drove us south until we were off of reservation land and then pulled over to the side of the road. He got out of the car and walked a few feet away. I stayed inside to let him have his thoughts to himself, but this time it didn't really work. The bond between us had grown so strong that we were almost one person. In his deep emotional state his feelings were broadcast to my heart so that I knew how he was kicking himself over lost opportunity. My father had offered me to him at a time when I would have consented. But he was kicking himself for nothing, and his lack of faith in the situation was upsetting to me. Obviously he was not the man God wanted me to have as a husband, nor was he even interested in me as a woman, so nothing but more pain and trouble would have come from our getting engaged. It was best having things as they were.

Before long, my partner returned to the car and tried to get his emotions under control. With clenched fists he sat once more behind the wheel and worked to slow his heavy breathing before saying, "Jenny, I know you're right. But if you only knew the dreams I've had. Vivid dreams, waking dreams that just–pop up without warning or provocation. I feel them as if they're actually happening! Over and over again, God shows me the two of us traveling and ministering together in awesome power. And I just can't shake it no matter how I try. I know what you said about an appointed time for it, but–" *The thought of losing you is more than I know how to take!*

"If you'll trust God and believe that he'll keep us close, you won't have such a broken heart."

"I know that, too. I feel so blessed when I just let go of my fears and believe God, but it's too hard to keep up. This whole thing is so–weird! It's being in love when you're not."

"But we've talked about that. We know what it is."

"Yeah, but why just us? Do you think everybody else who's serving God has this deep stuff going on? Why don't I feel this way about anybody else? I doubt if most husbands and wives experience love like this."

"Look, take my advice and quit trying to figure it out."

"It wouldn't be so bad if it didn't haunt me all the time. It's driving me nuts!! It'd be so much easier for me if you could share the visions, too, instead of me having it alone. And that doesn't make sense."

"Will you can it already?! God's got his reasons and that's got to be enough! If he's not telling, for Pete's sake, don't kill yourself trying to find out. Quit thinking about the future and try to enjoy what we have now."

He sighed deeply and made a strong effort to resign himself to the situation. "You're right. I'll do my best." Then he pulled me close and held me tenderly for a good while. With my arms around him I pressed my ear to his chest and listened to his quickly beating heart. Gradually it slowed to a normal pace, and peace settled upon us both. Then just as I was about to close my eyes and snuggle closer, Teddy's arms tightened around me in a gentle squeeze, he pressed his lips to my head and gave it a Dutch rub.

"Hey! Quit it!" I yelled and searched for his ribs to find a ticklish spot.

"Oh! Oh! Don't do that! Jenny–"

I had the advantage, given my position under his arms and with him being against the door. To escape, Teddy opened up the car door and we both went tumbling out onto the dirt and plants. Now the melancholy was all gone and we were both a couple of kids again.

FRIDAY, MARCH 14:

Friday was pleasantly different. Georgia dropped in at school, bringing Noel with her. After a nice chat with Mrs MacGregor, she came to hang out with the ADG at noon time and discuss the Case of the Missing Mommy.

"I'd say that looking in Los Angeles is pointless," my cousin said. "Unless we can actually go there and stay for a few weeks. It's pretty obvious that she had a stage name that most people knew her by. I mean, who'd try to make it in show business with a name like hers?"

"I agree," said Fletcher. "Without the trip and lots of leg work, it would be virtually impossible to pick up the trail."

"It'd be easier," said Billy. "To go back to England and get somebody who'd know how to pull information out of those servants and townspeople. That's unheard of, small town folk that don't gossip. Son, you musta gone about it all wrong."

"I did my best," Noel responded. "I think the problem was that I was the one doing the asking. They'd just as soon not cause problems for themselves if they can help it. That's easily understood, with my family being what they are."

"Now, are you sure she was a singer and not an actress?" asked Margo.

"Oh, I'm sure. The one person that would say anything about her told me that, only she couldn't remember her professional name. Mother seldom mentioned it."

"How'd your parents meet?" asked Tommy. "Did she say?"

"Yes. She said it was just at the end of the war when Daddy came home with her."

"Just as I thought," said Tommy. "You haven't told us everything. Come on. Every detail is important. So it was at the end of World War II?"

"Right. She was very beautiful, with long dark hair and dark brown eyes, not very tall but rather shapely. That's how she described her. I've got her mouth, the woman said. Anyway, she said that she'd come into town on occasion and stay at the inn whenever there were problems with her and my father. Usually she'd play piano and sing for the people just for the pleasure of it, because she missed it so. She played jazz and torch songs. Right, she was a torch singer."

"Was your father in the armed forces during the war?" asked Margo.

"Yes, the RAF. A bit of a hero, he was."

"If he met her during the war, she was likely entertaining the troops."

"Check with the USO," said Fletcher. "They might have kept some sort of record of the people who traveled with them overseas. It's a long shot, but anything's worth a try. Still it might be that Billy is right about England being your best bet. Somebody there must know what happened. If you're patient and can wait until you go back, just hire a detective. He'll know how to do the research and talk to people."

"They wouldn't tell you how she died?" asked Georgia.

"Haven't a clue. They've only said that she died when I was an infant."

"Who knows?" said Estrelita. "She may not even be dead, if the situation was that nasty. Maybe that was just their way of putting her out of their life and yours."

"I never thought of that," said Noel. "I can only hope you're right. I'd like very much to find her alive."

"Careful," said Bill. "Don't give yourself any false hope. It's better if you think of her as dead. There's no telling what you might find."

"I think she is dead," declared Katie.

"I do, too," said Georgia.

"Why do you say that?" asked Noel.

Katie replied, "How many mothers would give their child up to be taken to a foreign country and brought up in a place where she can't go because she's not wanted?"

"Where she was not wanted," I said. "And where she had no desire to be. Noel, if everything your father has said about your family is true, then the problems weren't just between your parents. I'd be willing to bet money that it was your father's family that made it the roughest on her."

"Well, the old woman did say that it seemed they were very much in love at the first."

"That makes perfect sense," said Georgia. "Johnny had married too far beneath him. She was just an entertainer, a torch singer. Of course, they'd have looked down on her."

"Let's establish the time line," I said. "Noel, you were born in 1948 in Los Angeles, California. Your mother died when you were too little to remember her."

"Let's say you were no more than three years old," said Mr Fletcher. "I know I can't remember anything much before that. My clearest memories start around age four. Now, if you did go to Los Angeles, that would give you a time frame to work in to find an obituary for your mother; more than likely that's where she died. If her name was never legally changed then it would be Rebecca Angrahm. Then if she was a singer of any real significance–especially if she worked in the film industry–all the local papers would have written her up when she passed away. Also, there are some famous night clubs from that era still in existence. If I were doing the leg work, I think it'd be worth a try to make the rounds in Los Angeles hangouts to see who might recognize some of the pieces of your story."

"Wait a minute," I said. "Noel, even if your mother wasn't well known, you father was. When obscure people marry important people, it very often lifts them into the lime light. And since Johnny's exploits as a pilot make him a part of history, following the trail of the local society columns, or even the London Times might turn up something, even if only a photograph. And since he brought her home at the end of the war, you'll know just where to start looking."

"Excellent idea!" Noel's eyes lit up with hope. "It'll have to wait till I get back home, but it's sure to turn up something. I just don't know if I can stand waiting that long."

"Well, on that same note," said Georgia. "The L.A. papers might also have some tidbits in the social columns. That'd certainly be worth a try."

Before the discussion could go any further, the bell rang and lunch period was over. Noel was positively delighted, though, with what we were able to do with what little he had to give us; he was now even more anxious to solve the mystery about his mother and only had to decide which direction to go in order to find out more. All this was a relief to me. With so little information, it seemed unreasonable to bother David about it. Besides, how could he possibly give us the name of some obscure singer who died nearly twenty years ago?

While getting myself ready for the service that evening, I remembered my date with David on Saturday night. I had meant to mention it to Georgia but hadn't had the opportunity. With others always around, it wasn't likely I'd get the chance to tell her until after it was all over. I didn't dare forget, so before I left that evening, I wrote myself a big note in code and put it on the mirror of my vanity.

But how was I going to look my prettiest for my man without drawing some attention? That occured to me suddenly in the middle of getting set up and tuned at The Rock. I seldom wore makeup for anything but school. Then what about my hair? It looked as if I might need to stop at Georgia's before going over to David's. After the meeting I hurried to put my things away so I could run off to talk to my cousin. But it wasn't necessary. She came up along with Noel and Veronica to speak with Teddy and me.

"Want to go for coffee with us?" she asked.

"No, I'm afraid not," said Teddy. "Whenever the weather is good we go out on the streets and witness. You three should try it. It's a real blessing."

"Could we go with you?" asked Veronica.

"We only go in groups of two or three," I said. "Sorry."

"Well, I could go with you and then you'd have the maximum. Can I?"

Teddy and I looked at each other. Sometimes the other teams took an extra person when needed, but we had never had to. We both felt a little odd over the idea because we were so used to it being only the two of us.

"But what about us?" asked Noel. "What will we do?"

"Well," said Teddy after adjusting to the situation. "We'll go in my car so that we can take Veronica with us; we'll also take her home when we're done. As for you two, I'd suggest you split up and go with different teams, or get with someone who's without a partner for the evening so you can stay together. They'll help you with that upstairs. Just let them know what you want and they'll fix you up."

"What do you say, George?"

"Fine with me, but what's wrong with going in a group?"

"We go out in big groups sometimes," I said. "Usually on Saturday night or at special events such as a rock concert, but there are advantages to not approaching people with a mob."

"Yeah, I guess so. Then we'll go on up and see what they can do about putting us with somebody else."

"I'll come with you. I need to ask you something." Quickly closing my guitar case, I jumped off the stage and went along with Georgia.

"So what's up?" she asked.

"Favor," I replied. "Feed bag at Joe's para Lizzy mañana noche. It's Ritz. Gotta hit Olga's. Hep?"

"Iffy. Olga's flighty, but hinges swing; picker 'neath rug, rock or whatever. Dig?"

"Dig. Word next."

"Flash."

A spare key would be at my disposal tomorrow so that I could make use of Georgia's apartment if she was out. She would call me as soon as possible to let me know how she would get it to me.

As I walked away I heard Noel asking Georgia if we'd been speaking in our detective's code and begging to be let in on the secret. It wasn't the official ADG code, but still it wasn't for anyone else to know. For the sake of Georgia's nerves I hoped he wouldn't persist.

So Noel and Georgia were placed with someone whose partner was out that evening, while Teddy and I took Veronica with us. After prayer we explained to her about street ministry and how we did things. Then we headed out in Teddy's car, not to our usual territory, but further east on Central to rotate with one of the other teams. All three of us sat up front which put me in the middle next to Teddy; a position that–after being out and about for a few minutes–brought on a familiar feeling; one that reminded me very much of Helen Bombardner.

As usual, Teddy and I sang and prayed intermittently as we rode along, looking for an opportune place to share the gospel. And Veronica? Not knowing the songs well, she listened, adding a part every now and then, occasionally peering around me at Teddy with a wide eyed expression.

It wasn't quite the intense jealousy that dear Helen had projected, but I did sense some envy and the feeling of being in the way. Poor thing. My little cousin, though not quite as well endowed, was just as pretty as her sister, with much the same coloring of hair and eyes, but with a slightly darker complexion. Still, she didn't stand a chance with Theodore. Now, how to tell her.

There were a couple of nightclubs in the area where we eventually stopped. We spent the next couple of hours sharing Christ with several of the patrons, either coming or going, as well as one or two passers by. At first it was only me and Teddy doing the outreach. Then after two or three encounters, Veronica felt bold enough to chime in and share her faith as we were doing, and discovered what a blessing it could be.

"Oh, that was fun!" she remarked as we went back to the car. "Praise God! Can I go with you again next week?"

Teddy and I looked at each other. Our immediate answer was both the same: no. But we didn't tell her that because we both recognized the selfishness of our motives and so decided to let God call this one.

"That's something we'll need to pray about," he told her. "If the Lord says to make you a part of our team, then fine. But usually when Janette and I go out, we like to take her motorcycle, and that only holds two people."

"Oh. Well–I hope God says yes. I'd really like to go again."

After dropping Veronica off at home, it was then straight home for both Teddy and me.

SATURDAY, MARCH 15:

After Saturday chores I touched up my perm, set my hair and climbed back into bed for an hour or so until Georgia came by bringing the spare key she had made. It was a copy I was to keep, should other such occasions arise. She wouldn't be gone the entire evening, but would be out when I needed to come by. I called her with the details of the evening ahead before she ran off. The rest of the afternoon was filled with my usual routine of Torah study before getting ready to go.

Excitement built inside me as I packed makeup, hair goods and perfume into my purse and the time drew closer. I had already told Mommy not to set my place at dinner because I was going out, so there was little else to be done. Finally I couldn't take it any longer and left. It was only a quarter to six and David wasn't expecting me until seven. An hour and fifteen minutes was more than I needed. So at Georgia's place I took my time and tried to make everything perfect. Then I rode slowly over to David's so as not to muss myself; and just for fun, I made myself five minutes late.

A delicious aroma greeted me in the hallway as I reached the top of the stairs. This time I rang the bell and waited.

The door opened and there stood David in evening attire: a gorgeous white dinner jacket with black tie and satin cummerbund. Before I could find words for comment, he drew me inside and gathered me up in his arms.

"You're late," he said and kissed me. "You mustn't torture me like that."

"You need a little torturing, you vain thing, you. Oh, David, you look scrumptious! Why the evening clothes?"

"We can't date quite like other people, so I wanted to do something special for us."

"But what about me? I'm just–"

"Don't worry. I bought you something."

"Oh? What did my sugar daddy get me this time?"

"Come look." He led me through the livingroom, down the hall and around the corner to his bedroom where, laid out on the bed was a sleeveless, sky blue silk dress with a full skirt, a square neckline in front and cut low in back.

"Do you like it?"

"Yes, it's beautiful."

"Then put it on. I like seeing you in dresses."

"Okay."

"Oh, and in the bathroom you'll find a few accessories." With that, David left and shut the door behind him.

It was a strange sensation standing there alone in that room, much like when he'd given me the key to his apartment. I looked at the furnishings and personal items lying about and a few seconds of that made me too nervous, so I concentrated on getting undressed.

In spite of a comfortable room temperature, I shivered as I changed clothes. The trembling of my hands slowed me down and made zippers and buttons hard to handle; but being happy and excited helped to hurry me along. Before putting on the dress I checked the bath for the accessories and found a pair of white sandals with two inch heels, coffee colored hose, a garter belt, bra, slip, and a gorgeous diamond necklace with earrings and bracelet to match. Also on the counter were hair pins, jeweled clips, a small vase of white roses, and a comb and brush set with gold handles, accompanied by a note card that said, "Just for her." So I took the dress and hung it inside the bathroom door, then put on the under things first.

With my outfit complete and my hair falling in curls around my shoulders, I surveyed myself in the full length mirror and smiled. It was indeed lovely, but I wasn't accustomed to seeing myself in modern dresses. The tapered hemline, though just below the knee in the back, was just above the knee in front, making me look closer to my age. Somehow I didn't think he had bargained on that, so I tried something different with my hair. I brushed it up and back from my face, which always did the trick when I wanted to look older. Using the clips, I pinned it up and back on the left side while letting it cascade down my back and hang over my shoulder on the right. Then I was ready. Anxious to see David's reaction, I stepped out of the bathroom and ran smack into a vision.

There was David's king size bed in front of me. It had been perfectly neat when I came in earlier, but now the covers were turned down and he was underneath them—and so was I. In another second, this unexpected preview of coming attractions was gone and all was as it had been. It frightened me too much to ponder its meaning, but for the moment I couldn't think of anything else. Shaking my head, I pulled myself together and accepted it first of all as a warning, one that didn't seem necessary since I had no intention of falling into that kind of trap. But I would heed it anyway. I then wondered if it was a forward look into the marriage I had committed myself to. Later on I would pray for more understanding. Presently, however, it wouldn't do to keep my man waiting; so I gathered my wits and went to present myself.

The fireplace was aglow, the lights were dimmed and soft music played on the stereo as I entered the living room. The drapes were opened to show the lights of the city, and David was at the window looking out.

"Well, here I am," I announced happily. "Like me?"

With arms extended, I stood still for a moment while he looked me over, then turned around so he could see the rest.

"Yes, I do. You look very lovely. Now, come here so I can look closer."

Touch was what he meant. I went and let him hold me close so that his hands could feel the soft fabric against my skin and the low back of the dress hidden beneath my hair.

"Now," he said once he'd kissed me. "Let's have dinner."

The table he'd set was magnificent. Fine white china plates with a border of burgundy and gold were flanked by gold ware and sparkling cut crystal for water and wine. Fragrant red roses at the base of two white tapers made a lovely centerpiece. The food in matching china dishes looked as perfect and delicious as the pictures in a fancy cook book.

David held my chair, and when I was seated, poured the wine. "You get to have two glasses," he said. "After that there's Kool-Aid for you."

After ha motzi he prepared a plate for me. It felt strange to have him wait on me like this. I rarely got this kind of service in restaurants, so it made me a bit uncomfortable.

"Did you have this catered?" I asked casually after taking my first bite of roast duck.

"No. You know I can cook. Does it taste all right?"

"It's delicious! Honey, you're hired. Now, can you sew and do ironing?"

"No, the dry cleaner takes care of all that. But when we get married you can save me quite a bit on those bills."

"I beg your pardon?"

"And I don't plan on getting dish pan hands, either."

"You don't get dish pan hands. You have a dish washer."

"Oh. Well, anyway, it'll sure be handy to have a woman around to do a woman's work. It is getting hard to find good domestic help these days."

"I know. It's all this Black Power business that throws a monkey wrench in it."

David laughed and dropped his fork. "Janette, you are priceless! Where have you been all my life?"

"In the mind of God, mostly. I sure wish he hadn't waited so long to bring us together. I like you an awful lot."

"Well, that feeling is mutual. Hey, how about a little dancing later on? Would you like that?"

"Yes, I'd would."

Talk about a night to remember. After dinner we danced before having dessert. One love song after another played on a big reel to reel while David held me tenderly. Then, as if that wasn't enough, my heart lost its steady rhythm when he started to hum along. When he began to sing softly, "'This is heaven. . . .'" I almost went to pieces. I knew he wasn't singing just to give me a thrill; he meant the words for the two of us. I wanted to sing with him but couldn't find my voice. Finally tears welled up in my eyes and rolled down my cheeks. Then he pulled me up closer and kissed me with a tender passion sweeter than I'd ever imagined.

I didn't know so much romance actually existed in the world. All this time I had thought it was only in Hollywood movies. But here I was in the arms of the most delicious thing in a pair of pants and there were no lights or cameras. Reason told me I'd better wake up because I must be dreaming; but my heart knew better, and got me hopelessly lost in the ecstasy.

"Are you ready for dessert now?"

"Hmmm?"

The music had stopped and for the moment there were no more records. I hadn't even noticed.

"Come on." David drew back a little and helped me to keep standing. "We'll have it in the living room so we can look at the fire."

In the state I was in, David had to walk me over to the couch and place me there. I sat in a daze waiting for him, thinking only of him and wanting his arms around me. When he returned with dessert, he put the radio on to play softly. Then we sat and fed each other spoonfuls of chocolate mousse, sometimes pressing our lips together between bites. When it was all gone, he drew me close and made love to me again.

From that point on the rest of the world ceased to exist. I lost track of time, forgetting that there was even a tomorrow. All I ever wanted was with me right then and there and he was in no hurry for me to leave. But finally, as the one o'clock hour approached, David decided that it was time for me to go home. Slowly the rest of the world began to come back into being, but I didn't want it to. I was doing just fine without it. But when I hesitated too long, David gently insisted that his "little Miss Jail Bait" get going.

Tears again threatened to rise when I had to put my old clothes back on and go home, so I took my sweet time doing it–all the while thinking of how Cinderella must have felt. The flowers, the comb and brush set and all of the things there that were now mine made me anxious for the day when I wouldn't have to go because my home would be there with him. Now, in that state of mind, can you imagine trying to drive–and on a motorcycle? David must have considered it because a big cup of coffee was waiting for me to drink before I left. A lot of good that did. I still can't remember how I made it home.

SUNDAY, MARCH 16:

During Sunday morning prayer with Teddy, I found myself distracted with thoughts of my Mr Wonderful. Then all during the mass it was a constant struggle to stay focused. In some distant corner of my mind there was a vague thought, a warning of being dangerously off kilter. I had other business, important business to be about that was being neglected. But the thought remained vague and slipped away completely until mass was over and I got a big fat reminder.

Teddy's mood was much too sober, but I barely noticed. Then at the first opportunity he got me alone back in the sacristy. The first words out of his mouth stunned me.

"Where were you last night?"

I didn't even have to answer. The look of joy and guilt on my face told him exactly where I had been.

"Yeah, I knew it," he said angrily, turning to grab an empty hanger for his robe. "It was late, but I tried to reach you over at Georgia's after calling your house. She didn't want to tell me where you were but I could guess. I knew you were with him and I told her so."

"Well, uh, I'm sorry I wasn't there for you. What was it you wanted to talk about?"

He replied with sarcasm, "Oh, nothing real important."

"Oh. Well, we have all afternoon."

"I'm busy this afternoon."

"I see. Got another girlfriend?"

Teddy turned to me with rage and incredulity pouring from his eyes. One quick step in my direction and his strong hands grabbed me by the shoulders, lifted my little body from the ground and shook me. Through clenched teeth he said, "Janette, I don't understand you! Shouldn't you be a little more careful with this man than to spend a Saturday night at his apartment–without your chaperon?! Georgia should have been there and she could have been. What on earth is the good of having a chaperon if she's not going to be there? Or maybe somebody didn't want her there?"

"Don't! Please!" His vehemence frightened me to the point of tears and his grip wasn't the greatest feeling, either.

"I'm sorry." Teddy released me immediately and then took a moment to calm his self. "Did I hurt you? I didn't mean to."

"No, I–I'm okay." Pulling myself together, I wiped the moisture from my eyes and said, "Look, if I'd thought we really needed Georgia then she'd have been there. Honestly. Teddy, I'm not stupid. Believe me, I have no intention of ending up in bed with David, so I wish you'd stop worrying."

"I can't help it. And I don't think you're stupid, it's just that you're human. Honey, haven't you noticed? Your brain doesn't have a whole lot to do with it. People are anything but sensible when they fall in love, and that includes you. All morning you've been drifting off to cloud nine."

He was sure right about that.

"All right. The next time David wants to do something like that, I'll insist on Georgia being there."

"Promise?"

"I'll do my best."

"Not good enough."

"Okay, I promise."

"Good girl. First chance I get I'll have a talk with Georgia about it, too."

"So what are you doing this afternoon?"

"Spending it with you, that is, if you want to come along. We are partners and we should stick together."

"Look, let's get out of here. I'll fix you something special for dessert."

"No, mate, listen to me. I want you to go somewhere with me. It's what I called about last night. I already told your mother about it. See, Iggy Hernandez and his wife invited me to come out to the reservation for dinner. But it'll be more than that. They're going to have some other people come later and we're going to talk about the Bible and the baptism of the Holy Spirit. I asked if I could bring you along so we could have a little music for our meeting and they said fine. But that was just an excuse to get you there. I need you for a lot more than music. Are you game?"

"Sure."

"Glad to hear it. Now, just forget all about lover boy and put your head back on straight, will you? This is serious business and we can't have any foolishness to distract us. Can you do that?"

"I can do it."

Teddy was now going far beyond the assigned research. He'd taken to spending most of his days on local reservations, but focusing mainly on Isleta. He talked to priests and lay people to try and get the whole picture, and as he worked he shared his testimony to the power of God. At Isleta he gained inroads through people from his parish who were delighted to introduce him to their friends. Now more than happy to complete his project, Teddy hoped also to see these people's lives transformed.

For this outing, since I wasn't a nun or even Catholic, I doubted that my words would carry much weight with these people. My main job was to provide prayer and moral support for Theodore. Even though I might know what the Bible said, I had come to learn that how to say it was just as important for getting a point across. Talking to Catholics in their own vernacular was something I was still learning to do, and what better teacher to have than a priest.

Ignacio "Iggy" Hernandez was a Hispanic man married to an Indian woman and living on Isleta with their six children. Teddy had spoken to him on several occasions and found that the man was more than just religious, having believed strongly in God from an early age. He usually came alone to folk mass, while his wife, Manuela, preferred the more traditional service at 11:30, usually taking the children with her. But for two Sundays in a row she had been willing to accompany her husband to hear the marvelous priest that he raved about. Now that priest was coming to dinner.

"You know what," said Teddy as we turned off the main highway onto the reservation. "I'm going to see if the archbishop will give me more time to pursue this study. If things keep going the way they are, you just might see a revival on this reservation."

"Great. How long will you ask for?"

"Well–I'd like to see if I can get some regular meetings going and stay long enough to get the people established in how to study the Bible. Another six months might do it."

"Why not just stay here for good? Would they let you?"

"They might, but I'm not sure I ought to. Don't think I haven't considered it because I have plenty of reason to stay. But Chicago keeps calling my name. I don't know. It's tough because this is starting to feel a lot like home, too. Maybe I'll come back after a while."

"You belong here."

"You really think so?"

"I know so." And just as soon as I said the words, I knew that if he belonged here, then so did I.

Sunday dinner with Iggy and his family was nice, even though the food had a touch more fire in it than Teddy cared for. Conversation centered around the importance of Bible study. Then the meeting afterward was very fruitful. Nine others came, some of whom Teddy had already spoken to. My part was much as I had thought it would be until Teddy hit an impasse because of his Anglo heritage. Then it was time to back him with more than prayer. Still I couldn't speak as a Catholic but only as myself, simply saying what was needed to address any anger and confusion. Then Teddy and I joined together to share some of the great changes God had worked in our own lives that transcended the cultures we were brought up in.

The meeting ended on a wonderful high note and Teddy and I couldn't have been happier. On our way out to the car we felt as if we walked above the ground a few inches.

"I can hardly take this," said Teddy, chuckling, as he got behind the wheel. "That was fantastic!"

"It was rather amazing," I said.

"And if you hadn't been with me, I don't know what I'd have done."

"I guess that's why we're a team."

"You've got that right." Teddy started the engine and turned the Chevy back toward the main highway. He started up a song and we sang a chorus together until he said, "Jenny, tonight you got a small taste of what I've been seeing in my dreams and visions."

"Oh, yeah?"

"Well, sure. What do you think I've been talking about, that, uh–what is it you always say? Oh, yeah, 'side-show Christianity.' No, none of that stuff for us. Just the real McCoy. I mean, think about what just happened and how those people's lives were touched. Isn't that what you want?"

"Well, sure I do."

"Then why give it up?" He pulled the Chevy to the side of the road and turned off the motor. Turning to me in the darkness, the joy he felt radiated in his smile and the excitement in his eyes. "Jenny, I could go on like this forever. Forever! Why don't we, just the two of us?"

His question rendered me speechless. It wasn't just the words that struck me; it was the power of the connection between us and the way he pulled my spirit to his with the joy and love flowing from his heart. Completely surprised and disarmed, I sat riveted while he slipped his hand along the back of my neck, then leaned close and tenderly kissed my cheek. Waiting for him to say something more, I didn't even try to speak. I needed something in addition to this to help me refuse his proposal. When I didn't reply, he grew confident and gathered me up in his arms.

MONDAY, MARCH 17:
The next morning found me still dazed and confused from Teddy's odd attempt at wooing me. Had it not been for the foundation of knowledge I'd already laid, I might have been at home packing my bags for a trip to Illinois and wondering how to get my hair under a veil. But while I had been shaken considerably, deep down I knew better and held tightly to that knowledge. And while I worked to cloak my discombobulation in nonchalance at the start of school, when he greeted me, the tender smile and the love light in my Mr Conrad's eyes, along with his excitement at my nearness, helped to put my head back on straight and in short order. As the day drew on, the daily routine further erased the haunting doubts that my friend had inspired, restoring much of my peace.

Then just when I was about to lose the shakes entirely, another challenge presented itself. In the Journalism room at lunch time, Margo snagged me before I could even sit down.

"Lady J, can you come by my place after school?" she asked casually.
"Uh, well–sure."

Something was up and it was serious. Margo had smiled as she spoke, but her big blue eyes told me that this wasn't just for kicks, and I hadn't the remotest idea what the problem could be. I hesitated because of the evening ahead with Teddy, but this had to be important, and getting myself ready for dinner wouldn't take too much time.

"Yeah, I'll come by, but only for a minute. I've got plans."
"It shouldn't take long. Just swing by here after school."

At least for the time being I had something different to worry over, except that I had no idea what this new problem could be. So it ended up that my thoughts volleyed back and forth from one enigma to the other until school was out, and that made it a very long day.

I stopped by the Journalism room and then walked home with Margo, but she waited until we got inside and were comfortable in her room to tell me what was up.

"Well, kiddo," said Muggsy as she handed me a drink. "I heard something on the grapevine that I want to put a stop to right away. I've already tried to trace down the rumor and I'm almost positive I know where it came from."

"I don't want to know who started it, so don't tell me."
"Are you sure?"
"Not unless it would be dangerous not to know." The feeling I got in my stomach was not a good one. It could only have to do with one thing. "Is it by any chance about me and David Conrad?"

"Why, however did you guess? Noticed any whispers or stares lately?"
"I can't say that I have. But what else is there to talk about?"
"Well, maybe you haven't seen heads turning yet, but don't be surprised if you do because I've heard it from a couple of student body sources, and so has one other Guild member. I mean, the whole world knows you're teacher's pet, so that's old news. But this is a little different because of the

added dimension of hanky-panky. What I've been hearing is not very nice, so I won't go into detail. But so you don't get too upset by it, you'll be happy to know that some people don't believe you're that kind of girl, and I think that goes for most of the crowd. After all, you don't dress or carry yourself like someone who's cheap, plus everybody knows how religious you are. But something else you should know is that as soon as I got wind of it, I started a counter rumor. I've said that Conrad is getting married soon to his childhood sweetheart and moving back to Los Angeles. Next I'd like to get one going about you and that guy I've seen you riding around town with. I mean that yummy looking blonde hunk of beef I saw you with the other night. Who is he anyway, and why haven't you told me about him?"

"Oh, that's just Teddy. No, please don't use him. He's a Catholic priest and I don't want to get him in trouble."

"Are you serious? A priest?"

"Yep."

"What a horrendous waste!"

"Tell me about it."

"Well, all the same, he's still a man."

"Look, I don't mind you starting a rumor about me, but can't you have me going around with someone imaginary?"

"Sure, but that's not nearly as good. Do you have any other men stashed away that you're not telling me about?"

"There are two guys here at school that like me a lot, but I don't want to encourage them. It'll have to be somebody that I know is safe."

"You can always pick somebody from the ADG."

"It's got to be believable, Muggs. . . . Wait a minute."

"Who?"

"Remember Noel and the *Case of the Missing Mommy*?"

"Yeah! He's perfect. And you know what'd really work?"

"What?"

"Getting him to play along, naturally. Have him show up at school to carry your books. Things like that."

"I don't know. I think we could trust him, but–no, I don't think we can trust him. The problem is that he gets all excited over our detective business, and I'm just afraid–"

"Oh, yeah, I get the picture."

"And at the same time I'm not real keen on just using him."

"Well, you can say that there's someone you want to make jealous. That's an easy, believable ploy."

"I have a better idea. I can talk to Georgia and have her let him know that I don't have a date for the prom. Get me?"

"Yeah. I'm sure she can set it up for you. And who knows? He's not bad looking. Maybe you two will hit it off."

"Looks aren't everything, Muggs. He's not my type."

"You're right, he's not. Okay, so Noel it is. I'll get to work on it. That'll be great, since he's already made one campus appearance."

"Oh, and if you're having trouble tracing down the source of that rumor, I hope you're also looking amongst the faculty. If it's got a nasty sexual twist to it, then it has to be Conrad's former girlfriend, Miss Marshall."

"Maybe, but I think she's too smart for that. However, it could be one of her cronies. If it's who I think it is, I can hardly wait for Fletcher to tell Old Mac."

With the problem being handled, I was all set to finish my drink and get going, but Margo had one more topic to discuss.

"Uh, before you go, Jan, I was wondering if you've been able to come up with anything new on The Fox."

"No, not since Christmas vacation, and I already told you about that." Until now, I'd almost forgotten David's hidden past. At the moment it seemed so unimportant.

"I just thought I'd ask. You know, as tight as you are with him now, you might just take a chance and ask him."

"Hmmm. . . . You've got a point there. But still I'll have to play it right. Thanks for the reminder."

I breathed easier once I'd left Margo's and was on my way home. From then on I determined to dwell on nothing but my evening with Teddy.

Though I wanted very much to make it special, I had mixed feelings about our St Paddy's Day dinner, especially in light of what happened the night before. I'd worn my usual orange to school but changed to something green before heading down to St Basil's. But I was in no hurry. Teddy's words and tender wooing rose up again to try and undermine my love for David, so after freshening up, I practiced the piano before loading up the Scout with my guitar and the gifts. It was then I found the relief I needed.

As words and troubled thoughts danced in the back of my mind, suddenly a familiar phrase was formed out of them: *Saint Patrick's Day, although I may be seen wearing green with a Paddy . . .* I sat bolt upright at the piano and gasped before laughing out loud. Then I sang the rest of the verse out loud. "'I'm always sharp when playin' the harp, 'cause my heart belongs to daddy.'" The Cole Porter song became the theme for my ride to the church. By the time I arrived, the heavy doubts were dead and gone.

The rectory was always a quiet place, but with the others away and Teddy and I there alone, it echoed with singing, laughter, and the sound of pots and pans. We set a time limit on ourselves so as not to run into the other priests returning from their evening out. Then when time was up, we would put things away and take off to finish our celebration over in the sanctuary where we would not be disturbed.

As we finished putting potatoes and cabbage on the stove, I couldn't help but feel apprehensive about Teddy's skill as a cook. He was such a manly jock type that I doubted he'd had much experience in the kitchen except looking to eat what someone else had prepared. His constant hesitation over little details told me that I was right. Fortunately he was bright enough to follow a recipe, and with some items being prepackaged, all that was needed was to heat them up. The only thing he lacked was the speed that comes with experience, so we would eat a bit later than planned.

"Now, that's everything," said Teddy, mentally going over the things he was supposed to do. "I think...."

"We need to set the table."

"Yeah, right. Now the plates are in–that one."

I didn't fault him for not knowing his way around this kitchen since the housekeeper did all the cooking. Still I could imagine times when one of the residents wanted a midnight or between meal snack and had to know where things were. But then I remembered how Teddy loved his burgers and realized that this room was quite foreign to him.

"Wish I had a camera," I said. "Your mother should get a load of this."

"Huh? Oh, yeah. She wouldn't believe it."

"You need to give me her address. I want to write and let her know what her baby is doing."

"Oh, no. If I could be sure my dad wouldn't find out, there are lots of things I'd like her to know. I've always been able to talk to her and I miss that. Miss it a lot. She may not always agree or understand, but she'll listen. You remind me of her in that way. You remind me of her in a lot of ways."

"Really?"

"Yes, you do."

"I'm flattered." And I was–deeply. Knowing how high her pedestal stood, this was quite a complement.

"But I have been writing to Terry, though, and telling her a good deal of what's happened to me these past few months. From the last letter she wrote, she's starting to experience some of the Holy Spirit for herself. And she's been reading–no, studying her Bible, too."

"Praise God! That'd be great if your sister got zapped. Then it'd be easier to share it with the rest of your family."

"You're right about that. You know what'd be fun? Adding Terry to our team–eventually."

Ah! Here we go. "Yes, and we'll need to add David, too."

"Huh?" He froze, then turned to look at me. For about a minute he was silent while the meaning sank in. "Jenny, how can you–I thought last night that you'd come to your senses."

"Oh, stop it. Nothing changed last night. How could it?"

"But you– "

"I'm not going with you to Chicago, and I didn't say that I would. As a matter of fact, I didn't say anything last night."

"That's why I thought you'd decided to–"

"You're deluding yourself, Teddy. I'm not going to become a nun in any shape form or–" Rather than repeat what I'd said before, I took a different route. "Look, when God connected you to people from Rock of the Witness, who's life changed direction?"

"Mine."

"Correct. Now, have you stopped to consider that maybe God teamed us up, not so that I could go in your direction but so that you could go in mine? That may be a tough concept for you to handle, but the fact is, God brought you out of what you've always known so he could give you what you've always wanted but never had. But you keep trying to drag me in the direction of a life that never satisfied you while insisting that it could somehow satisfy me. Now, does that make sense?" He was too stunned to answer, so I went on. "Teddy, I understand that you need to stay a priest right now, and I wouldn't drag you away from that for all the tea in China. But I have to go in the direction God has called me. How on earth you and I are going to stay together is beyond my understanding, too, but I know it's going to happen. I know it like I know my own name."

"You do? How?"

"Do I love you?"

"Yes."

"Then trust me. Since you don't have the faith for this, you'll have to hook into my faith. No, I'm not going to give up David, but Teddy, I don't want to lose you any more than you want to lose me. There must be a way."

"All right. I'll do my best."

"Good. Now let's get back to our little party."

Teddy looked down at the table, now set for two. "Okay, that looks complete to me. Would you say that's everything?"

"Uh, what's to drink?"

"I got a six pack of beer and I got you some ginger ale."

"Great. I love ginger ale, but I like water, too. Let's find a pitcher for that and then we can sit down."

He set out the drinks after checking the stove. "Man! This is hard work."

"Yeah, for you. You'd make a lousy house wife."

"Finally!" Teddy dropped himself into a chair at the table and it groaned from the impact. "Now what should we do?"

"Have some music." I got my guitar from its old hard case. Beneath the instrument were sheets of the songs I'd found at Fielding's. I laid them out on the table and began to play.

"That's real nice," said Teddy. "What is it?"

"It's a hymn called St Columba. They had it with three different sets of words, but I like this one the best."

I handed him the music and let him read the lyrics to "The King of Love My Shepherd Is."

"Fantastic! 'I nothing lack if I am his and he is mine forever.' It doesn't look familiar. Let's hear how it goes."

We didn't even get to the other hymns. After singing this one through a couple of times with all the verses, Teddy went and got his cello. We played and sang it until the timer went off to signal that dinner was ready.

Corned beef, cabbage, boiled potatoes, and Irish soda bread were a new combo for my palate. Not certain if I would like it, I prepared to ingest it without complaint. I kept my servings small and let Teddy take the first bite.

"Well?" He watched as I chewed corned beef with a little cabbage.

I was undecided. The taste wasn't bad, but it didn't exactly thrill me, either. "Not bad," I said. "But it needs salsa. Ow!"

Not having moved fast enough, Teddy's hand caught me on the back of the head.

"Now, behave yourself," he said. "And tell me the truth. Does it taste okay to you?"

"Yes, it's fine. You did good, Molloy. Give yourself a pat on the back."

Halfway through the meal the taste began to grow on me. Still I didn't eat much. As I knew he would, Teddy consumed most of everything while I got my kicks from watching him do it. Then because he had been too afraid to try making a dessert, we had ice cream and cake from the market.

"You know," said Teddy after his last bite. "That really wasn't bad at all. I may try cooking again one of these days."

"Oh, I love seeing you in an apron. I'll buy you one for your very own. One that's got ruffles on it."

"Can the smart remarks or you won't get your surprise."

"You got something for me?"

"Maybe. I know you got something for me. You go first?"

"Okay." Still in the hallway were the gifts I'd bought for Teddy. But my first gift was musical, so I picked up my guitar again. "First of all, you get copies of the hymns that I brought with me. But now here's a song especially for you."

MacNamara's Band was a popular tune for the Irish in America, but I wasn't sure where it originated. The melody was something I had pulled out of my memory and worked up on my guitar. I changed the words to make it a Christian song and even wrote a verse for Teddy which went,

> *Oh, my name is Theodore Molloy, and I would like to say*
> *That Jesus Christ, the Son of God, he is the only way*
> *To enter into heaven's door and find salvation's plan.*
> *So put your trust in Jesus Christ, who is the Son of Man.*

Teddy laughed joyfully as I sang and the look on his face was one of sheer delight. "I love it! Jenny, you're too much! And my own verse, even. Do you have one, too?"

"I'm still working on that. It was tough enough writing this out because of the time factor, but I'm glad you like what little I was able to do."

"I certainly do, and I want a copy of it."

"Already done. Okay, now it's your turn."

Teddy went to the laundry room just off the kitchen and returned with a big sweater sized box wrapped in Kelly green paper with white pinstripes. "Happy St Paddy's Day," he said and placed it in my hands. My suspicions of finding wearing apparel were correct. Underneath all the wrapping and tissue paper was cashmere!

"That comes from Ireland via Chicago."

"Oh, Teddy!" I brushed my fingers across the woven softness. "Oh, and there are two of them."

"There should be a third one."

"Yes, here it is."

On top were two simple little pullover sweaters with short, slightly puffy sleeves, one in pale mint green and the other in egg shell white. Third was a black, long sleeved turtleneck.

"Why don't you try one on?"

"Okay, but which one?"

"The black one."

There was one restroom downstairs. I found it and hurried out of my blouse. The sweater fit just fine, and it felt wonderful on my skin. After putting my hair back in order, I quickly returned to show Teddy and got another surprise. He was wearing a sweater just like it.

"Why–you've got one, too. We can be twins."

"That's right. Here, put this on."

Out of a bag he pulled a broad, flat cap made of brown leather. He tossed it to me and then brought out another for himself. I laughed and placed the hat carelessly on my head.

"No, no. Now, do it right." Teddy put his hat on and then he arranged mine. "There. Now we're twins."

"Pat and Mike indeed! Does this make me Irish?"

"Almost. But we'll get you there before the night's over."

"Okay, my turn again."

Running back out to the hall I grabbed the first box from my bag and set it before Teddy. He tore off the green and white shamrock paper and gasped when he found the green, white and black sweat shirts I'd had made. Underneath them were several T-shirts with the same design, done with colors reminiscent of the Irish flag. Atop his leonine family crest was his surname. Beneath the crest it said Ireland.

"Oh, Jenny. . . . Where did you–? How–how did–? The crest–I've only seen it once before."

"I got it right? I found several and just picked what I felt might be it."

"Oh, you got it right, all right. Man! I'll send one of these T-shirts to my old man. And I'm going to let him know it was you who had them made. Thank you, sweetheart. This means a lot." He gingerly placed the clothing back in the box and gave me a look of love and deep gratitude. He sighed heavily before saying, "All right, now it's my turn again."

He brought out another box, slightly smaller than the first. Inside was more clothing, more wool, but this was much different. The fabric was

smooth, tightly woven and plaid; a pale green plaid of complementary colors on an off white background. Lifting the garment up, I found that I held in my hands a pleated skirt with fasteners on the side. "It's a kilt," he explained. "An Irish kilt."
"Oh, it's beautiful."
"Now, go put it on. You'll find some stockings there, too."
He had planned my outfit. The heavy tights were black to go with my turtleneck. Back I went to the restroom to get out of my jeans. But this time I was more careful as I put on the hosiery and worked with the lengthy skirt.

Compared to the Scottish type kilts I'd seen, this was longer, more streamlined, and with a lot less flounce. It opened at the side where there were adjustable fasteners–and it fit like a dream! With my narrow waist and broad hips, that was no small miracle. Amazed at the perfection of fit, I kept looking at myself in the mirror on the door. Not a pucker or bind anywhere. Nor was it too long. The hem came just above the middle of my calves.

Tearing myself away, I hurried back so Teddy could see.
"Well, now." He nodded with approval as I turned around. With a brogue he said, "I think there's a strange young lass come in. Now, what on earth happened to that tomboy?"
"Oh, Theodore! This is absolutely gorgeous. Thank you so much!" I threw my arms around his neck and kissed his cheek.
"Now you're Irish."
"Oh, with this I can sure feel the part. It's fabulous! I've never had a ready-made skirt fit like this. It's perfect!"
"I'm glad you like it. I was hoping I got the right size. Now is that it?"
"I've got one more for you."
"All right."

This box had a small card with it, and the verse inside I had written myself. Teddy smiled as he read the little rhyme, then said it aloud. "'Theodore Francis John-Joseph Molloy is a Catholic priest from Illinois. Filled with the Holy Ghost and joy is Theodore Francis John-Joseph Molloy. God bless him!'" He blushed slightly and looked at me, then set about opening the gift. "Hmmm, kind of heavy. Now, what could this–be?"

His reaction was just what I'd hoped for. He was totally speechless as he lifted the black leather jacket from the box and held it before him.

Picking just the right jacket had taken some effort. The store clerk had shown me many contemporary styles, some of which were quite nice. But when I saw this old fashioned, Brando-esque biker's jacket with zippers and plenty of shoulder room, I knew it was made for my Chicago man.

"I was going to buy one of these second hand at the place where I got your punching bag," he said at last. "But it didn't fit me. Oh, Jenny . . . Jenny, thank you!"
"Glad you like it. Now, turn it over before you put it on."

Teddy flipped the jacket over and his eyes grew wide in disbelief. On the back was his boxing name, Wild Irish Rogue, in green, black, and white over a pair of wings; underneath in smaller print were the words, "To God Be the Glory."

As he studied the emblem, tears came rolling out. "Oh, God. . . . Praise God! This is–this–I'll never part with this as long as I live. Never." He laid the leather out on the table and stared at it, stroked the heavy applique, then looked at me. As if seeing me for the first time, he studied me from head to toe. His jaw tightened and anger mixed with sorrow radiated from his eyes. Suddenly he reached for me, wrapped me in his arms, and pulled me close in a tender, yet desperate embrace.

The wails that emanated from the depths of Teddy's soul echoed on the kitchen walls and down the hallway. Tears arose in my own eyes as I pressed myself to him. My clothes grew damp from the tears as he pressed his face against me. As he sobbed I stroked his golden curls and kissed his head, letting my heart be full also from the powerful bond between us.

In only a moment or two the wailing subsided and the tears stopped their flow. My other love slowly released me and managed a sober smile. "You know what?" he said. "I don't care how many men you marry–Jenny girl, you're stickin' with me always. You hear me? Always and forever."

"Always and forever, Teddy."

His heart was filled with things he wanted to say but couldn't express. I could feel it, the gratitude to God and to me for such deep and unconditional love. It brought him healing, the way I accepted and loved him freely, not putting him down or trampling on those things sacred to him. He also realized that it was God who had put such a love in my heart in order to express his caring for him on an intimate and tangible level. Teddy felt that he couldn't have asked for more, and that he had far, far more than he could ever deserve.

"Look, let's get out of here." Releasing me, he got up and hurriedly began to clean the table. "Let's skip the chapel. Get out of that kilt and then stow your gear in my car. I want to go for a walk."

We managed to get things back to normal quickly and then I jumped into my jeans. We left on foot and went for a walk along the irrigation ditches, going so far that we got ourselves lost. Lost in the most incredible way.

TUESDAY, MARCH 18:

"So what'd you do for St Patrick's day? Were you out with that priest?" David spoke casually *en Français* while adding the cream to his coffee, but I could sense the underlying anger and answered with caution.

"Well, sure. So what?"

The deadly look in his eyes over his rimless glasses told me "what."

"Had I thought about it sooner," he said. "I'd have put a stop to it. Where'd you go? I tried calling you."

"We had dinner down at the–at St Basil's."

"Then what?"

"Huh?"

"At half past five I left a message for you to call me when you got in, and I never heard from you."

"And I never got the message."

"You didn't?"

"No. Who did you leave it with?"

"Your mother. She said she would leave you a note."

The house had been dark by the time I got home, and that was well after midnight, so I didn't see the note. But I wasn't about to say so. "Well, I don't know what happened to it."

"What time did you get in?"

The last thing I wanted was to continue this subject, but I didn't know how to turn it off. Rather than escalate into a full blown argument by answering, I just clammed up. Then I got a revelation and grabbed a pen. Tearing out a sheet of paper from my notebook, I wrote out the St Patrick's Day verse from "My Heart Belongs to Daddy" and gave it to him.

Leaning back, David read the words and chewed his bottom lip for a second. Then looking up at me with softer eyes, he sighed and said, "I like that. It's kind of cute."

"It's what I was thinking of yesterday."

Now he smiled broadly, folded the paper and put it in the inside pocket of his jacket. Then we left off of the topic and got down to the usual routine of Hebrew studies.

Had I not seen Margo in the hall that morning, I would have forgotten what she had told me the day before about the ugly rumor. Thinking about it was a real bring down, but it was something that needed immediate attention. So that I wouldn't forget again, I called Georgia as soon as I got home and talked to her about it while changing clothes.

"Hi, I'm glad you're home," I said when she answered. "It's me. Anything turn up on the job scene?"

"Nothing. Absolutely nothing. I can't believe it. Nobody's calling. Maybe I'm over qualified or something, but I don't think so. Maybe God is trying to tell me something."

"I thought of that. Could be he's got something special that you'll have to wait for, or maybe he just wants you to do something else."

"Well, whatever it is he wants, I hope it happens pretty soon. This is very frustrating. So what's up with you?"

"Got a problem at school."

"Oh, yeah?"

"Somebody's spreading rumors about Lizzy and Joe. Muggsy told me about it yesterday."

"Are you sure they're just rumors? Maybe somebody's seen or heard something when they were together."

"I never even thought about that. The reason, I guess, is because they're both so careful. If she goes to his place for anything other than lessons, she takes a different route and makes sure she's not followed. Then she parks in back and uses the elevator. You know the kind of routine; it's nothing new. In public, for all intents and purposes they talk either music or religion. I don't know exactly what's being said, but the general idea is that it's not very nice, which means that it's just someone's evil thinking. I figure somebody's upset or jealous and wants to cause problems."

"I hope you're right. Well, have you thought about having them stage an argument? You know, have a little spat in front of just the right people?"

"It crossed my mind this afternoon, but it didn't sit right with me. I don't know why, but somehow I felt that it would only confirm just how close we–I mean, they are. I would rather have Joe do something like keep a Bible in view so that people will see that as the binding force of their relationship. Then with the counter rumors Margo is spreading, no one will believe whatever twisted things are being said."

"What kind of manure is she broadcasting?"

"She's got Joe marrying his childhood sweetheart and moving back to L.A. Then she wants one to go around about Lizzy and some fella, but I don't have any candidates. The best I could think of was Noel because of the time you sent him to come pick me up here at school. I figured that if Lizzy was seen enough with him then that would give Margo plenty of compost. Then if you could drop the hint that she doesn't have a date for the prom, she'd be mighty beholdin' to ya.."

"Good idea. I'll see what I can do."

"Just make sure he knows that she's got a boyfriend, so that he won't get any ideas. All she needs is another man coming after her. I figured we could let him know that there's a little intrigue going on without letting him in on everything. That way he won't get hurt or taken advantage of."

"That's good. Sure, he'd be tickled pink. I can just see it now. Noel will be perfect to escort Lizzy to the prom, since he's so well mannered and all. I just hope she doesn't mind that he's not going to be up on the latest American dances."

"Oy vey. I never thought about that. Have you ever seen him dance?"

"I've seen him do stuff like a Fox Trot, and he's good at that. But somehow I suspect that he's not much better than your average white boy when it comes to popular dances."

"Well, you can't have everything. First let's see if he'll go along with this, then maybe we can work on showing him the latest moves. To be honest, I've just learned them myself."

"Okay. I'll give Noel a call tonight and see what I can do. I think it'll be a good start to let him know that I'd like him to do a favor for someone special and try to down play the intrigue. But whatever I say, he won't be told Joe's name or anything really important, so Lizzy shouldn't worry. Then I'll give you a call back to tell you what to expect."

"Great. Look, I'd better go. I've got homework and music to practice.

Talk to you tonight."

By the end of the evening it was all set. Georgia talked to Noel and he was more than happy to be a substitute for my boyfriend. What he believed was actually happening, though, was beyond me, because he was even willing to take me out on dates other than the prom, if I thought it necessary. But I wasn't anxious to look too closely at this particular gift horse since it was sure that with this attractive Englishman around, the nasty rumor would be dispelled in no time at all.

WEDNESDAY, MARCH 19:

Eager for a pleasant diversion, Noel wasted no time getting started. The very next day he was walking around campus at the end of the school day looking for me.

"What a nice surprise," I said when I found him just inside the gate. I really was a little amazed to have things moving so fast.

"You oughtn't be too surprised," said Noel. "I'm delighted to–well, you know."

He took my school books and carried them along to the car. Perfect. I was tempted to look and see who was watching.

Noel drove Georgia's little red car again. He opened the door for me and offered his free hand to help me in.

"Georgia says that you don't have a date for your school promenade," he said as he pulled the car out into the street. "And that you're seeing a fellow who for some reason or other won't be able to take you?"

"Yes, that's right."

"Well, I think it's perfectly dreadful. Would you mind if I escorted you? Or would he be too terribly jealous?"

"Oh, I wouldn't mind at all. As for my boyfriend, I'm–sure that, uh, he'll be–very understanding. Noel, thanks for thinking of me. I don't know what it's like in England, but here the senior prom is a very important event."

"So I understand and it's why I want to help. Well, consider your problem solved. And I promise to do everything in my power to make it a memorable evening."

Noel was a bit difficult to get rid of that afternoon. He wouldn't just drop me off but came inside and then waited for me, even though I told him there was no need to give me a ride to my lessons. He wanted to take me there and then wait around till I was done. I was ready to sneak out the back door and leave him sitting in the living room when he remembered he'd promised to meet Johnny and Aunt Laura somewhere for something. Then before he could change his mind and turn around, I took off for the northeast heights.

I had planned to tell David every bit of what was going on regarding Noel and the rumor, but my courage dwindled with each flight of stairs up to his apartment. Then I remembered that I would see him again anyway at our study that evening and so decided to postpone it till then.

With so much to think about, I forgot to use the key. As I rang the bell the knot in my stomach began to ease. By the time David let me in I was able to behave as usual.

As soon as he opened the door I noticed that something was different about the way David looked, but couldn't figure out what. On my way to the piano bench I looked at him again and again. His hair was the same and there was nothing out of the ordinary about his clothes. Finally I just set my music down and stared at him.

"What's the matter?" he asked, smiling slightly. "Don't you like them?"

"'Them' what?"

"My contact lenses."

"Contact lenses? So that's it!"

"I thought I'd give them another try. I wore them a few years ago, but glasses are an advantage in the classroom. So, what do you think?"

"Well, I think you're vain enough to already know how good looking you are, but I'll tell you anyway. Honey, you look delectable!"

"Thank you. I'm glad you approve."

"But I do like you with glasses. They make you look–more vulnerable somehow; more approachable."

"But don't you think that glasses make me look older?"

"I don't know. Maybe a little bit."

"They also get in the way when I want to get close to you. But the best thing is, I can see more with these lenses, and that's important to a man."

"Mmmm . . . it's important to women, too." I continued to study him as I sat down at the piano. I'd seldom seen him without spectacles for more than a few moments, and now I could enjoy the full effect of his beauty. "David, you're a little hard to take like that. No wonder you wear glasses. You look like a movie star."

"Well, I won't wear them for anyone else but you."

"I certainly hope not."

Once David got his first couple of kisses, he was supposed to leave me alone. But as I opened my book of Hanon and set it in front of me, he got up and closed it, pulled me off the piano bench and sat down again with me on his lap.

"Honey, don't," I said as I helplessly lay my head on his shoulder. "We won't get anything done if we start like this."

His response was to raise me up and look straight into my eyes. Without the glasses it was almost like being in the arms of a stranger. A fiercely handsome stranger. His eyes, blue-gray and full of longing, pierced my heart and pulled at my soul. I closed my eyes to give myself the chance to gather strength to pull away, but the gentle touch of his hand on my hair made me weak again.

"I need to hold you, baby," he said softly. "Sometimes I just need to hold you as close as I can, and that's what I need right now. Please?" He kissed my cheek gently. "Please?"

Before I knew it my arms were around his neck and his tongue was teasing mine. If I got a lesson that day, it sure wasn't in music. After a flurry of kisses, though, he behaved himself and simply held me close with only an occasional caress of the hand.

"Are you mad at me?" he asked at the end of the hour.

"No. How could I be?"

"I'm glad you humored me. I was about to go crazy. But you'd better go home now."

When I saw my sweetheart again that evening at Georgia's, true to his word, there were the rimless glasses back in place. That was a relief for me. I liked him better that way because it seemed friendlier and more familiar.

As before, the three of us prayed together and then Georgia went to her bedroom to hit the books and listen to music. She kept the door ajar, however, so as to be available if needed. But before David and I got into our study, he had something else to talk about.

"I bought some more dresses." He smiled wistfully and touched my hair. "Would you like to come over next Saturday evening and try them on?"

"I don't know. You're going to have to stop buying me clothes, honey. I'm not used to this."

"You're going to be my wife. Now, why shouldn't I buy you things?"

"Does it have to be now? Maybe you should wait until we get married."

"If you can tease me with chocolate kisses and love notes, why can't I be your sugar daddy? It's fun for me to express my feelings that way."

"I know that. I'm sorry. It's just that–it's all starting to overwhelm me again. It would be different if all this were out in the open and everybody knew, because then I could let it all out. But instead I have to keep all the excitement inside me most of the time."

"I'd still like you to come over next Saturday. This time dinner won't be quite so fancy, and we can do whatever you like. If you want, I'll even dig out my old photo albums."

"Really?"

That sure lit my fire. But then David always had a way of doing just the right thing to get me going. It sounded like a perfect setting in which to deal with things in David's past. Ready to say yes, I suddenly remembered the promise I had made to Teddy.

"Can Georgia come, too?"

That struck him funny. He thought for a moment before saying, "I'd rather she didn't. There's something I want to talk to you about that–well, I'd like to stay between the two of us."

What could that be? Is he ready to talk about his past all of a sudden? Still it didn't matter. I had made a promise. In order to break it I'd have to get Teddy's permission. Now, how was I supposed to explain that to David?

"Uh–honey, look, I'd like to come over, but I just may have something else going that night." Something else, like staying home, and yet I felt I had to go. It looked like the chance I'd been waiting for. "Let me check things out first, and then I'll let you know if I can. Okay?"

"Okay."

That evening, getting into the Scriptures and prayer was very tough going. For some unknown reason there was no feeling of God's presence and it was getting me down. Things got confused and there were no little nuggets of revelation. It was such a total failure that I ended it early and said that I didn't feel good and needed to go home. It was no lie. Deep down I knew that something was very wrong.

When I got home and shut myself in my room to get ready for bed, a knock came on the door. It was Charlotte and she carried the telephone. She said it was Teddy.

"Hi, hon. How ya doin'?" he said.

"I don't know. Not too good," I told him.

"Me neither. That's why I had to talk to you. The Lord's been telling me that things are getting out of line with you and David and that it needs to stop."

"What? I–I don't get it. We don't–I mean, we haven't done anything."

"All I know is what God told me. I've been praying about it heavily, and what he says is that David is seducing you."

"Are you sure? I mean, he doesn't touch me where he shouldn't."

"Well, he's doing something. Maybe he hasn't gotten you into bed yet, but that's where he wants you; and if things don't change, that's where you'll end up. Honey, trust me. I'm not just trying to rain on your parade. I care about you, and I don't want to see your life or your reputation ruined. I've wanted to say something about this ever since Sunday, but–well, I don't want to look like the bad guy and have you think I'm just jealous and trying to spoil your fun. But the Lord wouldn't let me alone on this. I was even afraid I might be too late. Were you with him tonight?"

"Yes, over at Georgia's."

"I thought you might be, so I was praying. And I want you to know I've been praying hard for his salvation. I know you love this guy, but honey, you need to do things right. Now, what does Georgia do when he's there?"

"She goes into the next room to study, so she's there but she's not. She leaves the door open."

"Then it's the times that she's not with you that are the real problem. I know what I heard the Lord say. What happens at your lessons?"

"Usually he gives me my lessons."

"After twenty minutes of making out?"

I didn't answer because today there had been no lesson, which reminded of that vision from my dinner date at David's apartment, not to mention the evening itself. "Well, he has been turning up the heat a bit lately."

"Oh! Now I get it. He's doing it gradually to break down your resistance. That's it. He knows that ordinarily he'd never get you into bed, but if he can get you turned on enough to lose your inhibitions, then he's got you."

"I see what you're saying. Yeah. Makes a lot of sense."

"Good. Can you fix it?"

"Oh, yeah, I can fix it."

"I hope so. And please don't let it get like this again. If it does, Jenny, I'll have to talk to your father."

"Okay."

"Actually, I'd say it's time for you and David to talk with your parents and let them know what's happened with you two. You ought to make it as soon as possible."

"Why so soon? He's still not saved."

"Well, they're going to have to find out eventually, but then so will everyone else. It'll look better for you if your parents have been in on it long before the announcement. Also, he won't be so quick to take advantage of you—in any way."

"Hmmm. That sounds good, but what if my folks don't go for it? Or what if I get pushed into marriage before he becomes a believer? That's one reason I've wanted to hold off on this."

"You don't have to get pushed into anything, Janette. You know what's right and all you have to do is stand your ground. As for them liking the idea—well, that's something to pray about and then trust God for. I mean, if God really wants you to marry this character then you shouldn't have a thing to worry about; the Lord can take care of your parents and prepare them for the shock. If not, then you'll know that marriage isn't what God had in mind for your relationship."

"And if they accept him, it'll get them off of your case."

Teddy laughed. "Yeah, I never thought of that. But, you see, that just goes to show you. I'm ten or eleven years older than you and I have a mediocre income; if they aren't bothered by that, then David ought to be a shoo-in. And it's not as if they don't already know him."

"You're right. I'm sure glad you called. I feel better now."

"So do I. It's like a giant weight's been lifted."

"Look, I'd better get to bed. I'll give you a call later after I talk to David and let you know what's happening."

"Good. I'll be praying for you."

I stayed up for another hour or so, praying over the whole situation, including anticipating David's reactions and how to counter them. For not only could he not be trusted, I was beginning to feel that I could no longer trust myself when we were alone. What he had awakened in me would be very difficult, if not impossible, to put back to sleep.

The instruction I got wasn't particularly to my liking. The Bible studies had to stop altogether because David had enough now to work it out by himself, if he truly wanted Y'shua. Any heavy necking was out, too, and I had to watch how much extra time I spent with him. Things had gotten hot and heavy, and I was becoming too vulnerable to his advances.

THURSDAY, MARCH 20:

Sleeping later than usual the next day, I had my morning meal at home. David gave me a quizzical look when I came into French, but I ignored it. I was beginning to think it would have been better to have it out that morning at breakfast, but the Lord assured me I'd been correct to do as I had done and that after school would be soon enough.

"Un moment, mademoiselle," said David as I headed for the door after French class. He didn't say my name but the tone had Janette West written all over it.

"Oui, Monsieur?"

When the last student was gone he stepped close and asked, "Where were you this morning?"

"I just slept a little late."

"Were you still not feeling good?"

"No, I'm fine. It's just that–well, we're going to have to make some changes, especially regarding Bible study. We can talk about it later."

"When?"

"After school, if you have the time."

"I don't like this."

"I didn't think you would and I'm sorry. But it's not something we have a choice about. I've got to go or I'll be late. Is after school all right?"

"That'll be fine."

"Good. I'll see you then." I escaped before he could think of anything else to say and lost myself in the crowd.

David was moody and distracted all day, but I maintained a calm and sober front, not allowing myself to be worn down by pity for what he might be going through. Afraid that Noel might show up after school again, I called Georgia between classes and asked her to keep him away at all cost. Then I told her what was happening and she applauded Teddy for being so on top of things. She had felt something might be a little amiss but hadn't been sure what to say. If at all possible, she would set aside the time when I would be with David that afternoon as a time of prayer.

When David greeted me at the door, I held back, putting my hands up to make sure there was a little distance between us as he embraced me. Nor was there any passion returned when he kissed me. I also made sure that the kiss was brief.

"All right," he said. "Let's have it. You're mad at me about something."

"Yes, I am." I settled myself in the arm chair instead of the couch. David prepared himself to pace.

"I had the feeling you were upset, but I can't for the life of me figure out what I've done."

I decided the best way was not to mince words. "You've been trying to seduce me," I said plainly.

At first he was speechless. Then he sputtered and stuttered till he finally said, "Oh, come on! I've–I've never tried to seduce you. When have I ever touched you in a wrong place or–or tried to get your clothes off? Come on!"

He couldn't look at me as he said this, which of course betrayed the lie. I'd have felt better if he had just fessed up.

"David, I know what you've been doing. Last Saturday you poured it on hot and heavy in more ways than one: with the clothes, the dinner and dancing, and an hour–one full hour–of love making. Then, not to mention the contact lenses, you wouldn't give me my music lessons yesterday so you could keep the heat turned up. This Saturday you would have taken another step in breaking down my resistance; that's why you didn't want Georgia to come along."

He took a seat on the couch and was quiet for a moment. "Okay, I confess. Guilty as charged."

"But why do you have to seduce me now? Why can't you wait until we get married?"

"Well, Janette, desperate men do desperate things, not to mention foolish. But don't get me wrong, baby. It isn't that the things I said and did weren't from the heart; it means a lot to be able to give you things and make you feel special. It's always been that way, remember? Look, nothing, not even one word of it was phony, and I want you to know that. It's just that the timing was all wrong. The reason I let go of restraint is that I just can't stand the thought of you being with that–that Teddy character, and thinking you might choose him instead of me. I guess . . . I guess I just wanted some insurance against losing you. But I also want you to know that the thought of going that far with you severely bothered my conscience because of the problems I knew it would create for you. Who knows? Maybe I'd have stopped short and not gone through with it. But it was wrong to even think of it, and I'm so sorry that I did. Please forgive me, honey. I swear it won't happen again. The last thing in this world I want is to hurt you."

I didn't respond right away but thought about the whole thing of David's jealousy, his insecurity and how his being outside of God's kingdom made it nearly impossible for him to understand or fully have faith in what God was doing. The only solution was that David had to know God for himself.

Finding the right words wasn't easy. Again I wanted to reassure him that there would never be anyone else, and that unless God himself changed things between me and Teddy, he had absolutely nothing to worry about. From those thoughts came the revelation I needed.

"I do forgive you, David. I just wish you hadn't done this because it kind of spoils our love making."

"Please, Janette, I truly am sorry. I promise you I'll be good from now on. You can trust me."

"Honey, I understand how you feel about me and Teddy, but I've got to tell you that you're barking up the wrong tree. Don't worry about what Teddy might do. You need to concern yourself with what God might do."

"Huh? What do you mean?"

"I mean that the only way you'd lose me to Teddy or to anyone else would be if God changed my heart toward you."

"Why would he do that?"

"You should know the answer to that."

"Because of me doing things like trying to seduce you?"

"Yes, but that's not all. There's something else that's very important."

"What's that?"

"Well, what have we been studying in the Scriptures?"

"About the atonement. About–about Y'shua being our atonement and the reasons we need salvation."

"Right."

"So you're saying that if I don't receive the atonement that God might take you away from me?"

"I don't know. But I do know that he's the only one who can. I also know that even though I love you and want to marry you, I can't unless he tells me I can."

"I didn't know that."

"So, if you don't want me spending my summer in a convent in Illinois, you need to work things out between you and the Lord, and you need to do it real soon. Once you do, everything will be fine. Then you'll have some real insurance."

"Are you sure?"

"Yes. A hundred percent sure."

I was glad he didn't try to keep me there when I rose to leave. That was all I had to say, and it was plenty. David was now, of course, very somber, which was appropriate for the situation. As I left I was tempted to say, "Call if you need me," but held my tongue. This was now between him and God, and there was nothing else constructive I could do aside from pray.

Once home, the first thing I did was call Georgia and tell her what had happened. She was pleased and agreed that it had been necessary. Teddy got the news that evening at rehearsal. He applauded me as well, and expressed to me how relieved he was. However, the news also brought pain. Even though he held to the idea of David's salvation being God's only purpose in the love affair, he also knew that David coming into God's kingdom could mean losing any chance of taking me with him for the summer. It meant that there would be nothing to keep me from getting married once I was eighteen. To Teddy it was like giving me up altogether.

Chapter Ten
My Hand in Marriage

FRIDAY, MARCH 21:
My dreams on Thursday night were strange. I can't recall them very well, but I do remember that my spirit was in constant prayer. Then when I got up to go to school the next morning, I felt incredibly light. A strong sense of God's presence greeted me as soon as I opened my eyes and stayed with me throughout the morning.

Breakfast and morning devotions were done at home, and still I was among the first to arrive for French. I had expected to wait a bit for David to open the door, but minutes passed and the crowd outside the classroom grew larger all the time. Then the bell rang for class to begin and still no Mr Conrad. The students were getting a rather concerned, but while I was puzzled and a little inclined to worry, there came a feeling that everything was fine. After the little talk I'd had with him the night before, it was only natural to think he'd had an adverse reaction and done something foolish, but peace and joy was the answer each time I asked God what was going on.

About five minutes into class time, someone went and got a teacher from down the hall that sent to someone else and got a key. That person let us in and we sat around the rest of the period trying to figure out what might have happened to Mr Conrad. No substitute teacher or anyone else came with an explanation. The other students kept asking me about him, which made me a little uncomfortable; but at least I could answer in all honesty that I didn't have a clue.

So I kept praying in order to maintain my peace as the day went on. I figured when it came time for choir that either David would be there or someone would have an answer of some sort. I was wrong on both counts. There was a substitute who sat back while the accompanist rehearsed us. No one knew a thing, except that he did call to say he wouldn't be in.

By the time class was dismissed for lunch, I was resigned to the fact that David wouldn't be at school. I was certain to find out about it that evening, so I tried to let it rest.

While making my way out into the hall, I saw the door to the auditorium opening. Mr Johnson came out and looked around until he spotted me in the crowd. Calling my name, he gestured for me to come over. When I did, he pulled me by the arm and took me inside.

There was David seated on the edge of the stage in dim light. I almost ran to him but then I remembered Mr Johnson's presence and slowed my pace. He hopped down and stood with his arms open to me and waiting, but I hesitated and stopped short of reaching him.

"Go ahead," I heard Mr Johnson say. "It's all right."

David nodded in confirmation and smiled, so I jumped into my lover's arms and held him like I hadn't seen him in years.

"Well, I guess absence does make the heart grow fonder," he said, laughing. David kissed me sweetly, then just held me.

Something was different. He was different. I could feel it and I could see it as he looked down at me and smiled.

"What happened? Where have you been?" I asked, even though I felt I knew the answer. "You–you look different."

"Well, I am different. A saved man ought to be different. What do you think, Bob?"

"You're right about that," said Mr Johnson, beaming happily. "A saved man is definitely not the same."

I didn't know whether to shout or faint. Being completely overwhelmed and overjoyed, I couldn't find my voice.

"Well, say something," David said to me.

"I don't think she can," said Mr Johnson.

"Janette? Say something, honey."

"No, leave her that way. There's nothing like a woman who can't talk." That helped me find my voice again through laughter.

"You stinker!" I turned and pushed Mr Johnson lightly, but immediately turned again to my sweetheart. "Oh, David–I can't believe it."

"I'm having trouble myself," he said. "But it's true. I didn't know it was possible to feel this good. I feel so–I don't know–so new inside. I'm really amazed that my feet are touching the ground. Man! I wish to God I'd done this years ago."

"Just be glad you didn't put it off any longer," said Mr Johnson, eyes moist with joy over seeing his prayers finally answered. "I was ready to give up on you until you and Janette got together. When I saw how well you two were getting along, I felt sure God would use her to get hold of you."

"So, you told him all about us?" I asked David.

"Uh, huh. This morning during forth period."

"He started by asking me to be the best man at his wedding," said Mr Johnson. "I almost had a heart attack when he told me who the bride was."

"Well, baby, what do you think?" As David spoke there was no fear, no insecurity behind his words. He knew now as I knew, by the Holy Spirit, what God wanted for us both.

"I think it's a wonderful idea. We just need to set a date."

His response to that was another kiss. Somehow even that was different.

"Okay, you two," said Mr Johnson. "Enough of that. You'd better be careful. Anybody could walk in on us."

"All right," said David, letting go of all but my hand. "I guess we do need to keep our heads about us."

"So, tell me," I said to David. "When did it happen? What happened after I left yesterday?"

"Well, once you were gone, I had no idea what to do. My motive was all wrong, but it was all I had, so I began with that and plainly told God what I felt, what I wanted and why. Telling him why is what got me going in the right direction. I went over how miserable and empty my life had been, then ended up bawling like a baby and asking him to help me. I told him every rotten detail I could think of to show him why I needed you, but while I was pouring it all out, it occurred to me that all those things were reasons why I needed him and the atonement. You could love me, sure, but you could never clean out all the junk, the pain, and the disappointment. Only he could do that, so I asked him to. I told him I believed in his power and wanted it and that I needed it now. That's when it hit me, or rather, that's when it started to hit. Man! He brought up stuff I'd long forgotten about just so he could deal with it. It scared me a little at first, but only for a short while. Then his power kept coming like waves. How long it went on I don't know, but it lasted for hours. All I did was hang loose and let Y'shua do whatever he wanted. Then at some point I must have fallen asleep–at least I think I slept. Well, whatever happened, I came out of it around 8:45 this morning. I've been in seventh heaven ever since."

"A little difficult to teach when you're like that," Mr Johnson remarked."

"You've got that right. That's why I've been hiding out. I want this to last as long as possible, so I've been singing some of your songs and–oh! I read a little in my Bible this morning, too, and–man, oh, man! I couldn't believe the difference! Things were jumping off the pages at me, and I could understand it so much better because it seemed alive."

"Oh, David, that's wonderful! I am so happy."

"You and me both, baby. I feel free. I really do feel free."

"Why don't we go somewhere and get lunch?" Mr Johnson suggested. "I know where we can get a quick bite."

"Sure, why not," said David. "Let's take my car. We can go out the back way."

We managed to escape unseen by anyone and found the little hole-in-the-wall restaurant Mr Johnson had mentioned. It seemed that as soon as we got there it was just about time to turn around and go back. But we got our "quick bite" anyway and got it to go. Then while waiting for our order, we talked discreetly about the secret courtship between David and me, answering some of the questions Mr Johnson had.

"Look, Bob," said David, once we were out the door with our food. "I think I'm gonna kidnap Janette for the afternoon. Can I just drop you off near the school so no one'll see us?"

Mr Johnson shook his head and laughed. "All right. But you two had better be careful."

We dropped Mr Johnson off just around the corner from the campus and took off.

"And where are you kidnaping me to?" I asked David.

"I'd like to kidnap you to a jewelry store to look at wedding rings, but that can wait. I don't know. I just want to find a place where we can be alone and talk."

Albuquerque is full of little parks. We drove to one that was five or six miles from the school and sat in the car under a tree with the windows rolled down, eating our lunch.

"I want to get married as soon as possible," said David. "As soon as school is out."

"In that case," I said. "You'll need to talk to my parents."

"Yes, and I've been dreading that. However, I do feel better about it now that it's so much easier to trust God."

"Oh, David, my parents think the world of you. They always have. I'm sure there won't be much of a problem, if any at all."

"Well, in that case, I might as well do it and get it over with. It might be more painless that way. When do you think would be a good time?"

"This Saturday evening you could come to dinner. Sunday afternoon would also be good. Take your pick."

"Dinner is out. I couldn't eat under those circumstances. Of course I could just come after dinner."

"That would work, but I'm thinking Sunday afternoon might be best. With my brothers and sisters outside playing, we could talk to my parents without interruption. Yes. I think Sunday afternoon is best. My parents are generally more relaxed then, too."

"All right. I'll give them a call tonight."

When we were done eating, David and I took off again and drove up to Sandia Crest for the remainder of the afternoon. There in the cool quiet of the mountains we were able to do more than just talk about our life together. For the very first time we prayed together as believers.

As soon as I got home, I took the phone into my room and called Georgia to give her the latest news. All the news, which included a new job offer.

"I knew he'd come around soon," she said happily. "Praise God! Have you set a date?"

"Well, not yet. That's going to depend a lot on Olga."

"Olga? Why?"

"Because if Olga doesn't except Joe's job offer, they'll have to wait until July if they want a decent wedding."

"Job offer?"

"Yes. Since Olga hasn't been able to find work, and since she wanted to help put their wedding together, Joe and Lizzy thought it would be good to pay her to do just that. She can do all the running around and talking to people and ordering things and stuff that they can't do because of school. What do you think she will say?"

"She'll say yes! Maybe that's why she couldn't find work."

"Could be. Anyway, we'll get started on that next week after Joe has a nice little chat with Lizzy's folks. They'll need prayer for that, too. Lot's."

"You said it."

"And how."

"Olga will run out tomorrow and buy a wedding planner and some bridal magazines. She can hardly wait."

Just before dinner, David called and talked to my father, saying, "Janette and I have been discussing some rather important details concerning her future, and we'd like to let you in on it and get your approval. Would you mind if I came by on Sunday afternoon?"

"Oh, not at all," was Daddy's reply. "Come by for dinner, if you like. We usually eat around one or one thirty."

"Thank you, but no. I'm sorry, but I already have plans. Would 3:30 be okay?"

"Yes, 3:30 is just fine. We look forward to seeing you."

When I was told about it at the table, I took the opportunity to give my family the news of David's recent transformation, which allowed me to share parts of my relationship with my teacher that they knew little or nothing about, thus preparing them a tiny bit for what was to come.

Later, while I went to Rock of the Witness, David went to temple services. That was how it would have to be until our engagement was official and out in the open, and until the uncomfortable situation with he and Teddy was resolved. I did, however, suggest he try the Sunday service, since Teddy could never be there.

When I got to the church, my partner was already setting up. Teddy smiled at me as I came in and continued to tune his cello. Then he sat down at the drum set and played around a bit. Once I was done getting set up, I went to get my hug.

"Are you on drums tonight?" I asked.

"Yeah," he said. "Tony is sick, so I'll switch off between the fast and slow numbers. So, uh, how did it go?"

"He did it," I said. "He got saved."

"You're sure? You're sure it's for real?"

"I'm sure. The Lord told me even before David did. It's real, all right."

"Good. That's a relief. I'm happy for you, Jenny."

And he was. Teddy was only sad for himself because his last chance to get me to Chicago had just gone bye-bye.

"And just as you suggested, he's coming on Sunday to talk with my parents and get permission to marry me."

"Oh. So I guess I'd better not come by. Don't want to spoil things. Just don't let him make a habit of coming over. Do you mind? I'd still like to be able to see you and your family, especially on the weekends."

"Oh, you won't have to worry about that. We don't dare let the whole family in on this because they could never keep the secret and then it would be all over town."

"Good then. That'll keep me alive a while longer."

We had both forgotten about Veronica until the sibling trio showed up. They came early to get a good seat. When Teddy and I saw her we looked at each other and shook our heads. This of all nights was not a good one for her to tag along.

When the meeting was over, Veronica approached the stage and waited for an opportune moment to speak.

"Hi, Janette. Hi, Teddy." Her voice was shy and hopeful. "Have you guys prayed about adding me to your team?"

I started to answer and say that I hadn't, but Teddy got his in first.

"Yes, I have, and I'm afraid the answer's no. It's not that we don't want you along; if the Lord had said yes, then we'd take you. But–that's not the case. I'm sorry, Veronica."

"Oh. . . ." Her smile faded with her hopes, but she tried hard and forced it back as she said, "Well–maybe I'll see you on Sunday, then. I've been trying to talk the others into going to your church again. I'd come every Sunday, if I could, but I can't get a ride out there. It's pretty far."

"I wish you would come, and please tell Georgia that I said so. We had a great time when you were there before. Why don't we do it again?"

Now Veronica perked up. "Okay. Great! I'll go tell Georgia." She ran off immediately to find her sister. As I watched her disappear I debated whether or not to warn Teddy, or at least have a talk with her.

"She's awful cute." Teddy locked my head in his arm for a moment and released me. "Let's go kid."

"Are you up to it?"

"I think so."

For Teddy it was difficult at the start, but we did have a prosperous time on the street. It seemed to be the night for reaching out to backsliders and praying for the needs of hurting people. We also gave out a lot of spare change. Then as activity dwindled down to nothing, we called it quits.

"Hey, don't forget," I said, once we were parked again on the lot behind the church. "We do our switch tonight."

"Huh? Oh, yeah," he said. "You'll be at that other church on Sunday."

"So where's the blanket?"

"I cleaned the car today. It's in the trunk."

Teddy helped me fold and position the blanket in the front seat of his car. He watched me as I climbed in and got settled behind the wheel.

"How is it?" he asked.

"Fine. Don't worry, it'll be fine."

Teddy sighed and was silent for a moment before asking, "I suppose you'll be getting married real soon?"

"David wants to get married as soon as school is out, but I don't think it'll be practical if we're going to have any kind of a wedding. Looks more like the end of June'd be better."

"Well, I guess those visions I had really are for sometime in the distant future. I don't understand why God is doing things this way. It doesn't seem quite right to me, but then again, his ways aren't the same as ours."

"Teddy–I've prayed about this a lot, and what I get is that–well, neither of us is truly ready for what he's shown you. We may want it and even be capable up to a point; after all, we are doing it now on a very small scale. But it isn't possible the way things are now–especially logistically. That's why it has to wait, or at least that's part of the reason. It will come to pass, so whatever you do, don't lose the vision. Just be patient for it and consider the fact that I'll be a married woman, so take care on your interpretation. Whatever it's all about, God will make it happen at the proper time."

"But what will it take to be ready? I don't quite understand."

"A deeper knowledge of him and the way he does things–and why. Teddy, we may have learned a lot, but at the same time we're just getting started. I've only been in this for a couple of years, and you started studying the Bible on a deeper level only a few months ago. From what I've seen others do in ministry, I know we've both got a ways to go before we can handle the responsibility of anything like what you've seen. If we're to get to the place where we can be used of God like that, the important thing is to make sure we learn whatever he wants to teach us and not fight against it."

"I guess that last part goes without saying. I just don't want to go it alone. When I get back to Chicago, I'll go see Terry and tell her more about what I'd like to do. Maybe she and I can get something going, even if only in the realm of prayer."

SATURDAY, MARCH 22:

Early Saturday morning, right after breakfast, "Joe" called, wanting "Lizzy" to come see him that evening.

"I don't know, baby," he said. "I'd just feel a little better if I could see you before I see your parents tomorrow. Maybe we could pray together about it. I'm really getting uptight."

David had truly changed and I felt I could trust him, but still I had made a promise to Teddy.

"Can Olga come?"

"Olga? Well–sure, I guess. Why? I'd rather just see you."

"Uh–"

"What's the matter? You're not afraid of me, are you?"

"Uh–"

"Well, all right. Bring her if you want to, but it won't be necessary. I really have changed, honey. I promise not to get carried away like before. I've already promised God, and he's going to help me save all the good stuff for the honeymoon and our life together."

The Spirit confirmed his words and I felt it would be fine to go alone, once I had talked to Teddy. "So, should I come for dinner?"

"Yes, I'd like you to. Half past six. Is that okay?"

"I'll be there."

"With Olga?"

"I don't know. We'll see."

It took a while, but I eventually got in touch with Teddy and told him what was up. I was pleased when he, too, felt peace in his spirit about my safety in being alone with David, and so gave his consent.

Dinner was excellent, though much simpler this time. Still we dined by candle light while soft music played. Talk was pleasant but light, and it was then that I remembered about singing the next morning at First Presbyterian and realized that I hadn't once mentioned it to him.

"You know, there's been so much going on lately that I completely forgot to tell you that Bill Fletcher asked me to sing at his church. I'll be doing it tomorrow. Why don't you come, too?"

"Sure. As a matter of fact, I was thinking I'd go to church tomorrow."

"At Rock of the Witness?"

"No, but I have been asking God to prepare me for that. Of course, now it doesn't terrify me the way it used to, but–you know, I just wish you were going to be there on Sundays so we could go together. It'll feel strange not knowing anybody."

"You'll know David Richardson."

"Oh, that's right. I'd forgotten. I met some other people as well at the picnic last year."

"You'll know Georgia, too. She and her sister Veronica both go there along with their future step brother Noel."

"Well, then, I'll give it a try the next Sunday and sit with Georgia. Then anything I don't understand she can explain."

"Good."

"Also, one of these days I'll give Friday nights another try, but not for a while. I just–cannot stand seeing you with that priest. When is that going to change?"

"In about five months. That's when Teddy's assignment here will be over, unless he can get the extra time he wants. Otherwise, he'll be back in Chicago before we're back from our honeymoon."

"Then I'll have you all to myself. Even if he's still here when we get back, you're not going to see that man at all unless he shows up at church; and I don't want him touching you. You belong to me, not him."

Those words didn't do a lot for my faith in the situation. To keep my chin off the ground, I tried changing the subject.

"Oh, I've been wanting to ask, how are dance rehearsals going?"

"Good thing you asked. I'll be needing you next week. The show's coming along fairly well. The kids are talented and they really have been working hard. There won't be anything in that show to be ashamed of by curtain time."

"I just love the music you've chosen. My folks will dig it, too. Benny Goodman, Count Basie, Duke Ellington and–whatever made you choose Louis Jordan's hit songs? I thought we'd be doing more of the stuff that's on the radio, like the Dorseys and Glen Miller."

"Well, aside from personal taste, I had several inspirations, Alan Haskell being the main one. That's why he's got the solo on 'Beans and Cornbread'. I figured it was perfect for him as a preacher's kid."

"Yes, and it's a scream!"

"Well, I thought that if I was going to do this thing that I ought to get some personal enjoyment out of it. But that's not all. Just wait to you see what else is in this show."

"Oh, yeah?"

"I told Alan not to mention it to anyone, but he and I are featured in one of the dance routines."

"You're going to dance in the show? That's great! Will you sing, too?"

"Yes, I'll be singing."

"Hot dog! Whatever you do, just make sure the police are there for crowd control. What's the song?"

"'Lulu's Back In Town.' I got the idea from something Dick Powell did with the Mills Brothers."

"Well, I'm sure looking forward to that."

"Oh! I just remembered something. Would you happen to have the phone number to your friends up in Colorado? I'd like very much to go up there some weekend."

"Sure. I know it by heart. I'll give it to you tonight."

When dinner was over we sat together on the couch, talking over what we should say to my parents on Sunday, laying every detail of the circumstance before the Lord until we both felt confident that it would turn out fine. David also wanted to talk over wedding plans, so we discussed the ceremony. Then to end the evening, rather than make out as we once did, we simply sat on the couch, holding each other and saying very little, while watching the fire crackle and burn.

SUNDAY, MARCH 23:

Sunday was to be a full day and a fun one. Instead of driving straight to the church, I was meeting Bill at his place. Margo was coming, too, and we would ride together in the Chevy. David would meet us at the church.

In those days, people often left doors unlocked; Bill was one of them. When I arrived, I knocked, then turned the door knob while calling out hello.

"Janette?" responded Fletcher. "Oh, uh–come on in."

When I stepped inside, there stood Margo and Bill in the front room, and she was wiping his mouth with a tissue. It made me shudder and think of how he was forever cutting himself with his razor.

"Hi," I said. "Did you walk over, Muggs? I didn't think about it, but I could have come by and gotten you."

"I like early morning walks," she said. "You know that."

Fletcher lived a little less than a mile from Margo's house in the middle of a big, old apartment complex. With the day as lovely as it was starting out to be, I could well understand why she would rather walk.

"Well, let's go," said Bill. "Get your purse, Margo."

She turned to where there was a waste basket, and as she made her toss I saw what was on the tissue she had just been using. Expecting to see spots of blood, it was instead the same shade of pink lipstick Margo wore; and she had been wiping his mouth. Not his cheek, but definitely his mouth.

The wheels in my head began to turn, going backward over the time since Margo first had Bill as a teacher. That was her freshman year in highschool. They had taken to each other right off. Then she developed a big crush on him that she'd had a rough time getting over. Or did she get over it?

Well, well, well! And here I thought that I was the only one with a secret love affair. No wonder she kept egging me on toward David. It had certainly worked for her. Haut boy! Had it ever. Hmmm, maybe we could have a double wedding? Naw. But it would be fun to double date.

While Margo helped Bill with his jacket, I quickly picked up the evidence from the waste can and slipped it into my purse to confront her with later.

The church was not as large as I had thought it would be. Unlike the other religious edifices downtown, this one had a sanctuary that only seated about four hundred. It was decorated in a subdued fashion, with a plain cross that hung suspended in front of a blue velvet curtain behind the simply carved, wooden pulpit. The arched stained glass windows were only colored glass, lovely and restful to look at, but with no elaborate scenes. The carving on the pews and all the woodwork was attractive but simple, as if whoever was behind it all had wanted to make sure that in this place God was adored, and not the house in which he was worshiped.

After I met the pastor, Margo helped me to get set up. As soon as my guitar was in tune, we looked up to see David walk in the door.

"You didn't tell me he was coming," said Margo with a twinkle in her eye. "Far out!"

"I didn't ask him till the last minute because I almost forgot."

"Finally got used to him, huh?"

"Oh, ages ago."

David approached us smiling and with a church bulletin in his hand. "Well, good morning, ladies," he said. "Nice to see you when you're not in school or chasing criminals."

"Good morning," said Margo, with a puzzled smile. "My! But aren't we chipper. You smile like a politician who just won by a landslide."

"I'm a new man. I got saved Thursday night."

"You did? Wow. . . ."

"You ought to try it."

"I'll say."

"So where's Bill?"

"Bill? He was here a minute ago. I'll get him. I've been here a few times, so I should be able to track him down."

As soon as Margo was off on her search I whispered to David, "Honey, guess what? Margo and Bill are sweethearts just like we are."

"Really? Well, what do you know."

"Yeah, but they don't know that I know. Why don't we have some fun, okay?"

"Oh, yeah. Sure."

We made our plans and waited, and in just the next minute, Margo was coming along with Bill right behind her.

"Well, this is a surprise," said Fletcher to David as they shook hands. "Janette didn't mention that you were coming."

"I didn't hear about this until last–uh, until yesterday."

"Well, I'm glad you decided to come."

"Mr Conrad," I said. "Tell Bill the news."

"Oh, yeah. I got saved last Thursday night."

"You did? Say, that's great!"

"It sure is. I've never felt better or happier in my life."

"Say, why don't we go find our seats," said Margo. "It's almost time for the service to start."

"All right," said Bill. "How about over on this side so we'll be close to where Janette will be singing."

We picked out the fourth row from the front. Bill and Margo led the way, and as he allowed her to step into the pew I took a big step and hurried in right behind her. David, being inches behind me, followed, leaving Bill last to sit on the end.

As soon as Margo realized what had happened, her mouth drew up into a disappointed and angry pink pout. However, I pretended not to notice at all. Turning to see Bill's face, I saw a man who was bewildered and dismayed and trying desperately not to show it, his features twitching with the effort. Neither David nor I made any comment.

"You know what?" said David. "I just thought of something. Janette, you're going to have to get out into the aisle when it's time for you to sing. Why don't you sit over on this side of me? It'll make it easier for you."

"Good idea," I said, and immediately got to my feet.

As soon as I was up, David slid over into my place and I took his. From the look on their faces after the change, Bill and Margo seemed to think too late about changing the arrangement for their benefit. Seconds later the organist took her place and began the prelude. The church was almost full and they didn't dare start playing musical chairs. So for the duration of the service, the two secret love birds were apart.

Thoughts on Bill and Margo made it tough to concentrate on the service, even though the hymns were great and the singing pretty good. I was tickled pink over their love affair and wondered why no one had figured it out before. They were together almost all the time, but then that was nothing new. Something that was relatively recent was the two of them living so close to each other, ever since Bill had made the move to his current apartment a year ago. Margo was intelligent, attractive and a ton of fun. Why shouldn't he fall for her since she'd matured? But given my situation, I couldn't go over all the angles. I had to pay attention to the service so as not to miss my cue.

Two songs just before the sermon, was my set. A touch of nervousness hit me just before my performance, and then I heard the mention of my name as the pastor introduced me. Both songs were my own and fit his topic well for that Sunday (trusting God), but I didn't cut loose like I would at The Rock. Gearing my performance for the conservative crowd I had them pegged to be, everything went fine.

The people were uncertain whether or not to clap when I was done. After the first song, a few of them probably forgot where they were and let go with some applause which quickly died. At the end of the second song there was only silence. It was after the service that people expressed their enjoyment of my songs. Quite a few complemented my voice as well, saying that it was beautiful and very well trained. With David standing so close by, I just had to say that I'd never had a lesson in my life. Bill and Margo howled.

"What?!" David frowned and hit me with his rolled up bulletin. "How can you say that? And in church, too!"

"I'm just teasing. I'll tell the truth," I said and introduced him as my voice teacher.

Shortly afterward, the four of us made our way through the crowd and out to the parking lot.

"Well, where shall we go for lunch?" asked Margo.

"I know a good place," said David as I knew he would. "Ever hear of a place called Minnie's House of Chow?"

"Yeah!" said Bill excitedly. "But I hear it's expensive."

"It's worth it. Let's eat there and put lunch on my tab."

Once again it was time to have fun with the seating arrangement. In David's car, Margo and I sat in the back seat together. At the restaurant, David and I worked it so she sat next to Bill, but not without a little difficulty in getting there. David and I watched as the two tried not to show what they were going through in being separated, and once together again, not being able to react openly to restore the little rift in their bond through close contact. Hugs or touching of any kind would be a dead give away.

As usual, David was able to get the most comfortable seating in the coziest corner of this restaurant that catered to the American palate. It touted the best recipes, the finest ingredients and generous portions. But the atmosphere was anything but down-home. The decor was like an uptown restaurant, with big booths of dark brown, overstuffed vinyl and fine linen on the tables. Mirrors decked the walls, and potted palms were everywhere.

Before we were served, Bill excused himself to make a phone call. Until then I hadn't known when to bring up the evidence, but this looked to be as good a time as any.

"Muggsy," I said, my expression serious though struggling to hold back the chuckles. "Now that Fletcher's gone, I want you to come clean."

"What?"

"I want you to confess and tell me everything."

"Everything about what? I haven't done anything."

"I'll be the judge of that."

"I don't believe this! What's this all about?"

"About this." I reached into my purse and brought out the tissue, opened it up and spread it before her. "Do you recognize this?"

"No."

"You should. It's your lipstick, Muggsy. The very same lipstick you wore on the morning in question at the home of one William Henry Fletcher. The very same lipstick I saw you wipe from Bill Fletcher's mouth, and the very same lipstick you're wearing now."

For a brief moment she caught onto the fun I was having but then the glow faded from her cheeks as she realized that the jig was really up. She sat looking down at the tissue, turning it around and around in her hand.

"I should have known someone would find out sooner or later," she said. "To be honest, I'm surprised no one's figured it out before this."

David and I both took that moment to release the laughter we'd been holding back. Realizing just how she'd been had, Margo responded in a clear but subdued, almost frightening manner that was designed to turn the tables.

"I'll get you for this," she declared, anger flashing in her vivid blue eyes. "I'll get you for this if it's the last thing I do. Nobody plays Muggsy for a chump. Nobody, see?"

"Edward G. Robinson," said David, not the least bit fooled. "Or was that from a George Raft movie?"

"It wasn't from any movie," said Margo, now laughing with us. "But I meant every word of it. One of these days–"

"Well, I think it's great about you and Bill," I said. "I just wish you'd told me before. Are you guys getting married?"

"Yes, as soon as I turn eighteen."

"Great! So tell me about it. How'd it happen?"

"Oh, you remember that big crush I had on him at first. Well, I was still a little thing then. He saw what was going on, so we had a nice long talk that helped straighten me out. But then I guess I started growing up and so he got a crush on me. That was almost a year ago, a month or so before summer vacation. Bill didn't try to kiss me or anything like that. He just took me aside one day and said that he wished he hadn't discouraged me from being in love with him. We kept things kind of–well, out of the passion pit to start, especially in light of the Noonan case. He didn't want me to get the wrong impression of his feelings for me, and he felt it was just good common sense to go slow and not do anything we'd both be sorry for. The other thing was that Bill wasn't too sure whether he was really in love with me or just lonely. Well, with my mother working and partying with her friends most of the time, we were able to spend almost the entire summer together. We got along fine. So he asked me to marry him and we've been planning our life together ever since. As soon as I'm eighteen, I will become Mrs William H. Fletcher of Boston, Mass."

"Well," said David. "I'm glad you decided to confess and tell all. So I guess we ought to come clean ourselves and tell you about–well, what's happened with us."

Margo's eyes lit up and her mouth flew open. "Uh—uh, you mean—you guys, too?"

"That's right," I said.

"Fantastic! I was hoping there was some truth to those rumors."

"What rumors?" asked Fletcher as he approached the table. "Just ask me. I know all about rumors."

The three of us were silent for a moment and then broke out in laughter.

"All right, you guys," said Bill. "What's going on here?"

David shook his head and I did the same, saying, "Don't tell him. He can find out later."

Margo turned to Bill and then back to David and me.

"Uh, uh. Sorry, folks. I just don't have the heart. Besides, haven't you two put us through enough already?"

"What's going on here?"

"Bill, Janette and Mr Conrad, here—"

"David. Call me David, please."

"All right. Janette and David here have been playing games with us all morning. Remember how we couldn't sit next to each other in church? That was done on purpose."

"What? But why? I mean, do they know–about–"

"Yeah, they know all about us."

"Oh, I see."

"Here's what gave us away." Margo showed him the tissue. "I guess I shouldn't have taken those last few kisses."

"Congratulations," said David to Bill. "I hope you'll be very happy."

"Thank you." Bill perked up a little. "I'm sure we will."

"Although I can't imagine," I said. "That you'll be nearly as happy as we'll be."

"What?!" Bill jumped, he was so shocked and surprised. "Well! I only thought that you two–I mean, with all the books, the music, and the Bible study, I never gave it much thought. And nobody seriously believes anything romantic is going on with you two. To be honest, Connie MacGregor and I were pretty jazzed about Janette feeding you the Scriptures every day–and so this is the result. How funny!"

"Well, for most of the time it was strictly legit." I told him. And any feelings we had for each other stayed hidden, not just from other people but from ourselves as well, until we worked everything out."

"I'm sure glad that no one's been seriously suspicious," said David. "I'll feel much more relaxed from now on."

"Well, I'm actually glad that you caught us," said Margo. "It's a relief to have somebody else in on this. Now I'll have somebody I can talk to about me and Bill."

"Well, you might as well clue Georgia in on it, too," I told her. "She knows about us. She's our official chaperon."

"So how long have you two been involved?" asked Bill.

"Just since February," said David.

"That's not very long," said Margo.

"Guess whose fault that is?" said David. "This hard headed little thing thought it was beneath her dignity to fall for a man who teaches for a living."

"A living?" I said. "It's a hobby you get paid for."

We spent the next hour or so laughing and sharing some of the secrets of our courtships until it was nearing time for David and me to take care of business for that afternoon.

"David," I touched his arm and showed him my watch. "We'd better get going pretty soon."

"Oh, yeah." His smile faded as he grew quiet and slightly pale.

"He's asking for my hand in marriage today," I explained.

"I don't envy you," said Bill. "We're still working that one out. Margo thinks it would be better to just elope after she turns eighteen."

"Maybe," I said. "But Margo's mom really isn't all that bad. We all know why she drinks so heavily; it started when her husband left. I could be wrong, but I think, if you approach her right, that you just might find out she'll be thrilled to know that Margo found a decent man to take care of her. Sure. The more I think about it, the stronger I feel that she would appreciate knowing and would gladly give her consent. Just because she's not always there for Margo doesn't mean she doesn't love her. Staying busy has just been another way of drowning her sorrows. She doesn't know Jesus, so she has to escape into something."

"Asking her permission would certainly make for a better relationship with her in the future," said Bill. "I've gotten to know Mrs Townsend a little over the past couple of years, so I've had some of the same thoughts as you about this. You just gave me the confirmation I needed."

"Look, once you get her permission, you'll have the whole summer for your honeymoon and for getting settled in before school starts in the fall."

"Well—I guess," said Margo, still skeptical and somewhat sobered by the topic. "I guess it's worth a try. She couldn't really stop us anyway."

"I think it'll work out fine," said Bill. "I sure hope things go well for you two this afternoon. I'll be praying for you."

A few minutes more and we were out on the parking lot saying our goodbyes. I took Bill and Margo back to the apartment while David went home to change clothes before going over to my house.

Once home, I hurried to freshen up and change into a nice little day dress. Then when David came to the house, I made sure I was the one to greet him at the door. While changing, I had thought of something that might take the edge off and help my sweetheart to relax. I had been saving it for just before the wedding because of what it suggested; but it was funny, and I knew the shock and the laughter would snap him out of that bad case of jitters as well as provide added incentive to make it through the afternoon. So I came to the door with chocolate in hand: almond bark in a red envelope with a note that said, "J-a-n-e-t-t-e, what you get is what you see: cho——colate!"

"You don't look too good," I whispered as I opened the screen door.

"I don't feel too good," he said, lacking color and sweat beading up on his forehead. "I wasn't this scared in Noonan's apartment."

"Maybe this will cure what ails you."

David smiled wanly when he opened the envelope and saw the candy. He read the note, then grinned and chuckled.

"Oh, really? Young lady, I thought we were supposed to be turning the heat down, not up."

"Uh, oh."

"Which reminds me," He laughed again as he stuffed the envelope in his pocket. "That's a subject we need to discuss."

Oh, no! What have I done?

A moment later my parents came on the scene to greet my Mr Conrad. As we all went into the family room, I hoped and prayed that no one else would be listening in like I certainly would have been.

Mommy and Daddy were all smiles as they sat down on one end of the big, long couch. I couldn't help wondering how long the smiles would last once they heard what David had to say. This was going to be a rather large bomb to drop on these poor, unsuspecting people.

Placing David in one of the big easy chairs, I pulled up an old hard back chair and sat a few inches away from him.

"Oh, I almost forgot," said Mommy. "What can we get you to drink?"

"Bourbon, please," said David. "Neat."

"Had a rough day?" asked Daddy.

"A busy one," said David.

"I'll get it," I said. "Does anybody else want anything?"

"I'll have a beer," said Daddy.

"Nothing for me," said Mommy.

"Now," said Daddy, beer in hand. "Let's hear what you two have been talking about. Have you finally picked a college?"

"Yes," said David. "As a matter of fact, I've been able to talk Janette into staying in Albuquerque and going to UNM."

"What?!" they both exclaimed. Mommy asked, "How on earth did you accomplish that?"

"It took some doing, believe you me. But I've convinced her to at least start out there. After all, they have a music department that's fairly decent and they're offering her a full scholarship."

"Wonderful, wonderful," said Daddy. "That'll save us a tremendous amount of money. Thank you so much."

"Oh, you're more than welcome. You know, Mr and Mrs West, the first time I came here and talked to you about Janette, I didn't know much more about her than what I had heard. Since then I've gotten to know her very well, and I must say it's been quite an experience."

"I can believe that," said Daddy.

"What I mean to say is, you do have a lovely daughter, and I have very much enjoyed having her in my classes. I've learned as much from Janette as she has from me."

"That's nice," said Mommy. "Thank you for saying so."

"I mean it sincerely. She's more than just talented, she's kindhearted, intelligent, levelheaded, and in many ways she's more mature than some women twice her age. It's because she's the kind of person she is that Janette has become so special to me. I don't know whether or not she's told you, but because of her, I've given my life to Y'shua–uh, to Jesus."

"Oh, yes," said Mommy. "She mentioned something about that just the other day."

"Well, I'm saying all this because I want you to see that knowing Janette has made some wonderful changes in my life. That's why I've come to love her very much. It's why I want to marry her. I hope you'll give us your permission."

The smiles froze and then faded from my parents' faces and their eyes grew wide. Never before had I seen two people so dumbfounded, with both expressions virtually the same. Then as they sat, thought and stared, their heads tilted first to the right, then to the left simultaneously.

At last my mother broke the silence. "How long has this been going on?" she asked, angry and suspicious.

"I guess you mean how long have we been, uh, romantically involved. Only since February."

"February 17th," I added.

"Of course I've been in love with her much longer than that," said David. "It's just that the situation was such a–difficult one."

My parents were thoughtful for a while longer, then turned to each other and whispered together.

Turning to me, Daddy said, "Janette, you go upstairs with your mother and talk with her while I talk to Mr Conrad."

Mommy and I left together and closed the door behind us. We then went up to my room for our little talk and did our best to keep our voices low.

"Janette," she began, still angry and incredulous. "Have you lost your mind? That man must be twice your age."

"I know. But we love each other anyway."

"Are you pregnant?"

"No, Mommy. I haven't done anything to get that way."

"You're sure?"

"That would be a very difficult thing not to notice."

"Then you do understand all about sex? I know we talked about it once or twice before."

"I know enough. Don't worry, Mommy, I'm still a virgin. And please keep your voice down."

"Here I was wondering just how much you were carrying on with Teddy, and then here you come wanting to marry your–your music teacher! Janette, your Mr Conrad is a good man but he's much too old for you. At least Teddy's a little closer to your age. Why don't you marry him?"

"He isn't interested in marriage, to me or anybody else. He has too much to lose. Like I've been trying to tell you, he and I are best friends, brother and sister. That's all it ever has been and ever will be. But even so, I fell in love with David before Teddy ever came along."

"But you and Teddy always hug and kiss and carry on. Have you been having two boyfriends?"

"No. What you see Teddy and I do is as far as it ever goes: hugs, pecks and slapping each other around. That's just how it is with us. It's something special and it's completely innocent."

"That is mighty hard to believe."

"Should I swear on a stack of Bibles? I'm telling the truth!"

"Well, all right, all right."

"Look, I know how much you and Daddy like Teddy, but it's his religion that has kept us from being sweethearts. It's the most important thing in the world to him and I could never compete with it. But David Conrad is a wonderful man who loves me sincerely, and unlike Teddy, he does want to marry me. Can I tell you how it happened?"

"Of course. I want to hear everything."

While I was giving my mother the details, which included a peak at my ADG file on David, Daddy was downstairs trying to give my sweetheart a hard time.

"You know what?" Daddy looked from his beer to David's bourbon. "Now I know why you didn't want ice tea. I think I'll fix myself one of those."

David waited quietly, trying to keep his stomach from knotting up anymore. He slowly sipped his drink while my father poured his own.

"So, you want to marry Janette." Daddy sat down again and shook his head in disbelief. "For real?"

"Yes, very much so."

"Is it because you have to marry her?"

"No, sir, she's not pregnant."

"I hope for your sake that she's not. The doctor can check it out, so I suggest you be completely honest."

"I wouldn't be anything else, Mr West. I genuinely love Janette. I love her with all my heart. If I didn't I wouldn't be sitting here asking to marry her."

"Well, there's no doubt that you're able to support her, but don't you think you're a little old for a seventeen year old girl? You can't be much younger than my wife and I."

"Mr West, if your daughter was typical of girls her age, I would agree with you one hundred percent. But Janette is far from typical, and I'm sure you know that. Her maturity and wisdom are some of her most attractive qualities, and I doubt seriously that a younger man would value those things as highly as I do. To be honest, falling in love with Janette took me completely by surprise. I mean, it's not as if I've ever had any problem finding women my own age. You see, in the beginning, what concerned me most was making friends with her so I could stay off of her death list. Look, Mr West, I get teenaged girls coming after me all the time and never give one of them a second thought–or even a first one. But Janette—Janette is not like anyone I've ever met. On the first day of school, I thought she was a new teacher or a teacher's aid because she didn't look like a student. You've seen what she wears to school."

"Yeah, those old clothes she got from that fashion designer. They do make her look older."

"Yes. Older and very attractive. You've seen what women are wearing these days."

"I know what you mean. Janette wears makeup, too, which she didn't used to do. That also makes her appear older and more sophisticated. I get the picture."

"I'm glad you do. But it was more than the way she looked; that only got me interested. Janette has more talent, brains, and personality than any eligible woman I've met in a very long time. She also has a pretty good sense of humor."

"Laughs at your jokes?"

"Most of the time."

"Can't beat that."

"And think about this: because she's so young, there are no ex-husbands, or children, or all the other baggage that a lot of woman carry around."

"That's a very good point."

There weren't many other real reasons for Daddy to object to David wanting to marry me. But like my mother, he had carried hopes for me to marry Teddy, his newly adopted son. That hope was now destroyed.

"Well," Daddy sighed. "I'll be honest with you. Both my wife and I were hoping Janette would marry someone else. She's been very close with a young man she brought home a few months ago that we just think the world of. We thought sure they were in love with each other, so this comes as even more of a shock. Do you really want to marry her?"

"I most certainly do. I wouldn't have anyone else."

"What about children? Do you want any?"

"Yes, we plan to have a few."

"You won't be able to start right away, though, with Janette going to college."

"Oh, we'll go ahead as long as she doesn't mind being pregnant while at school. Of course she's never been pregnant before and can't really know what that'll be like."

"That'll be quite a hardship on her, don't you think?"

"No, I'd never let Janette wear herself out with both school and babies or anything else. I already have a very good housekeeper, and I can hire more help when needed. And once she does start having children, I'll stop working so we can do things together. After all, they'll be my children, too."

"Then I guess Janette will be well taken care of. You can afford to take care of her even without working?"

"Oh, yes, indefinitely. I have much more to draw upon than my salary as a teacher. I own quite a bit of real estate, and I have other investments as well. Janette will never want for anything as long as I live."

"Well, then," Daddy paused and thought a while, nodding and then shaking his head. "If you two really love each other, I don't see why you shouldn't get married. I guess you've known each other long enough and spent enough time together to know whether or not you'll get along. Still I want to discuss it with my wife and see what she thinks. From what we've seen of you, you seem to be a decent and responsible person. It's just a little odd, you being her teacher and all."

"I know. By the way, please call me David."

"All right. And you can call me Richard. But before I go get the wife, why don't you tell me a little more about yourself? Didn't you come out here from California?"

"Yes, that's right." David had hoped my parents already knew enough about him to accept him as their future son-in-law. He had always side stepped questions about his past very well, but now the last thing he needed was to appear as if he had something to hide–which he did. Believing he would tell me all when he was ready, I trusted that those dark years would never have anything to do with us anyway, so I hadn't asked him about it on Saturday, even though it had crossed my mind. Since David wasn't the criminal type, I was certain sure he wasn't hiding anything like grand larceny or a murder rap. But that was me, and Daddy wouldn't be so understanding.

Another danger in talking about his past was that it would reveal his age. From my estimation, David was pretty close to my father's age while Daddy was figuring eight or ten years younger, just as Margo and I had done. Any parent would find such a thing difficult to accept.

"Now, you were born and raised in Los Angeles?"

"Yes."

"I went there once, but that was years ago. It was a lot of fun. Had a wonderful time. You know, Hollywood, nightclubs and all that. So, uh, have you been married before?"

"No."

"Why not?"

"Well—uh, career, mostly. That's how it was at first; just too busy or not ready to settle down. Then when I was ready, finding the right woman wasn't as easy as I'd thought."

"You've got that right. I was sure lucky to find the woman I did. Some of my friends didn't do so well. Some of them married women with looks as fine as my wife's, but that doesn't mean happiness. Do you have any children?"

"No."

"Not that you know of?"

"I've always been very careful; too big of a price to pay."

"Amen to that. So you and Janette haven't–"

"No, we have not and will not until we're married. As far as I know, your daughter is still a virgin."

"I'm very happy to hear that. But that reminds me of something I was thinking of a moment ago. When was the last time she actually got a music lesson?"

While Daddy was making David squirm, Mommy and I were having a good time over the story of my romance with The Fox. She was impressed by my ability to exercise such control in the situation and found delight in the way things had finally come together. It was fun for her as I fit together the pieces of things like the Anthony Vaughn concert and the day I came home late after school with the costumes. We could have talked all afternoon, and would have, if Daddy hadn't knocked on the door.

"Janette, you can go on back down," said Daddy, poking his head inside the door. "I want to talk to your mother now."

They left my room and went down the hall to their own while I rejoined my sweetheart downstairs.

Now that David and I were alone, I wanted to be close to him. I took his hand and pulled him out of the chair and over to the love seat.

"How did it go?" I asked, slipping my arms around him.

"Good–I think. I don't know. It would seem fine and then he'd put the screws to me again. It went back and forth like that and I was just too nervous once you were gone. I hope he doesn't think I lied about anything."

"Or was holding something back. Did he ask your age?"

"No, thank God."

"He probably made an educated guess like I did and didn't think the question was necessary. Well, honey, anybody would be nervous, especially in your shoes, so you shouldn't worry. Besides, my mother's on your side. That ought to make you feel better about the outcome. She wasn't too thrilled at first, but she's all excited now. She thinks it's wonderful."

"That's sure nice to know."

I reached up and smoothed the worried frown from David's brow, drew him closer and kissed him. "It'll work out," I told him. "Don't worry."

Studying my face with a tender look in his eyes, David smiled and was about to kiss me when the door opened and my parents appeared. We jumped apart.

"No, don't stop on our account," said Daddy, closing the door behind them. "Go ahead. I've got to see this."

David and I looked at each other but didn't make a move.

"Aw, come on," said Daddy.

"Oh, Rich," Mommy chided and hit Daddy's arm. "Don't embarrass them like that."

As Mommy and Daddy took their seats, I moved over next to David and leaned against him. This seemed to relax him a little and he slipped an arm around me. Still he was nervous enough to make him sick.

"All right, you two," said Daddy. "I guess you'll want to get married as soon as school is out."

"Yes," I said. "As soon as school is out."

"What? Are you both agreed?" David asked. "We can get married?"

"Sure you can," Daddy answered. "But I'm warning you, if you decide you don't like her, don't even think about bringing her back."

"That will never happen." Close to tears, David held me tight with his face buried in my hair and said, "Oh, God. Oh, Jesus, thank you. Thank you, Jesus."

"I'm seeing it, but I still don't believe it," said Daddy. "Absolutely incredible."

"Look," said David, head up and smiling again. "Would you mind if we went somewhere for coffee or something? I know you've already had your dinner, but I feel like celebrating. Then we can talk some more about the plans Janette and I have made."

So that we could relax and talk with complete freedom, we decided to go to David's apartment rather than a restaurant. Afternoon quickly faded into evening as we talked over champagne cocktails, putting together plans for our secret engagement and wedding. With the date finally set for June 21st, the reality hit David so hard that he was almost beside himself. Before the night was over, Daddy got to see the kiss he'd asked for much more than once.

Chapter Eleven
Nedra Bates

MONDAY, MARCH 24:
"He never misses school," said Donna Gilbert.

"I know," said Mike O'Connell. "Either he was sick last Friday or something terribly important came up."

"He sure looked fine this morning. Not only that, he was beaming! See? There he is."

David Conrad came into the teacher's lunch room with a slap happy gin on his face and a bounce never before seen in his step. As he carried his tray along, he virtually danced his way across the floor.

"Say, Bill," he called out. "Come sit with me."

"Sure," said Fletcher and rose to leave.

"Wait a minute!" Bonnie Smith protested. "You just sat down. You haven't told us anything."

"Say, Dave," said Bill. "Why don't you come tell these people what happened to you last week?"

"Sure," said David. "Be glad to."

"Uh, oh," said Smith. "I've got a feeling."

Bill moved over a space and let David sit down.

"I guess everybody wants to know why I wasn't in school on Friday. Well, it's really very simple. The fact of the matter is, I got saved."

"You mean it took all day?" said O'Connell. "And I thought I was bad."

David laughed. "Actually it happened Thursday night, but God wouldn't let go of me for quite a while. I must have been up till three or four in the morning. When I finally woke up, it was too late to go in for morning classes. Then I just had to go see some friends and tell them about it. When something this great happens you've got to tell somebody, and the last thing you want to do is go to work. The way I felt, I wouldn't have been able to teach anyhow, so I just stayed away."

"You really did it, huh?" said Linda Armijo. "So how do you feel now? Happy, no?"

"That's an understatement," said David. "I'm so high now, I feel like any minute I could float away. See, the thing is–"

A crowd soon gathered as David explained the joyous relief he had found. No one scoffed openly or argued, but many mouths hung open and one or two asked questions. The change in him was overwhelmingly obvious. He was so alive with the very joy he talked about that it altered his appearance, giving him a youthful glow. So accustomed were they to seeing the old stoic, "man of few words" demeanor, that some wondered if he were actually the same man.

At the edge of the group of faculty members was Vicky Marshall, her expression one of haughtiness and disdain. But she hung on every word, and several times betrayed her amazement in the change she saw in the man she'd once been intimate with. Standing a few paces from her was Constance MacGregor, a broad and knowing smile on her face, happy enough to dance a jig over the sight of her prayers being answered so abundantly.

Meanwhile, in the Journalism room, Margo and I had a howling good time over the secrets we now shared. We sat back in the morgue whispering low with our heads together as I gave her the details of Sunday afternoon and getting my parent's permission. I gave the most vivid description possible of the looks on their faces, sending Margo into hysterics. Then I told her how my mother squealed with delight at the info I'd shown her from my ADG file on David.

"Look, Jan," she told me at the end of the lunch hour. "We've got to talk some more. Can you come over after school, or maybe tonight?"

"I can't, kiddo," I said after thinking over my schedule. "The best I can do is come by tomorrow after school. David called another dance rehearsal after school today and then tonight I've got some phone calls to make, with Teddy being one of them. Plus I've got to study and practice my music."

"You really are busy this year, aren't you?"

"Like I never dreamed possible. What with two church rehearsals–"

"And with two men, as well. My goodness! I want to hear some more about that priest of yours. Poor Joe almost couldn't get his foot in the door with your parents because of him. He must really be something."

"He is, believe me. That's one reason I'm so glad to have Joe, because it'd be a drag if I didn't and ended up in love with a Catholic priest. God sure knows what he's doing."

"I guess."

The bell sounded and reluctantly we got to our feet.

"Well," said Margo. "If you can't come by tonight, then I guess I'll go see Bubba."

Again I laughed out loud at the unlikely code name she'd chosen for Bill Fletcher.

"Pick another name, Margo. Please! I can't handle that."

"What's the matter? I think it's perfect. It describes everything he's not."

"All right. Well, be sure to tell Bubba that Lizzy says hey."

The rest of the afternoon whizzed by and soon school was out. With thoughts of the day and the evening ahead being uppermost in my thoughts, the last thing I expected was to see Noel strolling about the campus looking for me.

"Hullo! Janette!" He waved at me from the middle of the courtyard and then came running to meet me. "I hope it's not inconvenient, but I thought I might make the scene here for your benefit. Georgia seemed to think it was a good idea. Shall I take you home? I have my own car, now."

"Well, I wasn't going home, actually. I have a rehearsal in a few minutes. But let's go anyway, and you can take me home to change."

"Wonderful. Now, let me have those."

Noel reached for my books, which I gladly gave him. He then escorted me to the black Corvette he had just purchased.

"Nice," I said, as I settled back against the soft leather seat. "I've never ridden in one of these before."

"Don't be too impressed. It was used for a few months. But whoever owned it first put in all the extras and then some. It's like driving a rocket ship!"

At that he accelerated to sixty miles an hour to demonstrate his space vehicle, and I found myself pressed even further back into the leather.

"Far out! But don't get a ticket. And don't pass my house."

"Honestly, Janette, sometimes you're so uptight. Can't I drive you around just a little bit? As you can see, it won't take much time."

"Okay. I've been wanting to ask you something anyway."

"Oh? What about?"

"Noel–if I tell you something, could you keep it a secret? It's something very important."

"Yes, I can keep a secret."

"Good, because I need you to do a special favor for me. See, my boyfriend and I are engaged to be married, but only my parents and a few very trustworthy people know about it. Anyway, I've finally decided on what I'd like to get him for a wedding present."

"How can I help you with that?"

"Noel, for you to do a portrait of me, would I have to be there sitting for you all the time?"

"No, not at all. Just pick a setting and what you want to wear in it, then I'll take some photos and work from them."

"Good. That way it won't take so much time. How much will it cost?"

"Well, for you, since you're a friend and all, and since I'm on holiday–you still couldn't afford it on your allowance, whatever that may be."

"You'd be surprised. How's five hundred for starters?"

"Oh, my! Yes, that will do quite nicely. I'll need that in advance, of course. Then we'll set up a time."

"Sure. Just remember, this is a surprise gift for my certain someone, so don't breath a word of it to anybody, except maybe Georgia, since she knows about him. Promise?"

"Yes. You have my solemn promise. Georgia said this business with your fellow was hush-hush, and that's why she wanted me coming 'round to see you here, to get people off the track. I think it's excellent fun!"

Around the school we drove and then to my house. I was ready to have him drop me off without coming in, but then I remembered having Teddy's car and that I had driven it that morning and it was parked at school. So, running up to my room, I quickly changed into jeans and T-shirt, and then Noel took me back to the school.

Rehearsal was fun, or at least it started out that way. Before too long it became a lot of hard, sweaty work and heavy concentration. The routine David had worked out for me really was quite simple, even using some of the steps I had learned in Jewish folk dance. Still the combination of singing and dancing with others would take more energy and concentration than I was used to putting out on stage.

David was still flying pretty high as he took us through the routine. It was catching, and before I knew it we were both laughing as we danced, making it rather difficult to stay focused. While we laughed, tripped, and slammed into each other, the rest of the dancers soon stopped and stared. But they weren't all laughing with us because some had heard the tale going around, whether they believed it or not. The story was that we had been sleeping together.

Even when I had come in to stretch and warm up with the others, I had noticed a few odd looks along with whispering directed at myself. But knowing something was being done about it, I determined to stay in a good mood. And now David and I were practically giving ourselves away, almost falling over each other because of the happiness we had and losing control. So I stopped the dance and the entire rehearsal in order to explain.

"Stop it!" I shouted at David, still laughing. "This isn't going right. Will you stop that? Stop it!"

"I'm sorry. I–I can't seem to help it. Maybe if I–" He laughed instead of finishing his sentence.

Pulling on his arm, I made him bow his head to my level and whispered in his ear. "You'd better tell the kids about getting saved last week or they'll think there's hanky panky going on with us."

"Okay." But as he raised up and began to talk, only laughter came out.

"Listen, everybody," I said, projecting my voice around the stage. "Can everybody come out? Laughing boy, here, can't seem to talk, so I guess I'll have to give you the news."

By the time they all moved in close, David had collapsed into a sitting position on the floor, giggling uncontrollably. And though I was faced with a sea of curious faces, some with sober expressions, the sight did nothing to take away my joy.

"Maybe you haven't noticed," I began. "But since last week when Mr Conrad was absent, he hasn't been quite the same. Have you noticed?" Heads nodded and many voiced their agreement. "Well, the reason why he's changed, and the reason he's behaving so strangely right now, is that he finally gave his life to Jesus. He got saved last Thursday night."

As they all began to talk at once, I heard a few praises to God amongst the many comments and questions. Then came smiles followed by laughter. I laughed, too, and looking down at my Mr Conrad, kicked him with the side of my foot. He guffawed and so I pushed him over.

"Looks like rehearsal's over, you guys. Can someone please help drive him home?"

A couple of the bigger boys got David up from the stage and eventually to his car. After receiving directions, they drove him in the Jag while I followed in the Chevy. After getting him upstairs, I dropped them off at their houses. Then it was home for dinner, practicing and catching up on things with Georgia over the phone.

"I have been dying to talk to you all day," said Georgia. "Not only do I want to hear what happened with you, there are a few things I really need to tell you."

"Oh, yeah? Did you go to mass?"

"Yes. Veronica wanted to go and said Teddy had specially invited us."

"So what happened?"

"No, you go first. How'd your parents handle the news?" Georgia chuckled as I gave the details of Sunday afternoon *en Français*. when I told her our chosen day, she was relieved. "At this late date, it'll be tough to get a place for your nuptials. June is so popular for weddings, and since you're going to have such a massive one, we need to book the venue as soon as possible. Already I've been looking around at sanctuaries, as well as trying to find a place for a big reception, and there's not a lot to choose from."

"I was afraid of that. But let's talk about it later. I want to hear what happened yesterday."

"Well, it was funny, but tragic all at the same time."

"Veronica?"

"She is so gone on that man. Can't say that I blame her, but then she doesn't realize what she's up against, even though I've been trying to tell her like you told me. Well, we went to mass and Teddy preached another good one, even though he didn't seem quite as confident as he usually does."

"That's because I wasn't there. But he's going to have to get used to that."

"Really. Anyway, Ronnie was all gussied up in a new dress and smelling up the car with perfume on the way there; I had to make her wipe some of it off. Then at church she just had to sit on the aisle so that when Teddy came by to pass the sign of peace, she'd be the one to shake his hand."

"She's not talking about becoming Catholic yet, is she?"

"No, not yet, but she does want to check into joining the worship group over at The Rock."

"Oh. Well, what else happened? Did you go out to eat?"

"Yeah. It was real cute, too, since we were only four instead of five."

"Oh, no! Couples!"

"You got it. I did my best, but she just had to sit next to Teddy. Even when I said something to her in front of him, she just shrugged it off and did what she wanted."

"Oh, brother! I knew I should've had a talk with her the other night. So how'd Teddy handle it? Did he even notice?"

"Oh, he noticed, all right. She hasn't learned yet how to be subtle–or patient. She sat close to him right off the bat. He moved over to give her room, but as soon as his head was turned, there she was right next to him again. That definitely tipped him off, and he got a little red faced at first.

But your priest is pretty good when it comes to shooing away the dames; then again, I'm sure he's had lots of practice. He ordered a burger with onions, a side of raw unions, and chili cheese fries with onions. Then he pulled a Jerry Lewis and kept spilling things, especially in Veronica's direction. You should have seen her dress by the time we got out of there. He even did the old gag with hitting the ketchup bottle, and I could have sworn he aimed it right at her."

"My goodness! Was she discouraged?"

"She was almost in tears at the restaurant, and she did cry on the way home. I haven't been able to get her to talk about it, though. Noel is aware of her feelings for Teddy and tried to comfort her, but I don't know if it's done any good."

"Too bad. I feel so sorry for Veronica. Teddy could have taken a different approach."

"Well, maybe so, but when you're put on the spot like that, you don't have a lot of choices. Besides, with all of those onions, Teddy must have paid a bit of a price himself."

"Don't bet on it."

"Are you planning to talk to him about it?"

"I sure am. I was going to call him tonight, anyway, to ask how things went, as well as give him an update. Maybe what she did was stupid, but I know how she feels, and I don't like the idea of her being crushed like that."

"I feel the same way, but then again I did try to warn her. That's the kind of thing that happens when you don't listen to the voice of experience."

"Yeah. Well, look, let me get off the phone and call Teddy before it gets too late. Maybe tomorrow or Wednesday we can talk about wedding plans."

"Would tomorrow at lunch work? I know you've got rehearsal tomorrow night."

"Yeah, good idea. Nope, bad idea. Madrigal rehearsal is tomorrow at lunch. Wednesday at noon is another dance rehearsal. I'm even trying to squeeze in some time for Margo because–uh, because–"

"Because what?"

"Well–"

"Is it about the Case of the Missing Mommy?"

"More like the Case of the Future Mommy."

"What?!!"

"Don't jump to conclusions. It's not what it sounds like."

"Okay, who's pregnant?"

"Nobody. I told you not to jump to conclusions. I said 'future' in the context of marriage and the possibility that comes with it."

"Oh. So she knows about Lizzy and Joe?"

"Yes, and I know all about her and Bubba."

"Bubba? Who's that?"

"Take a wild guess."

"Bubba. . . . If I can guess then he's got to be somebody I know. Somebody in the ADG. But she's never liked any of those guys that I know of. I don't know of anybody Margo's ever liked aside from Bill Fletcher."

"Bingo."

"Are you serious?!"

"Mum's the word. Top secret and all that. I wasn't even going to tell you, but I know you won't spread it around."

"I sure won't. I wonder if they need help with plans for their wedding."

"Could be. I'll ask. She knows you're doing Joe and Lizzy's. Wednesday night we can talk about that, too."

"Right. But can we make it at Joe's? Noel and Ronnie have started dropping by unannounced since Noel got his new car."

"Okay. Maybe I can even get Joe to put on the feed bag."

"Sounds good."

"Look, I'd better go before it gets too late. I'll give you a call tomorrow after I talk to Joe."

"Okay. Mañana."

As soon as there was a dial tone, my fingers began dialing the number to St Basil's. Teddy must have been waiting for my call. It was he who answered the phone.

"Janette? Hi, sweetheart. I tried to reach you this afternoon but you weren't home. Did you get my message?"

"No, I didn't. That's unusual."

"So, how's my car doing?"

"Just fine. We'll make the switch tomorrow night, okay?"

"Great. So, how'd it go yesterday?"

"The ministry went well, and then getting permission from my parents worked out fine. You were right. It took a little effort, but they both gave their consent. We're getting married at the end of June."

Teddy's spirit's couldn't help but droop a little. I could feel in my own heart what was happening in his, but he wouldn't let it show in his voice. "Good," he said assuredly. "Then I'm sure things will work out for the best."

"So, how were things for you yesterday?"

"Oh, not bad. It was sure different without you, though. The band sounded different, of course, and the presence of the Lord wasn't quite as strong. But still it went okay. I'll be glad when I get you back."

"Did Georgia and company show up?"

"Yes, they did. We went out for lunch afterward."

"I know. Georgia told me what happened–ketchup and all."

"Oh. I take it you're a little upset?"

"Teddy, you made Veronica cry and you ruined her dress. Don't you think you went a little too far? The onions should have been enough."

"Maybe. But you're right. I did get a little carried away. It's just that once I realized she was after me, I could see what she's been up to all along. You know, with wanting to come witnessing with us and everything. Georgia did try to stop her, but she just kept on coming. I only wanted to put a stop to it once and for all. Look, she'll get over it."

"In about ten or fifteen years, maybe. Oh, I don't know. Maybe I'm being a little too concerned, but still, something should be done to help her get over it. That had to be very traumatic. I know how I'd have felt if it'd been me."

"So, what would you suggest I do? I don't want her to get ideas again."

"I don't know. Could you at least pray about it?"

"All right, I'll pray about it."

"Thank you."

"Say, I've been wearing the jacket you gave me. Everybody thinks it's a gas, all except for–"

"Frick and Frack? No surprise there. How about the nuns?"

Teddy laughed. "They were a little shocked at first, but the Reverend Mother is half Irish, you know. She gets a kick out of it in her own way. The others just smile and try not to look too interested."

"Those poor nuns. I'd sure hate to be in their shoes. I think half of them are in love with you. Then I go and give you something sexy like that jacket to wear."

"Oh, I don't know. Maybe, but so long as they don't come after me, I never think about it."

"Well, look, I'm going to hit the hay a little early. I just wanted to talk to you a bit since I didn't see you yesterday."

"I'm glad you did call. I wanted to hear your voice. See you tomorrow night, babe."

TUESDAY, MARCH 25:

David was still in a dangerous state of euphoria the next morning, even though he had no idea how he had gotten home on Monday afternoon and was a little embarrassed.

"I hope that doesn't happen again," he said. "But at the same time–"

"I know what you mean. I almost ended up like you did but I resisted. Which reminds me–there's something I need to tell you. It's kind of important."

"Oh, really? Should we talk about it now?"

"Well–no. It's not that important. It can wait until later. Actually, there are some other things far more important. First of all, can Georgia and I come over tomorrow night? We need to discuss wedding plans."

"Sure."

"Can we have dinner?"

"Anything you want. Anything my lover's heart desires."

"Don't say things like that in public. It wouldn't be proper to have me all over you."

"Then I'll have plenty of things like that to say to you tomorrow. I'd love to have you all over me. It's not like I can get your affection anytime I want."

"Now, stop that. You're going to make me forget what else I wanted to say.... Oh, I remember. You know, next week is Passover and we haven't made any plans yet."

"Oh, uh—I'm glad you mentioned that. You see—I have made plans."

"You have? Good. What are we going to do?"

"Well, I hate to tell you this, honey, but 'we' aren't going to do anything. I'm heading up to Alef Tav for Passover. Last night I called your friend Reuben and talked for a couple of hours. He invited me, and I really felt it was what God wanted me to do, so I said yes. Sorry, honey, but you'll have to work up your own plans for a Seder."

"What? That's not fair! You get to go to Alef Tav for Pesach without me? I want to go."

"But you know you can't. You have school till Thursday."

"I know. But I was looking forward to having a Seder with you: our first Seder together. Now how on earth will I be able to put together a Seder?"

"Well, let's see. You could have one at my apartment; there you'd have everything you need. Then invite Georgia and whoever else you want. Invite the priest, even. Who knows? Maybe you can convert him."

"Fat chance. Besides, it's also holy week, so he'll probably be too busy."

"Well, I'm sure you'll be able to get a few people together. I have a beautiful Seder plate and a full set of dishes and cookware just for Pesach. Or if you like, I could mention to my rabbi that you have no place to keep the Passover, and I'm sure he would be glad to have you at his home."

"Hmmm. . . . No, I'm not in the mood for that right now. I want to be with friends, not strangers. I don't know. Let me get over the shock of this and then pray about it."

"You know, I don't see what would be the harm in doing both. You could keep the first Seder at the rabbi's, then have your own when it's more convenient. Give it some thought and let me know what you want to do."

"The first Seder is on Wednesday night. Are you skipping school?"

"Yes and your lessons. I'll be leaving right after choir."

"How long will you be staying?"

"Till Sunday. Since we get Monday off as well as Friday, I thought it would be nice to have a day to recover from the long drive. Maybe you and I can spend that day together."

"Sure. That would be nice."

Nice, yes, but not enough to make up for David being gone at Passover. All day I thought about what to do, but my heart just wasn't in it. It wasn't so much whom to invite. I knew I could come up with a small group of friends, but I'd never led or put together a Seder before, and I had so been looking forward to both David and I doing it. It was a mom and pop sort of operation, and now "pop" would be out of town. But with or without him, I decided to go on and have a simple Seder and invite a few close friends. It was better than nothing.

After school, I stopped by the Journalism room so I could walk home with Margo as I had promised. She and Bill were on my list to invite for Passover.

"I'm making Bubba get some glasses like your Joe's," said Margo as we headed toward the gate. "I've been used to him in the horned rims because that's what he wore when I first met him, but it's time for a change."

"It'll sure look better in your wedding pictures. Joe will probably wear his contact lenses for our wedding."

"Contact lenses? I never thought of that. I used to think that if Mom had the money then I'd like to have some. I don't know if Bubba can wear them with his heavy prescription. Even if he got the lenses, I know he'd end up stepping on one or just losing them altogether. He can be such a klutz."

"So, are you two planning to have any kids? I can just see you with a whole brood of spectacled children."

"Yeah, that'll be cute. Once I get out of college, we'll get started with that. Otherwise, it'd be pretty tough, financially and in other ways. How about you?"

"We're not going to wait at all. Joe wants to stay home and take care of the kids and get us a housekeeper."

"Far out! Must be nice to be able to afford that. You sure have got a together setup. Still, if I were you, I'd rather have a couple of years to enjoy life without the responsibility of kids. Bubba and Francine want to do some traveling first."

"Well, Muggs, I know what you're saying, but Joe's had to wait too long already to have a family. At his age, he can't afford to put it off, unless he's not particular about seeing them grow up."

"Really? Good grief! How old is he?"

"I'm not sure exactly, but I figure he's at least 43, maybe even 45. Hopefully not much older. But I'll find out for sure pretty soon."

"Been waiting for the right time?"

"Yep."

"That's right. I would never have pegged him to be that old. How'd you find out?"

"His childhood pictures hanging on the wall. One's got a Model T in the background, remember? And the clothes they're wearing aren't exactly the latest thing: 1920's, early 1930's at best."

"What if he is older? It's not too likely, but would you still marry him?"

"Sure, I would. I love him too much not to."

"Hmmm, the mystery behind the mystery man. I guess you'll solve it one way or the other."

"I hope to solve it before the week is out."

We walked the last few feet to the house in silence. Once inside, we parked in Margo's room and kicked off our shoes.

"I'm glad you've got a double bed instead of a twin." I leaned against the wall on the lower half of the bed while she took the upper. "I'm not in the mood for a chair right now."

"Rough day?"

"Sort of. I've got a little disappointment to deal with. David's running out on me next week for Passover, so I've got to go it alone to put together a Seder. Would you and Bill like to come? It's next week. Wednesday night."

"I don't know. I think his church has got something going on that night that he's involved in. But I tell you what, I'd much rather go to your Seder. Church I've seen plenty of, and after a while it's all the same. But I've never been to a Passover Seder, so count me in."

"Thanks. I appreciate it."

"You want a snack? A drink, maybe?"

"I'm a little thirsty."

"Name your poison."

"Got any white wine?"

"Sure."

"Put just a touch in a glass of Bubble Up on the Rocks. Oh, and add a twist, if you've got it."

"Sure. Comin' right up."

As I waited for Margo to bring my drink, I grabbed a pillow for my head, closed my eyes and thought of David. Sometimes it was still hard to believe he loved me so much. June was such a long way away. First was graduation and then our wedding day. With it all being too good to be true, I couldn't help but pray nothing would happen to foul things up.

"So you're still going to live in good old Albuturkey, huh?" Margo handed me the drink and joined me again on the bed with her own concoction in hand. "I hope for your sake that David changes his mind."

"Me, too. I envy you going to Boston. Sure, we'll be able to travel and see other places, but—it would be so nice to live some place else for a change. I wouldn't even mind moving to Los Angeles, except that his mother lives there and I don't know what she's like."

"Bill's family is in Boston, but I've met his parents, and they really are sweet people. I think it'll be nice. Plus, once we do start having kids, it'll be handy to have them around."

"I imagine so. I don't suppose your mom could do too much to help out."

"That reminds me. I've been thinking about what you said the other day about my mother. You know, when you're a kid, there are a lot of things you don't understand. You blame yourself for things, and your parents . . . . Even God. For the first time I—well, after you said what you did, I thought about what it would be like if somehow I suddenly lost Bill and what it would do to me. I didn't dwell on it too long because it was just too heart wrenching, but it gave me an idea of what my mother has been through and now I can see her differently. It also made me wonder how a person is supposed to deal with something like that. How do you survive that kind of pain and still go on to be normal and happy? Is that what religion helps people to do?"

"It's what Y'shua helps them to do. With him in our lives, coping with problems is much easier, no matter what the size. It's part of the reason it pays to get saved and have him close to our hearts everyday so that he doesn't seem distant when the tough times come along. Since trouble is a part of life for everybody, whether we like it or not, it's better to have God to call on for the strength to get through problems rather than to deal with hopelessness."

"Hopelessness is right. But what kind of hope would that give someone like Mom? Would Jesus bring my father back?"

"Not necessarily. Something like that I couldn't really tell you about because I've never been through it. All I know is he can heal broken hearts and give us something worth living for. It doesn't matter how deep the wound goes, he knows how to take care of the pain so we can deal with our circumstances and go on to better things. The only problem is that we have to let him do it in order for it to happen."

"I don't know if she'd listen, though. She hasn't been to church in years. After the first time or two that I went with Bill, he invited her, too, but she wouldn't go. She even laughed, saying they'd probably just throw her out."

"Why don't you talk to her?"

"I would, but I don't know that much about it. All I've ever learned is what's supposed to be wrong with it. Since my father ran out on us, I can count on my fingers the number of times I've been to church, and I don't know the Bible very well, so I'm sure not the one to tell her anything."

"If you knew from first hand experience, then you'd have something to tell her."

"Oh. You mean I should get saved."

"Haven't you thought about it?

"Yeah, I guess. Especially since I know it would make Fletcher happy. But I'm not sure if I'm ready yet. I can accept it as being real because of what I've seen with you and now with Conrad, but—I just don't know if I want to spend the rest of my life like that, and end up like all those average people with average minds and average lives, until I'm just like one of those little old ladies with the hat and gloves and a placid smile. Jan, sometimes it's so boring in church I could scream."

"Do I look bored? Can you picture me like one of those little old ladies?"

"No. I've got to hand it to you; your brand of religion is different, much more my speed. But I'm not marrying you, I'm marrying Fletcher, and his brand is from square's ville."

"That's where prayer comes in. You must've heard the old expression, 'prayer changes things?'"

"Yeah, sure."

"That's what's so great about being a believer, because then you can go right to God and he can rearrange things for you. It's a trip and a half, and I oughta know. The thing is, you need to get to know him and learn how he operates, because he doesn't always do things the same way. And if you're not careful, sometimes you can mess it up for yourself and circumvent the answer to your own prayer."

"So you're saying that if I go ahead and get saved, that I can go to God and ask him to do something as trite as getting Bill to change churches?"

"Sure, but something like that isn't trite. What you get in the way of teaching and fellowship is very important. Going to the wrong church can even do some serious damage."

"Okay. Well, I have to admit that it's sounding better all the time. What's your church like?"

"Remember me and my friends at the talent show?"

"Yeah, that was excellent."

"That's what my church is like."

"Really? Great! I thought that was just something you did when the pastor wasn't looking. I'd sure like to check that out some Sunday."

"Don't wait for Sunday. Come to a Friday night service. They're much better, anyway. I always go on Fridays. Sundays I'm at Teddy's church."

"Well, I'm not doing anything this Friday night. I'll come then, and if I like it—who knows? Maybe I'll take the plunge. But before I do, explain something. What exactly is the big deal about all this? Sure, I know people who believe in Jesus who seem pretty happy and live good lives, but so do a lot of other people who don't buy into the Gospel. You can find happiness and satisfaction in a lot of things, Jan. I mean, the only difference between you and me right now is that you've got this big faith thing going on and I don't–and that's pretty much it, from what I can see. So what's in it for me outside of a place to go on Sundays–or Fridays, as the case may be, and a ticket to heaven when I cash it in?"

Thinking of what I'd experienced over the past couple of months, especially with Teddy, I paused to choose my words carefully. "Well–it all depends on how deep you want to go."

"Oh, yeah?"

"It's like this: the deeper you dig, the more you'll get; and when you do, life takes on a strange sort of supernatural–something. I can't really describe it, because if I told you even half of what I've seen and done the past few months, you'd think I was nuttier than a fruitcake. But it's fun, just sort of scarey sometimes."

"You intrigue me. Tell me more."

So I told her about Teddy, his transformation and our unique partnership with its deep supernatural bond. Still I was careful how much I shared, just as I've been in this narrative.

"That's very interesting." Margo nodded and smiled thoughtfully. "So you really connect with this priest guy. What about The Fox?"

"He's too new to it. No time yet for it to develop."

"So if I jump in with all four feet, do you think that Bill and I could–?"
"It's likely. Pull him in deeper and anything's possible."
"Far out. Yeah, I can dig it. You just may see me next Friday night."
"Cool."
"Now, before I forget, one thing I wanted to ask you is, would you be maid of honor at my wedding?"
"Sure, I'd be happy to. Thanks for asking. You'll be in my wedding, too, won't you?"
"Oh, sure."
We talked then of wedding dresses and ceremonies, until time for me to head for home.

WEDNESDAY, MARCH 26:
As much as I dreaded it, I couldn't put off telling David about the rumor and the solutions Margo and I had come up with. If I waited much longer, he was liable to learn about Noel through someone else, which would be disastrous. So rather than wait until the evening and risk spoiling that time together with an argument, I told him at breakfast where he was limited on how much anger he dared display. Then he would have the rest of the day to get used to the idea.

After we sat down together in our usual spot, I thought it best to get right down to cases.

"Honey," I said, using Hebrew for such an affectionate word. "I hate to mention something so unpleasant first thing in the morning, but have you heard the nasty rumor that's been going around about us?"

"I'm afraid so. I caught wind of it last week. I've also heard some other things about me since then, and I can't imagine where they've come from."

"Do you mean the one about you getting married to your childhood sweetheart and moving back to Los Angeles?"

"Something like that."

"Well, more than a week ago, Margo told me that there was dirt being spread around about us. She jumped on it as soon as she heard it and started counter rumors. The one about your childhood sweetheart is one of them."

"I suppose the other one is about you and someone else?"

"Yes, it is. The only thing is that in order to give it enough credibility to kill the rumor, we had to come up with someone to act out the part."

David was silent as he worked to keep jealousy and anger from rising within him. His jaw tightened and his countenance darkened as he grew more and more agitated. I even thought I saw steam coming from his ears. Leaning back in his chair he avoided my gaze as he casually said, "Who is it this time? Am I just going to have to get used to sharing you with other men? Every time I turn around you've got another one. Janette, I do not like you being cozy with other men. I won't have it."

"We won't be getting cozy; it's only for appearances sake. Don't you think it's for a good cause?"

"Well. . . ."

"Of course you do. Now, there's nothing to be uptight about. You know that. Those little boys don't have anything to offer me in the least."

He didn't say, "What about that priest," but I could feel him thinking it.

"Nor am I interested in being the secret wife of a Catholic priest, having fifty million and one kids and trying to survive on his pittance of a salary. No thank you."

"That's an interesting way to put it. Is that what he'd do?"

"What else could he do? Teddy isn't ready for marriage and he knows it. For one thing, he's in transition. Another thing is that he has too much to lose if he's found out. Look, when it comes to the priesthood, the man means business. Even if you weren't in the picture, believe me, I'd think a long, long time before I got into anything deeper with him. I've gotten a very valuable education these past few months."

"All right, Janette, all right. I'll try to accept this. It isn't that I don't trust you. Even though it doesn't seem like it, I believe what you say. It's just that I'm terrified of–of anything that presents the slightest chance of losing you. I'd like to be sensible and logical about this the way you are, but that's just not possible. Maybe I shouldn't be jealous of the guy who's the decoy, or even you and that priest, but there are times when it tears at my gut until I want to strangle somebody. I mean it. Prayer helps, but only for a little while. I swear, if I were a lesser man I'd–"

"You'd what?"

"I'm not sure. But I want to do something to keep you all to myself. I don't want other men having their arms around you. When you were seeing Alan Haskell, I wanted to do something then. The only reason I didn't was because I couldn't. If things weren't the way they are, I'm sure I'd think of some way to break up you and that–that priest. Maybe the Lord can do something to cure me of it."

"Of course he can."

"He has to. I can't go on being tormented like this every single time you happen to–"

"Look, let me give you some of the details so you'll know what's going on. His name is Noel. He's a believer and he's the son of the man that Georgia's mother is engaged to. The main reason I picked him is that I can be reasonably sure he won't try any monkey business, and he's willing to go along with the program. He's just going to be a decoy and he knows the setup with me having a fiancé. So far, all he's been doing is picking me up from school once in a while and making himself seen doing it."

"How long is this going to go on?"

"Just until the prom."

"I see. That means he'll be taking you."

"Right."

"Do you really need to go to the prom with a date? Aren't there other girls going alone?"

"Only the real dogs. Look, even Margo has an escort. I'm only interested in stopping the talk that's going around. And Noel is well aware that I'm already spoken for, okay?"

"Okay. You only get to have one senior prom, so I guess you ought to go to it. Just don't dance too close to him. Please? Not even for appearances."

"I won't. I promise. Honey, I love you with all my heart. We're going to be married soon. Try thinking of that again."

"June is sure a long way off. You won't change your mind, will you?"

"Of course not, and you know it."

"You're right, I do. But I just can't help it. And the funny thing about it is that since I've gotten saved, it makes me feel absolutely rotten. I've never liked what jealousy does to me, but now I really hate how it makes me feel. I mean it. I get so afraid and angry that sometimes I think I could lose complete control. When I get this way I–"

"Let's not talk about this anymore. I wish we hadn't had to talk about it at all. We have so much to look forward to."

"We do, don't we?"

We tried to focus on the future with the time we had left, but it didn't help much to change the mood. My sweetheart's anxiousness made it obvious that the dark things lurking in his past were still there in the present. That seemed strange, given the way he had come into the Kingdom of God. It didn't make sense with all the repentance he had gone through, that there should be such a strong lingering of this problem. That meant it went very deep, or else he was holding certain things back; so if this mystery wasn't solved, it could cause some serious problems for the future. It was time to have a talk.

As I went through the day, I prayed for David. He prayed too, as he struggled with his feelings. During French he often appeared distracted, but by noon time he was doing much better. However, in the penthouse that afternoon I saw that anguished look in his eye again and felt that same desperation as he took me in his arms. He had no desire to give me music lessons. His fear of losing my love prompted the same kind of amorous behavior that had gotten him to try and seduce me. All he wanted was to make love. Instead of letting me sit down at the piano, David pulled me toward his chair.

"Oh, no you don't." I dug my heels into the carpet and held my ground. "David, we need to stick to our routine."

"We'll get to the music, honey. Just sit with me for a bit."

"I've heard that one before."

"Please?"

"All right, but not there. Let's sit on the love seat." I now pulled his arm, but he was just as reluctant to follow. "Come on, honey. We need to pray through this thing."

"I've been praying all day. I don't feel like it anymore."

"Come on. We'll just pray in the Spirit."

At last he got up and joined me on the little Victorian love seat. He wrapped his arms around me and kissed my hair, sighing deeply as he closed his eyes for prayer.

I started out softly praying in tongues. He remained silent but that didn't bother me. I kept it up and put my focus where it belonged—on Y'shua. Then I heard him begin to use his spiritual language; it was faint and sporadic to start, but at least he was praying. Then as he prayed, I felt his tears fall warm onto my shoulder and the erratic heaving of his chest with the release of emotion. Soon after, David was peaceful.

"Mmmm . . . praise God." David breathed a deep sigh and rubbed his forehead. "I guess it's more powerful when we pray together. I'll have to remember that."

"Now, wasn't this better than making out?"

"Well, I honestly have to admit that it was. I am feeling much better."

"Good."

"But can't we cuddle just a little bit? It's been a while."

"What about my lessons? And don't you have to fix dinner for a couple of ladies that are coming over?"

"Why don't you stay and help me? You told your folks about tonight, didn't you?"

"Yes, they know. All right. I'll call and let them know I won't be home at all."

After lessons, I called home. Then we went into the kitchen to start dinner. David put the apron on me himself, stealing kisses as he did so. Then it was down to business.

It amazed and embarrassed me to watch David in the kitchen, slicing and dicing and whatnot. He was so adept at preparing food that I was almost in the way. Of course he'd had a few more years of experience than I, and his kitchen was new to me. Still it made me feel like I was going to be the one to come home from a hard day and say, "Honey, I'm home. What's for dinner?" It was apparent that I would have to rethink the domestic aspects of my role as wife and mother.

Before long, David's concoction of beef and vegetables was together and on the flame, as was the rice it would cover. Together we set the table, and shortly after that was done, the doorbell rang.

"Would you get that, babe?" said David. "I need to check on dinner."

"Sure."

Checking my watch, I knew it had to be Georgia, so I could answer the bell without any surprises. I hurried to the door and there she was.

"Hi, kiddo," said Georgia and greeted me with a hug.

"Hi, George. Come on in."

"Say! This is nice. Give me a tour."

"Yeah, sure. Look," I lowered my voice. "Can you find an excuse to skip out early? Say around eight or eight thirty? There's a mystery that's long over due in being solved and I'd like to do it tonight."

"Okay. No problem."

While David was in the kitchen, I showed Georgia the music studio, the balcony and then took her down the hallway to see the old photographs I'd told her about. But not wanting David to inadvertently catch a word or look regarding them, we didn't linger long. Back we went into the living room where I set about fixing us both a drink.

"Fix me one, too," said David, as he stepped out of the kitchen. "Hello, Georgia. How are things?"

"That depends on what things you want to talk about. But fine overall. Say, I hear you're a good cook."

"I do all right."

"It smells delicious. Will it be long?"

"Oh, about twenty minutes."

"Then why don't we get started now? I'm afraid I'll have to cut out kind of early tonight and I want to make sure you get all the information I've gathered."

So we sat down together in the living room to hear and discuss what Georgia had to tell us. Then we continued at the dinner table.

First we worked on selecting a place for the ceremony. Hundreds of invitations would go out, and if even half of the people showed up, we could be in trouble. If the wedding was held outdoors, there was the weather to contend with. Rain might not be an issue, but wind could make plenty of trouble, especially if it brought sand with it. Since there was no synagogue in town large enough, the solution was a Baptist church, newly built and conveniently located. Completed less than two months ago, its sanctuary, which held seventeen hundred people, was not booked solid with weddings in June. The only problem had been getting past the snotty church secretary who didn't seem to like the idea that we weren't Baptists. Fortunately someone more reasonable was in charge of weddings. For the reception, there was only one place in town with a hall big enough and David was opposed to it. The magnificent Broadmore Hotel had a giant ballroom that would hold five hundred people with room to spare.

"That place is a death trap," he said. "It ought to be torn down."

"Really?" said Georgia. "When was the last time you saw it? I stayed at the Broadmore with my family for a good little bit before moving into my apartment and it looked pretty good to me. They've done a lot of remodeling."

"I don't know. What if they're just covering over? If we could have the place inspected and get a good report from the fire marshal, then I'd consider it. If not, I'd just as soon have a smaller reception at one of the other hotels near the airport or on the east end of Central."

"I love the Broadmore," I remarked. "That grand ballroom is absolutely gorgeous. If it's in good shape, I'd rather have the reception there."

"Well, since the reception is my responsibility," David said. "I'll look into getting an inspection as soon as I can."

"I tell you what," said Georgia. "Since you're pressed for time, why don't I go ahead and book the ballroom anyway? We don't want somebody to beat us to it. It's open right now for your date."

"Well—all right. Go ahead and book it. And while you're at it, book all the empty rooms as well for our guests. I'll get started tomorrow by phone on what I need to do."

There were so many details to putting together our wedding that it was staggering, and I hadn't even started on choosing a gown. It made me want to yank my hair out.

"Well, I can tell you this," said Georgia as she prepared to leave. "We're going to need more man power, especially to get those invitations sent out."

"That's for sure," I said. "But now that my parents know, my mother can help. In the meantime, maybe we can come up with somebody else we can trust that's able to help out."

"Bob Johnson's wife only works part time," said David. "I'm sure she'd be glad to lend a hand."

"Great," said Georgia. "And the sooner the better."

A few minutes more and David and I were alone. Still feeling light headed, I sat down again on the couch with pictures of wedding cake and ballrooms whirling in my head. I didn't dare think of the things we hadn't talked about. Something in my schedule was going to have to make room for wedding preparations, but I didn't know what to cut out.

"So, are you excited?" asked David as he joined me in front of the fire.

"Huh? Well–overwhelmed is more like it."

"Don't worry, baby. We'll get it all done. Your cousin is handling this very well. She really knows her stuff."

"Thank God she does."

"That's right. Try to look at it like I do. For one, all of this preparation will make the time go faster. But also, each one of these things means that it's actually going to happen. I don't know about you, but sometimes it doesn't seem real to me."

"You're right, it doesn't."

"Well, have you decided what you want to do for Pesach?"

"Yes. Yes, I have. I'm going to have my own Seder and invite my friends. Margo's already said that she'd come, and there'll be Georgia, of course. I think I'll invite Noel and Veronica, too. That'll probably be it."

"What about going to the Rabbi's?"

"Naw. I've got other things to tend to. I'd even thought about driving up to join you at Alef Tav, but after tonight, I know exactly what I need to be doing. Plus I've got a surprise for you that I need to get working on."

"A surprise?" David put his arm around me and I happily leaned against him. "What kind of a surprise?"

"A wedding present."

"Is it bigger than a bread box?"

"Not now it isn't."

"That's a strange answer. But it doesn't matter. I'm sure I'll love whatever it is. Honestly, honey, the only wedding present I'm interested in is you." He shifted his position a little bit and reached into his pants pocket. "But speaking of surprises, here's one for you."

David brought out a black velvet ring box and held it in front of me. All I could do was gasp.

"I hope you like this set. If not we'll just get you another."

Taking the little box in trembling hands I opened it and gasped again. "Oh! Oh, honey! I've never seen anything like it. Oh!"

"It's an original design from the jeweler," he said as he lifted the rings out. "Let's see how it fits."

First he took the engagement ring and placed it on my finger. The fit was perfect, of course. Rather than bore you with a full description, I'll just say that the big stone was a three karat blue diamond with rows of smaller diamonds on either side. They were set in a sweet floral pattern of white gold. I stared in delight and amazement at its beauty, almost unaware that he slipped the wedding ring on. It had diamonds, too. Seven of them! I turned my hand from side to side and studied my sparklers.

"Do they fit snug enough?"

"They fit just right," I said and threw my arms around my sugar daddy. "Thank you, honey. This is wonderful."

I kissed my man and he responded tenderly at first, then passionately, holding me tighter and pressing his fingers into my flesh. As he drew the breath from me, I forgot the questions I had about getting him his ring. I forgot a lot of things until he took his lips away and I lay my head on his chest, listening to the beat of his heart.

Nestled against his firm body, I soon noticed something. David felt different. Oddly enough, leaning against his chest suddenly felt akin to leaning on Teddy's well developed muscles. One caress of his upper arm and shoulder told me it hadn't been my imagination. "What have you been doing?" I asked. "Where did these muscles come from?"

"It's about time you noticed. I started working out a few weeks ago to get in shape for the spring concert."

"Oh, so this isn't just for my benefit."

"No, but I was still hoping you'd notice."

"Yes, I like it, but keep it up and you'll need new clothes."

"Maybe, but I hope not. That'll just be one more item in a long list of things to do."

"David—"

"Yes, honey?"

"How old are you?"

He paused long. "Does it matter?" he said at last.

"No, not really, but I would like to know."

"Well, all right. I don't want you to go on thinking you're getting one thing and then find out you've been had." He paused again and I could feel him tense up inside. "I'm forty five years old. Are you sure that doesn't make a difference?"

"Oh, I'm sure. I've already had time to think about it."

"You knew?"

"Your photographs in the hallway told on you. All I had to do was make an educated guess."

"Oh. It honestly doesn't matter at all?"

"Of course not. Other people might find it appalling, but we're not getting married to them."

He sighed with relief and smiled. "You know, I've wanted to tell you for a while now, but just couldn't bring myself to do it. Forgive me?"

"Of course I do. I understand."

"Well, baby, I want you to know that I'm in good health. I've always tried to take good care of myself, and everything you see is real; not one artificial thing. No hair coloring, no face lifts, no false teeth, no false anything. You're welcome to inspect any time you like."

"For now, I'll just take your word for it."

"Oh, yeah? After that note you gave me last Sunday?"

"That was only to cheer you up. Actually I had been saving it for much later."

"Oh, I get it. Well, I'll look forward to whatever else you want to tease me with, Mrs Conrad."

Smiling, he kissed me a peck and relaxed. But I was just getting started. Letting a moment or two pass in silence, I lovingly stroked his chest and asked, "Honey, why have you never been married?"

The tenseness returned. He didn't reply but thought for a long while. Finally he said, "Well, you have the right to know about that, too. Besides, you're not the only one who's going to wonder, and–it's time I finally talked about it.

"The summer of 1953, I landed a job as a music director with one of those TV programs that interviewed famous people. I liked being around celebrities, and as you see from the autographs I've collected, I do admire great talent; but I've never been one to get star struck or fawn all over anybody. Well, one day one of my all-time favorites became a guest on the show. I didn't always interact closely with the guests because I only handled the music which was usually just in the background; but this one star, I was determined to meet up close and personal because I'd been a huge fan of hers since I was in short pants. So I made it a point to be on the set as soon as she arrived.

"It was early in '54 when we met. I don't know if you've ever heard of her, but her name was Nedra Bates. There's a picture of her in the hallway from the height of her career that she autographed for me. Nedra was an actress from the age of silent films. She did a few talkies, but worked mostly in the theatre and in silents. When I was a kid I developed something of a crush on her, and I'd seen every single one of her pictures several times over. But even though she'd stopped working in front of the camera years before, she was still well known in Hollywood. Her husband was a movie producer and director up until his death, while she never stopped being active in entertainment organizations and charities, and socializing with the industry elite. So both she and her late husband were well known and loved in that town, and it was a long time before the papers stopped printing bits about either one of them, even once they were gone.

"Nedra had just turned sixty when we met, and she was still very beautiful. While getting up the nerve to say hello to her, I noticed she seemed upset, which gave me second thoughts about intruding, until I realized she was just nervous. So I figured the best way to cheer up an aging actress would be to ask for her autograph. It worked. She was delighted to know anyone even remembered her films, so she latched onto me and confessed how afraid she was of going on the program. It had been a long time since she'd been in front of cameras, and she wondered who would remember her anyway, outside of her Hollywood social circle. So I took the few minutes I had to let her know that there were still plenty of people who remembered and adored her, and that she'd be beautiful from any camera angle. It did the trick. She went on the show and did fine. Afterward she came looking for me and asked if I would have dinner with her; she wanted to say thank you. Needless to say, I was very flattered and gladly accepted her invitation. So we went some place quiet and exclusive and spent the evening together. We had a wonderful time, and we discovered that we had quite a lot in common.

"It was hard for me to believe. Being with Nedra Bates was a fantastic dream come true. But it turned into a big fat nightmare when it got to be more than I anticipated. We hit it off so well that she wanted to get together again. There was a big party coming up–a fund raiser–and she wanted to know if I'd be so kind as to escort an old lady. Again I accepted her invitation, and that's how it all got started. See, Nedra had no family. She was orphaned as a child and then married young, not long after she started in pictures; her husband died of heart failure about a year or so before we met. Her only son was killed in WWII over in France. But that was just her situation. At the time we met, I was still on the mend from–a seriously broken heart, so we really needed each other. At the end of each evening, it was always tough going when we had to say goodbye. We'd drag it out as long as we could. She'd always ask me in for a night cap and usually her chauffeur would drive me home. But one night, after about the third or fourth party, she got on this kick about trying to get me in front of the camera. She made the comment that I was more handsome than any of her leading men, and then I was foolish enough to tell her how I used to fantasize about being in their shoes. When I remarked how I'd often wondered what it would be like to kiss her, she gave me the chance to find out. Then to make matters worse, I didn't go home that night. Then we started seeing even more of each other. It was great at the beginning because we both needed the relationship so desperately. Under the guise of helping my career (and by the way, she helped me get a lot of good work) we saw each other constantly. Of course some people saw through it, although we were very discreet in public. Still most of Nedra's really close friends were more or less happy for us because they got to know me and saw how much we loved being together."

"What about her other friends?"

"They thought I was simply out for what I could get."

"And your friends?"

"They advised me against it, but they weren't too hard on me since they knew what I'd been through before. But I also assured them my head was still on straight and that it was just a passing thing. I wasn't going to go on with her indefinitely because it wouldn't be right."

"So you weren't in love with her?"

"No, but we became the best of friends; in that way I grew to love her very much. Still it had to be short lived because I wanted to have a family, which was something she couldn't give me–and we did discuss it. So after about–oh, seven or eight months, I was pretty well mended and ready to move on. I was working myself up to telling her, dropping hints to let her know that one day I wouldn't be so handy. Then in the meantime I met a wonderful girl who thought I was pretty wonderful, too. I had just started working at MGM. She'd been in several of their films and was finishing up another at the time we met. Well, outside of having lunch at the commissary, I didn't want to date her until I'd moved on from Nedra, but I never got the chance. A few weeks later, she was gone. When I tried calling her, she wouldn't talk to me except to say she'd gotten a contract job over at Fox and to stop calling her. Now, that really upset me, but I got over it fast since I hadn't known her long. Then before anyone else could come along, I had a very honest talk with Nedra and told her exactly how I felt, that I did care very much for her and appreciated all she'd done for me, and not just career wise. Then I said that neither of us could have expected our affair to go on forever and that it would be much easier to end it now than later. We could still be friends, but then I could go on to find the right girl to marry and have children with. Well, she let me go, but not without a big fight and a lot of tears. She still needed me badly; at her age, what I had given her wasn't easy to come by and she wanted to keep it. I'd given Nedra her youth again with all the excitement of a first romance, plus it was like having back the son she'd lost in the war. (He'd only been a year older than me.) So freedom from Nedra came with a degree of guilt for leaving her alone again, but that was–well, just one of those things. I had to go on with my life. It wasn't as if I would abandon her entirely. She really meant a lot to me.

"Well, it turned out that she only made a pretense of letting me go. Even though I tried putting some distance between us, she'd always show up, still inviting me to parties and pulling strings for my career. She even talked me into performing again, so I had a few bit parts in a musical or two, and somehow I always ended up going back to her. It took me a while to figure out what else she was doing to hold on to me. In show business there are plenty of beautiful and talented women, and I wasn't exactly shy and retiring when it came to getting acquainted. I naturally went to parties with my old friends and with co-workers, but seldom could I get a girl to go out with me more than twice; sometimes not even once, if she was someone I worked with. I knew there was nothing wrong with me, but still it began to cause a slight ego problem. Then I noticed a pattern and saw how people whispered and looked at me funny. Single women I hadn't even said hello to avoided me at all cost. I was talking about it to a guy I worked with who told me I was being watched and that any girl I was seen getting close to would be warned to stay away from me."

"What were they told to make them avoid you?"

"Usually that they'd lose their jobs and never work in the industry again. As a result I was labeled as poison by virtually every single woman in Hollywood."

"Didn't you try dating women outside of the industry?"

"A few times. It didn't work. They were led to believe I had a jealous wife and a house full of kids or some such rot."

"Oy v'voy."

"Well, I confronted Nedra with what I knew and she owned up to it. She wasn't proud of it, though. She even apologized and begged my forgiveness. But then she started in again with how much she loved and needed me. Then she said that if I would just stay with her for now, that it wouldn't be long and I'd be free again. But I knew she'd never let go and I told her so. That's when she told me about the cancer. She assured me that her doctor diagnosed her as terminal, giving her six months to a year to live. That was a tough one to deal with. She pointed out that I had my whole life ahead of me while hers was almost over. What was a year or even a couple of years to someone my age? Well, I could see her point, but I still didn't want to be hers exclusively. I had a new girl in my life; she and I were falling in love, and I told her. But she said no to that because she was in love, too, and needed more than just friendship. I didn't have to marry her, but she said that if I would be her lover, when she died her entire estate would go to me. There were no heirs who could contest the will, and I could be in on all the legal arrangements so I'd know she meant business. But if I refused, I'd never work in Hollywood again, nor would any of my friends. And after seeing what she'd done thus far, I didn't doubt that she could do it. Hurting my career was one thing, but I couldn't let it happen to my friends. So I gave in. I put my life on hold and took care of hers. And you know what happened? She lived for three more years before the cancer finally killed her. It was more than just a bad diagnosis by her doctors. I had all that checked out personally because Nedra insisted. But because I kept her happy, I also helped to keep her alive. If we hadn't been together, I'm sure she would have gone a lot sooner."

"Well, having you gave her more to live for. I can sure understand that. But what were those years like for you?"

"Overall–miserable. I got into a pit of the doldrums that I'm still climbing out of, so even now I'm not really the same guy I was before that whole mess started. You'll see. Oh, sure, there were some good times; wonderful, even. Once I got used to the idea of being stuck with Nedra, I managed okay. But no one in his right mind likes to be imprisoned—in any way. Even though I loved her, and even though I got to do things with my career that I might not have had the opportunity for without her, I couldn't get over the suspicion that it was mostly because of her clout and not necessarily my abilities. I was told that my work was good, and once I was even nominated for an award on a movie I scored, but no man worth his salt wants everything just given to him. That's where she couldn't stop being my mother. Giving me this and arranging that. I hated being a kept man, so I just buried myself in work."

"Did you live with her?"

"Not at first. That was one thing I absolutely refused to do when she asked. I had to have some sense of freedom, whether it was real or not. It wasn't until the last year and a half, just before she seriously started to decline, that I moved in. Then I stayed as close to her as I possibly could."

"So did you get her estate when she died?"

"Every bit of it. I said I didn't want her dough, but she insisted. With no family, there wasn't anyone else to give it to, and she didn't want the government to get it. She'd already given loads to charity and wanted someone that she loved to have the things she loved, and that was me. So, instead of a will, she set up a trust. A year and a half before she died, Nedra showed me her entire estate down to the last nickel and put me in charge of her business affairs so I could get comfortable with everything. Some things she just gave me outright before her passing, like the Monet. How word got out, I don't know; but people talk no matter where you go and what you do. Now, her close friends understood because they knew her and they knew me and that I wasn't out to take advantage of her. But when people are jealous or don't understand—well, I won't go into that."

"So others thought you were taking advantage of Nedra when all the time it was the other way around, and your reputation suffered, not hers."

"That's putting it mildly. It wasn't just ruined by word of mouth; the gossip columnists really did a number on me, especially in the trades. They showed no mercy whatsoever. That's why I stopped working in the months before Nedra died."

"Then what did you do?"

"Well, I desperately needed to find myself again, so when she died I shut up the house and went to Europe alone. I ended up in Paris, staying for almost a year and living like there was no tomorrow. But I'm not that big a fool, so I could see fairly soon that it wasn't making me feel any better inside. Then I went to Israel to see if God was there and had anything to offer. Living on a kibbutz for six months or so helped straighten my head out a little, but I never found the spiritual lift I was looking for. So I came home and dealt with Nedra's things. Most of her memorabilia and personal possessions I gave to her best friends and the charities she always supported. Then I put the house up for sale and decided on a new career. Show business was ruined for me. I didn't want any part of it, and I didn't think I'd be that welcome in most of the circles that I used to run in. So someone suggested teaching. I gave it a try and found out I liked it a lot. Not really being known except in the industry, I could stay in Los Angeles without any problems, plus it gave me the support I needed from my family. Then I came to New Mexico for a change of scene, and because I have friends and family here."

I paused to think over all I had heard and tried to imagine how deeply it must have affected him to lose his freedom and the chance to fall in love. With what it must have done to him emotionally, I was beginning to understand how he'd had a problem making himself vulnerable again. It also helped me understand and empathize with his jealousy and see that it wasn't going to be so easy to overcome. But though this story explained a great deal, it didn't tell me everything.

"Well, now you know why I've never been hitched and just why you mean so much to me. Sure, I've met some nice women over the years that I might have married, but none of them ever had what it took to snap me out of that depression long enough to make me feel anything strong enough to call love. It was like being under a spell, and you're the one who finally broke it. Now I guess the shoe's on the other foot. I'm the old man after a young woman. Maybe you can love me now, Janette, but I just can't help thinking that someday you'll want a younger man."

"David, I've already thought all of this through. I think I know what could happen and what will happen pretty much when you get up in years. It still makes no difference to me. It will never change the way I feel about you. I love you and I want to be your wife."

David lifted me onto his lap and kissed my mouth, then planted kisses about my face and neck. His hands caressed me with love and tenderness, and joyful tears welled up in his eyes. "Sweetheart, I love you so much," he said. "Janette, you've made me the happiest man in this whole lousy, stinking world. I'll do everything in my power to see that you never have any regrets about marrying me. I swear it."

David seemed to have very little idea just what he was giving me with his love, and I wasn't too sure I should try telling him–at least not yet. Even though his best years would soon be behind him, he was still quite a prize, and I was just glad that I got him when I did. That I got him at all.

"You know what, honey? I'm glad you made me get this out in the open. I talked to God about it, of course, when I got saved, but lately he's been telling me to let you in on it. I didn't because, as you can imagine, it's not easy to talk about."

I remained on David's lap for a while, greatly satisfied at his telling of the tragic tale that robbed him of so many years of happiness and fulfillment. It made sense of most of what Muggs and I had puzzled over. And since it was obvious that his years with Nedra were primary in changing the course of his life, I wanted to leave that other business alone and let this be enough, especially for one evening. But that nagging desire which came from my training was joined by the voice of wisdom, both of which told me emphatically that such willful ignorance, born of fear, would be foolish to entertain.

As I touched his face and let him kiss me, I only wanted to place a sweet balm on the pain that had risen from his recalling the memories. Yes, it was enough for one evening, but it could not be enough. No matter what it might mean, before we made our vows, whatever dark business David was holding back, it was going to see the light of day.

END OF BOOK TWO

NEXT IN THE WAR THIS SIDE OF HEAVEN

KILLING OLD GHOSTS
Book three in The War This Side of Heaven series

A series of events reveals the murder of Roxanne Jordan--a beautiful woman who was once very intimate with David Conrad and whose killer is yet to be found. Also known as Rebecca Angram, she returns to haunt him, not only in her memoirs, but in the form of her son Noel and her cuckolded husband, British war hero Jonathan Angrahm. Accusing Conrad of the murder, Angram is hell bent on taking his long overdue revenge. To end the conflict, young Janette West must track the murderer over a trail that's been cold for twenty years.

ABOUT THE AUTHOR

Sharon Evans is an award winning jazz vocalist and entertainer, and a writer/producer of variety shows in the classic style of early 20th Century entertainment. Miss Evans has been a fan of detective fiction in film, television, and in books since early childhood. Some of her influences have been Erle Stanley Gardner, Howard Pease, Sir Arthur Conan-Doyle, Raymond Chandler, Alfred Hitchcock, Rod Serling, and Ray Bradbury, along with writers of gothic romance such as Charlotte Brontë *(Jane Eyre)*, Phyllis A. Whitney, and Daphne du Maurier.

A native of Los Angeles, California, where she currently resides, Miss Evans spent her college years at Friends University in Wichita, Kansas where she majored in music. She also lived several years in Albuquerque, New Mexico, where her stories are set. Her husband and all-around business partner is entertainer/entomologist, Rick Rogers.

You can find Sharon Evans online at www.sharonevansauthor.com, www.sharonevansauthor.blogspot.com, www.evansandrogers.com, as well as on Facebook.

Made in the USA
Charleston, SC
25 October 2015